Robert Trojanowicz   Michigan State University
Victor E. Kappeler   Eastern Kentucky University
Larry K. Gaines   Eastern Kentucky University
Bonnie Bucqueroux   Michigan State University

COMMUNITY POLICING

A CONTEMPORARY PERSPECTIVE

2nd Edition

anderson publishing co.
2035 Reading Road
Cincinnati, OH 45202
800-582-7295

Community Policing: A Contemporary Perspective, Second Edition

Copyright © 1990, 1998
Anderson Publishing Co.
2035 Reading Rd.
Cincinnati, OH 45202

Phone 800.582.7295 or 513.421.4142
Web Site www.andersonpublishing.com

Library of Congress Cataloging-in-Publication Data

Community policing : a contemporary perspective / Robert Trojanowicz
. . . [et al.]. -- 2nd ed.
    p.   cm.
Previous edition entered under Robert Trojanowicz.
Includes bibliographical references
ISBN 0-87084-876-3 (pbk.)
1. Community policing--United States. 2. Crime prevention--United States--Citizen participation.
3. Public relations--Police--United States. I. Trojanowicz, Robert C., 1941-
HV7936.C83C663   1998
363.2--DC21   97-38448
                                                                          CIP

Cover design by Tin Box Studio/Cincinnati, OH
Cover photo credit: Guildhaus Photographics/Cincinnati, OH

EDITOR Gail Eccleston
ASSISTANT EDITOR Elizabeth A. Shipp
ACQUISITIONS EDITOR Michael C. Braswell

In Memory
Robert C. Trojanowicz

On Friday, February 11, 1994, Dr. Robert C. Trojanowicz, 52, Professor of Criminal Justice and Director of the National Center for Community Policing at Michigan State University, died of a heart attack at his home. Dr. Trojanowicz, who was scheduled to receive an MSU Distinguished Faculty Award on the following Tuesday, served as Director of the MSU School of Criminal Justice for 10 years. A Fellow in the Kennedy School of Government at Harvard University, Bob was the author of 12 books and numerous articles, as well as the recipient of many honors for his work. Despite his wide-ranging work in juvenile delinquency, police management, and policy analysis, Bob was perhaps best known for his tireless efforts in research and technical assistance on community policing.

Dr. Trojanowicz first offered his vision of community policing in a 1976 *Crime and Delinquency* article, followed by his comprehensive research on Neighborhood Foot Patrol in Flint, Michigan, funded by the C.S. Mott Foundation in the late 1970s. These efforts led to his creation of the National Center of Community Policing at Michigan State University in 1983. Through the Center, Bob provided research, technical assistance, and training on community policing to police agencies both in the United States and in such diverse locations as the United Kingdom, Brazil, South Africa, the Sheikdom of Dubai, Japan, and South Korea. His two books on community policing have become "the bibles" for many police departments, as well as staples in many college classrooms. It is both a tribute and an irony that in the year of his death, community policing became a major cornerstone in the federal government's policy for crime control.

Bob will be remembered by friends, colleagues, and co-workers as a vigorous, hard-working, and generous person. He always made time for people and inspired others to pursue excellence. Bob was a modest person who would get embarrassed when his accomplishments were cited; Bob was a friendly person who always made the extra effort to help another; Bob was a visionary who was driven by hard work and an ideal for a better society; Bob was a giving person personified by the phrase so often heard from him by those who knew him, "Can I help?"; and Bob was a friend on whom you could rely for a word of encouragement, a laugh, or help in solving a problem. Bob Trojanowicz will be missed.

For those interested, contributions to the Robert C. Trojanowicz Fund for scholarships and the NCCP can be sent to:

Dr. Merry Morash, Director
School of Criminal Justice
Michigan State University
560 Baker Hall
East Lansing, MI 48824-1118
(517) 355-2197

ACKNOWLEDGMENTS

Revisiting *Community Policing: A Contemporary Perspective* was a tremendous opportunity and difficult undertaking that would not have been possible without the advice and assistance of many people who provided us support, encouragement, or materials throughout the process.

We would like to thank the police executives and law enforcement officers who were generous enough to provide us with information about their departments and community policing programs. We also extend our gratitude to the police officers who took time away from their families and already demanding work to write the "Community Close-Ups" that appear at the end of this book. These essays are an important part of this book.

We would like to acknowledge the efforts of the staff at Anderson Publishing Co. Mickey and Susan Braswell deserve special mention. Mickey and Susan have been a growing source of encouragement and friendship to us over the years. We have had the good fortune to share some of life's twists and turns with them and have greatly benefited from the experience. Gail Eccleston, our editor, did a wonderful job of working with us through the final stages of preparing the manuscript. Gail is always a delight to work with, and she made a difficult undertaking quite enjoyable.

We would be remiss if we failed to acknowledge the tremendous amount of support, love, and encouragement we receive from our families. They are, and continue to be, the source of meaning in our work.

PREFACE TO FIRST EDITION

Community policing, the first major reform in a half-century, changes the way the police think and act. This revolutionary movement broadens the police mandate beyond a narrow focus on fighting crime, to include efforts that also address fear of crime, social and physical disorder, and neighborhood decay. The community policing philosophy provides an organizational strategy that challenges police officers to solve community problems in new ways. It says that the police must form a partnership with people in the community, allowing average citizens the opportunity to have input into the police process, in exchange for their support and participation. Community policing rests on the belief that contemporary community problems require a new decentralized and personalized police approach, one that involves people in the process of policing themselves.

This book also details the evolution of the Community Policing Officer (CPO), who acts as the police department's community outreach specialist. Freed from the isolation of the patrol car and the incessant demands of the police radio, CPOs operate as full-fledged law enforcement officers, but their expanded mission allows them the flexibility and autonomy to develop short- and long-term, community-based efforts to improve the safety and quality of life in the communities they serve.

Much of the challenge in writing this book has been to keep up with the ways in which this new way of policing continues to evolve—it is like trying to mount a butterfly to a board while its wings are still beating. The goal has been to describe as fully as possible what community policing can and is doing, without pinning it down in ways that might inhibit its continued growth. As Professor David Carter has said, community policing is at the "cutting edge" of what is happening in policing today, which means that no single book can hope to capture all the creative ways in which it is and will be applied.

Most promising of all, perhaps, are the ways in which community policing addresses the pernicious problems posed by illicit drugs in this society. We have all recoiled in horror at the sight of what armed troops have done to average citizens on the streets of Beijing, a grim reminder of why we must explore all police alternatives before succumbing to the temptation to send our military troops into areas of our major cities where open drug dealing has careened out of control. As a result, we have devoted two chapters to how community policing offers new ways in dealing with the drug problem, which may well be the most serious criminal justice issue of our times.

As the police stand poised on the brink of the twenty-first century, the need to provide a comprehensive look at the Community Policing movement seemed a particularly urgent task. This book was written with today's criminal justice student in mind, because of the need to make tomorrow's police officers—and ultimately the police administrators of the future—aware of the community policing contribution. Yet the book is also intended to provide today's police professionals an important resource that may spark new ideas that they can implement now.

This book is also intended for government policymakers and administrators, community leaders, and concerned citizens. For community policing to succeed in fulfilling its promise, everyone in the community must understand what it can and cannot be expected to do. Community policing is not a cure-all for society's ills as much as it serves as a catalyst to involve people in the process of making their neighborhoods better and safer places in which to live. Maybe the biggest obstacle to community policing's widespread acceptance is that it requires a profound, but subtle, shift in thinking. It is not a simple tactic that can be conveyed in a catchy slogan, but a new way of looking at old problems. Embracing the community policing approach means more than tinkering with the system; it implies re-thinking the way in which the police deliver service to those they serve.

The authors also hope this book will inspire debate and discussion. While the necessity of putting ideas into words on paper is akin to pinning down those fluttering butterfly wings, readers should not infer that the authors assume that they know what the future will bring. Much of the impetus in writing this book was to inspire a dialogue about community policing with others who are equally concerned about helping the police contend with the exciting and daunting challenge of finding new ways to achieve excellence. We hope that this book serves as an important first step in developing a new roadmap that will allow us all to find the best route to a better future.

Robert Trojanowicz
Bonnie Bucqueroux

PREFACE TO THE SECOND EDITION

When Robert Trojanowicz and Bonnie Bucqueroux wrote *Community Policing: A Contemporary Perspective* the environment of American policing was very different than it is today. The nation was in the midst of a deep recession and policing faced a crisis in public confidence. The police institution lacked a clear direction that was meaningful in the lives of a majority of people. The lack of institutional direction was met with challenges to the very idea of public policing. In an era of fiscal conservatism where deregulation and privatization ruled, most police executives saw departmental resources decrease and the federal government abandon its responsibility to urban centers. Shrinking budgets were met with an increased politicization of crime. Political leaders accelerated the rhetoric of law and order, promoted crime-fighting rather than peace-keeping and problem-solving; a self-reliance approach to human problems filled the air. Political leaders pandered to the public's fear of crime and demanded that police focus on violent urban crime despite substantial decreases in both criminal victimizations and the federal government's contribution to urban coffers. As political leaders played shell games with public resources, police executives were forced into a downward spiral of focusing more and more of their shrinking budgets on serious crime.

Despite the fact that the professional model of policing had passed the apex of its potential, police executives were forced to make any adaptation or innovation in practice directly applicable to the narrow war on "serious" crime. From Trojanowicz's view, policing had become detached from the needs and desires of the people. As policing became increasingly meaningless in the day-to-day lives of people, confidence in the police diminished and administrators were experiencing great pressure from the public and politicians to reform the institution. Policing had to become meaningful to the quality of peoples' lives. During this bleak moment in history, Trojanowicz offered a hopeful approach for the future.

Shortly after the publication of *Community Policing: A Contemporary Perspective,* the picture of policing and American politics began to change. Transformation seemed to come overnight. The nation moved out of the recession into one of the largest and most sustained economic expansions ever experienced by this country. The politics of self-reliance and deregulation began to be tempered with talk of community and collective responsibility. Community policing replaced political pandering to public fear of crime and get-tough approaches to human problems as the cornerstones of political agendas. States and municipalities, largely through their own initiatives, were able to recapture lost shares of their coffers. Victimization and crime rates continued their downward spiral. In less than one decade, community policing provided law enforcement a unified direction as well as the public and political support necessary to sustain that direction.

While many of the reforms in American policing during the last decade are the result of a broad range of social and political forces, many can be directly traced to Trojanowicz's vision of communities and their police. During a less-than-hopeful period of recent history, Trojanowicz spread what he was too humble to call the "gospel" of community policing and his book became known to many as the "bible" of community policing. All too quickly after the publication of his book and just as policing began to find firm political and economic support along the road to substantial change, Robert C. Trojanowicz passed away.

Robert C. Trojanowicz was a hopeful visionary who provided policing with a road map to a brighter future. His work, however, did not suffer the utopian tendencies of many visionaries; he understood too clearly how the real world worked. He not only understood what policing needed for it to remain a viable and meaningful social institution, but he understood the difficult historic pitfalls that could resurface along the road to reform.

It is in the spirit of cautious optimism that we undertook revision of *Community Policing: A Contemporary Perspective*. We have attempted to extend the road map that the father of community-oriented policing sketched and bring it back into contemporary focus. In doing so we have tried to remain true to the spirit and vision that underscored the original work both in terms of its hopefulness and its cautionary pragmatism. We hope that he would be pleased.

Victor E. Kappeler
Eastern Kentucky University

THE TEN PRINCIPLES OF
COMMUNITY POLICING

1. Community policing is both a philosophy and an organizational strategy that allows the police and community residents to work closely together in new ways to solve the problems of crime, fear of crime, physical and social disorder, and neighborhood conditions. The philosophy rests on the belief that people in the community deserve input into the police process, in exchange for their participation and support. It also rests on the belief that solutions to contemporary community problems demand freeing both people and the police to explore creative, new ways to address neighborhood concerns beyond a narrow focus on individual crime incidents.

2. Community policing's organizational strategy first demands that everyone in the department, including both civilian and sworn personnel, must investigate ways to translate the philosophy into practice. This demands making the subtle but sophisticated shift so that everyone in the department understands the need to focus on solving community problems in creative, new ways that can include challenging and enlisting people in the process of policing themselves. Community policing also implies a shift within the department that grants greater autonomy to line officers, which implies enhanced respect for their judgment as police professionals.

3. To implement true community policing, police departments must also create and develop a new breed of line officer, the Community Policing Officer (CPO), who acts as the direct link between the police and people in the community. As the department's community outreach specialists, CPOs must be freed from the isolation of the patrol car and the demands of the police radio, so that they can maintain daily, direct, face-to-face contact with the people they serve in a clearly defined beat area.

4. The CPO's broad role demands continuous, sustained contact with the law-abiding people in the community, so that together they can explore creative new solutions to local concerns involving crime, fear of crime, disor-

der, and community conditions, with private citizens serving as unpaid volunteers. As full-fledged law enforcement officers, CPOs respond to calls for service and make arrests, but they also go beyond this narrow focus to develop and monitor broad-based, long-term initiatives that can involve community residents in efforts to improve the overall quality of life in the area over time. As the community's ombudsman, CPOs also link individuals and groups in the community to the public and private agencies that offer help.

5. Community policing implies a new contract between the police and the citizens it serves, one that offers the hope of overcoming widespread apathy, at the same time it restrains any impulse to vigilantism. This new relationship, based on mutual trust, also suggests that the police serve as a catalyst, challenging people to accept their share of the responsibility for solving their own individual problems, as well as their share of the responsibility for the overall quality of life in the community. The shift to community policing also means a slower response time for non-emergency calls and that citizens themselves will be asked to handle more of their minor concerns, but in exchange this will free the department to work with people on developing long-term solutions for pressing community concerns.

6. Community policing adds a vital proactive element to the traditional reactive role of the police, resulting in full-spectrum police service. As the only agency of social control open 24 hours a day, seven days a week, the police must maintain the ability to respond to immediate crises and crime incidents, but community policing broadens the police role so that they can make a greater impact on making changes today that hold the promise of making communities safer and more attractive places to live tomorrow.

7. Community policing stresses exploring new ways to protect and enhance the lives of those who are most vulnerable—juveniles, the elderly, minorities, the poor, the disabled, the homeless. It both assimilates and broadens the scope of previous outreach efforts, such as Crime Prevention and Police/Community Relations units, by involving the entire department in efforts to prevent and control crime in ways that encourage the police and law-abiding people to work together with mutual respect and accountability.

8. Community policing promotes the judicious use of technology, but it also rests on the belief that nothing surpasses what dedicated human beings, talking and working together, can achieve. It invests trust in those who are on the front lines together on the street, relying on their combined judgment, wisdom, and expertise to fashion creative new approaches to contemporary community concerns.

9. Community policing must be a fully integrated approach that involves everyone in the department, with the CPOs as specialists in bridging the gap between the police and the people they serve. The community policing approach plays a crucial role internally, within the police department, by providing information and assistance about the community and its problems, and by enlisting broad-based community support for the department's overall objectives.

10. Community policing provides decentralized, personalized police service to the community. It recognizes that the police cannot impose order on the community from outside, but that people must be encouraged to think of the police as a resource they can use in helping to solve contemporary community concerns. It is not a tactic to be applied, then abandoned, but an entirely new way of thinking about the police role in society, a philosophy that also offers a coherent and cohesive organizational plan that police departments can modify to suit their specific needs.

CONTENTS

CHAPTER 1
The Idea of Community Policing

The legitimate object of government is to do for a community of people whatever they need to have done, but cannot do at all, or cannot so well do for themselves, in their separate and individual capacities.

—Abraham Lincoln

The Community Policing Revolution

Community policing is perhaps the first substantive reform in policing since American policing embraced the professional model of policing more than one-half century ago. It is a dramatic change in the philosophy that determines the way police departments interact with the public. It incorporates a new philosophy that broadens the police mission from a narrow focus on crime to a mandate that encourages the police to explore creative solutions for a host of community concerns, including crime, fear of crime, disorder, and neighborhood conditions. Community policing, in its ideal form, is not merely a means to address community concerns, but it is a philosophy that turns traditional policing on its head by empowering the community rather than dictating to the community. In this sense policing derives it role and agenda from the community rather than dictating to the community. Community policing rests on the belief that only by working together will people and the police be able to improve citizens' quality of life. This infers that the police must assume new roles. In addition to being enforcers, they must also serve as advisors, facilitators, and supporters of new community-based initiatives. Community policing is a grassroots form of participative democracy rather than a representative top-down approach to addressing contemporary community concerns.

Community policing also embodies a new organizational strategy that allows police departments to decentralize police service and reorient police patrol (Skogan & Hartnett, 1997). The focus is on the police officer who is detailed to work closely with people and their problems. This Community Policing Officer (CPO) has responsibility for a specific beat or geographical area, and works as a generalist who considers making arrests as only one of many options that can be used, if only temporarily, to address problems. As the community's conduit for positive change, the CPO enlists citizens in the process of policing themselves. The CPO also serves as the community's ombudsman to other public and private agencies that offer help. If police officers are assigned to geographical areas, they are able to not only focus on current problems, but also become directly involved in strategies which forestall long-range problems. Also, by giving citizens the power to set local police agendas, community policing challenges both police officers and private citizens to cooperatively find creative ways to solve both old and new problems in their communities.

What started as an experiment using foot patrols and problem-solving in a few departments has now exploded into a national mandate. As a result of the Crime Bill, most police departments in the United States now say they ascribe to community policing. McEwen (1994), in a national survey of police departments, found that 80 percent of the responding departments stated that they were using community policing. Additionally, community policing has become a standard in a number of other countries. Police departments all over the world now embrace the *language* of community policing. It has become ingrained throughout departments as managers attempt to develop strategies and tactics to deal with day-to-day issues and problems.

Despite this impressive progress, many people, both inside and outside police departments, still do not know precisely what community policing is and what it can do. Although most everyone has heard of community policing and most police departments say they have adopted the philosophy, few actually understand how it works and the possibilities it has for police agencies and communities. Indeed, it is viewed from a number of different perspectives. Does community policing work in practice or is it just a pipe dream? Is community policing simply a new name for police-community relations? Is it foot patrol? Is it crime prevention? Is it problem solving? Is it a gimmick, a fad, a promising trend, or is it a successful new way of policing? Perhaps, David Bayley (1988:225) best summarizes the confusion about community policing:

> Despite the benefits claimed for community policing, programmatic implementation of it has been very uneven. Although widely, almost universally, said to be important, it means different things to different

people—public relations campaigns, shop fronts and mini-stations, re-scaled patrol beats, liaison with ethnic groups, permission for rank-and-file to speak to the press, Neighborhood Watch, foot patrols, patrol-detective teams, and door-to-door visits by police officers. Community policing on the ground often seems less a program than a set of aspirations wrapped in a slogan.

Much of the confusion surrounding community policing stems from three basic factors:

- Community policing's introduction into American policing has been a long, complicated process. It is rooted in team policing, police-community relations, crime prevention, and has become tactical in nature (Kappeler & Kraska, 1998);

- The movement continues to suffer because some police departments claim to have implemented community policing, but they violate the spirit or the letter of what true community policing involves and demands; and

- Community policing threatens the status quo, which always generates resistance and spawns controversy within police organizations. This is because community policing challenges basic beliefs which have become the foundation for traditional policing. It requires substantive changes in the way police officers think, the organizational structure of police departments, and the definition of patrol officers' work.

Elements of Community Policing

Before discussing these factors in detail, the following is a basic definition of community policing:

Community policing is a new philosophy of policing, based on the concept that police officers and private citizens working together in creative ways can help solve contemporary community problems related to crime, fear of crime, social and physical disorder, and neighborhood conditions. The philosophy is predicated on the belief that achieving these goals requires that police departments develop a new relationship with citizens in the community, allowing them the power to set local police priorities and involving them in efforts to improve the overall quality of life in their neighborhoods. It shifts the focus of police work from handling random crime calls to addressing community concerns.

The community policing philosophy is expressed in a new organizational strategy that allows police departments to put theory into practice. This requires freeing some patrol officers from the isolation of the patrol car and the incessant demands of the police radio, so that these officers can maintain direct, face-to-face contact with people in the same defined geographic (beat) area every day. This new Community Policing Officer (CPO) serves as a generalist, an officer whose mission includes developing imaginative new ways to address the broad spectrum of community concerns which exist in every community. The goal is to allow the CPOs to co-own and identify with their beat areas. Such co-ownership allows officers to develop the rapport and trust that is vital in encouraging people to become involved in addressing problems in their neighborhoods. The CPO acts as the police department's outreach specialist to the community, serving as the people's link to other public and private agencies that can help. The CPO not only enforces the law, but begins, supports, and facilitates community-based efforts aimed at local concerns. The CPO allows people to set day-to-day, local police priorities in exchange for their cooperation and participation in efforts to police themselves.

Community policing requires both a philosophical shift in the way that police departments think about their mission, as well as a commitment to the structural changes this new form of policing demands. Community policing provides a new way for the police to provide decentralized and personalized service that offers every citizen an opportunity to become active in the police process.

Our definition of community policing and the Ten Principles at the beginning of the book imply that police departments must make profound changes in the way they conduct business and fulfill community expectations. Essentially, community policing consists of three broad operational strategies: police-community partnerships, problem solving, and community engagement (Dietz, 1997). Though an oversimplification, traditional policing implies that the police department imposes law and order on the community, while community policing makes the all-important shift to understanding that the police role must be to encourage and support people's efforts to improve their communities and create their own order.

Though these ideas and themes will be examined many times throughout the book, the following are key words that can help distinguish the philosophy of community policing from many of the programs that have developed under the umbrella term "community policing:"

- **Philosophy/Strategy/Tactic** – Though a semantic debate about whether a new concept is a philosophy, a strategy, or merely a tactic may sound like quibbling, experience shows that a failure to understand how broadly a new concept must be applied can doom a promising new idea before it has a chance to demonstrate what it can do. In this context, *a philosophy* is defined as what you think and believe, a *strategy* is how you put the philosophy into practice, and a *tactic* is one method that can be used to achieve a narrowly defined goal.

A police department's philosophy sets the stage for the development and implementation of strategies and specific tactics. A philosophical change, as required with the implementation of community policing, generally is enumerated in a department's mission statement. For example, the Madison, Wisconsin, Police Department had the following mission statement:

> We believe in the DIGNITY and WORTH of ALL PEOPLE.
> We are committed to:
>
> - PROVIDING HIGH-QUALITY, COMMUNITY-ORIENTED POLICE SERVICES WITH SENSITIVITY;
> - PROTECTING CONSTITUTIONAL RIGHTS;
> - PROBLEM SOLVING;
> - TEAMWORK;
> - OPENNESS;
> - PLANNING FOR THE FUTURE;
> - PROVIDING LEADERSHIP TO THE POLICE PROFESSION.
>
> We are proud of the DIVERSITY of our workforce which permits us to GROW and which RESPECTS each of us as individuals, and we strive for a HEALTHFUL workplace.

Source: M.A. Wycoff & W.K. Skogan (1993). *Community Policing in Madison: Quality from the Inside Out.* Washington, DC: National Institute of Justice.

This mission statement greatly expands the traditional mission of policing, but it hardly embraces the full meaning of the community policing philosophy. The mission statement fails to endorse the most essential aspect of the community policing philosophy–giving citizens the power to set the police agenda. Also note that for this mission statement to be implemented, it must find its expression in coherent strategies. That is, strategies must be employed that will further the overarching philosophy or mission of the department. The same can be said of the tactics which are used by officers as they attempt to attend to problems and concerns. A philosophy serves as the department's rudder, which helps guide the department as it serves the public.

This helps explain why it is crucial to understand that community policing is a new philosophy that offers a coherent strategy that departments can use to guide them in making the structural changes that allow the concept to become real. Community policing is not just a tactic that can be applied to solve a particular problem, one that can be abandoned once the goal is achieved. It implies a profound difference in the way the police view their role and their relationship with the community. Just adopting one or more tactics associated with community policing is not enough. In fact, such an approach could cause considerable damage to the community's perception of the police department. Conversely, departments that embrace community policing must not only change the way they think, but the way they act.

- **Foot Patrol** – Adding to the confusion, many people have good reason to wonder whether community policing and foot patrol are the same thing since the two terms have in the past been used interchangeably. The distinction is that community policing is a philosophy, while foot patrol is just one tactic that can be used to put line officers in closer contact with people. A police department can have true community policing without using foot patrol, and a department can have foot patrol without a true commitment to community policing.

  The reason the misnomer of foot patrol stuck for so long stems from the fact that community policing has its roots in two experimental foot patrol programs, one in Newark, New Jersey and one in Flint, Michigan, which were launched and evaluated during the late 1970s and early 1980s. In Newark, the initial foot patrol experiment used foot patrol as a limited tactic—the goal was to see whether simply putting officers back into the community on foot would deter crime. The Flint experiment went substantially further, using foot patrol officers as part of a strategy to involve officers directly in community problem-solving, with the officers trained to do far more than act as a visible deterrent to crime. Both experiments reflected the growing realization that something important may have been lost in the process of putting officers into patrol cars, and that there might be a way to update the role of the old-fashioned beat cop to address contemporary community problems. The Flint program was sponsored and evaluated by Michigan State University, which spawned the label "community-oriented policing" as a result of the new focus on citizens.

- **Problem-Oriented Policing** – Confusion also surrounds the relationship between "community policing" and "problem-oriented policing," which are very different, and not always compatible concepts. Problem-oriented policing evolved as a result of the writings of Herman Goldstein and work by the Police Executive Research Forum (PERF). Goldstein (1979; 1990) observed that American police had evolved into call-takers. That is, police officers typically rapidly responded to calls for service, attempted to deal with problems or issues as quickly as possible, and then returned to their cars so as to be available to respond to another call. Goldstein noted that the police did little substantively when responding to calls for service, and if the police were to be effective, officers must devote more time and attention to calls. They must attempt to understand the issue at hand and provide some meaningful, not just short-term, solution. In other words, the police should engage in problem solving, rather than focusing solely on responding. Goldstein's idea eventually evolved into problem solving, a process which now has fallen under the umbrella of community policing.

  Another point of confusion is between "location-oriented policing" (Strecher, 1997) and problem-oriented policing. Problem solving is an analytic method whereas location-oriented policing is a technique for the specific application of tactics. Far too often the problem-oriented policing tends to narrowly focus on geographical policing. That is, the police focus on areas as opposed to problems. While a narrow focus on areas allow officers to understand crime trends and typically places individual instances of crime into a framework, location-oriented policing seldom addresses the broader social causes of problems. Location-oriented policing without a problem-oriented method suggests that a technique like crime mapping or crime analysis would alert the department to the persistent problems at a corner, but does little to address the underlying causes of the problem. An officer skilled in problem solving would more readily recognize trends and problems and investigate them. Problem solving not only focuses on crime, but it also results in officers asking "why" the problem is occurring and "what" can be done to prevent future problems.

Essentially, problem solving is a four-step process (Spelman & Eck, 1987). First, officers must identify and specify the problem. This requires that officers study the problem and develop a full understanding of it. Second, there must be a careful analysis of the problem and its attributes. In many cases a problem is easily identified, but the cause of the problem may be very complex. Officers must endeavor to identify causes. Third, officers must identify a host of possible solutions. Officers should consider every possible solution and enact a solution only after it is determined that the solution very likely is the most effective. Finally, officers should implement a solution and evaluate its effectiveness. CPOs must ensure that their solution is effective. If it is not, then the problem should be re-evaluated, and other solutions determined and implemented. Every effort should be made to ensure that the problem ultimately is dealt with or eliminated.

It is, however, possible that police departments adopt problem solving without embracing the spirit of community policing. Problem solving aimed only at crime or problem solving derivative of a unilaterally developed police agenda without involving the community in the problem identification and solving process can erode into traditional policing with citizens both isolated from the police and police advancing their own agendas. In this situation problem solving becomes little more than a public relations effort or police tactic that can cause greater alienation of the police and community. When problem solving is used based on the philosophy of community policing, citizen's have the power to identify their concerns and implement their solutions, not just law enforcement responses.

In addition to problem solving, the police often engage in situational crime prevention. Situational crime prevention is a form of problem solving and comprises, "opportunity-reducing measures that are, (1) directed at highly specific forms of crime, (2) that involve the management, design, or manipulation of the immediate environment in as systematic and permanent a way as possible, and (3) so as to increase the effort and risks of crime and reduce the rewards as perceived by a wide range of offenders" (Clarke, 1992:4). Adherents to situational crime prevention believe that crime is a product of "rational choice" where criminals weigh the likelihood of being discovered with the potential benefits of the act (Cornish & Clarke, 1987). Of course this is a highly speculative and narrow view of criminality that implies that traditional enforcement efforts can affect crime. Proponents of this perspective often see increases in the difficulty of committing crime or the likelihood of apprehension resulting in reduced levels of crime.

Situational crime prevention also relies on routine activities theory. Routine activities theory postulates that crime occurs when a motivated criminal converges on a suitable target when there is a lack of guardianship (Felson, 1994). For example, increases in residential burglary during the 1960s and 1970s have been attributed to decreased guardianship because of the increase in empty homes. Yet, decreases in the burglary rates in the 1980s and 1990s did not follow an increase in the number of guardians available to protect so-called "targets." Also, proponents of this perspective find that there are large numbers of crime on routes leading to bars, taverns, adult bookstores, and other entertainment spots. As criminals travel to and from these locations and their homes, they discover opportunities to commit crime. One method for reducing crime, according to supporters of the theory, is to increase guardianship. Guardianship can be increased through neighborhood watches, police presence, and increased citizen activity. Yet, little is understood about how criminals modify their "routine activities" to correspond to changes in crime control tactics. An obvious goal of community policing is to increase the role of citizens in guardianship, but it is only one tactic that has become loosely associated with crime prevention and community policing.

Traditional police, trained to think solutions lie in responding to calls and catching criminals, must be educated to make the shift from an agenda driven by isolated incidents to one focused on solving the underlying problem in new ways. One side of the scale, critics of problem solving worry, is that this kind of solution does not do enough to apprehend criminals, and that problem solving, especially when crime prevention is used as a solution, will simply displace crime. Others argue, hopefully, that crime is opportunistic, and anything that the police can do to make it tougher for people to commit crimes holds the promise of reducing crime (Eck & Weisburd, 1995). The displacement of crime, however, is a real crime control issue—whether crime is displaced from one community to the next or whether it is moved from the streets into suites. The displacement of crime can lead to aggressive and more intrusive law enforcement practices as police attempt to follow the path of crime from public to private locations. Such practices are fraught with the potential to eroding any public support gained from citizens as police attempt to investigate and reach into citizens' homes to ferret out crime—inevitably, mistakes are made. On the other side of the scale, critics argue that problem solving, divorced from the spirit of community policing, erodes into nothing more than an elaborate law enforcement tactic that uses the language of community policing and the scientific method to exert greater control on communities and give the police more power, which can result in less police accountability (Kappeler & Kraska, 1998; 1998a).

Community policing approaches problems very differently than traditional policing and mere problem solving in that it focuses on quality of life concerns. In most instances, crime and disorder have far-reaching consequences for victims or those who are affected. Traditionally, the police have responded only to that portion of the call that met departmental criteria as being important. If the problem did not meet some police criteria, e.g., constitute a criminal offense or appear as an obvious violation or problem to the responding officer, little was done. Complainants were commonly told to get a warrant, take civil action, or that there was nothing the police could do about their particular situation. Community policing dictates that officers delve deeper into problems than required by official criteria. Community problems and the consequence of crime, regardless of their nature or extent, are of concern to the CPO.

- **Working Together** – The professional model of policing was institutionalized in the early 1900s. It dictated that police officers remain aloof and detached from the citizen-clients they served. Police administrators believed that if officers were "professional" in their interactions with citizens, as defined by this aloofness and detachment, then there would be less possibility of police corruption and political intervention into police affairs, which were two significant problems at the time (Bracey, 1992).

  This professional model, as represented in popular culture, was perhaps best typified by the popular 1950s television police show "Dragnet." The main character in the show was Sergeant Joe Friday who always quipped, "Just the facts, ma'am," anytime a witness or victim became overly verbose or strayed from the facts in his or her description of what had occurred. Sergeant Friday was portrayed as a professional, uncaring bureaucrat who cared only about making the arrest and little about the emotional or physical welfare of citizens with whom he came into contact. Police officers commanded respect and demanded answers; they were the persons holding all the power in any interaction with the public. Sergeant Friday's narrow mandate, to solve the crime, meant that he could not allow anything to interfere with achieving his goal. He had no time to listen to anyone's petty concerns, such as rowdy kids in the neighborhood, barking dogs, or potholes in the street. Sergeant Friday showed little sympathy or concern even for frightened victims, since their emotions simply got in the way of his opportunity to get the facts.

  Community policing drastically departs from the Joe Friday mind-set of policing. Today, CPOs are concerned with health issues, zoning laws, rowdy kids, barking dogs, or potholes, and it is just important for officers to attend to victims' emotional needs, as it is to attend to their injuries. The community policing philosophy rests on two important departures from the past:

- **Developing Trust** – Community policing suggests that to get "the facts, " the police must do more than attempt to impose their authority and order on a community, that they must find new ways to promote cooperation between citizens and the police. Information is the lifeblood of both traditional and community policing. Without facts, police officers cannot solve crimes or social problems. The challenge the police face in getting information is that there must some level of trust for citizens to cooperate with the police. Historically, the rich and middle class had a great deal of trust for their police, but relationships with most poor and minorities left a great deal to be desired (Kappeler, Sluder & Alpert, 1994; Carter, 1985; Scaglion & Condon, 1980). In many instances, the police were seen as armed, uniformed strangers who could hurt you, but would not help you. The police were intimidating. Today, officers must foster better relations with all segments of society. They must attempt to gain all citizens' trust so that they can also gain their cooperation.

A prime example of the trust problem occurred in New Orleans in the mid-1990s. During that period, the police department was rife with corruption and the police were known for their brutality. The police essentially were out of control. The problem came to a culmination with the shooting of a police officer by another officer who was committing an armed robbery. During the period, citizens had good reason not to trust their police. Some citizens stated that when cases went to court, they would have more faith in the defendants' testimony than that of police officers. Not only did citizens not trust their police, they were afraid of them. After national attention and substantial public outcry, the city began a reform of the police department. History shows that it is a long and arduous process for a police department to reform itself and regain public support and trust (Kappeler, Sluder & Alpert, 1998).

In contrast, a central part of community policing is building trust. An important strategy is for CPOs to directly communicate with as many individuals and groups of people as possible. CPOs not only attempt to portray themselves as friends and partners in the community—they must become friends and partners with the community. This philosophy ultimately fosters greater trust and cooperation.

- **Sharing Power** – The second dramatic departure from the past is that the CPO's agenda is influenced by the community's needs and desires, not just the dictates of the department. Historically, police administrators have set the agenda for policing, often without any regard or input from the citizens who were being policed (Cordner, 1978). The police, from chief to line police officer, must recognize that citizens have a legitimate right to make demands upon the police and control their agenda. Police departments in addition to being law enforcement organizations, should be service organizations, and as such, they should provide the best level of service possible. This means asking *all* citizens, not just those supportive of the police, about the kinds and levels of services they need and want.

  Empowering citizens also requires an important adjustment in the line officer's thinking. Traditional officers who believe their authority should be sufficient to demand compliance may find it difficult to make the shift to sharing power as demanded by community policing. A traditional officer might find it difficult or unwieldy to chat with citizens about seemingly petty concerns, but this is an important part of community policing. It builds a bond between the police and citizens, and it allows officers to gather information about what they should be doing. The best CPOs understand that people are not obstacles the officer must overcome to do the job, but a tremendous resource that can be tapped to make the community a better and safer place. It also takes the sustained presence of a CPO to persuade people that the department now sees them in this new light, and that the commitment to sharing power is real.

The CPO's challenge also includes involving people directly in efforts to solve problems in the community. Not only does community policing encourage people to act as the eyes and ears of the department, it solicits their direct participation in solving problems. Community policing goes well beyond other programs such as neighborhood watch, crime prevention, or police-community relations in this regard. It might mean encouraging volunteers to help staff the local office. It could mean urging groups of parents to volunteer their time to coach summer athletic activities for kids. It often means asking businesses to donate goods, services, or expertise for neighborhood projects. The goal is for the CPO to recruit as many volunteers as possible, so that the community has dozens of people working together to make a difference. Generating community involvement is one of the most difficult aspects of community policing (Skogan & Hartnett, 1997).

- **Creative** – The Community Close-Ups at the end of this book demonstrate that community policing will work in any kind of police department, from large municipalities to small towns. Community policing can be successful because it is not a static program. It represents a philosophy whereby problems are identified and strategies and tactics are determined by the community not just the police. Community policing is a form of accountable creativity whereby CPOs are allowed to experiment and try a variety of tactics. Accountability is interjected into the process because CPOs are forced not only to successfully address specific problems and community concerns but to seek community involvement into the solutions to be implemented. This is a departure from traditional policing whereby a police department had a limited repertoire of enforcement-based programs, and all were essentially addressed using the same strategies and tactics. Also, officers in traditional policing were evaluated on response times, the numbers of arrests they made, and the numbers of citations they issued. These measures have little to do with community policing or quality police work (Stephens, 1996).

- **Crime, Fear of Crime, Disorder, and Quality of Life** – We have long debated the primary role of the police in society (Wilson, 1968; Harring, 1984; Manning, 1997), and over the last 30 years we have come to the point whereby everyone accepts that the police role expands well beyond law enforcement and "crook catching." In fact, reviews of police activities show that the majority of calls and the vast amount of time police spend on the job is of a non-crime nature (Whitaker, 1982; Greene & Klockars, 1991). The advent of community policing has resulted in a broader police mission evolving. Today, police see crime, fear of crime, disorder, and the general quality of life all as being important parts of the police mission. Indeed, all of these societal factors are intertwined and interact with one another.

Community policing recognizes that fear of crime can be as much of a problem as crime itself. It is fear of crime that can trap the elderly in their homes or can make people afraid to venture out alone. Traditional policing efforts have had little, if any, ability to reduce fear. Fear was not even a consideration or objective in traditional policing. Periodically the police would make arrests that might have had a short-lived impact on fear, but for the most part, people sustained a fairly significant level of fear for which the police did little. This fear adversely affected people's daily lives. An important ingredient in community policing is active police involvement with citizens through a wide range of programs designed to involve citizens in fear reduction. CPOs must get people out of their homes and actively involved in their communities. CPOs must also be careful not to promote unnecessary fear of crime to gain support.

- **Community Policing Officers (CPOs)** – CPOs are a new breed of officers who see themselves as community members and problem-solvers, and not just as crime-fighters or call-answers. A CPO answers calls and makes arrests, just like any other police officer, but these activities actually are only a small part of the job. The CPO acts as an innovator, looking beyond individual incidents for new ways to solve problems. The CPO is the police department's direct link to the community, providing policing with a human touch, an officer who people know on a first-name basis and as a friend who can help. The CPO acts as a catalyst, involving people in efforts to police themselves. The CPO is a mini-chief in a beat area, with the autonomy to do what it takes to solve problems. The CPO also acts as a referral specialist, the community's ombudsman who can link people to the public and private services that can help and who can jog reluctant bureaucracies to do the jobs they are supposed to do. The CPO acts as the crime prevention and police-community relations specialist, not just as a law enforcer.

    The hallmark of community policing is that policing is tailored to neighborhood needs. In some programs, the CPOs operate out of offices in schools, public housing, or even in shopping malls. Police service and access are decentralized so that the police are more approachable by citizens. When the police are accessible, citizens are more likely to cooperate with them, have a reduced fear of crime, and be willing to provide crime-related information.

    Some CPOs walk the beat, while others may ride a horse or a bike. The mode of transportation is not as important as the commitment to ensuring that the CPO has the time and opportunity to talk with people formally and informally. The police mode of transportation is merely the vehicle by which CPOs get into contact with the members of the community. It is also important that CPOs take calls like any other officer, though some departments have decided to phase this in over time, as a way to reduce internal dissent by allowing the CPOs to prove their worth first.

- **Particular Geographic (Beat) Area** – The importance of stationing a CPO permanently in a specific beat area rests on allowing the officer to *co-own* that particular piece of turf. The optimal size of each beat can differ dramatically from place to place. The goal is to keep the geographic area small enough so that the officer can get around the entire beat area often enough to maintain direct contact. In high-density areas, a CPO might only be able to handle a few blocks at most, while in a relatively tranquil residential area of single-family homes, the CPO's ability to cover the physical distance might be the primary limiting factor.

  Another important consideration in setting up beats is for the department to identify areas of community cohesion. Whenever possible, it pays to not divide a distinct neighborhood so that they fall into two or more beat areas. Along these same lines, it is not a good idea to have more than one distinct neighborhood group in the same beat area. The goal is to decentralize police service by dividing the area into natural and manageable units, so that people can receive *quality* police service regardless of whether they live in little-town, Texas, or mid-town Manhattan. Beats, where possible, should be as homogeneous as possible.

  A major misunderstanding about community policing stems from the misconception that the goal in freeing the officer from the patrol car is so that the officer serves as a visible deterrent to crime on the street. While that may be a useful by-product of freeing CPOs from the patrol car or even a specific tactic in a high-crime area, the more important purpose is to involve the officer in the life of the community. This allows the to CPO integrate into the community. Obviously, the size of the beat significantly affects the quality of this integration process.

  In the Flint foot patrol project, there was roughly one foot officer for every 2,500 people. Some residents complained that they were not seeing officers often enough. Regardless, police resources are limited, and community policing requires more personnel than traditional patrols. CPOs must set priorities and schedule within their beats to maximize contact and goal accomplishment. The department had to educate people about how community policing worked, so that the citizens understood the program and did not develop false expectations.

- **Direct, Daily, Face-to-Face Contact** – Community policing also rests on maintaining the same CPO in the same beat every day. The goal is to involve CPOs so deeply in the life of the community that the officers feel responsible for what happens in their beats, and the people who live there learn to trust them and work with them, and hold them accountable for their successes and failures. CPOs should not be used as pinch *hitters* to fill vacancies elsewhere in the department, nor should they be rotated in and out of different beats. The only way that community policing can work is when both the officers and the residents can count on the CPOs continued, daily presence. This breeds familiarity on the part of the officers and citizens, which is an important ingredient in community policing.

There is considerable debate around the question of whether CPOs should be allowed to use cars for at least part of their shifts, simply to get around their beat areas more quickly. The optimal situation allows CPOs to walk or ride a horse, motor-scooter, or bicycle around the beat area, at least some of the time. These modes of transportation make it easy to stop and chat and to reassure people that the officer is concerned with them and their problems. Freeing officers from patrol cars altogether may be an essential step in reversing the pitfalls of traditional policing.

The danger in the traditional system's reliance on the patrol car is that the patrol car becomes a barrier to communication with people in the community. Officers trapped inside cars are segregated from the public. They become slaves to the police radio, which serves less as a link to people in the community than as a means for the department to control the officers' behavior and activities. This is especially true in large cities where officers run from one dispatched call to another. In some jurisdiction, officers never have the opportunity to talk with pedestrians or business owners in their beat areas.

There is an obvious danger in suggesting that police administrators can consider the elements that make up community policing as a shopping list from which they can pick and choose the things that sound easy to adopt and ignore those that are difficult to implement. We will discuss the consequence and practice of picking and choosing among the various programs and tactics that have become associated with community policing in the concluding chapter of the book. Yet, community policing can take different forms in different areas, depending on the internal dynamics of the department and the external situations in the community. Ultimately, the sincerity of the commitment to the concept probably matters more than the particular strategies or tactics, and some departments may have good reason to phase in aspects of the approach over time.

What Community Policing Does Not Constitute

The above sections provide a fairly in-depth discussion of the idea of community policing. Community policing is a comprehensive philosophy which affects every person and part within a police department. It is also an overarching philosophy which dictates a department's operational strategies and tactics. To reinforce understanding of what community policing is, it is important to understand what community policing *is not*. By understanding what does not constitute community policing, we get a better idea of what needs to occur if it is to be implemented correctly.

- **Community policing is not a technique.** The two philosophies that have dominated modern policing are traditional (professionalized) policing, personified by the aloof or detached motor patrol officer traveling to the scene in a patrol car to respond to a call for service or attempt to apprehend a criminal, and community policing, embodied in the accessible CPO working with neighborhood residents to find new, creative solutions to problems. These two philosophies represent ends on a continuum, and most police departments fall somewhere in between (Toch, 1997; Gaines & Swanson, 1997). Many police departments have moved away from the old quasi-military model, but many others are rapidly embracing military type tactics under the language of community policing (Kappeler & Kraska, 1998; Kraska & Kappeler, 1997). Additional movement and redirection by many departments is required if they are to embrace the spirit of community policing successfully. Regardless, community policing is not a technique that departments can apply to a specific problem, but an entirely new way of thinking about the role of the police in the community. It says that the police must focus on addressing community concerns, rather than their own agendas.

- **Community policing is not public relations.** Improved public relations is a welcome by-product of community policing, though not its sole or even primary goal. The idea of police-community relations grew from work by the National Conference on Christians and Jews which led to the establishment of the National Institute on Police and Community Relations at Michigan State University in 1955 (Radelet & Carter, 1994). "Between 1955 and 1967 more than 1,100 police officials representing 180 agencies participated in conferences" sponsored by the institute (Strecher, 1997:91). By the 1960s, most larger police departments had police-community relations units. These units, however, tended not to attempt to help the community or focus on community needs, but rather they were designed to sell the police department to citizens. The underlying philosophy was that a substantial amount of dissatisfaction with the police was the result of citizens not understanding the police and the difficulties facing them as they enforce the law (Wintersmith, 1976). Police-community relations programs were seen as vehicles to educate the public and lessen the strains between the police and citizens.

  Community policing, on the other hand, enhances the department's image because it is a sincere change in the way the department interacts with people in the community. Police-community relations, by and large, was appearance, while community policing is substantive. It treats people as partners, a new relationship based on mutual trust and shared power. The traditional system often makes people feel that the police do not care about their needs. In traditional departments, officers often see people in the community as *them*, those nameless and faceless strangers whose reluctance to cooperate and share what they know makes them indistinguishable from the criminals (see Van Maanen, 1995). Community policing instead treats people in the community as an extension of *us*.

- **Community policing is not soft on crime.** Critics suggest that community policing's broad mandate and its focus on the community as opposed to crime and using tactics other than arrest to solve problems detract from a proper focus on serious crime. CPOs often face ridicule from fellow officers who call them *lollicops* or the *grin-and-wave squad*. The reality is that CPOs make arrests just like any other officer does, but CPOs deal with a broader variety of community concerns *in addition to* crime, not as *a substitute* for addressing serious crime. As discussed later in this volume, patrol officers typically spend vast amounts of uncommitted time on random patrol, which has little, if any, real impact on serious crime (Kelling et al., 1974). In contrast, CPOs spend their time between calls on a variety of proactive efforts designed to prevent crime and solve problems. CPOs remain engaged with the community throughout their shifts not just when called.

Crime analysis routinely shows that the majority of calls for service come from a relatively small number of locations (Sherman, 1987). An important ingredient of community policing is to focus on these "hot spots." But merely focusing on the so-called "hot spots" fails to recognize that police behavior and programs influences who will and who will not call the police for assistance. Furthermore, applying location-oriented policing based on traditional notions of what calls are worthy of a police response violates the spirit of community policing. CPOs must dissect these areas, determine what is occurring in terms of problems and develop strategies for reducing problems. CPOs must also be mindful that their behaviors, programs, and data collection techniques, at least in part determine, what a "hot spot" is. By way of example, one rarely hears police speak of a concentrated group of drug users as a hot spot for the transmission of HIV. Community policing dictates that CPOs consider strategies and tactics which include, but are not limited to, arrest and suppression. This does not mean that community policing is soft on crime; it means that community policing is open to more suggestions as to how to solve broad social problems, with arrest being only one alternative.

- **Community policing is not flamboyant.** When a SWAT team successfully disarms or kills a sniper or a barricaded person, their work makes the headlines. When a CPO helps organize a summer softball league for idle neighborhood youngsters, the long-term impact may be equally as dramatic, but the effort will not rate a lead-off feature on the nightly TV news. It very likely will not be picked up by the media. The media reinforces the image of the macho police officer whose job is glamorous, tough, and often dangerous (Kappeler, Blumberg & Potter, 1993, 1996; Kasinsky, 1994). The hero myth and "warrior fantasy" also appeals to police officers themselves (Kraska, 1996; Crank, 1998), which accounts for a substantial degree of resistance to true community policing. Community policing recognizes that the job gets done through steady, hard work. CPOs must learn to defer gratification and notoriety and focus on the job and its long-term benefits.

- **Community policing is not paternalistic.** Police departments are organized as a paramilitary hierarchy where those at the top, to some extent, expect to set the department's agenda, based on their experience and expertise. This organizational structure and mentality often extends beyond the police department itself and is manifested in the way officers typically inter-act with the community (Kappeler, Sluder & Alpert, 1998). In its most extreme form, the message to the average citizen is that the police think peo-ple do not know enough about police work to do much more than pay taxes and respond to officers when questions are asked. The traditional, paternal-istic police attitude suggests that crime is so complex and difficult that it must be left in the hands of skilled professionals specifically trained for the job. Community policing threatens those who enjoy the traditional system, because it requires that police superiors empower officers and citizens with the decision-making authority to properly serve communities.

- **Community policing is not an independent entity within the depart-ment.** Ultimately, the community policing philosophy must inundate the entire department. There are a number of ways of implementing community policing, including doing so gradually. Piecemeal arrangements include the formation of a special unit or concentrating on specific geographical areas. In fact, it is virtually impossible to suddenly and comprehensively implement community policing in all but the smallest departments. When community policing is implemented piecemeal, it can generate tremendous pressure on the CPOs, who are the most visible expression of the new commitment. The challenge is finding ways to demonstrate to non-committed members of the department how the community policing philosophy works.

     Patrol officers in particular must be shown that CPOs not only help them by providing information, but also that they help ease tensions between the police and the community, which can be a particular problem in minority neighborhoods. In the Flint, Michigan experiment, a foot patrol officer arrived on the scene shortly after patrol officers had responded to a call about a man brandishing a gun. The foot officer was able to tell his motor patrol peers that the man inside was known as a heavy drinker, and that his wife routinely vis-ited her sister when he got drunk. A phone call there confirmed that the wife was safe and had her children with her, and that the man was probably asleep in the back bedroom. When the officers entered, they found the man passed out in bed as predicted. By working together, the motor officers and the CPO solved the problem with the least risk to themselves and others and avoided using a SWAT team. This is quite a different approach to the problem when compared to the use of paramilitary teams using force to extract citizens from their homes. CPOs are able to assist other officers because of the intimate knowledge they amass as a result of close ties with the community—thus, hopefully reducing the need for force-based actions.

- **Community policing is not cosmetic.** Unlike crime prevention and police-community relations programs, community policing goes beyond providing information and expressing goodwill. Community policing requires that departments make substantive changes in how the department interacts with the public. Community policing broadens the police mandate to focus on proactive efforts to solve problems. CPOs are simply the patrol officers who serve as community outreach specialists, offering direct, decentralized, and personalized police service as part of a full-spectrum community policing approach that involves the entire department in new community-based efforts to solve problems.

Unlike limited proactive or community-relations efforts of the past, community policing not only broadens the agenda to include the entire spectrum of community concerns, but it offers greater continuity, follow-up, and accountability. It is important to understand that community policing goes beyond handing out brochures, making speeches, talking with community leaders, telling people how to guard against crime, and urging fellow officers to treat people with respect. As line officers directly involved in the community, CPOs have the opportunity to make real, substantive changes.

In Florida, a CPO concerned about the poverty and high unemployment in his beat area actively solicited leads on jobs which he posted in the neighborhood community policing office. Officers in the Jefferson County, Kentucky, Police Department participated in neighborhood programs in public housing where youngsters were tutored in reading and mathematics. Community policing's proactive focus goes beyond target hardening, street sweeps of so-called hot spots, and other relatively superficial solutions, to initiating creative efforts that attack the very social fiber of problems. Such solutions hold the promise of long-term changes whose full impact may not become fully evident for years.

- **Community policing is not just another name for social work.** The broad constellation of problems that plague society, especially in the inner city, defy simple solutions. Yet critics of community policing think that involving officers in efforts that have not traditionally been viewed as part of the police mandate is not only wasteful, but silly. Traditionalists insist that the police have their hands full trying to battle serious crime, so efforts that detract from that effort not only waste valuable time and money, but they can erode the credibility and authority of the police. Their attitude is that the police should leave social work to the social workers, so that the police can focus all their energies on their real and important job of fighting crime.

  Yet, this position ignores the fact that crime constitutes only a small portion of what the police are called upon to do (Kappeler, Blumberg & Potter, 1996). Indeed, if the police actually attempted to limit their mandate solely to crime, it would be almost impossible for most departments to justify the bulk of their budgets. The fact is, police officers are already involved in many non-law enforcement activities which have little, if anything, to do with serious crime. These activities include: crowd control at public events, protecting politicians, issuing traffic tickets, providing people with directions, investigating accidents, or helping stranded motorists. The issue is not whether the police should become involved in efforts that do not directly focus on serious crime, but what kinds of other services should the police provide.

As the only government social agency open 24 hours a day, seven days a week, people call the police for help with a host of problems that have little or nothing to do with serious crime. Yet, if the police refuse to help, if only by offering advice on alternative solutions, this further alienates people from the police, which can make people less eager to cooperate when the police later need their assistance. Furthermore, government has a moral obligation to serve its constituents, and the police are most often in the best position to do so. The fact is, social work has always been an important element of police work.

Community policing not only embraces this role, but it broadens it by urging officers to focus on addressing community problems and concerns. As discussed in succeeding chapters, traditional policing at best has only a limited impact on most serious crime. For example, the officer is almost never there when a drunken husband unexpectedly reaches for a knife in a family fight, when a clandestine dope deal goes sour, or when a mugger in an alley panics and shoots someone. Yet many people believe society's crime problems would be better served if the police just cracked heads and the courts locked everyone one up for long periods of time. This mind-set ignores three important realities:

- **Rebellion** – Many people respond to aggression with rebellion. If the police limit their approach to *getting tough,* they risk alienating the very people they are sworn to serve and protect. As we have learned from psychology and sociology, real or implied violence simply begets more violence. The police must find more effective ways to reduce the level of violence in this culture, not only because it is morally right, but because it is also in their enlightened self-interest. Unnecessary aggression today may play a role in creating tomorrow's *cop haters.* At a practical level, limiting an officer's response to a get-tough approach can also limit effectiveness. A helping hand can often be far more effective in solving a problem.

- **Justice system limitations** – Another obvious obstacle in the get-tough approach is that there is not enough jail and prison space to lock up everyone. The reality in many areas today is that there is barely enough room to keep the most serious offenders behind bars.

  Not only does this mean that arresting more people may ultimately prove futile, experience shows that prisons fail to rehabilitate. In fact, most correctional systems today do not even put on the pretense of attempting to rehabilitate offenders. The system can do little to turn around a serial rapist, which is why scarce prison space should be devoted to keeping the most violent offenders off the street.

Longer-term solutions may lie in urging the police to explore new ways to intervene with youngsters who are at the greatest risk of pursuing criminal careers as adults. This means taking the so-called petty crimes of juveniles far more seriously than the current system does. The sad fact is that the traditional police approach often gives short shrift to crimes like vandalism, despite the fact that spending a little more time on a young offender's problem today may save resources and time in the future. An additional irony is that it is far easier for the police to have a positive impact on a youngster who is only beginning his or her criminal career.

A community policing approach assists the police in finding new ways to handle juveniles at risk, especially since it encourages officers to consider arrest as only one option they can employ. So CPOs who are skilled in employing a range of innovative approaches to encourage positive change are the logical candidates to develop new strategies aimed at kids. The benefit to the community is that this approach holds the promise of making streets safer in the future, without the need to keep building more and more jails and prisons.

- **Scope of service** – The third reality ignored in a narrow, get-tough approach is that roughly four of every five calls for service to any police department do not involve a crime in progress. The romantic vision of the officer as crime fighter, tracking down vicious killers or clever jewel thieves, bears little relationship to how most police officers spend their days and nights (Kappeler, Blumberg & Potter, 1996). It is far more likely that someone calls the police needing help with a barking dog, a loud party, a disheveled panhandler who is scaring customers away, or a drunk sleeping in the hallway.

    By labeling these as *nuisance* calls, the police send the message to people that they do not appreciate being asked to waste their time on these annoyances. Yet, if people who call the police for relatively minor problems are made to feel they are merely bothering the police, the department should not be shocked to find that people are increasingly reluctant to risk their own personal safety to help the police by providing information or direct assistance, or when they refuse to pay more in taxes for police service. People resent a system where the police always seem to have the time to issue them a traffic ticket for speeding, but they cannot find the time to have an officer help stop the neighbor's dog from barking all night. It should be remembered that if a citizen calls the police, very likely, the problem is very important to the citizen regardless of what the police think!

The police officer must be many things, law enforcement officer and peace officer, armed symbol of authority and part-time social worker (Cumming, Cumming & Edell, 1965). It is this blend of force and compassion that makes the job so potent and unique. No other job in civilian society permits a person to choose from an array of responses that range from flashing a friendly smile to using deadly force. For many years, the British bobbies were famous for not needing to carry guns because they were not only respected but loved by the people they served. Though that has changed, it serves as a reminder that verbal aggression and physical force can never solve contemporary social problems.

- **Community policing is not elitist.** One of the biggest difficulties that CPOs often face is that they are heroes in the community, but objects of sarcasm and scorn among their peers. Some of the resentment stems from CPOs receiving seemingly preferential treatment or special consideration by the department or citizens. Left unchecked, this friction can erupt into outright hostility. Departments that launch new community policing efforts must pay particular attention to educating everyone in the department about the community policing philosophy, the role of the CPO, and how this new way of policing can benefit everyone in the department directly. It takes constant reinforcement from the top to explain that CPOs are not being treated like an elite corps, but as the department's direct link to the community. It is also important to establish standards CPOs and allow everyone the opportunity to become involved. If everyone is given an opportunity to participate, it generally reduces some of the hostility.

- **Community policing is not designed to favor the rich and powerful in the community.** The dramatic surge in drug-related murders in Washington, D.C., at the end of the 1980s prompted more than one commentator to suggest that if these murders were occurring in an affluent enclave nearby such as Georgetown, the police would be forced to take more action. That damning indictment that the police pay more attention to the problems of the rich and powerful deserves a closer look because it offers more than a kernel of truth.

    The fact is, of course, that the odds are that an upscale community like Georgetown will never suffer a similar spate of drug-related murders. The mistake is to think that this is because most of the residents of Georgetown obey the law, while the majority of those who live in poor neighborhoods in the District of Columbia do not. But what it does mean, is that the high price tag required to afford to live in Georgetown means the community does not suffer from poverty, unemployment, illiteracy, over-crowdedness, substandard education, declining health care, or despair, the myriad of social ills that plague many inner-city neighborhoods. Crime clusters in neighborhoods that already suffer from social and economic problems, and these problems can overwhelm the citizens forced to live there.

Yet there may well be more than a little truth to the persistent allegations that the police often accede to pressures to pay more attention to the wants and needs of the rich and powerful. Though this can include paying attention to even the most serious crime of murder, any gap in the level of service between rich and poor is likely to grow even wider in the level of response for less important calls for service. In fact, one of the most common complaints from inner-city residents is under-enforcement of the law (Walker, 1994). Inner-city residents complain that the police do not give their problems the same consideration that they give to problems in more affluent communities.

It is easy to see why the police might hustle faster to investigate an abandoned car, up on blocks with no wheels, if the call comes from a senator in Georgetown rather than someone from a bad section in the District. The first reason is that the police in Georgetown may well be far less busy, because there are fewer emergency calls demanding an immediate response. Second, that abandoned car would be a relative rarity in Georgetown, which makes it seem more suspicious. And the unfortunate and unavoidable third reason is that a Senator who is unhappy with the police response can do far more to make problems for the department. The Senator may well know the chief personally and would have few qualms about calling at home to complain. Senators also have access to the media, a bully pulpit from which they can denounce the department's inefficiency. Poor people, on the other hand, seldom have any access whatsoever when they feel grieved as a result of government inaction or insufficient action.

Community policing is egalitarian in the sense that it says that regardless of whether you have money and power, and despite whether you do or do not vote or pay taxes, all citizens deserve direct assistance and support from the police. Community policing requires that every area within a jurisdiction be evaluated and serviced. Community policing mandates that the police not disregard the needs of the poor, disadvantaged, or least powerful in society.

- **Community policing is not a panacea.** Perhaps the greatest lesson this country has learned in the past few decades is that social problems do not lend themselves to simple solutions. Part of the difficulty in educating people about community policing is that it cannot be captured in a slogan. It is not a nifty, new tactic that can be instituted overnight to solve a particular problem. Community policing is instead a sophisticated, subtle, logical, and flexible approach that focuses on street-level problems and concerns. It will not fix all problems (Buerger, 1991), but it fully does better than other models of policing when addressing problems or responding to citizens.

- **Community policing is not "safe."** Allowing officers the freedom to attempt creative solutions to problems carries with it the risk of mistakes that can range from the embarrassing to the disastrous. The traditional system instead focuses on routinizing tasks and codifying procedures as a way to eliminate the potential for mistakes that can threaten the department's reputation.

Table 1.1
Traditional Versus Community Policing Models

Question	Traditional Policing (TPM)	Community Policing (CPM)
1. Who are the police?	A *government agency* principally responsible for law enforcement.	*Police are the public* and the public are the police; police officers are those who are paid to give full-time attention to the duties of every citizen.
2. What is the relationship of the police to other public service departments?	*Priorities often conflict.*	The police are *one department among many responsible* for improving the quality of life.
3. What is the role of the police?	Focusing on *solving crimes.*	A broader *problem-solving* approach.
4. How is police efficiency measured?	By detection and *arrest rates.*	By the *absence of crime and disorder.*
5. What are the highest priorities?	*Crimes* that are high value (e.g., bank robberies) and those involving violence.	Whatever *problems* disturb the community most.
6. What specifically do police deal with?	*Incidents.*	Citizens' *problems* and concerns.
7. What determines the effectiveness of police?	*Response* times.	*Public cooperation.*
8. What view do police take of service calls?	Deal with them only if there is no *real police work* to do.	Vital function and great *opportunity.*
9. What is police professionalism?	Swift/effective response to *serious crime.*	Keeping close to the *community.*
10. What kind of intelligence is most important?	*Crime intelligence* (study of particular crimes or series of activities crimes).	Criminal intelligence (*information about* individuals or *groups*).
11. What is the essential nature of police accountability?	*Highly centralized*; governed by rules, regulations, and policy directives; accountable to the *law.*	Emphasis on *local accountability* to community needs.
12. What is the role of headquarters?	To provide the necessary *rules and policy* directives.	To preach organizational *values.*
13. What is the role of the press liaison department?	To *keep the "heat" off* operational officers so they can get on with the job.	To *coordinate* an essential channel of communication with the community.
14. How do the police regard prosecutions?	As an *important goal.*	As *one tool* among many.

Source: M. Sparrow (1988). *Implementing Community Policing.* Perspectives on Policing, pp. 8-9. Washington, DC: National Institute of Justice and Harvard University. Italics, model labels, and numbers added.

At issue, of course, is whether police officers are educated professionals who can be trusted to do their jobs. Community policing dictates that police departments must learn to suffer the occasional mistakes, so that officers can bring the full impact of their education, training, experience, professional instincts, and imagination to bear on solving community problems. History shows that the traditional approach is far from being error-free, and that problems cannot be eliminated by treating personnel as if they cannot be trusted.

The preceding sections have laid out the idea of community policing. Our discussion shows that community policing represents a significant departure from the past. In an effort to summarize our discussion on what community policing is and is not, Table 1.1 is provided. The figure compares one author's model of traditional policing with community policing. We will discuss the implications of modeling community policing at the conclusion of the book. For now, however, the figure provides a basic contrast between the two forms of policing.

Summary

Community policing represents a new, bold approach to law enforcement. Not since the beginnings of the 1900s has law enforcement moved back to its social service roots. Community policing represents a comprehensive attack on community problems. It signals a time whereby the police are concerned with citizens and their problems as opposed to focusing solely on responding to calls for service and making arrests. Community policing truly is a paradigm shift.

It is important for the police administrator to not mistake some strategy or tactic for community policing. While community policing employs a number of strategies and tactics, the essence of community policing (empowerment of the community, community engagement, problem solving, and community partnerships) represent the glue that holds these strategies and tactics together. Community policing requires that the police work as closely as possible with citizens to identify and solve their problems. Under community policing crime reduction and "crook-catching" are not primary objectives, but represent strategies that are a part of a potentially rich over-arching philosophy.

References

Bayley, D.H. (1988). "Community Policing: A Report from the Devil's Advocate." In J. Greene & S. Mastrofski (eds.) *Community Policing: Rhetoric or Reality?*, pp. 225-238. New York, NY: Praeger.

Bracey, D. (1992). "Police Corruption and Community Relations: Community Policing." *Police Studies*, 15(4):179-183.

Buerger, M. (1991). *Repeat Call Policing: The RECAP Casebook*. Washington, DC: Crime Control Institute.

Campbell, A. & H. Schuman (1972). "A Comparison of Black and White Attitudes and Experience in the City." In C. Harr (ed.) *The End of Innocence: A Suburban Reader*, pp. 97-110. Glenview, IL: Scott Forsman.

Carter, D. (1985). "Hispanic Perception of Police Performance: An Empirical Assessment." *Journal of Criminal Justice*, 13:487-500.

Clarke, R.V. (1992). *Situational Crime Prevention: Successful Case Studies*. New York, NY: Harrow and Heston.

Cordner, G.W. (1978). "Open and Closed Models of Police Organization: Traditions, Dilemmas, and Practical Considerations." *Journal of Police Science and Administration*, 6(1):286-292.

Cornish, D.B. & R.V. Clarke (1987). "Understanding Crime Displacement: An Application of Rational Choice Theory." *Criminology*, 25:933-947.

Crank, J.P. (1998). *Understanding Police Culture*. Cincinnati, OH: Anderson Publishing Co.

Cumming, E., I. Cumming & L. Edell (1965). "The Policeman as Philosopher, Guide, and Friend." *Social Problems*, 12(3):276-286.

Dietz, S. (1997). "Evaluating Community Policing: Quality Police Services and Fear of Crime." *Policing: An International Journal of Police Strategies and Management*, 20(1):83-100.

Eck, J. & D. Weisburd (1995). *Crime and Places*. Monsey, NY: Willow Tree Press.

Felson, M. (1994). *Crime and Everyday Life: Insights and Implications for Society*. Thousand Oaks, CA: Pine Forge Press.

Gaines, L.K. & C.R. Swanson (1997). "Empowering Police Officers: A Tarnished Silver Bullet?" *Police Forum*, in press.

Goldstein, H. (1990). *Problem-Oriented Policing*. New York, NY: McGraw-Hill.

Goldstein, H. (1979). "Improving Policing: A Problem-Oriented Approach." *Crime & Delinquency*, 25:236-258.

Greene, J. & C. Klockars (1991). "What Police Do." In C. Klockars & S. Mastrofski (eds.) *Thinking About Police: Contemporary Readings*, Second Edition. New York, NY: McGraw-Hill.

Kappeler, V.E., M. Blumberg & G.W. Potter (1993, 1996). *The Mythology of Crime and Criminal Justice*, Second Edition. Prospect Heights, IL: Waveland Press.

Kappeler, V.E. & P.B. Kraska (1998). "Police Adapting to High Modernity: A Textual Critique of Community Policing." *Policing: An International Journal of Police Strategies and Management,* in press.

Kappeler, V.E. & P.B. Kraska (1998a). "Police Modernity: Scientific and Community Based Violence on Symbolic Playing Fields." In S. Henry & D. Milovanovic (eds.) *Constitutive Criminology at Work*. Albany, NY: SUNY Press.

Kappeler, V.E., R.D. Sluder & G.P. Alpert (1994, 1998). *Forces of Deviance: Understanding the Dark Side of the Force,* Second Edition. Prospect Heights, IL: Waveland Press.

Kasinsky, R. (1994). "Patrolling the Facts: Media, Cops, and Crime." In G. Barak (ed.) *Media, Process, and the Social Construction of Crime*, pp. 203-234. New York, NY: Garland Publishing, Inc.

Kelling, G., T. Pate, D. Diekman & C.E. Brown (1974). *The Kansas City Preventive Patrol Experiment: A Summary Report*. Washington, DC: The Police Foundation.

Kraska, P.B. (1996). "Enjoying Militarism: Political/Personal Dilemmas in Studying U.S. Paramilitary Units." *Justice Quarterly*, 13(3):405-429.

Kraska, P.B. & V.E. Kappeler (1997). "Militarizing American Police: The Rise and Normalization of Paramilitary Units." *Social Problems*, 44(1):1-18.

Manning, P.K. (1997). *Police Work*, Second Edition. Prospect Heights, IL: Waveland Press.

McEwen, T. (1994). *National Assessment Program: 1994 Survey Results*. Washington, DC: National Institute of Justice.

Radelet, L. & D. Carter (1994). *The Police and the Community*. New York, NY: Macmillan.

Scaglion, R. & R.G. Condon (1980). "Determinants of Attitudes Toward City Police." *Criminology*, 17(4):485-494.

Sherman, L. (1987). "Repeat Calls for Service: Policing the 'Hot Spots'." *Crime Control Reports*. Washington, DC: Crime Control Institute.

Skogan, W.G. & S.M. Hartnett (1997). *Community Policing, Chicago Style*. New York, NY: Oxford University Press.

Sparrow, M. (1988). *Implementing Community Policing*. Perspectives on Policing, No. 9. Washington, DC: National Institute of Justice and Harvard University.

Spelman, W. & J. Eck (1987). "Newport News Tests Problem-Oriented Policing." *National Institute of Justice Reports*, (Jan.-Feb.):2-8.

Stephens, D. (1996). "Community Problem-Oriented Policing: Measuring Impacts." In L. Hoover (ed.) *Quantifying Quality in Policing*. Washington, DC: PERF.

Strecher, V.G. (1997). *Planning Community Policing*. Prospect Heights, IL: Waveland Press.

Toch, H. (1997). "The Democratization of Policing in the United States: 1895-1973." *Police Forum*, 7(2):1-8.

Van Maanen, J. (1995). "The Asshole." In V. Kappeler (ed.) *The Police & Society: Touch Stone Readings*, pp. 307-328. Prospect Heights, IL: Waveland Press.

Walker, S. (1994). *The Police in America*, Second Edition. New York, NY: McGraw-Hill.

Walker, S. (1993). "Does Anyone Remember Team Policing? Lessons of the Team Policing Experience for Community Policing." *American Journal of Police*, 12(1):33-56.

Wilson, J.Q. (1968). "Dilemmas of Police Administration." *Public Administration Review*, (Sept./Oct.):407-416.

Wilson, J.Q. & G. Kelling (1982). "Police and Neighborhood Safety: Broken Windows." *Atlantic Monthly*, 29(March):29-38.

Wintersmith, R.F. (1976). "The Police and the Black Community: Strategies for Improvement." In A. Cohn & E. Viano (eds.) *Police Community Relations*, pp. 422-433. Philadelphia, PA: J.B. Lippincott.

Wycoff, M.A. & W.K. Skogan (1993). *Community Policing in Madison: Quality from the Inside Out*. Washington, DC: National Institute of Justice.

CHAPTER 2
A History of Community Policing

Perhaps it is not true that history repeats itself; it is only that man remains the same.

—Walter Sorrell

The Lessons of History

The saying that "people receive the kind of policing they deserve" ignores the role power plays in the kind, quality, and distribution of police service. The police are social control agents, an institution of government that imposes law on the public. Power, therefore, resides among those who make the laws and those who have the ability to influence the course of law. By extension, then, power is vested in those who determine police structure, set the police agenda, and choose the tactics that police employ.

In totalitarian countries, all power is vested in government leaders, an obvious invitation to abuse, since the system permits the few to impose their will on the many, with the police controlled by a power elite. In democratic societies, ideally, the people make the laws through their elected representatives, but the organization and operation of the police can vary greatly from agency to agency, and from place to place, depending on the ability of social groups to influence police practice.

A main challenge in the United States has been to fashion a structure for the police that insulates departments from the corrupting influence of politics, without risking a department so autonomous that it is isolated from accountability the citizenry. Finding the proper balance between the need for police independence and the need for public accountability has been difficult. Examining the history of American policing can help us see what we have learned—and forgotten—as modern policing evolved.

Policing shifted from an informal to a formal system, this progress also meant a shift away from direct community input and control. As we will see, most changes were the result of five interrelated pressures: (1) continued population growth; (2) the shift from an agrarian to an industrial economy; (3) increased complexity in the distribution of material resources; (4) the crowding of people into cities; and (5) advances in technology.

At the beginning of English policing, hundreds of years ago, people simply policed themselves. Policing functions were carried out by citizen volunteers. Policing, however, began to formalize by the adoption of regular night watches, manned by volunteers that ultimately culminated into paid forces that provided service around the clock. These forces underwent reform that *professionalize (bureaucratize)* and attempted to *depoliticize* the police. In this process police narrowed their mandate to crime-fighting, and motorized patrol replaced foot patrol with the police rapidly adopting modern technology. The bulk of modern policing's history shows that each succeeding advance inadvertently distanced the police further and further from the people they served.

Each effort to improve police efficiency and effectiveness was a response to an obvious problem, but few recognized that the downside to each change was increasing isolation from the community. The riots and civil unrest of the late 1960s were a vivid reminder that a democratic society will not accept a police force that is alienated from and systematically uses violence against any segment of society—regardless of the use of technology or the effectiveness or efficiency of the tactics.

The purpose in looking backward at the police is to identify the best of the past we must keep, as it warns us of mistakes we dare not repeat. The history of modern policing therefore serves to show why the emergence of community policing was a hopeful response to a system that had lost touch with its ideal function, which was to find ways to involve all citizens in improving society.

When people feel that the police do not understand or respond to their wants and needs, when police use violence to stifle progress or maintain an order that a significant number of citizens have no vested interest in, the result is either apathy, vigilantism, or revolution. History proves that safety and order are not commodities the police can effectively impose on communities; instead they are the hallmarks of communities that participate in social equity and self-governance to improve the quality of life for all citizens.

Policing's British Roots

The United States is undeniably a diverse society, with various ethnic groups who continue to arrive in search of the American dream. While this unlikely mix has blended together to produce a uniquely American culture, with its distinct way of doing things, most of this country's institutions still show the profound early influence of the British with a strange mix of Puritan values. Therefore, to understand this country's law enforcement tradition requires a brief excursion into British police history. According to William H. Hewitt (1965), the history of law enforcement in England can be divided into three distinct, successive periods:

- The era when citizens were responsible for law and order among themselves;

- A system where the justice of the peace both meted out justice and maintained the peace; and

- A paid police force (Hewitt, 1965:4).

From our modern gaze, it is hard to imagine a time when there were no paid police officers and the community residents policed themselves. Under Alfred the Great (870-901), citizens had to help apprehend wrongdoers or risk being fined. During that era, communities were organized into *tithings, hundreds,* and *shires.* Every 10 citizens constituted a tithing and every 10 tithings made up a hundred (Uchida, 1993). A *constable,* appointed by a local nobleman, was in charge of each hundred; his job was to make sure citizens reported problems and tracked down offenders.

A group of hundreds was organized into a shire, the rough equivalent of a county. Shires were supervised by a *shire-reeve*—or *sheriff*—whose role narrowed over time to apprehending lawbreakers. During the reign of Edward I (1272-1307), the constable was formally given an official police force to help protect property in large towns; the force was funded by pledges and manned by unpaid citizen volunteers.

In 1326, Edward II established a new office, *justice of the peace,* filled by noblemen appointed by the king. The justice of the peace, with the constable serving as his assistant, eventually refined his role to that of judge—the first official split of the judicial and law enforcement functions.

It is important to understand that the king and his noblemen had a vested interest in maintaining social order, because both crime and rebellion ultimately threatened the taxes upon which the feudal system depended. The citizens supported the upper classes, in exchange for which they received some protections. As economic pressures began to erode the feudal system, the pledge system that supported these local law enforcement efforts broke down and citizen participation decreased.

The dramatic rise of the Industrial Revolution in the eighteenth century dramatically accelerated the pace of social change, as people flocked to the cities and the older forms of community control broke down as newly vested interests arose with economic change. During the eighteenth century, Britain's population grew from about 6 to 12 million persons (Critchley, 1985). Ironically, citizens moving to cities looking for work found "increasing mechanization which meant that manufacturers needed fewer and fewer workers. Accordingly, many job seekers found themselves unemployed and impoverished. Because so many workers were displaced, resentment developed that often pitted the industrialists against labor—a condition that drastically changed the nature of policing" (Kappeler, Sluder & Alpert, 1998). Social conditions in the eighteenth century worsened for most citizens. While the rich isolated themselves in enclaves with private security forces, others faced more difficult times. Evidence of disorder could be found everywhere. Riots occurred throughout Europe over food shortages, high prices, the introduction of machinery and religious prejudice (Richardson, 1974). Public drunkenness became a common sight, and intoxicated mobs often engaged in unpredictable and violent activities (Rubinstein, 1973) many of which were directed at the industrialists and their factories. Urbanization was accompanied by homelessness, sewage, and air pollution (Hernandez, 1989). By mid-century, vast, crime-riddled slums had sprung up in the industrial cities, and frightened officials and citizens created a host of erratic and overlapping groups that launched a draconian war on crime. At one point, stealing a loaf of bread was a hanging offense, one of 160 capital crimes. In that era, citizens vied for rewards paid for turning in offenders, and the guilty were given long sentences or deported to America or Australia, yet crime continued to plague urban areas.

The need for new solutions became even more urgent when the citizens began to rebel against military intervention. In 1818, troops were called in to quell a disturbance at a lecture in Manchester and 11 people were killed, with many more injured. For the first time, the people balked at using soldiers to deal with civil unrest, and the resulting public outcry set the stage for dramatic reform.

Against this backdrop of chaos, Sir Robert Peel became Home Secretary in 1822, inheriting a fragmented system where there was one police force for business, one for shipping, one for parishes, as well as a host of vigilante groups. The visionary Peel, acknowledged as the father of modern policing, introduced the Metropolitan Police Act of 1829. How the bill passed without dissent remains a mystery, since it radically restructured the status quo. The Act abolished existing efforts and, in their place, established a Police Office, administered by *justices (commissioners)* in charge of planning. It also created the Metropolitan Police District, staffed by paid constables.

The virtually unknown Charles Rowan and Richard Mayne were the commissioners Peel appointed to organize and run the new department. The duo set up operation in the back of London's Whitehall Place, which opened onto a courtyard used by the kings of Scotland—Scotland Yard. There they fashioned a plan to deploy six divisions of 1,000 men each, with each division divided into eight patrol sections, with those sections divided into eight beats.

To be an officer, candidates had to provide three character references and prove they could read and write. Despite the dismal pay—and the fact that becoming an officer cost the men their right to vote in parliamentary and municipal elections—more than 12,000 applied for the 6,000 jobs as a *Bobby* (a nickname honoring Sir Robert). Most of the officers selected came from cities other than London which further distanced the police from the community (Richardson, 1974). The turnover was high, with more than 11,000 officers leaving the force during the first three years (Richardson, 1974), in part because of low pay (Stead, 1985), but also because of misconduct (Kappeler, Sluder & Alpert, 1998) and the public's initial resistance to the new police force.

After the first year, the citizens actually called for the force to be disbanded. Yet the police persisted, battling night-long riots during their first four years, with only their batons for protection, winning respect because the Bobbies never inflicted serious injury and did not resort to calling in the military. As the crime rate began to drop and the streets became safer, the *Peelers* gained acceptance.

Yet the twin problems of low status and low pay persisted even after the force won acceptance. For years, British police officers were considered unskilled laborers, and it was not until 1890 that they were granted pensions. A police strike in 1918 led to legislation the following year that established a police federation which set pay scales and adopted a professional code. Of the nine principles typically attributed to Peel (which were, in fact, drafted by Rowan and Mayne), the seventh addresses how the police should treat the public:

> To maintain at all times a relationship with the public that gives reality to the historic tradition that the police are the public and that the public are the police; the police being only members of the public who are paid to give full-time attention to duties which are incumbent on every citizen in the interests of community welfare and existence (Reith, 1952:154).

Colonial Law Enforcement in Cities and Towns

Against this backdrop of British history, we can now trace the American law enforcement tradition to its beginnings in Colonial times. Perhaps the earliest organized law enforcement effort was the *night watch*, first established in a Boston town meeting in 1636. Unless they could provide a good excuse, all males over the age of 18 were expected to serve. No doubt the most famous *night watchman* of all time was Paul Revere, the Revolutionary War hero who roused the citizenry with the cry, "The British are coming, the British are coming."

In New York, a *scout* and *rattle watch* was established in 1651. The rattle was an actual rattle, used to sound the alarm by a *rattle watcher,* who made 48 cents for his 24-hour duty. The system was not without problems, particularly because offenders were often sentenced to this duty as punishment. However, once pay rates rose, so did the number of applicants eager for the job.

Over time, watch systems in various towns became more sophisticated and more organized. By 1705, in Philadelphia, the Common Council divided the city into 10 patrol areas, each with a constable who recruited citizen volunteers to keep the watch with him. Incredible as it seems today, all these early law enforcement efforts only provided formal protection at night. In fact, captains assigned to various areas of New York (Colony) chose to interpret sunrise as occurring anywhere from 3 a.m. to 5 a.m., so they could shorten their duty. "In the larger industrial cities in the East and Northeast, a watch system was adopted. Because the South was more rural and agriculturally based, a county system of government emerged with the office of the Sheriff providing law enforcement services. As the Midwest and West began to develop, citizens preferred law enforcement services provided by constables and sheriffs—both of whom were elected officials" (Kappeler, Sluder & Alpert, 1994:39). Though the system had serious flaws, night watches functioned fairly well as long as America remained primarily an agrarian society—keep in mind that it was not until 1790 that six cities finally reached a population of 8,000. However, at the turn of the nineteenth century, the drawbacks were becoming difficult to ignore. One major problem was that local watchmen were notoriously lax, to the degree that they had become the butt of jokes about their ineptitude.

As commerce and population in the eastern states grew, crime problems there began to mirror those in England that were fueled by the Industrial Revolution. Meanwhile, continued western expansion into the seemingly unlimited frontier created a different set of law enforcement problems. How these different traditions were ultimately wedded into one distinctly American approach requires looking at each historical trend separately.

The Rise of Municipal Police

As noted above, early law enforcement efforts in the few American cities large enough to require organized efforts consisted primarily of night watches, manned by citizens who were supervised by constables assigned to various districts. Major problems with this system were that they operated only at night, enforcement was erratic and inefficient, and the competence and character of the individuals selected or forced to serve were often suspect.

Between the Revolutionary War and the Civil War, rapid population growth and increasing industrialization pressured police departments to become more effective and more efficient. However, the downside to organizing the police into one structured department was that concentrating power into the hands of paid police without providing the proper safeguards ushered in an era marked by widespread corruption.

Table 2.1
Comparison of Community Policing to Police-Community Relations

Community Policing	Police-Community Relations
Goal: Solve problems—improved relations with citizens is a welcome by-product.	**Goal:** Change attitudes and project a positive image—improved relations with citizens is a main focus.
Line Function: Regular contact between officers and citizens.	**Staff Function:** Irregular contact between officers and citizens.
A department-wide philosophy and department-wide acceptance.	Isolated acceptance often localized in the PCR unit.
Internal and external influence and respect for officers.	Limited influence and respect for officers.
Well defined role—does both proactive and reactive policing—a full-service officer.	Loose role definition; focus on dealing with problems of strained relations between police and citizens; crime prevention encouraged.
Direct service—same officer takes complaints and gives crime prevention tips.	Indirect service—advice on crime prevention from PCR officer but "regular" officers respond to complaints.
Citizens identify problems and cooperate in setting up the police agenda.	"Blue Ribbon" committees identify the problems and "preach" to police.
Police accountability is ensured by the citizens receiving the service in addition to administrative mechanisms.	Police accountability is ensured by civilian review boards and formal police supervision.
Officer is the leader and catalyst for change in the neighborhood to reduce fear, disorder, decay and crime.	Officer provides consultation on crime issues without having identified beat boundaries or "field responsibilities."
Chief of police is an advocate and sets the tone for the delivery of both law enforcement and social services in the jurisdictions.	Chief of police reacts to only the law enforcement concerns of special interest groups.
Officers educate public about issues (like response time or preventive patrol) and the need to prioritize services.	Officers focus on racial and ethnic tension issues and encourage increased services.
Increased trust between the police officer and citizens because of long-term, regular contact results in an enhanced flow of information to the police.	Cordial relationship between police officer and citizens but often superficial trust with minimum information flow to prevent and solve crime.

Table 2.1—*continued*

Community Policing	Police-Community Relations
Officer is continually accessible in person, by telephone, or in a decentralized office.	Intermittent contact with the public because of city-wide responsibility; contact is made through central headquarters.
Regular visibility in the neighborhood.	Officer seldom seen "on the streets."
Officer is viewed as having a "stake in the community."	Officer is viewed as an "outsider."
Officer is a role model because of regular contact with citizens (especially youth role model).	Citizens do not get to know officer on an intense basis.
Influence is from "the bottom up"—citizens receiving service help set priorities and influence police policy.	Influence is from "the top down"—those who "know best" have input and make decisions.
Meaningful organizational change and departmental restructuring—ranging from officer selection to training, evaluation, and promotion.	Traditional organization stays intact with "new" programs periodically added; no fundamental organizational change.
When intervention is necessary, informal social control is the first choice.	When intervention is necessary, formal means of control is typically the first choice.
Officer encourages citizens to solve many of their own problems and volunteer to assist neighbors.	Citizens are encouraged to volunteer but are told to request and expect more government (including law enforcement) services.
Officer encourages other service providers like animal control, firefighters, and mail carriers to become involved in community problem solving.	Service providers stay in traditional roles.
Officer mobilizes all community resources, including citizens, private and public agencies, and private businesses.	Officers do not have mobilization responsibility because there is no specific beat area for which they are responsible.
Success is determined by the reduction in citizen fear, neighborhood disorder, and crime.	Success is determined by traditional measures—i.e., crime rates and citizen satisfaction with the police.
All officers are sworn personnel.	Most staff members are sworn personnel but some are non-sworn.

Source: R. Trojanowicz & B. Bucqueroux (1994). *Community Policing: How to Get Started*, pp. 133-134. Cincinnati, OH: Anderson Publishing Co.

In Philadelphia, the first of a series of so-called "Negro" riots occurred, causing widespread death and destruction, including the burning of Pennsylvania Hall. The rioting broke out again in 1842 and 1844. Around 1835, a series of riots swept through the country. About 15,000 Irish citizens and firemen clashed in Boston in 1837; riots in Philadelphia left scores of citizens dead; and in 1844, Native American riots lasted for three months, leaving many persons dead or wounded and much property damage (Fosdick, 1969). Similar episodes of mass violence took place in most other major cities. In New York, for example, 1834 was christened the "year of the riots" following repeated outbreaks of civil disorder (Miller, 1977). "Since there were no full-time police forces, cities had to resort to calling out the militia to restore order. Given problems of civil disorder, coupled with an increase in citizens' fear of crime, many cities had few options other than to create full-time, organized police forces" (Kappeler, Sluder & Alpert, 1994). As a result, police forces were formed in New York City in 1845, New Orleans and Cincinnati in 1852, Boston and Philadelphia in 1854, Chicago in 1855, Baltimore in 1857 and St. Louis in 1861. By the mid-1860s police forces had been created in virtually every major city and several smaller ones in the United States (Johnson, 1981).

As early as 1833, Philadelphia made a dramatic effort to organize an independent, competent, 24-hour-a-day police force, supported by patron Steven Girard, who left a large inheritance to fund police reform. Philadelphia passed a model ordinance that provided two dozen police, who would serve both day and night, with officers appointed by the mayor's office and control of the force vested in one officer. In addition, the new law required that promotions would be based on skill and integrity.

While this sounds like a giant leap forward—and it was—within two decades, partisan politics undid Girard's good intentions, with the police force consolidated under a marshal (later a police chief), elected for a two-year term. While that change may sound benign, it meant that the police department was no longer insulated from partisan politics. Without safeguards, such as Civil Service, the *spoils system* prevailed. That term comes from the motto, "To the victors go the spoils," used in this sense to mean that the political party that wins can use *patronage* (political favors) as a means of consolidating and perpetuating its power. The *Spoils Era* in American history referred to the period prior to passage of the Civil Service Act of 1883 as a time when many federal officials considered a government post as a virtual private fiefdom. Once elected, politicians solidified their power by taking care of the cronies who had helped them win election. Every decision, from who would receive lucrative government contracts to who would be hired or promoted, was dictated by politics rather than merit.

State and local governments were far from immune to political corruption. Within local police departments, the spoils system meant that political favoritism dictated who was hired and who was promoted. In their dealings with the public, corrupt departments did the politicians' bidding, which meant looking the other way when politicians and their friends broke the law, while using the law to punish political enemies. This kind of corruption also promoted the harassment of African-Americans and other immigrant ethnic minorities, many of whom could not vote, and the police were also used to wage outright war against strikers who threatened powerful business interests. In short, police were used to control and regulate the two major economic engines of the time—slaves and industrial workers.

Adding to opportunity for corruption as well was the fact that the police in those days also handled a number of other administrative tasks totally unrelated to what we think of today as part of the police role. In many cities, the police issued licenses for everything from taverns to ice-cream parlors, boarding houses to dog breeders. Even honest cops who were not tempted by monetary bribes could do little to defy a system where such licenses were dispensed as political favors.

In the Spoils Era, police departments were routinely headed by a police chief whose sole qualification was that he would do the bidding of the politician or politicians who gave him his job. Lack of qualified and independent leadership at the top was a major problem in American policing for many years.

In cities such as Baltimore and Cincinnati, the police force was used primarily to rig elections. Until 1844, New York City had actually had two police forces, one for daytime duty, one for night-time duty, with each dispensing patronage. The New York police reform act passed that same year became a model for the American police system, though it lagged years behind Peelian reform in England. The major problem with the law was that it allowed aldermen and assistant aldermen to appoint the police captain, assistant captains, and patrolmen for their wards to one-year terms. The police chief, appointed by the mayor, was little more than a figurehead. While the new system attempted, in theory, to consolidate and upgrade the police into one unit controlled by a police chief, in practice, it institutionalized political corruption.

In some municipalities, police officials were elected; in others, they were appointed by the mayor, the city council, or some other administrative body. Even uniforms were not standardized. As late as 1853, New York policemen wore civilian clothes and could only be identified by the 33-inch clubs they carried. Initial efforts at standardization often did little to lessen confusion, since each ward adopted its own style. For instance, the summer uniforms in some wards consisted of suits made of white duck cloth, while others opted to wear colors, and some even chose to wear straw hats.

By 1860, Philadelphia decided to adopt a standard police uniform, which consisted of single-breasted blue frock coats with brass buttons, W pants with black stripes down the sides, and an old-style broad-top cap with a leather visor. It was not until the next year that a new badge was adopted, and a few years later the trousers were changed to matching blue, inaugurating the *blue* look associated with police uniforms today.

As these anecdotes demonstrate, the history of policing in this era was marked by occasional enlightened efforts to upgrade the force, but few efforts addressed the underlying corruption in any systematic way. For example, in 1871, leading police officials of the time met in Philadelphia, where they devised and implemented the first uniform crime reporting system, a valuable attempt to find new ways to identify crime trends. Yet, this development was a first major step toward institutionalizing the police and making them a crime-fighting bureaucracy of limited responsiveness to citizens concerns. It in effect created a measure of police performance based on reported crime rather than citizen input and concern. By that time, pay scales for police officers had also improved, and, by the mid-1880s, police officers in many metropolitan areas could retire at half pay after 20 years of service.

Graft was endemic. The Lexow investigation of the New York City Police Department in 1894 confirmed that officers had to pay to be hired, with higher payoffs for promotions. From their first contact with the department, rookies learned that bribery and political pull were part of the system.

Civil Service reform helped clean up some abuses, particularly in hiring and promotion, and periodic, highly touted investigations of corruption in big-city departments also spurred change, though in many cases, those gains faded when the headlines stopped (Kappeler, Sluder & Alpert, 1998). However, as long as police leadership remained deeply politicized, the taint of corruption hovered around many municipal police departments well into the twentieth century.

While nineteenth century law enforcement in the eastern United States was primarily a study in learning how to develop structures suited to increasingly populous cities, the law enforcement challenge in the Wild West during this period focused on how to make the frontier a safer place, which involved different kinds of problems, since people were scattered far apart and communication between settlements was almost non-existent. As we will see later, no sector of the United States was free of vigilantism, but, on the frontier, even authorized efforts dispensed street justice.

Frontier Justice

The westward expansion that characterized the nineteenth century meant that people ventured into the wilderness first and then formal institutions followed. Movies about this era tend to glorify the violence associated with the lawlessness of the frontier, but there were many bloody clashes between various interest groups—sheepherders versus cattlemen, farmers versus ranchers, settlers versus Native Americans, various ethnic groups against others. Settlers were also not only easy prey for con men and swindlers offering phony land deals, but isolated families alone on the prairie had little protection from thieves and rustlers.

The laws in place were also a curious blend of criminal codes and so-called *blue laws*, a peculiarly American phenomenon where religious groups successfully lobbied to make custom part of the criminal law. Many of these laws related to the selling and consumption of alcohol, either restricting sale to certain times or places or banning it outright in specific areas. In other cases, blue laws regulated everything from store hours to public dancing. There was a certain irony in the fact that many frontier communities had rigid laws governing such social behavior, when, at the same time, it was doubtful they had the mechanisms in place even to enforce the laws against major crimes.

In many cases as well, it was difficult to tell much difference between formal law enforcement and vigilantism. The typical system in most frontier towns was that the sheriff was the chief law enforcement official. When the town or territory could afford to do so, the sheriff was a paid official, but the candidates for the job often had few skills beyond a willingness to take what was often a thankless job. The sheriff could deputize citizen volunteers to track down offenders, and visiting circuit judges made periodic rounds of outlying territories to conduct trials.

Vigilantism

Because of an inadequate justice system and the violent nature of American frontier life, many people had few qualms about taking the law into their own hands. Drawing the line between responsible efforts of organized civilian volunteers and *vigilantism* can be difficult. After all, looking back on the British experience, groups of unpaid citizens constituted the bulk of early law enforcement efforts. However, as the concept of justice evolved, it recognized that victims and their families and friends must be removed from the formal process, since they should not be expected to be objective—if you damage my property, that should be a capital crime, whereas if I damage yours, that is merely a forgivable accident.

What makes vigilantism different from responsible citizen action is that it operates *in opposition to* formal legal norms. As more than one sheriff learned, standing in the way of vigilantes intent on enforcing their own brand of justice could often be more dangerous than dealing with the criminal. When citizens pursue suspected felons, they are assisting the police, but when they seek to inflict punishment, they have crossed the line into vigilantism. Vigilantes inject emotion into a process where reason should prevail; their subjectivity undermines their claim to justice.

Among the first recorded examples of vigilantism were the South Carolina regulators who operated between 1767 and 1769. This extralegal citizens' group served as a model for later vigilante efforts. Astute filmgoers will note that Marlon Brando played a regulator hired to kill rustlers in *The Missouri Breaks,* certifying this was the preferred term for a vigilante until the mid-nineteenth century.

According to Richard M. Brown in *Violence in America,* vigilantism is based on three rationalizations:

- **Self-preservation** — Just as self-defense is a valid defense for what would otherwise be murder, this idea justifies vigilantism by arguing that citizens must be willing to *kill or be killed,* when the official system fails to provide adequate protection. Newspapers of the era often endorsed this sentiment. An editorial in the *San Francisco Herald* in 1851 said: "Whenever the law becomes an empty name, has not the citizen the right to supply its deficiencies? (Gard, 1949:158).

- **Right of revolution** – Unlike the Canadians, for instance, citizens of the United States come from a tradition of violent revolution, and early framers of the Constitution argued that periodic revolt might be necessary to prevent government tyranny. Part of the American psyche embraces the idea that when something fails to work properly, revolution is as valid a response as reform.

- **Economic rationale** – The development and maintenance of an effective criminal justice system is an expensive proposition, and this position argued that frontier towns should not bear the expense, when vigilantism did the job efficiently for free (Brown, 1969:140).

Echoes of all three justifications can be heard in this particular warning, posted outside Las Vegas, New Mexico, in 1880, a citizen manifesto similar to many of that era:

> The citizens of Las Vegas are tired of robbery, murder, and other crimes that have made this town a byword in every civilized community. They are resolved to put a stop to crime, even if, in obtaining that end, they have to forget the law and resort to a speedier justice than it will afford. All such characters are notified that they must either leave this town or conform themselves to the requirement of the law or they will be severely dealt with. The flow of blood must and shall be stopped in this community and good citizens of both the old and new towns have been determined to stop it if they have to hang by the strong arm of force every violator of law in this country—Vigilantes (Otem, 1935:205-206).

The impulse to vigilantism may be understandable, but a system with no controls is an invitation to abuse. All too often, the innocent were hung along with or instead of the guilty. In addition, whenever groups operate with no oversight, there is nothing to prevent people's worst instincts from taking over. On the frontier in the South, and also in the major cities of the East, prejudice ran high against various groups—Native Americans, African-Americans, and immigrants. Many formal law enforcement efforts were often tainted by a two-track system of justice, where offenses committed by members of unpopular groups rated punishment far beyond what white Americans suffered, especially if the victims were white.

Because vigilantes, by definition, have no external restraints, lynch mobs had a justified reputation for hanging minorities first and asking questions later. Because of its tradition of slavery, which rested on the racist rationalization that African-Americans were sub-human, the South had a long and shameful history of mistreating African-Americans, long after the end of the Civil War. Perhaps the most infamous American vigilante group, the Ku Klux Klan, was notorious for assaulting and killing African-American men for transgressions that would not be considered crimes at all, if they had they been committed by a white man.

More than one Southern African-American was hanged by a lynch mob for such *crimes* as whistling at a white woman or failing to show proper respect to a white person. Adding to the climate of terror such outrages perpetuated was the fact that many law enforcement officers participated in or gave tacit approval to Klan activities, adding to the popular perception that some vigilante groups enjoyed a quasi-legal status or were at least tolerated by the establishment. The Civil Rights Act of 1871, which has become the modern-day foundation for police legal liability for civil rights violations (Kappeler, 1993, 1997), passed in large part because of involvement of law enforcement in the activities of the Ku Klux Klan.

Twentieth-Century Policing

While the foregoing might seem like a uniformly grim and pessimistic view of the history of law enforcement, there were undeniable problems in law enforcement at the turn of the century, including the taint of corruption, shortcomings and confusion in leadership, the threat of vigilantism, and inequities in application of laws. Though Civil Service reform helped introduce increased fairness into hiring and promotion without effective leadership at the top, many police departments continued to wallow in corruption.

Part of the problem was structural, since many big-city departments were controlled by police boards that rarely provided a single, strong leader who could speak with authority for the department and to the department. Awareness of this flaw led to efforts to invest leadership in one person, so that by 1921, only 14 out of the 52 cities in the United States with a population of 100,000 or more were still run by police boards. However, this reform served to highlight another major defect—too many departments were headed by men who had no practical or educational background in law enforcement.

Once New York City adopted the single-administrator form, during roughly the next two decades, a parade of army officers, newspapermen, lawyers, and professional politicians were tapped to fill the post. In Philadelphia, during the first 20 years of the twentieth century, the position of director of public safety was filled by a candy manufacturer, an insurance broker, a banker, an electric company official, and five lawyers.

This also indicates the tremendous problem many departments had with turnover, since Civil Service reforms often did nothing to insulate the top spot from politics. Not only were most top police administrators ill-equipped for the job, they served at the whim of politicians. Police Commissioner

Woods of New York City testified in 1912: "The police department is peculiarly the victim of this principle of transient management. Most of the commissioners are birds of passage. The force gets a glimpse of them flying over, but hardly has time to determine the species" (Fosdick, 1921:68).

At that time, New York had had 12 commissioners in 19 years, with an average term on the job of less than two years, and the shortest term only lasting 33 days. In comparison, by 1912, London had had only seven police commissioners during the preceding 91 years. The problem was not limited to New York; in the early twentieth century, the director, chief, or commissioner's office in major cities seemed to have a revolving door. For example, Philadelphia had 13 directors in 33 years; Cincinnati had 4 in 7 years; Cleveland had 5 in 12 years; Chicago had 25 in 49 years; and, Detroit had 9 in 19 years.

Adding to the host of problems that plagued police departments in that era was the legislative control that tied the chief's hands, making him an instrument of the law, so that he could not innovate or experiment. In addition, low pay for police added to problems with morale and increased the likelihood of bribery. In 1900, a blue-ribbon commission known as *The Fifteen* found New York City officers had been blackmailing prostitutes, requiring a sliding scale of payoffs to look the other way.

In September 1919, the Boston police went on strike for higher wages. That night, when word spread that there were no police on duty, people looted stores and smashed windows, forcing the mayor to call out the troops. A hastily organized group of citizen volunteers was deployed to maintain order, but when they killed two citizens, that touched off intermittent rioting and violence that lasted for days. A local political leader announced: "There is no right to strike against the public safety by anybody, anywhere, anytime" (Allen, 1959:44). In response, Boston recruited an entirely new police force, but the incident left a negative mark against the police that extended far beyond the city, since the story made headlines nationwide.

Corruption also increased with passage of the Volstead Act of 1919, which made Prohibition the law of the land. This ushered in the *Roaring Twenties,* also called the *Jazz Age* or the *Flapper Era.* It was a time when bootleggers and owners of *speakeasies* openly paid off police, and many people winked at the no-alcohol law. Mirroring in some ways today's problems with illegal drugs, the huge profits from rum-running often meant huge payoffs to police. While many decried this open rebellion, a large segment of society viewed Prohibition as a laughable nuisance, and even gangsters like Al Capone and Lucky Luciano became folk heroes.

The blatant disregard of Prohibition also fostered widespread disrespect for the law in general and, by extension, disrespect for police. The 1920s were a heady time, a live-for-today response to the grimness of World War I. It was also the era of the easy buck, when people could buy stock on margin for as little as 10 percent down, which meant even busboys and cab drivers were playing the stock market. More than a few became millionaires overnight, as a result of a stock tip from a well-connected patron with insider information.

It should also be noted that one of the quickest ways for an ambitious politician to further his career was to launch an investigation of corruption in police departments. In New York, both Theodore Roosevelt and, much later, Thomas Dewey, catapulted onto the national political scene by using the springboard of police reform. The press was also eager to jump on this issue, since expressions of moral outrage about police corruption, coupled with sordid examples of abuses, helped sell newspapers.

This is not to suggest that there were not serious problems within police departments, but honest and dedicated individuals who were trying to make a difference faced tremendous odds, in no small part because the general public held the police in such low regard. A widely read article of the period said:

> Every large American police department is under suspicion. The suspicion amounts to this: that for-money crimes are not only tolerated but encouraged. The higher the rank of the police officer, the stronger the suspicion. Now it is only one step from the encouragement of vice, for the purposes of loot, to an alliance with criminals. Indeed, in some of our large cities, the robbery of drunken men is permitted already by police on the profit-sharing plan (Matthews, 1901:1314).

The Stock Market Crash of 1929 and the resulting Great Depression ended the giddy atmosphere of the 1920s with a bang, touching off a politically volatile period of re-examination. The crisis of confidence in the police set the stage for the dramatic police reform movement launched in the 1930s that determined the face of American policing for almost the next half-century.

Police Reform in the 1930s

Just as the principles attributed to Sir Robert Peel provided the foundation for British policing, Oakland, California Police Chief August Vollmer is credited with launching the American police reform movement. As head of the National Commission on Law Observance and Enforcement established by President Herbert Hoover in 1929, Vollmer supervised the preparation of 10 principles he considered vital in reforming the police:

- The corrupting influence of politics should be removed from the police organization;

- The head of the department should be selected at large for competence, a leader, preferably a man of considerable police experience, and removable from office only after preferment of charges and a public hearing;

- Patrolmen should be able to rate a "B" on the Alpha test, be able-bodied and of good character, weigh 150 pounds, measure 5 feet 9 inches tall, and be between 21 and 31 years of age. These requirements may be disregarded by the chief for good and sufficient reason;

- Salaries should permit decent living standards, housing should be adequate, eight hours of work, one day off weekly, annual vacation, fair sick leave with pay, just accident and death benefits, when in performance of duty, reasonable pension provisions on an actuarial basis;

- Adequate training for recruits, officers, and those already on the roll is imperative;

- The communication system should provide for call boxes, telephones, recall system, and (in appropriate circumstances) teletype and radio;

- Records should be complete, adequate, but as simple as possible. They should be used to secure administrative control of investigations and of department units in the interest of efficiency;

- A crime-prevention unit should be established if circumstances warrant this action and qualified women police should be engaged to handle juvenile delinquents' and women's cases;

- State police forces should be established in states where rural protection of this character is required; and

- State bureaus of criminal investigation and information should be established in every State (Wickersham Commission, 1931:140).

Though some of Vollmer's specifics may seem dated, this progressive doctrine established important concepts that served as the underpinning for modern policing:

- The necessity of eliminating political corruption;

- The need for an independent chief;

- The importance of an educated and trained police force that would be compensated as professionals;

- The judicious use of the latest technology;

- An awareness of the benefits of preventing crime;

- The beginning of an expanded role for women;

- An understanding of the need for different police approaches for urban and rural areas; and

- The importance of the service role in policing.

In their analysis of this reform movement, Harvard University's George L. Kelling and Mark H. Moore propose that Vollmer's moral vision, coupled with O.W. Wilson's work in police administration, revolutionized policing in seven areas:

- **Authorization** – In the past, police authority rested *on politics and the law;* the Reform Era replaced that underpinning *with professionalism and the law.*

- **Function** – The reform movement also narrowed the police function from a broad array of *social services to crime control.*

- **Organizational design** – Reformers also shifted departments from their previous *decentralized* model into a *classical, centralized* form.

- **Demand for services** – In the past, police *responded* to a *community's needs,* but the reform movement instead *sold* the public on the police role as *crime-fighters.*

- **Relationship to environment** – To insure against corruption and improve professionalism, the police were encouraged to abandon their *intimate* community ties and instead adopt a sort of *professional aloofness.*

- **Tactics/technology** – The foot patrols of the past gave way to preventive *motor patrol,* with an additional emphasis on *rapid response* to calls for service.

- **Outcomes** – The police of the past sought to *satisfy both politicians and mainstream citizens,* whereas the reform movement *measured success* by how well the police *controlled crime* (Kelling & Moore, 1987:38).

As Kelling and Moore point out, big-city police departments took a lesson from J. Edgar Hoover, who made the Federal Bureau of Investigation (FBI) a widely popular and respected unit by narrowing its mandate to specific crimes that were both highly visible and relatively easy to solve, then selling the public on the force's successes. "The FBI has not been without criticism. Public policy analysts and agents alike have leveled scathing criticism against the FBI, especially when Hoover was Director. Historically, the FBI has experienced two different periods of decline and criticism: the Teapot Dome-Attorney General Stone era of 1924-1936 and the Watergate era of 1972-1977 (Poveda, 1990). The Teapot Dome scandal involved large-scale corruption in the Office of the President and Congress and resulted in numerous criminal indictments and convictions. During the 1960s and 1970s, the FBI sustained substantial criticism because of its spying on noncriminal groups. For example, it was learned that from 1962 through 1968, the FBI planted numerous wiretaps and hidden microphones to monitor the movements of civil rights leader Dr. Martin Luther King, Jr., and the FBI routinely maintained surveillance on political and civic groups that were deemed to be "enemies." President Nixon revealed in 1973 that the FBI had been involved in a number of illegal burglaries for the purpose of gathering intelligence" (Gaines, Kappeler & Vaughn, 1997:18-19). Despite the FBI's ability to cultivate a professional crime-fighting image, local police did not have the luxury of picking and choosing which crimes they would pursue, the reformers could see great wisdom in narrowing the police function to crime control, not only because relative success would be easier to measure, but because involving the police in a whole host of other duties, such as political spying and issuing liquor licenses, seemed to invite inevitable corruption.

It is also important to understand the panorama of societal change that provided the backdrop against which these reforms took place. Not only had Hoover professionalized the FBI, but this was a time when it seemed every problem, including social ills, could be solved by properly applying scientific principles and the new science of management theory. As proof, believers could point to the giant strides made by industry, where moguls such as Henry Ford introduced revolutionary concepts such as the assembly line that dramatically increased productivity by stressing efficiency. It was an era when change was synonymous with progress, and there appeared to be no limits on what could be achieved.

That seems naive today, now that we have learned there is always a price, though sometimes initially hidden, that must be paid when any new technology is introduced and that people do not always behave rationally. However, back then, as the country struggled to overcome the effects of the Great Depression, the idea that American ingenuity could create a perfect world was an article of faith, certified over time by examples such as this country's victory in World War II.

Vollmer's precepts signaled an organized approach to resolving the problems of the past, while offering a new course for the future. Change does not come overnight, but these principles gained momentum as the wave of the future for policing, which meant many metropolitan police departments adopted new ways to extract politics from the process. As Kelling and Moore point out, such efforts helped make many police chiefs more autonomous than any other local government official. For example, Los Angeles and Cincinnati adopted Civil Service examinations for chiefs, while Milwaukee provided police chiefs lifetime tenure, with removal only for cause. This insulation from politics, however, gave chiefs in these cities great power and autonomy. More recent history shows that these police departments have been plagued with police violence and the abuse of minority citizens as well as a focus on crime fighting to the exclusion of community service and responsiveness (see, Kappeler, Sluder & Alpert, 1998). LAPDs beating of motorist Rodney King and the subsequent acquittal of the officers involved by an all-white jury sparked the worst riots in American history; Milwaukee's mishandling of the Jeffrey Dahmer case which allowed a child to die at the hands of a serial killer brought renewed charges of a racist in the police department, and recent acts of brutality by police officers in Cincinnati, Ohio, have rekindled concerns over police violence (Kappeler, Sluder & Alpert, 1998).

As the reform movement took hold in urban police departments, the frontier and Southern sheriff tradition continued to evolve into the model for rural areas nationwide, and state police departments were initiated to fill important gaps between local and federal efforts to control society's economic engine as well as selected groups in society. Pressures to professionalize the police increased throughout the system, but history proves that concentrating groups of people into confined spaces in cities appears to increase the number and seriousness of crime and disorder problems, which means urban police face challenges in scope and scale beyond what other departments do. Because crime and disorder cluster together in poorer neighborhoods, because police have historically focused on minority populations for control, this helps explain why minorities can serve as convenient scapegoats for the frustrations of both society and its police.

The Police and Minorities

The history of policing is, in reality, a record of how one group of people attempts to control the behavior of others, as individuals and as groups. A closer examination of early law enforcement efforts in England shows that even within a seemingly cohesive culture, where everyone shared the same ethnic roots, the same language, and the same customs, differences in class determined how the law was applied. Under the feudal system, the nobility claimed rights that the serfs did not enjoy. A group of noblemen on a fox hunt could destroy crops. The infamous *droit du seigneur* gave landlords the right to deflower the virginal daughters of their tenants, a legalized rape.

While the United States was founded on the ideal of establishing itself as a classless society, in practice, various groups have been discriminated against because of their skin color, ethnic heritage, immigrant status, religious beliefs, gender, or income level. Since law enforcement is part of the overall social and economic fabric, these groups also suffered at the hands of police.

In addition, especially during the Spoils Era, it was not uncommon to find entire departments harassing minorities, as a way of solidifying mainstream support. In a capitalist society, supply and demand operate unfettered, at least in theory. This means the job goes to the lowest bidder, which therefore means that impoverished immigrants and disenfranchised African-Americans willing to work for low wages were perceived by businessmen as a boon— and as a serious threat by workers who feared being displaced. Until or unless these groups could establish political and economic clout, it was popular to use the police to "keep them in line."

In a capitalist, democratic society, money and votes mean power. Immigrants often arrived with little more than the clothes they were wearing, and the process of becoming a naturalized citizen takes fume. In the South, poll taxes and literacy tests were effective ways of excluding African-Americans from the electoral process, and statistics verify that African Americans have never enjoyed income levels comparable to whites in this country. Even today, the poor, the underclass, and many minority groups are the least likely to vote. The powerless make inviting targets for exploitation—and for society's frustrations.

Sadly, the history of modern policing includes countless incidents where police unfairly harassed minorities, and under certain circumstances, white skin was no protection against abuse. Jews faced widespread anti-Semitism, including harsh treatment by police, especially in cities like New York where immigrant Jewish families often settled. The Irish, Poles, Italians, Germans, and other central and eastern European immigrants also suffered injustice, a sadly predictable rite of passage in the transition to assimilation.

As this litany confirms, the have-nots, those without substantial clout, often had good reason to fear the police. Waves of immigrants hit this country's shores because of problems at home—the Irish faced famine, eastern Europeans fled revolution, the Jews tried to escape persecution. Lured by the myth that this country's streets were paved with gold, hordes of displaced persons flooded into the land of opportunity only to face the stark reality of low-paying and often dangerous jobs as unskilled workers.

One bloody episode occurred in 1897 when 21 Polish and Hungarian strikers who had organized a march outside Hazleton, Pennsylvania, were killed when the local police fired upon them after the owners of the local coal company convinced the police the protest was illegal. As this example demonstrates, police violence against minorities often exhibited the interwoven themes of rich against poor, as well as us against them.

As Jack L. Kuykendall explains, such incidents are evidence of power dashes that reinforce the negative stereotyping of one group by another (Kuykendall, 1970:47,52). Ethnic minorities cling together because of culture, heritage, language, and rejection and oppression by the mainstream, yet this in turn is perceived by the mainstream as evidence of secretive and clannish behavior that justifies further abuse. Completing the vicious cycle, minorities that suffer indignities and brutality at the hands of police learn, in turn, to see the police as paid thugs and oppressors. Once people are divided by the us against them mindset, it becomes much easier for each side to justify aggression against the other.

Though a white skin did not prevent discrimination, being white undoubtedly made it easier for ethnic minorities to assimilate into the mainstream. The additional burden of racism has made that transition much more difficult for those whose skin is black, brown, red, or yellow. In no small part because of the tradition of slavery, African-Americans have long been a target of abuse. The use of patrols to capture runaway slaves was one of the precursors of formal police forces, especially in the South. This unfortunate legacy persisted as an element of the police role. In some cases, police harassment simply meant African-Americans were more likely to be stopped and questioned, while at the other extreme, African-Americans have suffered beatings, and even murder, at the hands of white police. Questions still arise periodically today about the disproportionately high numbers of African-Americans killed, beaten, and arrested by police in major cities.

Most worrisome is that some law enforcement officials made it clear that they not only tolerated but encouraged their officers to keep African-Americans "in their place." Though we still wince at news footage of notorious southern Sheriff "Bull" Connor loosing police dogs on Civil Rights marchers in Selma, Alabama, the police in the North have not always treated African-Americans much better. More than one big city northern police chief has used racism to secure his power, by currying favor with whites by thinly veiled assurances that he will use police power against African-Americans.

Hispanics have fared little better, and border states in particular have a checkered record in their dealings with Mexican immigrants, dating back even before the notorious incident in the 1940s, when *zoot suiters* and police clashed in riots in Los Angeles in 1943. Cubans in Miami and Puerto Ricans in New York have also reported notable problems with police brutality. The same holds true for Native Americans in various areas.

Asian-Americans have also been the target of hostility. *Coolies* who worked laying railroad track were seen by some as taking jobs away from *real* Americans, which led to riots in 1871. American citizens of Japanese extraction were interned in concentration camps during World War II. Even today, the *boat people* from Vietnam and Cambodia face problems in many communities, where they are perceived as straining the local economy, as evidenced in the bloody clashes between white and Asian-American fishermen in Texas and California continues to be a hot spot for conflicts between citizens over immigration.

Initial Attempts to Reach the Community

The police reform movement launched by Vollmer in the 1920s, which took hold in the 1930s, seemed to offer the promise that society was on the brink of solving the riddle of crime. Police departments were now increasingly insulated from the political pressures that had spawned a variety of abuses, and they were organized according to the principles of scientific management theory, which promised increased efficiency and effectiveness. Over time, more and more departments were staffed by educated and highly trained officers, roaming the streets in new squad cars that gave them the mobility to swoop down quickly wherever problems occurred. As home telephones became increasingly affordable, it seemed there would soon be no way crooks could escape the ever-tightening net of police technology.

By the 1950s, however, blemishes had begun to appear in that model of perfection. Many police departments found themselves the target of mounting citizen complaints. Many accusations seemed relatively trivial—perhaps the officer appeared indifferent to the caller's seemingly petty concerns such as broken streetlights or barking dogs. Often the charges were serious and well founded, such as when minorities accused the police of harassment and brutality.

While concern about the isolation of the police from their constituency had not reached crisis proportions, the increasing pressure to find a way to build bridges to the community fostered interest in Police Community Relations (PCR) efforts. The best PCR programs were a sincere effort to reach out and address a host of community concerns. The worst were half-hearted, understaffed, and underfunded attempts to blunt public criticism without making any substantive change. The worst PCR programs were often little more than attempts to legitimize past police practices.

In 1955, the National Institute on Community and Police Relations, co-sponsored by the School of Police Administration and Public Safety of Michigan State University and the National Conference of Christians and Jews, convened to help police become aware of their problems. Later, the National Association of Police/Community Relations Officers outlined seven objectives of a good PCR program, paraphrased below:

- Improve communication, reduce hostility, and identify tensions between the police and the community;

- Assist both the police and the community in acquiring skills to promote improved crime detection and prevention;

- Define the police role, emphasizing equal protection;

- Adopt a teamwork approach, including the police department, the public, and other public service agencies;

- Instill in each officer a "proper attitude and appreciation of good police/community relations;"

- Enhance mutual understanding between the police and the community; and

- Stress that the administration of justice is a total community responsibility that necessitates total community involvement (NAPCRO, 1971).

As these laudable goals suggest, PCR efforts aimed high, but they fell short on structure and tactics. In practice, PCR units operated as separate entities within the department, never fully integrated into the police milieu. In the organizational scheme, the PCR unit was usually in the service track, not part of the operations bureau, which meant the jobs were filled with staff and not *line* officers. While this made sense, given the unit's mandate, it meant PCR officers were not viewed as *real cops*. The officer's mission was not to handle crime and disorder on a daily basis, but to "make nice." In some cases, the PCR director was a civilian, further distancing the effort from service-based policing.

With the benefit of 20/20 hindsight, another structural flaw was to have PCR officers communicate with the community through community leaders. Tactics included organizing an advisory council made up of civic and church leaders. Though this seemed wise at the time, experience shows that community leaders are not always fully in touch with the real concerns in the community, so PCR units rarely received the broadest possible input about the community's real concerns.

In part because of these structural weaknesses, PCR tactics often translated into well-meaning activities of limited scope. PCR officers staffed a speaker's bureau that gave talks on crime prevention or recruiting to various civic groups. Officers also made presentations in schools. Another typical PCR function was press relations. PCR officers also served as the liaison to other public and private agencies. Many PCR officers spent much of their day hosting tours of police facilities. Though PCR officers were encouraged to solicit *suggestions,* many were under orders not to handle actual *complaints,* but to refer those to the administration.

While most PCR officers winced at being labeled public relations flak-catchers, the structure of the unit and nature of their daily activities made it difficult for them to do more. The friendly PCR officer who discussed concerns with minority leaders often bore little resemblance to the tough motor patrol officer who arrived later to handle a call. Their role in press relations was often perceived as putting a good face on a department's mistakes.

PCR programs overall suffered two major interrelated problems because of the inherent lack of follow-up and accountability. Though citizens might feel flattered by the attention when a PCR officer asked for suggestions, the officer lacked clout within the department to address specific complaints. In addition, the PCR officer who gave the talk on crime prevention to the Senior Citizens Club was never the officer who had to handle the call later, if those preventive efforts failed.

The stated objective of using PCR officers to reverse minority abuse within the department was obviously doomed, since the most aggressive officers were usually the first to call PCR officers wimps. Also, especially in departments where PCR units were established as a reluctant gesture to defuse community criticism, police administrators used the unit as a dumping ground for problem officers, further undermining internal and external credibility. However, in spite of these structural and tactical drawbacks, many PCR efforts achieved notable success.

The 1950s also saw the introduction of new *Crime Prevention Units*, a proactive approach aimed at the community. Depending on the size of the department and the funding available, some departments provided a separate

Crime Prevention Unit or officer, while others rolled both Crime Prevention and PCR into one.

Like PCR, Crime Prevention was manned by staff rather than *line* officers. The unit's goal was to educate the businesses and community residents about specific measures they could take, such as target-hardening, to reduce their likelihood of victimization and thereby help decrease the crime rate overall. Obviously, the unit's strengths and weaknesses mirror those of PCR units, and although many such efforts helped inform the public about things they could do to help prevent crime, it was nevertheless an overly optimistic reliance on "scientific" solutions to human, political and economic problems facing communities.

The Challenge of the Late 1960s

Though PCR efforts were decidedly a step in the right direction, the program's inherent weaknesses became dramatically apparent during the domestic upheaval that began in the late 1960s. As Baby Boomers will attest, the early 1960s was a time of great optimism, fueled by the idealism of the millions of young people who dominated the culture by their sheer numbers. President John F. Kennedy tapped into this youthful enthusiasm when he challenged the entire generation to "ask not what your country can do for you, but what you can do for your country." His new Peace Corps attracted thousands of energetic young people who believed in their collective ability to change the world overnight.

Despite Kennedy's assassination in 1963, his successor, Lyndon Johnson, announced his commitment to carry on Kennedy's civil rights agenda, embodied in the Great Society programs that were designed to promote equality between African-Americans and whites and narrow the gap between rich and poor. This was the era when Martin Luther King's dream of a color-blind society seemed within reach. Within policing, it seemed that the continued adoption and expansion of PCR and Crime Prevention units would provide the last link in fulfilling the promise of a full-service, professionalized police force, capable of handling any challenge.

Shockingly, within just a few short years, the country was instead plunged into domestic chaos. Talk of revolution filled the air, as cities burned, and crime rates soared. The civil rights movement spawned the militant Black Power movement, which included groups such as the Black Panthers, whose bloody clashes with police heightened tensions on both sides. Race riots erupted summer after summer—in Watts, Newark, Detroit, then in cities nationwide the spring of 1968 when Martin Luther King Jr. was assassinated.

Meanwhile, protests on college campuses became increasingly violent, as the focus narrowed to the pressing issues of the Vietnam War and the draft. The nightly news was filled with images of students armed with lists of nonnegotiable demands taking over university administration buildings as riot police lobbed tear gas into the crowds. History repeated itself or, as we have observed at the onset of this chapter, the same mistakes were repeated. For, example the military units were called out to control a student protest at Kent State University which resulted in the killing of four students by national guardsmen.

The upheaval pitted hawks against doves, African-Americans against whites, students against the establishment, young against old, in an atmosphere of increasing fury on all sides. As representatives of the establishment whose job included maintaining domestic peace, the police often found themselves on one side of the barricades facing any one of a number of widely diverse groups collectively known as the New Left.

The New Left was a loose coalition of groups clamoring for a variety of social changes, under the overall umbrella term of social justice. Their unifying slogan was *Power to the People.* The agenda ranged from legalizing marijuana and other drugs to ending the draft, from sexual freedom to equality for African-Americans and women. Protests covered the spectrum from non-violent actions such as the bizarre attempt by the Yuppies to levitate the Pentagon by chanting to outright urban terrorism, including bombings conducted by small, ultra-radical groups like the Weathermen, who had split from Students for a Democratic Society (SDS) over the issue of violence. The underground Weathermen served as a model for other violent groups, such as the Symbionese Liberation Army (SLA) that made headlines when they kidnapped heiress Patty Hearst.

Gross characterizations took place. To the New Left, the police were pigs, brutal agents of establishment oppression. To the police, the New Left was made up of *hippies* and *longhairs,* an unlikely mix of spoiled college kids and draft-dodgers, who had turned their backs on the culture that subsidized them, and murderous African-American criminals, who cloaked their "reverse racism" in rhetoric about equality.

Perhaps the most dramatic confrontation occurred in Chicago during the 1968 Democratic convention, when TV cameras rolled as the late Mayor Daley's police waded into crowds of young protectors. Wielding nightsticks, their badge numbers hidden, the police *cracked heads* in what the Kerner Commission would later call a *police riot.*

The increasing polarization of society into opposing factions made it hard for the calm voice of reason to be heard above the shouting. Those on the political right issued a call for *law and order*—which those on the left interpreted as a euphemism for a heavy-handed police crackdown on minorities and students. Those on the political left protested against police brutality, suggesting the police had become the Gestapo. Despite the infusion of new technology funded by the Law Enforcement Assistance Act (LEAA), escalating criminal and political violence continued into the early 1970s, underscoring the need for the police to find new ways to heal old wounds.

In this climate, the growing rift within society could not be healed by well-meaning but often ineffectual PCR and Crime Prevention efforts. Quite obviously, the bitterness brewing between the police and various splintered and polarized elements within communities required a bolder approach. Though many police departments that had not previously adopted a PCR or Crime Prevention program now did so as a way of addressing the need to find ways to break down barriers between the police and the community.

As the limitations of both PCR and Crime Prevention efforts became increasingly obvious, numerous experiments were conducted to see if some new way could be found to build bridges to the community. One promising new approach that became popular beginning in the early 1970s was *team policing,* which involved maintaining a permanent team of officers that responded to crime problems within a particular geographic area.

Team policing recognized that one of PCR's main defects was its reliance on staff and not line officers. However, though team policing involved line officers, it was often applied as if it were no more than a limited tactic, rather than as a strategic approach, so it typically lacked the commitment required to make any substantive and lasting impact on improving overall, long-term police relations within the community. In essence, team policing also suffered because it was still basically a reactive approach, with officers rushing from one crisis to the next.

The Birth of Community Policing

As history demonstrates, many factors set the stage for the birth of community policing:

- The isolation of officers in police cars;

- The narrowing of the police mission to crime fighting;

- An overreliance on the scientific approach to management that stressed efficiency and effectiveness;

- Increased reliance on high-tech gadgetry instead of human interaction;

- Insulation of police administration from community input and accountability;

- A long-standing concern about police violation of human rights; and

- Failed attempts by the police to reach the community, such as PCR, Crime Prevention, and team policing units.

Most of these elements share two common themes—the isolation of the police from the public and a growing use of overt and symbolic violence to control groups in society. The resulting alienation fostered an *us* against *them* mindset on the part of both the police and the community. Community policing therefore rose like a phoenix from the ashes of burned cities, embattled

Collegeville Residents Feel Like Prisoners in Their Guarded Community

A 64-year-old public housing resident says she's a prisoner in her own home. Life around her modest, one-bedroom unit in the Collegeville public housing community has been compromised, she said, since the Housing Authority of Birmingham (Ala.) District (HABD) erected an eight-foot high fence of green iron bars around the complex in 1993.

"It's just like living in a jail cell," said the woman, a 33-year resident of the North Birmingham community. "Prisoners in the penitentiary have it better."

Along with the fences came four security stations manned around the clock with armed guards who control access into the area. A list of rules followed.

For years, this 571-unit housing complex was open to the public. People came and went as they pleased. But after the housing authority received Federal funding for the security project, the City Council voted to vacate the public status of the streets that run through the complex.

Now, when a resident leaves the premises and returns home, that person is expected to show picture identification to prove he or she lives there.

Names of friends or family members who want to visit residents inside first must be approved by the housing authority, and then be placed on a master list posted in the guard stations.

"If their names are not on the list, then we can't let them in," said C.W. Parker, Director of Security for Elite Security Specialists, Inc., the company contracted to handle Collegeville's security.

Gating Supposed To Make Life Easier

According to housing authority officials, the gates, guards and rules aren't meant to make life harder for Collegeville residents, but easier.

"It's a whole lot safer," said Louise Carroll, a resident since 1969.

But others, like 14-year resident Ora Bradford, say the security system often causes more trouble than it's worth.

"The people that live here have problems getting in," Bradford said. "And the people who have no business being here get in faster than we do."

Since the gates and guard stations went up, some residents says they've had trouble obtaining basic services normally available to every community.

Home newspaper delivery became so erratic that the 64-year-old woman, who spoke on the condition of anonymity, said she finally dropped her subscription.

Some complain taxi cabs regularly are turned away at the gates and others say even visiting preachers have problems getting in to pick up parishioners for Sunday service.

But HABD director Ralph Ruggs says security installations have reduced crime and upgraded living conditions at both Collegeville and North Birmingham Homes, the only public housing communities of the 18 in Birmingham with secured gates and monitored access points.

"So far, it has been positive in our efforts to control illegal activities in both communities," Ruggs said.

After rampant drug activity led to a 62.9 percent increase in total crime at Collegeville from 1988 to 1989, housing officials began searching for solutions.

Community Is Safer

HABD won the Federal Drug Elimination Grant to fund security projects at Collegeville in 1993 and at North Birmingham Homes the following year. Since then, crime has dropped about 5.5 percent at Collegeville from 1993 to 1996 after the gates and guardhouses were installed.

North Birmingham Homes show a 5.7 percent increase from 1994 to 1996 with guardhouses and fencing in place.

The latest statistics from Birmingham Police show both gated complexes were among only six public housing communities in the city without a homicide in 1996.

For the communities without guardhouses and fences, four had one homicide; three had two; and one—Elyton Village—had three.

But despite their success, HABD has no plans to replace existing nongated, foot-patrolled systems at the remaining 16 public housing communities.

Residents at most communities have responded negatively to the idea, Peguese said, and logistical problems also make such ventures unlikely.

But the guards and fences will stand at Collegeville and Parker knows her work is cut out for her.

"They don't like the security. The actual idea offends them," she said. "They feel like they're prisoners, and because of that, we get a lot of people questioning our authority."

For residents like the 64-year-old woman, the situation is a lost cause. "If they take it all down tomorrow, it wouldn't even matter," she said. "It might even be better."

Source: *Community Policing Digest* (1997). September 4, pp. 4-5.

campuses, and crime-riddled neighborhoods, a positive new response to the chaos of that turbulent era. Beginning in the early 1970s, the basic issues and ideas that would ultimately coalesce into the community policing concept were discussed in various books and articles, though the cohesive philosophy and the specific organizational changes that would have to be made to achieve these new goals had not yet solidified (Trojanowicz, 1973; Trojanowicz & Dixon, 1974; Trojanowicz, Trojanowicz & Moss, 1975; Goldstein, 1977, 1979). Later, in some cases, it was called foot patrol, then Neighborhood Policing, Neighborhood-Oriented Policing, Community-Oriented Policing, Community-Based Policing, or Community Policing. But regardless of the name used, this growing new movement learned from the past, saving the best from each successive advance.

A Summary of the Lessons Learned and Mistakes Not to Be Repeated

The reform movement of the 1930s brought about many changes in policing some of which are contained in the philosophy of community policing. Community policing retains, for example, commitment to upgrading the education and training of police officers. It also recognizes the limits of technology and science in dealing with human problems and encourages the judicious use of new technology. The philosophy embraces and encourages the recruitment and employment of talented women officers. Most importantly the movement seeks, the insulation of the police from politics, so that today's CPO cannot fall into the trap of the foot patrol officers of the past whose agenda was dictated by politicians and special-interest groups while recognizing that lack of accountability to the community can lead to abuse of authority.

The PCR and Crime Prevention movement also changed the face of policing and the lessons police must learn. Community policing retains from these lessons of history a sincere commitment to improving police relations with minorities and a concerted effort to end police brutality. Community policing embraces an outreach into schools, in the hope of preventing problems in the future and provides a liaison with other organizations and agencies. History, however, also instructs that policing too prone to use technology and gimmicks to enlist support and even well-meaning efforts are often undermined by the police themselves. Policing cannot rely merely on the pretense of service and commitment to community; they must embrace the spirit of service, accountability, and responsiveness.

To these lessons of history and practice, community policing, in its ideal form, brings:

- A new mandate that expands the police beyond crime-fighting;

- A proactive focus;

- Daily, face-to-face contact with the community, with the same officer in the same neighborhood, as a means of developing long-term rapport and mutual trust;

- An opportunity for meaningful community input into the police agenda; and

- An emphasis on encouraging the officer to experiment with creative and innovative solutions aimed at problems and not just isolated incidents.

No doubt changing times and changing needs will spawn yet another reform movement in the future, but today's community policing revolution is the most dynamic and innovative response to finding ways to involve the community in policing itself that has come along in 60 years. From its birth as pilot programs in places like Newark and Flint, to its widespread practical application nationwide today, community policing has made the crucial transition from being a promising philosophy to a professed norm.

The lesson of history teaches that the biggest challenge the police face is finding a way to enlist the cooperation and support of average citizens in efforts to make their lives safer and more enjoyable, a way to earn dignity and respect. Community policing reminds us of the importance of balancing efforts aimed at the top with those that focus on the street where most people live. It also reminds us that people are the police department's most valuable resource and should be treated as valued partners in the police process.

What history also shows is that change takes time and that, at any given moment, the past and the future co-exist together. Even today, some departments have not fully embraced all the reforms Vollmer outlined in the 1930s, meanwhile other departments are leading the way into the future that others will follow. Still signs of the past can often repeat themselves and reformers must be concerned that history finds well-meaning solutions to the problems of crime, policing, and accountability stifled and abused by institutional and social forces. What we do know today is that community policing has now reached critical mass and is beginning to transmute into forms that one of its founding fathers, Robert Trojanowicz, both hopefully envisioned and cautioned against.

References

Allen, F.L. (1959). *Only Yesterday.* New York, NY: Harper & Row, Publishers.

Bell, D. (1960). *The End of Ideology: On the Exhaustion of Political Ideas in the Fifties.* New York, NY: The Free Press.

Bittner, E. (1970). *The Functions of the Police in Modern Society.* Chevy Chase, MD: National Institute of Mental Health, Center for Studies of Crime and Delinquency.

Brown, R. (1969). *The American Vigilante Tradition, Violence in America, A Staff Report to the National Commission on the Causes and Prevention of Violence.* Washington, DC: U.S. Government Printing Office.

Crank, J.P. and R. Langworthy (1992). "An Institutional Perspective of Policing." *The Journal of Criminal Law & Criminology*, 83(2):338-363.

Critchley, T.A. (1985). "Constables and Justices of the Peace." In W.C. Terry (ed.) *Policing Society: An Occupational View.* New York, NY: John Wiley and Sons.

Davies, R.W. (1977). "Augustus Caesar: A Police System in the Ancient World." In P.J. Stead (ed.) *Pioneers in Policing*, pp. 12-32. Montclair, NJ: Patterson-Smith.

Douthit, N. (1975). "Enforcement and Nonenforcement Roles in Policing: A Historical Inquiry." *Journal of Police Science and Administration*, 3(3):336-345.

Drago, H. (1975). *The Legend Makers: Tales of the Old-Time Peace Officers and Desperadoes of the Frontier.* New York, NY: Dodd, Mead & Co.

Fogelson, R. (1977). *Big-City Police.* Cambridge, MA: Harvard University Press.

Fosdick, R. (1921). *American Police Systems.* New York, NY: The Century Co.

Gaines, L.K., V.E. Kappeler & J.B. Vaughn (1997). *Policing in America*, Second Edition. Cincinnati, OH: Anderson Publishing Co.

Gard, W. (1949). *Frontier Justice.* Norman, OK: University of Oklahoma Press.

Goldstein, H. (1979). "Improving Policing A Prom Approach." *Crime & Delinquency*, 25:236-258.

Goldstein, H. (1977). *Policing in a Free Society.* Cambridge, MA: Ballinger.

Haller, M.H. (1992). "Historical Roots of Police Behavior: Chicago, 1890-1925." In E.H. Monkkonen (ed.) *Policing and Crime Control.* New York, NY: K.G. Saur.

Harring, S.L. (1992). "Class Conflict and the Suppression of Tramps in Buffalo, 1892-1894." In E.H. Monkkonen (ed.) *Policing and Crime Control*. New York, NY: K.G. Saur.

Harring, S.L. (1981). "Policing a Class Society: The Expansion of the Urban Police in the Late Nineteenth and Early Twentieth Centuries." In D.F. Greenburg (ed.) *Crime and Capitalism*. Palo Alto, CA: Mayfield Publishing.

Harring, S.L. & L.M. McMullin (1992). "The Buffalo Police 1872-1900: Labor Unrest, Political Power and the Creation of the Police Institution." In E.H. Monkkonen (ed.) *Policing and Crime Control*. New York, NY: K.G. Saur.

Hewitt, W.H. (1965). *British Police Administration*. Springfield, IL: Charles C Thomas.

Johnson, D.R. (1981). *American Law Enforcement: A History*. St. Louis, MO: Forum Press.

Kappeler, V.E. (1993, 1997). *Critical Issues in Police Civil* Liability, Second Edition. Prospect Heights, IL: Waveland Press.

Kappeler, V.E. (1989). "St. Louis Police Department." In W.G. Bailey (ed.) *The Encyclopedia of Police Science*. New York, NY: Garland Publishing, Inc.

Kappeler, V.E., R. Sluder & G.P. Alpert (1994, 1998). *Forces of Deviance: Understanding the Dark Side of Policing*, Second Edition. Prospect Heights, IL: Waveland Press.

Kelling, G.L. & M.H. Moore (1988). *The Evolving Strategy of Policing*. (NCJ114213). Washington, DC: National Institute of Justice.

Kelling, G.L. & M.H. Moore (1987). "Prom Political to Reform to Community: The Evolving Strategy of Police." A paper produced at Harvard University's Kennedy School of Government: Cambridge, MA.

Kelly, M.A. (1973). "The First Urban Policeman." *Journal of Police Science and Administration*, 1(1):56-60.

Kleinig, J. & Y. Zhang (1993). *Professional Law Enforcement Codes: A Documentary Collection*. Westport, CT: Greenwood Press.

Knapp Commission Report on Police Corruption (1973). New York, NY: George Braziller.

Kuykendall, J.L. (1970). *Police and Minority Groups: Toward a Theory of Negative Contacts, Police, 15*, No. I :47 & 52.

Louis, P. (1989). "New York Police Department." In W.G. Bailey (ed.) *The Encyclopedia of Police Science*. New York, NY: Garland Publishing, Inc.

Matthews, F. (1901). *The Character of the American Police, The World's Work 2*. New York, NY: Doubleday, Page & Co.

Miller, W.R. (1977). *Cops and Bobbies: Police Authority in New York and London, 1830-1870*. Chicago, IL: University of Chicago Press.

Moore, M.H. & G.L. Kelling (1976). "To Serve and Protect: Learning from Police History." In A.S. Blumberg & E. Neiderhoffer (eds.) *The Ambivalent Force*. New York, NY: Holt, Rinehart and Winston.

Murray, C. (1985). "Images of Pear." *Harper's Magazine*, (May):41.

Nalla, M.K. & G. R. Newman (1994). "Is White-Collar Policing, Policing?" *Policing and Society*, 3:303-318.

NAPCRO (1971). *Get the Ball Rolling: A Guide to Police Community Relations Programs.* New Orleans, LA: National Association of Police Community Relations Officers.

National Advisory Commission on Civil Disorders (1968). *Report of the National Advisory Commission on Civil Disorders.* New York, NY: Bantam Books.

National Constables Association (1995). "Constable." In W.G. Bailey (ed.) *The Encyclopedia of Police Science*, Second Edition, pp. 114-114. New York, NY: Garland Press.

Otem, M. (1935). *My Life on the Frontier, 1864-1882.* New York, NY: The Press of the Pioneers.

President's Commission on Law Enforcement and Administration of Justice (1967). *The Challenge of Crime in a Free Society.* Washington, DC: U.S. Government Printing Office.

Pringle, P. (n.d.). *Hue and Cry: The Story of Henry and John Fielding and their Bow Street Runners.* Bangay, Suffolk, Great Britain: Richard Clay and Company.

Reichel, P.L. (1992). "The Misplaced Emphasis on Urbanization in Police Development." *Policing and Society*, 3:1-12.

Reith, C. (1952). *The Blind Eye of History.* London, England: Faber & Faber Ltd.

Richardson, J.F. (1974). *Urban Police in the United States.* Port Washington, NY: National University Publications, Kennikat Press.

Robinson, C.D., R. Scaglion & J.M. Olivero (1994). *Police in Contradiction.* Westport, CT: Greenwood Press.

Rubinstein, J. (1973). *City Police.* New York, NY: Farrar, Straus and Giroux.

Samaha, J. (1974). *Law and Order in Historical Perspective.* New York, NY: Academic Press.

Stead, P.J. (1985). *The Police of Britain.* New York, NY: Macmillan.

Strecher, V. (1995). "Revising the Histories and Futures of Policing." In V.E. Kappeler (ed.) *The Police & Society: Touch Stone Readings*, pp. 69-82. Prospect Heights, IL: Waveland Press.

Thorwald, J. (1966). *Crime and Science.* New York, NY: Harcourt, Brace & World, Inc.

Tobias, J.J. (1979). *Crime and Police in England, 1700-1900.* Dublin, England: Macmillan.

Trojanowicz, R.C. (1973). *Juvenile Delinquency: Concepts and Control.* Englewood Cliffs, NJ: Prentice Hall.

Trojanowicz, R.C. & S.L. Dixon (1974). *Criminal Justice and the Community.* Englewood Cliffs, NJ: Prentice Hall.

Trojanowicz, R.C., J.M. Trojanowicz & F.M. Moss (1975). *Community Based Crime Prevention.* Pacific Palisades, CA: Goodyear Publishing Co.

Uchida, C.D. (1993). "The Development of the American Police: An Historical Overview." In R.C. Dunham & G.P. Alpert (eds.) *Critical Issues in Policing: Contemporary Readings*, Second Edition. Prospect Heights, IL: Waveland Press.

Walker, D.B. & M. Richards (1995). "British Policing." In W.G. Bailey (ed.) *The Encyclopedia of Police Science*, Second Edition, pp. 41-48. New York, NY: Garland Press.

Walker, S. (1995). "'Broken Windows' and Fractured History: The Use and Misuse of History in Recent Police Patrol Analysis." In V.E. Kappeler (ed.) *The Police & Society: Touch Stone Readings*, pp. 53-67. Prospect Heights, IL: Waveland Press.

CHAPTER 3
The Changing Meaning of Community

The difference between the right word and the almost right word is the difference between lightning and the lightning bug.

—*Mark Twain*

The Importance of Definitions

Like any profession or highly skilled craft, policing abounds in jargon—terms understood by insiders, which function as a shorthand so that members of the profession can communicate ideas to each other easily and quickly. In a practical sense, of course, there is the danger that jargon can cause confusion, both inside and outside a profession, when people do not understand a term's true meaning. In a more abstract sense, words and phrases have embedded meanings, values and connotations. Words and phrases do not simply carry with them a variety of meanings that cause the potential for misunderstanding, they are abstractions from reality that provide bridges to other words, meanings, and history.

Some early experiments that paved the way for community policing relied on the tactic of using foot patrol officers to put police officers in daily, face-to-face contact with the community. This helped fuel misunderstanding about how modern, directed foot patrol differed from foot patrol in the past, and whether foot patrol and community policing were synonymous. Not only did this spawn confusion, but it also meant that the taint of corruption surrounding foot patrol efforts of the past raised concern about contemporary efforts. In this sense the phrase community policing acted as a bridge to foot patrol that carried with it a link to past police practices.

Confusion and misunderstanding can also arise when two people think they are talking about the same thing, when they both use the same term, without realizing each has a different idea concerning what the word actually means. The likelihood of this kind of misunderstanding is magnified with a phrase like "community policing," since those two simple words are used to convey a subtle but sophisticated philosophy, as well as an organizational strategy that police departments can use to put the philosophy into practice. Not unlike the foot patrol example, the phrase "community policing" has its connotations and linkages to the past.

Because accurate and complete definitions are so important, the first chapter defined the idea of community policing. The purpose of this chapter is to clear up any confusion concerning what the word *community* means in the context of community policing.

A History of the Meaning of Community

To understand the full implications of community policing requires a clear understanding of what is meant by community and how communities have changed over the course of time. The definition of community has evolved over time to take into account the changing social reality as the kind and character of communities themselves have changed. In the past, defining community was simpler, because a sense of community was based on a *community of interest* that typically overlapped a *geographic community*, but, as we shall see, that is not always the case today. Technological, economic, and communicative changes have had a dramatic impact on social life and have altered the very nature of modern communities.

The term "community" is perhaps one of the most difficult concepts to define and one of the most abused terms in modern sociology (Lowe, 1986). The term can be used in both the concrete and the abstract. In the concrete sense, according to Donald R. Fessler, (1967:7) sociologists define community as "any area in which people with a common culture share common interests." More often than not the geographic area referred to in the definition of community is a neighborhood. The problem with that broad a definition is that it could span "a rural village of half a hundred families" to "one of our major cities" (Fessler, 1967:7). Additionally, this definition fails to note the use of the term community in the abstract as well as the social ascriptions often thrust upon the term. Community does not always refer to an area, location or neighborhood; often it refers only to a group of people drawn together by common interests—like a "community of scholars" or the "religious community."

The German sociologist Tonnies (1887) made a clear distinction between community relationships that were defined by intimacy and durability where kin relations determined status, power, and behavior and where community relationships were rational, calculated, contractual, and based on merit and achievement. This later use of the term community is, as Fessler noted, not what people meant when they talked about community, because of the inherent depersonalization that dominates relations in large cities and mitigates against the cohesive sense of community.

At the turn of the century, when this country was primarily an agrarian society with less than one-half the population living in cities (Trager, 1979), the term community hardly seemed to require definition. Community expressed the idea of a distinct area where people shared both a common geography and a common culture, as well as elements of mutual dependence. Increasing industrialization drove people from the farms into the cities and in the first decade of this century more than 9 million people immigrated into cities, but the term community still seemed to serve fairly well in describing how even the largest cities broke down into smaller, often ethic-based, communities that still met these criteria.

In the 1920s, the *Chicago School,* comprised of sociologists such as Robert E. Park, continued attempts to refine the rural model so that it could be applied to communities within major metropolitan areas (Watman, 1980:35). According to sociologist Thomas M. Meenaghan (1972), the Chicago School technique relied on identifying central locators, such as businesses, churches, and schools, and then drawing the community's boundary lines by finding those living the furthest away who still used those services. As Meenaghan (1972:94) wrote in his treatise, *What Means Community,* ". . . Park saw the community as a group of people living in a specific geographic area and conditioned by the subcultural or life processes of competition, cooperation, assimilation, and conflict. The unplanned life processes created so-called natural areas that not only had a defined territorial frame, but also shared special or unique cultural and social characteristics."

In less formal terms, this means people take on identifiable marks of membership in the community just by living there and creating community-based social institutions that allow residents to interact; that even when individuals or groups within a community were in conflict, their constant interaction and interdependence, perhaps their shared interests, help shape their identity and values; and that living in the community is a potent force in influencing what people think, how they feel, and what they believe. People do not make a conscious decision to take on the colorations and nuances of their communities, but instead this occurs as a natural outgrowth of living in a community under a variety of conditions and bumping up against the behavior and attitudes of other community members in the course of daily life.

By the 1950s, there were so many definitions of community that George A. Hillery, Jr., of the University of Atlanta, attempted to classify 94 different definitions, by content, to see whether he could identify areas of common agreement. His conclusion was that, "Most . . . are in basic agreement that community consists of persons in social interaction within a geographic area and having one or more additional ties" (Hillery, 1955:111).

This makes it easy to see how the term community began to become synonymous with *neighborhood.* A neighborhood, however, "is a small physical area embedded within a larger area in which people inhabit dwellings. Thus, it is a geographic subset of a larger unit" . . . where "there is a collective life that emerges from the social networks that have arisen among the residents and the sets of institutional arrangements that overlap these networks. That is, the neighborhood is inhabited by people who perceive themselves to have a common interest in that area and to whom a common life is available. Finally, the neighborhood has some tradition of identity and continuity over time" (Bursik & Grasmick, 1993:6). In Hillery's time, a decade after World War II, when most cities were still dominated by clear-cut, virtually self-contained, ethnic neighborhoods, drawing such distinctions seemed like needless hair-splitting. But we must understand that depending upon what neighborhood or community one lived and the nature of the existing social arraignments and social networks often determined the conditions of social life and how people were treated by the dominate culture.

In her paper, "The Neighborhood," Suzanne Keller (1982) defined neighborhood in terms that echo past definitions of community, demonstrating that confusion about these terms persists today. "The neighborhood, viewed as an area or a place within a larger entity, has boundaries—either physical or symbolic and usually both—where streets, railway lines, or parks separate off an area and its inhabitants or where historical and social traditions make people view an area as a distinctive unit. Usually these two boundaries reinforce each other: the physical unit encourages symbolic unity, and symbolic boundaries come to be attached to physical ones" (1982:9). Common phrases like a person "comes from the wrong side of the tracks" captures the physical, economic and cultural separation between neighborhoods in the 1950s. Depending, of course, on which side of tracks one came from likely determined whether communities were a positive or negative force in one's life and often determined how people were viewed and treated.

Though community study had, to a great degree, fallen out of fashion in the 1960s, efforts to update and refine the definition of community in the 1970s focused on identifying new, unifying principles. The University of Chicago's Albert Hunter (cited in Watman, 1980), in his book, *Symbolic Communities,* noted the close association among the words *common, communication,* and *community.* He argued that both language and shared symbols help identify what he called the *natural community.* Meenaghan (1972:95) focused on social area analysis, which used census tract information to break out urban groups of 3,000 to 6,000 people, so that data on the homogeneity of economic, family, and ethnic characteristics could then be used to identify the boundaries of communities.

Finally, Worsely (1987) has argued that despite the complex and different definitional issues associated with the term community, there seem to be three base components to communities. First, there is the geographical aspect of the term that refers to human settlements within a fixed location. Second, the term refers to the network of social relations and interactions among a group of people who constitute a community. Third, community has been referred to as a quality of particular types of social interrelations where the phrase "sense of community" and "community spirit" capture the essence of this usage.

A Good Idea Sells Itself: Miami Reaps Harvest of Volunteers for Citizen Patrols

Miami police officials have unveiled plans for an ambitious citywide program that will use citizen volunteers to serve as the eyes and ears of the police in their own neighborhoods.

The program, tentatively called Citizens on Patrol, is modeled after similar efforts by police departments in Rochester, N.Y., Fort Worth, Texas, and a handful of other cities. It is expected to be formally launched sometime this year; a pilot program has been underway in Northeast Miami and the Model City neighborhood since last year.

While the plan is still in the nascent stages, calls from potential volunteers have swamped the Police Department since the Jan. 25 announcement, according to Louis Epstein, a community involvement specialist with the department's Community Relations Unit. At least 200 interested residents have inquired about the program, he said, and the agency has even received calls from outside its jurisdiction from people wanting to join.

"This is the first time I've seen this community come forward for such an event like never before," Epstein told Law Enforcement News. "They realize that crime is rampant and we've got to work together."

Participants in the program would undergo four to eight hours of training to familiarize themselves with the workings of the department and the duties of police officers, as well as crime prevention tips and clues to suspicious activities. They will be instructed not to attempt to stop crimes themselves, but to immediately report suspicious activities to police. Some participants will be issued police radios or cellular phones, and identifying T-shirts, caps and ID cards will be issued to active patrollers.

Because of an austere financial situation confronting the city, Epstein said, the department is seeking Federal grants and private donations to fund the patrol program. Help is starting to trickle in, he noted, with the donation of 70 cellular phones from the Motorola Corporation.

Under the plan, which has the support of Police Chief Donald Warshaw, unarmed volunteers would be assigned to patrol 14 neighborhood districts. Volunteers must be at least age 18, live in Miami, have no convictions for felonies or drug- or sex-related misdemeanors over the past five years, and pass a background check.

Training could start as soon as the end of this month, although Epstein cautioned that details were still being worked out and the target date might be pushed back. "It's on paper, but it's not quite in the works yet," he said.

Civilian patrol programs are nothing new, but they are getting a second look from budget-strapped police departments trying to stretch personnel and get more community input to solve crime problems. The Rochester, N.Y., Police Department's program, called Police and Citizens Together Against Crime, has been in existence since 1975, according to Lieut. Timothy Hickey, who oversees the effort. Up to 300 Rochester residents each month participate in the patrols, he said.

While PACTAC's impact on crime is difficult to measure, Hickey said the program does offer other benefits—increased involvement between the police and community and a reduction of fear among residents. A plan to start a "Junior PACTAC" program that would teach crime prevention techniques to young people is now on the drawing board, he added.

In Fort Worth, a Citizens on Patrol program involving nearly 2,500 participants has contributed to a double-digit decrease in reported crime in the city since it began in 1992, said a police spokeswoman, Lieut. Pat Kneblick. The program has proved popular with Fort Worth residents, she said, adding that training programs conducted by the department add about 40 new citizen patrollers each month.

Source: *Law Enforcement News* (1995). March 15, p. 5.

As these distinctions demonstrate, the terms *neighborhood* and *community* could be used interchangeably with little argument when most cities consisted of distinct ethnic enclaves. After the turn of the century, wave after wave of immigrants arrived in the United States, primarily from Europe, settling most often into expanding ethnic neighborhoods in major cities, where they could also continue to maintain their various cultural traditions. In addition, African-Americans from the rural South continued to migrate to northern cities in search of higher-paying jobs in industry and to avoid the treatment they received in the South. They settled in specific city neighborhoods, dictated not only by choice and economic status, but by discriminatory housing practices. Victor G. Strecher (1995a:210) describes this exodus:

> Between 1910 and 1963 it is estimated that more than 5,000,000 African Americans migrated from the South, mostly to the large cities of the North and the West, in two distinctive patterns. Between 1910 and 1940, about 1,750,000 migrants moved northward to the large cities directly in their paths ". . . from South Carolina to New York, from Georgia to Philadelphia, from Alabama to Detroit, and from Mississippi to Chicago." Between 1940 and 1963 migration largely followed the second pattern. During that period most of the 3,300,000 African Americans who left the South migrated to the western as well as to the northern cities. Frequently, the reason for moving was a desire to leave the South rather than a specific attraction of the destination (citations omitted).

The economic changes and the explosion of technology that have occurred since the end of World War II disrupted the status quo, so that established definitions of community and neighborhood began to take on new meaning. What many researchers failed to take into account was that a community of interest did not have to be tied to a particular geographic area. In particular, the impact of mass transit, mass communications, and mass media, as well as economic pressures, disrupted previously stable, but very often far less than equal, communities, leaving in their wake areas in many major cities where people still live together in a definable geographic area, but they do not interact in the same ways as before.

Assaults on the Community

A serious danger in any discussion about changes in what is meant by the word community, and changes that have occurred within communities, is that such discussion is unconsciously colored by a wistful longing for what may only *seem* like a better past. As Victor Azarya (1985:135) of the Hebrew University in Jerusalem wrote about many of the definitions of community analyzed by Hillery: "These approaches are clearly mixed with some nostalgia for a glorious past in which people were thought to be more secure, less alienated, and less atomized." Certainly there is a healthy measure of nostalgia and romanticism in the notion that communities of the past were all safe harbors and free of conflict. This certainly was not the case, nor is it the case today. Victor G. Strecher (1995:78) makes the following observations on today's notion and uses of the term community:

> An 'American community' is a warm, comforting phrase. In this concept there is the overtone of the small society—the community of neighbors who know each other (to the third generation), and whose offspring develop their self-awareness in an atmosphere of warmth, trust and a wish to become like those who have gone before. . . . The small, simple, pre-industrial, consensual, almost primitive aspect of community does not require much secular law. . .—not much beyond the Ten Commandments. There is no big government, no regulatory laws and agencies . . ., no tension between the sermons heard in church and the high school curriculum. 'Community' is a realization of the romanticized melting pot. Where do we find this small, uncomplicated, unspecialized, unstratified colony of believers who are clustered around an agreeable moral code? Chicago? Miami? San Francisco? Minneapolis? Maybe those are too large. Bangor? Rocky Mount? Wausau? Dothan? Waco? Nogales? Butte? Poplar Bluff? Bakersfield? Boulder? Eugene?

American society is, however, different today than it was decades ago. One major difference is U.S. cities have become poorer. The *white flight* of the 1950s from the cities to the suburbs was succeeded by the *black flight* of middle-and upper-class African-Americans that began roughly a decade later, serious social problems persuaded those who could to move to the suburbs. This shift was also fueled by the continuing rise in the overall standard of living created by an expanding economy, which allowed more and more people the opportunity to be upwardly mobile.

White flight from cities was also the result of a notoriously unethical real estate practice, called *blockbusting*. Blockbusting stampeded white home owners into selling their houses because of the fear that African-American families moving in would inevitably cause property values to plunge. Some unscrupulous real estate agents would intentionally line up an African-American home buyer for a house in an all-white neighborhood, and the agents would either keep the buyer's race secret or offer the seller an inflated price to ensure the sale would go through. Then they would prey on the racial fears of the other white home owners, warning them that unless they sold quickly, they would be trapped in homes worth a fraction of their current value. This practice exploited a self-fulfilling prophecy, since panic selling did depress price, which meant those previously stable neighborhoods quickly degenerated into chaos.

Not only did the influx of newcomers lack a shared history together, late arrivals were able to purchase homes for a fraction of what the early arrivals had paid, which often meant the new community suffered inevitable internal tensions in trying to blend people of vastly different socio-economic classes in one confined area. Only the real estate agents profited, since they were able to turn tidy profits on the huge volume of sales that blockbusting promoted.

The full implications of these dislocations were somewhat masked, as long as the rising standard of living held the false promise of offering ever-increasing opportunities for advancement to anyone willing to work hard— the American dream. Then the dramatic rise of oil prices in the early 1970s, followed by stagflation, then the recession of 1982, culminated in the loss of high-paid unskilled jobs in industry and manufacturing, with more of the new jobs created in the lower-paying service fields, and with many of those jobs in the suburbs. An increasing trend toward coporatizing American retail businesses dislodged many "mom and pop" operations. Manufacturing was moved to rural areas or foreign countries in search of inexpensive, often child-based, labor. This trend continued well into the 1990s with corporate downsizing and the decline of workers' real wages. Even when adjusted for inflation, median family income remained stable or declined somewhat over the last two decades. The shifting economic picture of American was coupled with a growing negative view of welfare and governmental assistance. People who were dislodged from jobs also found it more difficult to look to the government for a helping hand as they attempted to make the transition from industry to the service sector. As a society, we have not yet grasped the full implications of what it will mean if most people cannot expect to improve their condition, and the young have good reason to worry they may not be able to achieve the same standard of living enjoyed by their parents. Expression of this general cultural sentiment can be found among the X generations' apathy and willingness to reject the work ethic of the past and their adoption of an alternative culture and world view that gives up economic drive in favor of a freer life style.

Using Detroit as an example, between 1955 and 1990, the city lost over 850,000 people—enough to qualify as this nation's 11th largest city. According to the *Detroit Free Press,* during that same time, other important community assets have been also been lost: "Detroit has lost about 100 movie theaters, J.L. Hudson's flagship department store, the headquarters of the AAA-Michigan, Stroh's brewery, the Pistons professional basketball team, the Lions pro football team, countless factories" (McGraw & Blossom, 1988:2B). In addition, Cardinal Szoka announced in the fall of 1988 that he planned to close one-third (43) of Detroit's remaining Catholic churches, leaving the city with only one-half the number it boasted in 1968 (Ager, 1988:15A). In 1956, Michigan employed 412,000 in the auto industry, down to 288,000 in the second quarter of 1988 (Jackson, 1988:1C). While this suggests future workers will need more education to secure good jobs, two studies of ninth grade classes in Detroit (in 1982 and 1983) showed that roughly four of every 10 of those students left school by graduation (Finkelstein, 1988:1A). Detroit is still suffering the consequences of a shifting economy. The state of Michigan has recently begun a campaign to attract people to the state and into the service-based economy that is now emerging.

These economic shifts have contributed to a growing underclass in American society, more than one-fourth of American families now live in poverty. Among children from all kinds of families, one in four is born poor, and at least one in three will be on welfare at some point in their lives, with one in two living in a single-parent household headed by a female. According to Senator Daniel P. Moynihan, we have become "the first nation in history in which the poorest group in the population was the children. This is intensifying. Today, the poorest children are the youngest children" (Moynihan, 1988:7A).

The economic changes, particularly the growing division of labor and the complexity of the distribution of material resources, as well as the dislocations wrought by mass transportation, mass communication, and mass media, have ruptured the tie between geography and community. In the rural model of 100 years ago, individuals were forced to depend on each other, in great part because they had no connection to people who lived outside their immediate area. A farmer whose barn burned could usually count on his neighbors to help him rebuild. The altruistic impulse was bolstered because people stuck together since they also knew they might be the ones to need a helping hand tomorrow.

Affordable technology, such as the automobile, the telephone, and the internet now allow those with sufficient resources to make bonds based on community of interest without regard for geography or dependency. If trouble strikes, a person today picks up the telephone to call a friend across town or across the country. If the problem is serious enough, that friend can climb into a car or board a plane to come help. If someone is lonely they can access a chat-line on the Internet and simulate social interaction. In the same faceless sense, people now look to corporations to provide the necessities of life rather than looking to each other or someone in the community. Likewise, business decisions are made based on efficiency and cost rather than by a sense of community. Often community-based businesses suffer because people now have the ability and willingness to procure goods from hundreds of miles away with little thought to how these changing forms of commerce affect their neighbor's business or their community.

In the rural past and in city neighborhoods before the advent of the telephone and the automobile, people were forced to trust and depend upon their neighbors, whether they shared much in common or not. Today, it takes less effort to call a friend hundreds of miles away for advice, comfort, or assistance, than to walk 50 feet to the person who lives next door. This makes it far easier to associate with people of the same class, same educational level, same religion, same politics, and same interests, regardless of whether they live nearby.

These changes, of course, have altered the nature of police and community interaction. Citizens have become more dependent upon government and government ordering. In the same sense that a neighbor might pick up the telephone to call a friend hundreds of miles away rather than turning to a neighbor, citizens will call the police for assistance with the loud music coming from next-door rather than merely walking those same 50 feet to ask the neighbor to turn down the stereo. Our tolerance for diversity and our ability to solve human problems have been limited by reliance on formal social institutions and a growing alienation from community.

Though the effects of mass transportation and mass communication on the community have been well documented, the role of mass media also deserves mention. Journalists and advertisers alike understand demographics, which means that their audience breaks down in part by geography, but more strongly by *lifestyle,* made up of age, income, race, religion, marital status, education, career, politics, social status, and leisure-time interests. The advertising medium now attempts to capture cultural sentiments and accentuate differences for the purposes of increasing sales. Many in our society now define themselves by labels, reinforced by the mass media—Baby Boomer, born-again Christian, feminist, yuppie, New Ager or member of the X-generation. Some people identify most strongly with career, while others identify more closely with family and leisure activities. Freed from the link to place, many people can shift gears into and out of various communities of interest during the day.

Using politics as an example, it becomes clear how this context of community has changed. Before television, politicians and their supporters relied on campaigning door-to-door within neighborhoods for support. Today, the politician stages a photo-opportunity in a particular neighborhood where background symbols that appeal to particular demographic groups nationwide are manipulated to transmit a message to those who share that community of interests, regardless of where they live—community as media backdrop.

Cynics like Azarya can effectively argue that communities of the past were far from being glorious, but that does not mean today's communities do not fall ever farther short of that imperfect model. Likewise, it is somewhat simplistic to solely blame urbanization on the decline of "traditional" communities (see, Young & Willmott, 1960; Gans, 1962) the very nature of social interaction has changed and continues to change today well after the industrial revolution. Statistics alone do not tell the full story about the impact these changes in our sense of community make in the lives of people who find less fulfillment in community life than ever before. The answer in such cases lies not in looking at what science tells us, but at literature. As author Kurt Vonnegut notes, this need to be part of a community tied to a place where people interact together in their daily lives has universal appeal:

> This is a lonesome society that's been fragmented by the factory system. People have to move from here to there as jobs move, as prosperity leaves one area and appears somewhere else. People don't live

in communities permanently anymore. But they should: Communities are very comforting to human beings. I was talking to a United Mine Workers lawyer in a bar down in the Village the other day, and he was telling me how some miners in Pennsylvania damn well will not leave, even though the jobs are vanishing, because of the church centered communities there, and particularly because of the music. They have choirs that are 100 years old, some of them extraordinary choirs, and they are not going to go to San Diego, and build ships or airplanes. They're going to stay in Pennsylvania because that's home. . . . Until recent times, you know, human beings usually had a permanent community of relatives. They had dozens of homes to go to. So when a married couple had a fight, one or the other could go to a house three doors down and stay with a close relative until he was feeling tender again. Or if a kid got so fed up with his parents that he couldn't stand it, he could march over to his uncle's for a while. And this is no longer possible. Each family is locked into its little box. The neighbors aren't relatives. There aren't other houses where people can go and be cared for. . . . We're lonesome. We don't have enough friends or relatives anymore. And we would if we lived in real communities (Vonnegut, 1965-74:241-242).

Vonnegut says the craving for community runs so deep that people who have no drinking problem join Alcoholics Anonymous because of the extended family and sense of community it provides them. He cites the longing for community as a factor in drug use. "The fact that they use drugs gives them a community. If you become a user of any drug, you can pick up a set of friends you see day after day, because of the urgency of getting drugs all the time. And you'll get a community where you might not ordinarily have one" (Vonnegut, 1965-74:250). Vonnegut's observation only becomes more powerful when one looks at the consequences of the Internet, gated communities, and the power of the media to shape sentiments about social interactions. Take for example the AT&T commercial where a husband is jetting off on business to some far away location. The traveler faxes a message to his wife to meet him on the porch of their house for a "date." He then calls her up on a cellular phone while still in flight. Both are mutually satisfied by the technological encounter and business goes on. This commercial is aimed at changing the cultural sentiment about social relations and implies that technology is a viable replacement for real social interaction. If your views and personal/social relationships can be modified by the introduction of technology and the careful crafting of social sentiment by the media, our communities can be altered to an even greater extent. The emotional need to belong in a society where few opportunities exist has produced what "a proud but meaningless association of human beings" (Vonnegut, 1965-74:xv). The theme in many of Vonnegut's writings is that a true sense of community has been lost, replaced by the illusion of community that fails to satisfy the basic human need of belonging.

But even technological interactions are not evenly distributed across all segments of society. What is clear as well is that many who live in poverty, the underclass, lack the resources to enjoy even this weakened sense of community based solely on interests or the simulation of social interaction. While some may be able to tune in to the mass culture offered on TV, fewer have the money for a telephone, a car, or an internet connection so they have no easy access to people outside their neighborhoods. Different as well is the increased likelihood that the person behind the counter in the neighborhood store is probably not a member of the community. Chances are likely that the person behind the counter is not the owner, but a hired clerk, someone who has no authority to extend credit or make allowances for family problems. The underlying racial tensions, cultural differences, and pervasive mistrust make it far more likely that if the young boy shoplifts, the clerk will not confront the family privately but instead will call the police—or even take the law into his own hands. And somehow, though the face of the law makes no distinction, shoplifting from an impersonal corporation rather than the mom-and-pop stores of old is a different kind of crime.

These changes have accentuated the three-tiered hierarchy of community based on class:

- *Underclass and lower-class* inner-city neighborhoods house those who are too poor to escape, either permanently, through upward mobility, or symbolically and temporarily, by automobile, telephone, or internet. These blighted areas have lost many important anchors, including industry, businesses, shops, schools, and churches—interactions that not only helped hold the community together, but provided meaningful ways for citizens to fill their lives. Despite a shared geography and the common-thread fear of crime, many people in such communities are too fearful to interact in ways that can rebuild a sense of community.

- For the *middle class,* community spans a wide range of options. On one end are lower-middle class neighborhoods that may or may not show active signs of community life, filled with people who hope to rise higher, but fear slipping lower. On the other end of that spectrum are upper-middle class communities—gentrified areas in major cities and upscale suburban and ex-urban enclaves. In those areas, people usually have the resources that allow them to interact with others who share their interests, regardless of geography. These interactions, however, are becoming more meaningless, less direct, and certainly less social. As disposable income increases, people can also afford to partake of social and cultural activities both within the geographic community and elsewhere—movies, plays, clubs, sporting events, health clubs. The more money an individual or family has, the better they can afford to develop and enjoy a community of interests that need not be tied to the geographic area in which they live. Participation in any community life available within the geographic area where they live becomes voluntary, a matter of choice no longer based on mutual dependence.

• By virtue of their income, the *upper classes* can afford all the security they want and need, yet, even with bodyguards, the affluent cannot guarantee perfect safety, especially since their wealth makes them inviting targets for crime. There is also, no doubt, a sense of community associated with wealthy areas such as Palm Springs, California, and Grosse Pointe, Michigan, but community involvement usually means heading charitable organizations or becoming a patron of the arts, which implies service to others rather than mutual dependence. The affluent also have the wherewithal to travel wherever a community of interest draws them. Additionally, they have the resource to influence social policy and practices that are in their best interests rather than those of the community.

Not only has American society become stratified in this three-tiered hierarchy, communities have also changed because of the fairly recent emergence of planned communities. Hunter noted that a *natural* community springs up when people live together in places that also support an underlying community of interests and mutual interdependence. Planned communities upset the natural balance, whether it is a low-income public housing project or an upscale suburban enclave. What all planned communities share in common is that their rapid appearance thrusts large numbers of people together who have no history. Likewise, they are simulations of community and serve to isolate people from others and larger social problems.

Sparking an immediate sense of community is difficult because there is no established base upon which to build. In the case of many suburban developments, a sense of community may develop over time, because the people who move there share enough in common, though it may never run deep. This is far different than when an organic community assimilates an infusion of newcomers into an already functioning system. The emotional loss may be masked in affluent suburbs, because people in such circumstances often have the money to travel and indulge their hobbies and amusements. Among those who are financially strapped, however, the move from a stable city neighborhood to a new suburb offers undeniable improvements, yet it may also exact a penalty in the loss of an important source of social support, meaningful activities, and real social interaction.

In the case of public housing projects, the same kinds of barriers to generating a natural community exist, but experience also shows they are prone to even more serious problems. The kinds of low-income housing projects popular during the 1950s and 1960s put huge numbers of people into a confined space virtually overnight. Unlike the suburbs, such projects normally housed renters, not owners. This meant the new residents had less of a stake in maintaining the property, and they typically also had fewer resources to do so.

The lack of an existing cohesive community allowed people to exploit this lack of community, which, in turn, could prevent or at least slow the growth of a natural community. Unlike the suburbs, where home owners typically enjoyed a rising standard of living, many of the people trapped in housing projects found their standard of living declining instead, especially as welfare payment failed to keep pace with inflation. Home ownership also allowed those who bought a home in a new suburb to enjoy the benefits of increasing equity, inflating home prices, and a write-off on mortgage interest on their income tax. Their counterparts in low income public housing were not building any equity, and, for them, inflation simply meant an increased risk of rising rents and expenses beyond what their income could cover.

For those whose basic standard of living is comfortable, the loss of community may simply mean learning greater self-reliance or greater reliance on government, perhaps explaining the boom in self-help books offering advice to people on how they can become their own best friends and handle personal problems on their own, as well as the types of service calls police officers receive everyday. As Suzanne Keller (1984:288) wrote, "It is now possible for individuals to travel throughout the globe without ever leaving home, while others are at home wherever they set foot. Expanding spiritual and physical horizons have severed the original link between place and community." For those left behind without access to new technologies and a raise each year, the gap between the life of the *haves* and the *have-nots* can seem an unbridgeable gulf.

Without overly romanticizing the past, the alienation fostered by the loss of a sense of community takes an increasing toll on people. Membership in a strong community of the past implied belonging to a group of us who held fast together against the world. If community no longer provides that emotionally satisfying feeling of security and shared struggle, people are forced to rely more on themselves or on family. For those without the resources to enjoy the culture beyond what a TV screen or internet connection provides, the loss of geographically viable communities threatens to differentially erode the quality of life.

How Community Policing Can Build a Sense of Community

The purpose in this analysis is not to belabor or assign blame for the growing gap between rich and poor, the problems posed by racism, the blight of the inner city, and the pernicious problems of the underclass. Instead the goal is to examine today's reality and the dynamics that have eroded the strong communities of the past, to better understand the unique role community policing can play in meeting the obvious challenges.

Part of the challenge for community policing is to help revive the idea that those who live in the same area can improve the quality of community life by understanding how they share a community of mutual interests. Perhaps ironically, the threat of crime can be a catalyst to make people see that they do share a community of interest based on mutual geography. Of great consequence as well is that unless fear is channeled into positive change, it can degenerate into apathy, social isolation, or even vigilantism and riot. Community policing holds the promise of using fear of crime and disorder as an impetus to improve the overall quality of community life.

The issues of crime, fear of crime, and disorder within any geographic community offer police their best and most logical opportunity for unifying people in ways that help rebuild that traditional sense of community. Yet as the discussion of the three-tiered class hierarchy of community also shows, money can mask some of the downside of a loss of a sense of community, and community policing can play an important role wherever people cluster together. The department in Clearwater, Florida, for instance, first introduced community policing in the Greenwood Avenue area, a low-income, high-crime community. The approach's success there persuaded the administration to implement community policing on the beach, where many problems involved helping local businesses and residents cope with the influx of tourists. In the new effort, CPOs in shorts patrol the beach, easing tensions when young visitors who are far away from home often feel the urge to behave in ways they would not behave in their home communities—which also shows how a sense of community can shape people's behavior.

Regardless of the neighborhood, any new community policing effort starts first with face-to-face meetings with *average citizens*, not just so-called *community leaders*. This part of the start-up process involves average citizens in setting the priorities the police should pursue first and that alone can help people regain a sense of personal control over their collective destiny. One must be mindful, however, that initiatives must come from the community itself and not just from police or elites that desire to impose their vision of community onto a neighborhood. Bursik and Grasmick (1993:3) recount the consequences of this failed attempt at revitalization in the following observation:

> several cities also have experienced a sometimes violent resistance to the movement of upper-middle-class residents into traditionally lower- and working-class areas, that is, the process that has been referred to as gentrification. For example, the Knight-Ridder News Service released a story about the tensions that have evolved between the Polish, Italian, and German blue-collar residents of the Manayunk section of Philadelphia and the recent wave of artists, white-collar workers, and merchants who have tried to transform its working-class shopping district into a 'hip row of pastel-colored shops that some compare to Coconut Grove without the palms or

Sausalito without the San Francisco.' The resistance to this change rapidly escalated from the exchange of verbal insults to broken windows, scratched cars, and assaults (citations ommitted).

As Bruce Benson, who was a lieutenant in the Flint foot patrol experiment, noted, a survey comparing why people chose one bank over another, despite the fact all the banks in the area offered virtually the same services and benefits, related strongly to whether the patrons felt they received personalized service. If tellers smiled and made comments about anything other than the business at hand, people responded positively to this personalized attention. A police department infused with the community policing philosophy understands that the benefits of making people feel they are being treated as human beings not only makes the police more popular within the community, but it enhances the feeling of community cohesion. We must be mindful, however, that false responsiveness, technological gimmicks, and institutionalized niceties like cheerful bank tellers calling you by your first name because it appears on your bank deposit slip undermines the spirit of community policing and will be quickly detected as an attempt by police to manage their appearances and impose their will on the community.

Summary

In summary, we see that the sense of community that existed in many neighborhoods has disappeared, as a result of dramatic economic and technological changes in a relatively short period of time. Those above the poverty line at least have some opportunity to use their resources to find the emotional sustenance once provided by neighborhood life, but many problems are magnified where people cannot escape impoverished communities, either physically or symbolically.

In many ways, these changes occurred so suddenly that people stunned by the changes have not yet fully identified how to set things right. The advent of a society rich enough so that the majority can afford their own automobiles, telephones, televisions, and Internet connections seemed to offer unlimited progress. Given enough time, it seemed those left behind would catch up. What we see today instead, however, is a culture still reeling from change.

As our understanding grows, we see that a community based solely on a community of interest, with no geographic tie, can provide some level of emotional sustenance to some segments of society as long as it is reinforced with meaningful, face-to-face involvement. The problem of crime, however, requires that people who live in the same area find ways to revitalize that sense of community in their neighborhoods, especially in those places where people cannot afford to buy as much protection as they want and need.

Community policing is not a panacea—it alone cannot be expected to revive that sense of community overnight. What community policing can provide, however, is an important first step in many ways:

- CPOs can *bring neighborhood people together* in efforts to enhance the community, so that they can begin to re-establish a pattern of interacting face-to-face, which fosters the mutual trust and support that is necessary to build a sense of community;

- By *making communities safer and more attractive* places to live, people can begin to enjoy the emotional support that participating in community life can provide;

- By allowing people *direct input* into setting *the power to set the police agenda* for their area, community policing can help people develop confidence in their ability to control their collective destiny;

- In contrast to the adversarial relationship implicit in the traditional system, the community policing philosophy encourages the department to *humanize all interactions with citizens,* focusing on new ways to help them solve community concerns. By decentralizing police service through CPOs, and by personalizing all the department's interactions with average citizens, community policing helps foster an atmosphere of mutual trust and respect, which are essential in promoting a positive community atmosphere;

- Many community policing efforts specifically target the most vulnerable—the elderly, women, children. Singling them out for protection offers the promise of *encouraging everyone to participate* more fully in a community life enriched by their involvement;

- Fear of crime traps many people in their homes, where television reinforces the perception that the streets are even more dangerous than, in fact, they are. By encouraging people to band together for support and by providing personal protection, community policing *reduces the fear of crime* that stifles community involvement;

- At least initially, many cities using community policing focus new initiatives in inner-city neighborhoods. Besides the logic of addressing the most serious problems first, a renewed sense of community may provide part of the answer in addressing current social and community conditions. This offers the promise of involving the police in *new efforts to reach the underclass*, encouraging and supporting their efforts to make positive changes; and

- A welcome by-product of community policing is *improved race relations*, and racial tensions remain a major barrier in developing a true sense of community.

As this demonstrates, community policing attempts to renew the link to a place that was historically an important part of the definition of community. It says that people who live in the same place must again become sensitive to the need to care for their neighbors, and that the police must become good neighbors to the people they serve.

References

Ager, S. (1988). "Catholics Took Road to Closings." *Detroit Free Press*, (October 2):15A.

Angell, R.C. (1965). *Free Society and Moral Crisis.* Ann Arbor, MI: Ann Arbor Paperbacks/The University of Michigan Press.

Azarya, V. (1985). *Community in The Social Science Encyclopedia.* Ed. Adam Kuper & Jessica Kuper. London, England: Routledge & Kegan Paul.

Bursik, R.J. & H.J. Grasmick (1993). *Neighborhoods and Crime.* New York, NY: Lexington Books.

Church, G.J. (1988). "Are You Better Off?" *Time*, (October 10):28.

Fessler, D.R. (1976). *Facilitating Community Change: A Basic Guide.* San Diego, CA: University Associate.

Finkelstein, J. (1988). "Campaign Aims to Keep Students in School." *Detroit Free Press*, (August 26):1A.

Gans, H. (1962). *The Urban Villagers: Groups and Class in the Life of Italian-Americans*, Second Edition. New York, NY: The Free Press.

Hillery, G.A. (1955). "Definitions of Community: Areas of Agreement." *Rural Sociology*, 20(4):111.

Jackson, L. (1988). "State's Auto Jobs Continue Decline." *Detroit Free Press*, (August 15):1C.

Keller, S. (1984). "Community and Community Feeling." In A. Whittick (ed.) *The Encyclopedia of Urban Planning.* New York, NY: McGraw-Hill.

Keller, S. (1982). "The Neighborhood." In R.H. Baylor (ed.) *Neighborhoods in Urban America.* Baylor Port Washington, NY: Kennikat Press.

Kelly, R.M. (1977). *Community Control of Economic Development.* New York, NY: Praeger.

Lapham, L.H., M. Pollan & E. Etheridge (1984-1987). *The Harper's Index Book.* New York, NY: An Owl Book/Henry Holt and Company.

Lowe, S. (1986). *Urban Social Movements: The City After Castells.* London, England: Macmillan.

McGraw, B. & T. Blossom (1988). "Losings Deal Another Blow to a City Losing People, Businesses, Institutions." *Detroit Free Press*, (September 30):2B.

Meenaghan, T.M. (1972). "What Means Community." *Social Work*, 19(6): 94.

Moynihan, D.P. (1988). "America's Children: Half are Born Without a Fair Chance." *The Detroit Free Press*, (October 3):7A.

Nielsen Report on Television (1988). Northbrook, IL: Nielsen Media Research.

The State of Michigan Strategy—1988 Update of the 1986 Anti-Drug Abuse Act, prepared by the Michigan Office of Criminal Justice, a quote from Joel Gilliam of the Detroit Police Department, July 1988, p. 1.5-2.

The State of Michigan Strategy—1988, a quote from Detroit Mayor Coleman Young, p. 1.5-1.

The State of Michigan Strategy—1987 Update of the 1986 Anti-Drug Abuse Act, prepared by the Michigan Office of Criminal Justice, taken from *Drug Abuse Trends,* prepared by the Michigan Department of Public Health's Office of Substance Abuse Services, Statistical Division, by Richard Calkins.

Stengel, R. (1988). "The Underclass: Breaking the Cycle." *Time,* (October 10):41.

Strecher, V.G. (1995). "Revising the Histories and Futures of Policing." In V. Kappeler (ed.) *The Police & Society: Touch Stone Readings.* Prospect Heights, IL: Waveland Press.

Strecher, V.G. (1995a). "People Who Don't Even Know You." In V. Kappeler (ed.) *The Police & Society: Touch Stone Readings.* Prospect Heights, IL: Waveland Press.

Swickard, J. (1988). "Detroit Tops Big Cities in Rate of Youths Slain." *Detroit Free Press,* (September 11):15A.

Swickard, J. & M. Trimer (1988). "Jury Acquits 2 Vigilantes of Burning Down House." *Detroit Free Press,* (October 7):1A.

Taft, D.R. (1942). *Criminology.* New York, NY: Macmillan.

Tonnies, F. (1887, Eng. Trans. 1955). *Community and Society.* London, England: Routledge.

USA Today, (October 5):1.

Vonnegut, K. (1965-1974). *Wampeters, Foma & Granfalloons (Opinions).* New York, NY: Delacorte/Seymour Lawrence.

Watman, W.S. (1980). *A Guide to the Language of Neighborhoods.* Washington, DC: National Center for Urban Ethnic Affairs.

Worsley, P. (1987). *New Introductory Sociology,* Third Edition. London, England: Penguin.

Young, M. & P. Wilmott (1960). *Family and Kinship in East London.* Harmondsworth, England: Penguin.

CHAPTER 4
Community Policing and Crime

*Laws, like the spider's web, catch the fly
and let the hawk go free.*
—*Spanish Proverb*

Challenges to Traditional Crime Control

Since the police reform movement of the 1930s, the primary job of the public police has narrowed to that of crime-fighter. While the merits of paring down the police role to this narrow yardstick is debatable, the presence and absence of crime has been an occupational standard against which police programs were measured. Indeed, part of the impetus for finding new ways of policing stemmed from the failure of traditional policing to meet the challenge posed by the explosion of crime in the 1960s. Although criminal victimization has generally declined over the past 20 years (Kappeler, Blumberg & Potter, 1996), rates of serious crime in this country are far higher than for other Western, industrialized nations. Crime has become a media mainstay and it has emerged as one of the top issues in every presidential campaign of the past three decades. Media-generated fear of crime, public pressure to find new ways to "combat" crime, and the failure of the traditional policing model helped persuade police to experiment with new ideas, including community policing.

Though supporters of community policing can point to very recent data that suggest that the movement has at least contributed to the recent decline in crime rates (Kelling, 1997), it is also beneficial to remember Mark Twain's (1972:925) warning that there are three kinds of lies—"lies, damn lies, and statistics." It should be remembered that the professionalizion movement in policing was predicated on the assertion that police could control crime and that crime fighting was their mandate (Manning, 1995). Citizens wanted the

81

police to be accountable for their performance and police officials actively took responsibility for crime control as part of their professional mandate. As Alpert and Moore (1993:110) observed, "Citizens and their elected representatives have long sought a bottom line to measure police performance. The goals have been to reassure the public that hard-earned tax dollars were being spent to achieve important results and to hold police managers accountable for improving organizational performance. As police agencies matured, four generally accepted accounting practices became enshrined as the key measures to evaluate police performance. These include: (1) reported crime rates (2) overall arrests (3) clearance rates (4) response times." It then followed that these should be the measures of police performance and the idea became institutionalized. The professional model, however, had little direct impact on crime rates even after millions of federal dollars were poured into crime-fighting programs.

More recently, as the nation's crime rates were falling, unemployment was declining, as the country bounced back from recession and moved into one of the longest and most significant economic expansions ever experienced. At the same time as well, the percentage of the population in its most crime-prone teenage years was falling, as the last of the Baby Boomers matured and significant changes occurred in the American youth culture. Another obvious factor is that there has been a tremendous increase in private policing activities. The number of privately employed security personnel now far exceeds the number of public police officers. Some have effectively argued that the police institution's move from the language of crime fighting to that of service was, at least in part, a consequence of this private challenge to the crime-fighting mandate (Manning, 1995a). There has also been an explosion in the punitiveness of American society. From 1970 to today this country has increased its incarceration rate by more than 400 percent (Kappeler, Blumberg & Potter, 1996). The police are currently making more arrests than at any other time in American history. Of course this is not to suggest that arrest and incarceration have an appreciable impact on serious crime rates because the majority of the increase in the prison population came from the incarceration of relatively minor drug offenders, rather than the serious offenders on which the media and the public seem to focus. Yet, the United States leads all other industrialized nations in both crime rates and the number of citizens under control of the criminal justice system.

In a complex society undergoing rapid and constant change, there are simply too many variables to be able to determine, with any certainty, how much of a role any single factor may play in the rise and fall of overall crime rates. Unlike a controlled lab experiment, studying changes in the world at large depends on how wisely the researchers choose which factors they will look at. After all, during that same period, there were also dramatic increases in the number of coronary bypasses performed, as well as in the number of compact disc players purchased, yet few would argue these changes made any difference in overall crime rates. Another related problem in determining whether a particular social intervention effects crime is that of philosophy and measurement. Social scientists tend to focus on short-term interventions like crime prevention programs and police tactics and measure outcomes in terms of existing measurements and data that are readily available and easy to collect. When a major philosophical change occurs in a social institution that promises long-term intervention, new measurement instruments must be created and new data collected. Dennis P. Rosenbaum (1996:408) has remarked that, "Nearly all of the evaluation research on collective anti-crime strategies focuses on opportunity-reduction activities" (i.e., "victimization prevention" behaviors and programs). At present we know little about the effectiveness of neighborhood-based strategies that focus on social problems . . ." At least for a time, we must rely on logic and reason to determine which changes hold the greatest promise of making a significant impact on crime.

Police Measures of Crime—What Do We Know?

The answer to how much crime exists in the United States is simple—no one knows. At best, indicators such as the Uniform Crime Reports (UCR) statistics compiled by the FBI show trends, but they do not provide a true picture of the crimes actually committed at any specific time. Even when the police are notified, changes in reporting procedures, complications, and manipulations of the reporting system make the rates suspect. We do know, however, that police accounting practices and politics effect crime rates. Victor G. Strecher (1997:72-73) summarizes the findings of the Crime Reporting Audit in St. Louis in the following passage.

> This program was tested in the early 1960s; its purpose was to assure the accuracy of crime reporting. Certain dispatches were thought to be downgraded (for example, burglary to larceny, aggravated to simple assault) by reporting officers under pressure from district commanders to keep crime rates low. . . . Initially it was found that numerous calls were, in fact, being downgraded—in some cases improperly classified as "unfounded" reports. These inspection findings were given to field operations command for correction after each audit. In time it found that the proportion of calls being downgraded was equaled by those being upgraded (both now small numbers) to the disadvantage of the reporting unit. After this audit, it was thought the limits of accurate reporting had been reached. It was thought, how ever, that continued audits were necessary to assure the accuracy of crime reporting, given the pressures upon district commanders to keep crime rates low.

The problem of distortions in crime reporting is not merely a problem of the 1960s. Since the creation of the UCR, and even today, many police departments are involved in the distortion of crime rates. Skogan and Hartnett

(1997) noted that in the 1980s investigative reporters uncovered that members of the Chicago Police Department "killed crime" by fraudulently rejecting reports to keep detectives' loads low (see, Skogan & Gordon, 1982). While one can argue that the more serious the crime, the more reliable the figures, all suffer distortion. We assume that murder rates are the most accurate of all, since people are very likely to report the discovery of a dead body to the police. Yet even in this case, no one knows for sure how many people are murder victims. When figures for even this most serious of crimes cannot be considered complete, the less serious the crime, the more likely that the statistics should be considered highly suspect as an indicator of what is happening in the real world.

An important issue beyond mere numbers concerns which crimes we consider the most serious, as a society and as individuals. The UCR data focuses on eight so-called Part I (Index) or "serious" crimes—four violent crimes (murder, rape, robbery, aggravated assault) and four property crimes (burglary, larceny/theft, motor vehicle theft, arson). While it might seem that everyone would agree that these are the crimes that deserve the greatest attention—and nearly all countries in the world define these crimes as top priorities—they do not reflect the comparative harm caused by criminality.

Using murder as an example, the UCR figures show there are about 22,000 murders committed in the United States each year, but there are also about 40,000 traffic-related deaths every year, and almost one-half involve alcohol. Though a direct comparison of both problems ignores obvious difficulties, the realization that drunk driving kills nearly as many people each year as are murdered in this country has made us rethink our priorities. Research on the ability of the police institution to curtail drunk driving finds two serious and surprising barriers to effectively reducing this behavior. First, police officers have traditionally viewed drunk driving as a non-serious crime and officers in many departments have been reluctant to take enforcement actions (Mastrofski & Ritti, 1992). Second, despite training, a growing public concern about drunk driving, and a change in police attitudes toward drunk driving many police departments do not provide officers a structured work environment from which officers can take enforcement action (Mastrofski & Ritti, 1996). In essence, even when officers attitudes are changed and training in drunk driving enforcement is provided, if answering calls for service is a department's first priority and if a department continues to place a greater value on other police activities, very little progress toward solving this problems takes place. These observations reflect the reality that what we define as serious crime changes over time, that there is a relationship between how officers view police work and how police departments structure police activities and the ability of law enforcement to address crime-related problems. Crime and policing must be considered in a social and organizational context.

While monitoring trends for Part I crimes over time provides a blurry snapshot of what the police are doing and what citizens are reporting, the picture remains incomplete. Prior to the Sullivan Act, for example, narcotics were legal, whereas today, drug arrests constitute a significant percentage of all arrests made by the police. Manufacturing, selling, and consuming alcohol were illegal acts under Prohibition, but since Repeal, the police role has been narrowed primarily to controlling open drinking, public drunkenness, drunk driving, and problems with underage drinking. Thirty years ago, the crime of child abuse received relatively little attention, but now claims-makers argue that 2.9 million cases of abuse occur each year (Brott, 1995). The real number is closer to 350,000 (Potter & Kappeler, 1998). Yet, since the early 1970s, the number of unsubstantiated claims of child abuse has almost doubled, making questionable claims of abuse greater than founded claims (Kappeler, Potter & Blumberg, 1996).

Likewise, in the 1970s and 1980s, many states decriminalized *status offenses* (acts by juveniles, such as violating curfew or running away, that would not be considered as crimes if committed by an adult), but by 1997, well over 75 of the largest 200 American cities had reenacted or created rigid curfew laws designed to address the public's fear of juvenile crime, which means because of sensational media reporting and a failure to understand the realities of juvenile crime, the pendulum may begin to swing back.

Certain ideas about crime seem to go in and out of fashion, as our knowledge, sensibilities and media's focus change over time. For example, not only is increasing attention now paid to all rapes, but within the past few years, date rape has been more clearly defined as an offense that victims should report to the police for prosecution. Additionally, sensational media reporting and an attempt by political leaders to appease a fearful public has created new crimes like stalking and carjacking (see, Kappeler, Blumberg & Potter, 1996). Advances in technology and changes in business practices have also spawned new categories of crime. Prior to the widespread use of computers, unleashing a computer virus could not have been a crime. This country's increasingly complicated financial system has unleashed new variants of white-collar crime, including electronic embezzlement of funds and new wrinkles in stock manipulations. While street crime is estimated to cost Americans between $10 billion and $13.5 billion a year, white-collar crime is estimated to cost between $174 billion and $231 billion annually (Coleman, 1994; Clinard & Yeager; see, Kappeler, Blumberg & Potter, 1996).

Perhaps if we look at an extreme example we can begin to understand the comparative nature of crime as well as its context and consequences. In an elegant analysis comparing the impact of bank robberies versus stolen bikes, Edmonton (Canada) police inspector Chris Braiden questioned whether police are out of touch with the wants and needs of average citizens. His study showed that in a single year, 1,069 banks in Canada were robbed, with total losses of $2.8 million. Because of the importance of the crime and because such losses are typically recoverable by insurance or tax write-offs, bank robberies are almost always reported to the police.

In contrast, that same year, 182,000 bikes were reported stolen. Since the reporting rate for bicycle thefts is only 29 percent, Braiden conservatively calculated that these crimes cost Canadians $45 million that year. Comparing the two crimes shows that bicycle thefts involve roughly 100 times as many victims as bank thefts, with 15 times the dollar loss (Braiden, 1987). Yet he notes that when a bank robbery occurs, every available officer responds. When a bike is stolen, many departments will not even send an officer to investigate—instead they ask for a report over the phone.

Braiden's point is not that the police pay too much attention to bank robberies, but that they pay far too little to so-called petty crimes. This does not mean that a fleet of squad cars should come screaming to the scene of a bike theft, sirens blaring, but that the police must have a strategy that allows them to monitor and play a role in dealing with such offenses. In fact, such exaggerations have been used to rhetorically support police focus on street crime and support the traditional crime control model (see, Klockars, 1995). Far too many police officers think *wasting* time on finding the youngster who steals a bike; too many police organizations feel that they have no role to play in addressing white-collar crime because they feel that this detracts from the *important* job of catching bank robbers.

It is easy to understand the justification for relegating widespread but relatively trivial crimes to lesser status. Compared to an armed bank robbery, a bicycle theft does seem petty—except to the victim. In our quest for justice, we have tried to fashion a criminal justice system where the greatest resources are concentrated on what appear to be the more serious threats, but appearances are deceptive. The danger is that police departments can lose touch with average citizens and become indifferent to their valid concerns, and petty and white-collar crimes affect far more people than so-called serious street crime.

We expect crime victims to take their victimization seriously, but when the police fail to do so, that reinforces their already heightened sense of vulnerability and fear. Police departments that appear to ignore petty crime contribute to the pervasive sense of dread that crime is spiraling out of control—and that the system will not help because it does not care.

While the next chapter will deal in greater depth with the problem of fear of crime, any discussion of crime must include recognition of how the threat of victimization affects people. We expect the police to do all they can to protect us. We understand, intellectually, that if a serial killer is on the loose, the police department must shift resources from other services to help protect us from that threat, even though relatively few people are actually at greater risk and most police departments and communities will never have to deal with a serial killer (see, Kappeler, Blumberg & Potter, 1996).

While the media and the police community bombarded the public with national crime statistics, an average person on the street probably has no idea what the ups and downs in the statistics show about the crime rate in their neighborhood. But when the woman across the street returns home for the second time in six months to find the TV stolen or when a stream of late-night visitors frequent an increasingly dilapidated house two doors down, she may have good reason to fear that her personal risk of victimization is increasing.

Those incidents may not individually or collectively make a noticeable difference in the crime statistics, and even the most sophisticated crime analysis may not identify a trend, but someone attuned to life in that neighborhood knows problems are brewing.

To understand more clearly the special niche that community policing fills, it is important first to understand how traditional policing confronts the entire matrix of crime. Only then can we assess the impact community policing makes.

The Traditional Police Effort

Proponents of the traditional model of crime control and supporters of some of the more modern forms of crime prevention argue, based on a deterrence philosophy, that there are three times when police action can influence crime:

- Police action can prevent a crime from occurring;

- Police intervention during the commission of a crime can influence the outcome; and

- Police efforts after the crime has occurred can resolve the situation, ideally by solving the crime, arresting the perpetrator, and, in appropriate cases, restoring stolen property.

Traditional police efforts rely primarily on motor patrol as the first line of offense and defense. Special units, high-tech gadgets, sophisticated lab analyses, and investigative follow-up are all designed to complement the use of motor patrol as the primary tactics in the traditional police model of fighting crime. Yet even a cursory examination of this approach demonstrates serious shortcomings in how traditional policing approaches intervention into crime:

• **Prevention** – The rationale for having motor patrol officers cruise streets on free patrol is that their visible presence in the community should act as a deterrent to crime. It was thought that criminals would refrain from the commission of crimes by the mere presence of a police car or by creating the illusion that their was a significant chance that the criminally minded would be caught by the police should they attempt a crime. Yet, few research studies support the assertion that traditional random motor patrol is effective in these regards.

The controversial Kansas City (Missouri) Preventive Patrol study divided the South Patrol Division's 15 districts into three kinds of beats. In five reactive-only beats, routine preventive patrol was eliminated entirely; patrol cars were dispatched only when calls for service were received. In the five control beats, routine preventive patrol remained at the standard one-car-per-beat ratio. In the five proactive beats, the intensity of routine preventive patrol was increased by doubling or tripling the normal ratio.

The results of the Kansas City Preventive Patrol study had profound implications for the efficacy of the traditional crime control model. Among the findings:

- Rates of crimes reported showed no difference among the beats;

- Victimization studies showed the proactive approach made no discernible impact on the number of burglaries, auto thefts, larcenies involving auto accessories, robberies, or vandalism—the kinds of crimes considered to be most susceptible to deterrence through preventive motor patrol;

- Citizen attitudes toward police showed few consistent differences and no apparent pattern across the three different types of beats;

- Fear of crime did not decline;

- Citizen satisfaction with police did not improve in the experimental areas; and

- Experimental conditions showed no effect on police response times or citizen satisfaction with response times (Kelling, 1974).

The Kansas City study has raised serious debate and controversy. Some have even argued that the findings of the study have been misinterpreted to mean that all forms of patrol have no impact on crime (Cordner & Trojanowicz, 1992). Obviously such an interpretation is open to question. The study does, however, raise concerns about *random motor patrol's* immediate ability to prevent crime by its mere presence. It also shows citizen satisfaction does not appear to depend on how often they see a patrol car—not only did satisfaction not rise in the beats where patrols were doubled, but it did not decline in areas where officers only responded to calls. The assumption was that random motor patrol would provide short-term prevention, while the addition of Crime Prevention Units would address the need for longer-term, educational efforts. In part because of the finding of the study, others have reframed the basic question about motor patrol to focus on the more important issue of how police spend their time and how patrol activities can be restructured to be more effective in crime prevention (Krajick, 1980, Wilson & McLaren, 1977).

Perhaps, Victor Strecher (1997:17-18) said it best in his advice to police executives: "*Forget* the time-honored but mistaken imagery of an omnipresent "patrol blanket" over the entire jurisdiction. There is no blanket. There has never been a blanket. From the time of its enunciation by Vollmer, it has been an illusory doctrine which in recent years has revealed vast holes in its fabric."

- **Crimes in Progress** – In theory, this is the area where motor patrol's ability to provide a rapid response should make its greatest contribution to reducing and controlling crime, but another study done on Kansas City raised troubling concerns. It showed that response time was unrelated to the probability of making an arrest or locating a witness for serious crime. Success or failure depended less on how fast the officer arrived and more on how quickly the citizen reported the crime (Board of Police Commission, 1977). Other research confirms this conclusion. Most of the criminal or serious calls to the police are "cold" where the perpetrator has long absconded, or the victim waits an inordinately long period of time before calling the police. A national study of response times showed that approximately 75 percent of serious crimes were cold when the citizen notified the police (Spelman & Brown, 1984). Citizen delays in calling the police are attributable to:

  - apathy;

  - skepticism about the police's ability to do anything; and

  - citizens notifying other persons before calling the police.

  It seems citizens wait at least five minutes before calling the police in about one-half of the serious crimes that are reported. These studies clearly indicate that rapid response does not contribute to increased apprehensions in the majority of crimes. A second consideration with rapid response is citizen perceptions of police effectiveness. Untimely delays for a police response does cause citizen dissatisfaction with the police (Percy, 1980; Pate, Ferrara, Bowers & Lorence, 1976). However, this dissatisfaction can be reduced and controlled through proper police communications procedures. In most cases, discontent is the result of the police response being slower than that which the police dispatcher indicated or led citizens to expect. "In short, we have focused on using high-technology dispatching equipment and sophisticated deployment schemes to reduce police response time, when we should also have focused on reducing citizen delays" (Larson & Cahn, 1985) and informing citizens about police responses. Research confirms that rapid response led to response-related arrests for Part I crimes in only three percent of calls (Kelling, 1981).

- **Resolving Crimes Already Committed** – Traditional police efforts after the crime has occurred include both motor patrol and investigation. Again, the rationale for relying primarily on motor patrol's quick response is based on the assumption that the officers can therefore do a better job of preserving evidence and locating witnesses. After this initial assessment, many departments then assign investigators to follow up further. Criminal investigators, however, don't have a very good track record in solving crime already committed. The RAND study of the criminal investigation process (Greenwood & Petersilia, 1975) cast serious doubt on one of the basic planks in the traditional crime control model. Victor Strecher (1997:73-74) extracted and summarized the major findings of the study in the following list:

- On investigative effectiveness: Differences in investigative training, staffing, workload, and procedures appear to have no appreciable effect on crime, arrest, or clearance rates;

- The method by which police investigators are organized (team policing, specialists vs. generalists, patrolmen investigators) cannot be related to variations in crime, arrest, and clearance rates;

- On the use of investigators' time: Substantially more than one-half of all serious reported crimes receive no more than superficial attention from investigators;

- [A]n investigator's time is largely consumed in reviewing reports, documenting files, and attempting to locate and interview victims on cases that experience shows will not be solved. For cases that are solved . . . an investigator spends more time in post-clearance processing than . . .identifying the perpetrator;

- On how cases are solved: The single most important determinant of whether or not a case will be solved is the information the victim supplies to the immediately responding patrol officer. If information that uniquely identifies the perpetrator is not presented at the time the crime is reported, the perpetrator, by and large, will not be subsequently identified;

- On how cases are solved: Of those cases that are ultimately cleared but in which the perpetrator is not identifiable at the time of the initial police incident report, almost all are cleared as a result of routine police procedures (that is, additional information obtained while investigating other cases, or fortuitous results of traffic stops and field interviews, such as Timothy McVeigh being stopped for a traffic violation);

- On collecting physical evidence: Most police departments collect more physical evidence than can be productively processed. . . . [A]llocating more resources to increasing the processing capabilities of the department can lead to more identifications than some other investigative actions;

- On the use of physical evidence: Latent fingerprints rarely provide the only basis for identifying a suspect;

- On investigative thoroughness: In relatively few departments do investigators consistently and thoroughly document the key evidentiary facts that reasonably assure that the prosecutor can obtain a conviction on the most serious applicable charges;

- On investigative thoroughness: Police failure to document a case investigation thoroughly may have contributed to a higher case dismissal rate and a weakening of the prosecutor's plea bargaining position;

- On relations between victims and police: Crime victims in general strongly desire to be notified officially as to whether or not the police have "solved" their case, and what progress has been made toward convicting the suspect after his arrest; and

- On investigative organization and procedure: Investigative strike forces have a significant potential to increase arrest rates for a few difficult target offenses, provided they remain concentrated on activities for which they are uniquely qualified; in practice, however, they are frequently diverted elsewhere.

Subsequent research supports the RAND study's findings with a somewhat more positive twist. Eck (1983), upon attempting to refine our understanding of the investigative process concluded that there were three categories of cases facing investigators: weak cases that cannot be solved regardless of investigative effort (unsolvable cases); cases with moderate levels of evidence that can be solved with considerable investigative effort (solvable cases); and cases with strong evidence that can be solved with minimum effort (already solved cases). Eck found that cases within the "already solved" category did not require additional investigative effort or time, and the "unsolvable cases" should not be investigated because it would be wasted effort. Eck concluded that detectives should be assigned the "solvable cases." Such cases had the potential to be solved and they required additional effort. Brandl and Frank (1994) examined a number of burglary and robbery cases relative to Eck's triage of cases and found that cases with moderate levels of evidence could be successfully investigated. Thus, contrary to the RAND study, criminal investigations can have positive results, but investigators must focus on only those cases that tend to solve themselves.

Traditional motor patrol efforts has little discernible impact on preventing crime, very rarely do they thwart crimes in progress, and they accomplish less than people hope for in resolving crimes after the fact. These findings are offered as an effort to understand the structural limitations of a basically reactive response. Alpert and Moore's (1993:112) consideration of the traditional crime control strategy concluded that "enthusiasm for this strategy of professional policing has waned. The professional policing model has been ineffective in reducing crime, reducing citizens' fears, and satisfying victims that justice is being done. Indeed,. . . a majority of the population believes that the crime problem has become progressively worse during the past decade. Similarly, citizens have lost confidence in the criminal justice system to protect them" (citations omitted).

Let us step back from the research for a moment and put a human face on the consequences of a reactive policing model. Perhaps as early as 1964, there were ominous warnings that the traditional police approach, with its focus on reacting to calls for service, would prove unable to control serious crime. That was the year that Kitty Genovese was mugged and murdered in New York. Though she screamed for help for half an hour as her attackers stabbed and beat her, none of those 38 middle-class neighbors who heard her cries called the police. In a series of articles in the *New York Times*, some of those neighbors said they were too afraid to get involved, while others said they simply did not consider the problem any of their business—that it was a problem for the police to handle, not them (Goulden, 1989).

Some commentators tried to write off the incident as peculiar to New York City, but the case raised serious concerns that something had gone severely wrong with the relationship between people and the police and also that something was seriously wrong with the system. The traditional approach relies on that all-important call for service before the police can spring into action. The millions of dollars spent each year recruiting and training top-notch officers and equipping them with the latest technology ultimately relies on persuading just one person to lift up the phone.

What the *Genovese* case did was demonstrate that the police had over-sold themselves as society's crime-fighters, to the degree that people wanted to believe they could delegate all responsibility to police professionals—that crime was not their responsibility and getting involved was too risky. That famous case also vividly brought home the depth of the estrangement between people and their police. None of those people in Queens apparently saw the police as trusted friends who could protect them, but as nameless and faceless strangers that they dared not count on. Of course, the New York City police have done much historically to foster this public perception (see, Kappeler, Sluder & Alpert, 1998). This incident brought into stark relief the terrifying prospect that the alienation between people and their police was so profound that no one was safe. It drove home the point that a society in which people are not part of the police process cannot expect to control serious crime, and that the police had to find better ways to involve people in efforts to police themselves.

The Dynamics of Serious Crime

To understand the special contribution that community policing can make in extending the overall impact of the police, we will examine the most heinous crime, murder, to show how community policing augments motor patrol's attempts to prevent, thwart, or solve this crime. Homicide (including murder, nonnegligent manslaughter, and negligent manslaughter)—murder is often a crime of passion or profit. In more than 50 percent of the cases of known murders, the victim knew or was related to the killer. While TV dramas perpetuate the image of psychopathic killers roaming the country, picking off victims at random (Kappeler, Blumberg & Potter, 1996), the vast majority of murders committed in the United States stem from the escalation of domestic quarrels, arguments between friends or acquaintances, or battles that result from intoxication or those that erupt from conflicts about drugs and drug profits.

Murder can be premeditated or impulsive, but, in either case, the police face obvious limits on their ability to make a difference. As the murder of President Kennedy—and then his alleged killer—affirmed, even being encircled by police is not always enough to prevent premeditated murder. In impulsive murders that occur when a robbery or burglary goes awry, the police cannot hope to provide much protection except by striving to eradicate and control these other crimes. Ironically, the evidence suggests that the police can do the least with comparatively few senseless, random acts of violence with which we are most often concerned.

One of the most intractable problems is finding ways to prevent domestic violence from escalating to murder. When we look at the dynamics of murders involving family or friends, the reactive nature of traditional police efforts makes dealing with such problems extraordinarily challenging. Until or unless a call is made to the police, either by the victim or by neighbors or other witnesses, there is little chance that a patrol car driving by can have any impact on people arguing behind closed doors, so preventive patrol can do little. Once a call is made, motor patrol officers can reduce the likelihood of repeat violence that always holds the threat of ending in murder by arresting the attacker.

The Minneapolis Domestic Violence Experiment in 1981-1982 showed arrest was the most effective of the three standard methods police use to reduce domestic violence (the other two are *advising* or *sending the suspect away* for at least eight hours). The research showed that when the police arrested the suspect, the incidence of repeat violence over the next six months was only 10 percent, compared to 19 percent for advising, and 24 percent when the suspect was sent away (Sherman & Berk, 1984). This study also shows that factors traditionally considered outside the province of the police seem to play a role in this potentially murderous violence. One striking finding was that roughly six out of 10 suspects and victims alike were unemployed, while the overall unemployment rate in the area was only 5 percent. Also, 45 percent of suspects were the unmarried male lover of the victim; 35 percent were the victim's current husband. Eight of 10 victims said they had been assaulted by the same person within the past six months, and six of 10 had called the police to intervene within that same period. Slightly more than one in four couples were in counseling at the time. In addition, six in 10 suspects had a prior arrest, and four in 10 had been arrested for an alcohol offense (Sherman & Berk, 1984).

Under political pressure from feminists and other groups of citizens concerned with domestic violence, and facing the ever-increasing threat of lawsuits, legislators were quick to enact presumptive or mandatory arrest laws. Relying on the proof of the well-publicized Minneapolis experiment, they legislatively limited officers' discretion in an attempt to reduce domestic violence. Subsequent studies, which replicated the Minneapolis experiment, were conducted in Omaha, Charlotte, and Milwaukee. Using similar research designs, dramatically different results were reached: making an arrest did not result in fewer subsequent incidents of assault. The danger to the victim is not increased or decreased by an officer's choice to use mediation, to separate the parties, or to arrest the offender (Dunford, Huizinga & Elliott, 1986). While there is sufficient philosophical justification for treating domestic violence as seriously as officers would treat other forms of violence, evidence as to the effectiveness of mandatory arrests in reducing violence is at best uncertain. The Attorney General's Task Force on Family Violence (1984) noted that the process of mediation assumes equal culpability in a dispute, which seldom is the case in domestic violence cases. Even if arrest is not as effective as hoped, it remains a temporary solution for law enforcement, but community policing perhaps offers a better solution to the problem than merely relying on arrest.

This paints a vivid picture of couples struggling with problems beyond what a 10-minute visit from a motor patrol officer can hope to solve. Over and over, the police arrive to find a troubled couple, stressed by economic problems, where alcohol helped trigger potentially murderous rage. Yet research demonstrates social intervention can make an impact—if someone asks for help—and this is where community policing can begin to expand the police department's impact. One of community policing's stated goals is to boost people's confidence in the police as a valid source of help, so that they will be quicker to report crimes to the police. By focusing on domestic violence as an example, here are other ways a creative community policing effort could be devised to target murders stemming from this problem:

- CPOs could be charged with the responsibility to make follow-up home visits periodically, as part of their regular beat activity. If social intervention can substantially impact future violence, repeated visits by an officer at least offers some promise of convincing the aggressor that the police are watching him and that they take the matter seriously. But this is only one aspect of the CPO's role;

- In the role as liaison to other public and private agencies, a CPO might also be able to urge more of the three out of four troubled couples into appropriate and affordable counseling. CPOs can also offer information about alcohol abuse programs. COPs can also offer to escort the victim to a shelter for battered women; and

- Long-range, proactive community policing efforts, ranging from career counseling to providing lists of available jobs, help address some of the underlying dynamics, such as unemployment. In addition community policing efforts that provide relief for families under pressure, such as activities for juveniles, can help ease tensions that can trigger violence. Because we now know that children who see physical violence in their homes while they are growing up often learn to mimic that behavior when they become adults, community policing's added impact in reducing violence today also holds the promise of reducing such violence years from now.

The dynamics of so-called *crimes of passion* defy easy answers. While traditional, reactive efforts can help, the underlying factors that can impel some people to murderous violence require longer-term interventions, which is where community policing offers the promise of playing a broader role. The difficulty in outlining precisely how community policing can dramatically extend the police role relates to the fact that its strategies and tactics are bounded only by the imagination of the officers involved. Perhaps in ethnic neighborhoods where macho male behavior tacitly condones wife beating, the CPO might work with local religious leaders to develop workshops on how to change cultural attitudes. Prevention efforts might also include having CPOs talk on domestic violence in various high-school classes aimed at both sexes, separately and together. The CPO's opportunity to work with young people, one-on-one and in small groups, in informal give-and-take conversations over a long period of time, can also help to counter-balance the negative impact of growing up in a violence-prone environment. This, however, requires that CPOs become educated in the context, not just the control, of crime. Another quality of community policing is that it does not rest on a rigid, textbook approach, but instead each effort can be tailored to the needs of the particular community.

The purpose of this lengthy discussion has been to identify how departments that adopt community policing can address a far broader range of the dynamics involved in murder, as a way of illustrating the principles that apply to a wide array of other serious and petty crimes.

As the dynamics involved in these most serious violent crimes indicate, the traditional police response offers little opportunity for officers to make meaningful interventions that hold the promise of making people safer. All too often, the best the police can hope to do is deal effectively with the problems after the fact, and even in that regard, community policing's ability to generate more and better information holds the promise of doing a better job than traditional efforts. Moreover, because of community policing's emphasis on treating citizens as partners in the police process and on encouraging CPOs to develop their interpersonal skills to the maximum, it allows the department to do a better job of working with victims and witnesses.

Police Substations in Fast Food Restaurants Efficient, Provide Security

The cop at McDonald's may be woofing down a hamburger, but sometimes he's really on the job.

Police substations at fast food restaurants and convenience stores, tucked into neighborhoods that want both hot french fries and good policing, are proving to be a good deal, police say.

"I guess the issue becomes availability to the citizens," said Steve Chermak, assistant professor of criminal justice at Indiana University. "Community policing makes it easier for the public to meet with the police."

Since 1992, the number of these ministations in Indianapolis has increased from one to at least 15, said Indianapolis Police Department Patrolman Fred Smith. They are in McDonald's, Burger Kings, Pizza Huts, Thorntons, Village Pantries and other places scattered around some of the city's most crime-plagued areas.

"The main purpose is to deter criminal activity," Smith said, sitting at a familiar table at a McDonald's.

Although the police department doesn't have specific figures on the crime rates around these mini-stations, those who patrol, work and eat at the establishments agree: The number of problems has dropped significantly.

"They Know You're There"

"It's a pro-active approach," Smith said. "It's high visibility. They know you're there."

All the workers on Smith's route know him—and vice versa. People seem at ease in a rough area of Indianapolis' inner city, some stopping by to ask directions or anything else that comes to mind.

"We have that sign on our foreheads: 'Ask me anything,'" he said, laughing, and making a swipe across his brow.

But he's often there for more than chatting. He's there to work. Most substations are clearly marked and have at least one phone line dedicated to police business—whether that is making calls or hooking up their portable computers. Officers keep a stack of the most common police forms in the kitchen.

"You could use your own phone, but you wouldn't make contacts," he said. "I know the criminals. I know the victims. You know everybody will know you."

That makes people like Donald Welton feel more comfortable. He lives in the neighborhood just south of Interstate 70 and said the more police presence, the better.

"I think I could let my teenager come up here now to get some food," he said, adding that that wouldn't have been the case five years ago.

Manager Cliff Jones said the police presence has altered the clientele base at the McDonald's.

"We have more eat-in customers since the officers have been here," he said. "We lost some of the undesirable customers here who made trouble. We gained the steady customer. They approach me all the time, saying they feel more comfortable."

The cost of the phone lines, signs and cubicles for the officers have paid for themselves many times over in a reduction of robberies and other crime, he said.

"It's worth it," he said. "Not only does it help business, it helps the community."

Idea Catching On Elsewhere

The idea has caught on. In Washington, D.C., 33 restaurants opened substations last year. Substations also have opened in Maryland, Hartford, Conn., and Chicago.

Ed McGarrell, director of the Hudson Institute's Crime Control Policy Center, said the move toward substations is a national trend toward police building ties with the community.

"For the past 30 years, police have primarily been known to the community as officers in cars who drive by," he said. "In many ways, it's a return to the officer on the beat."

Mary Rhinehart hopes the trend continues. "I feel more safe," she said. "I live in the neighborhood. A lot of things can happen here. We need all the protection we can get."

Source: *Community Policing Digest* (1997). September 4, pp. 1-5.

Community policing's focus on solving problems rather than just answering calls, making arrests, and handling crimes as individual incidents also makes better sense than traditional efforts because of the relative difficulty in making a difference in the dynamics that result in serious crime. CPOs gather information beyond what traditional efforts can achieve, which allows the department to concentrate its efforts where they will do the most good. CPOs provide a sustained presence in the community, so that they can initiate efforts targeted at troubled families and potentially explosive situations in ways that traditional approaches never could. As people learn to trust their CPOs, they turn to them for help, and CPOs skilled in knowing other communities resources that can be tapped for assistance have made dramatic strides in helping to defuse the overall climate of violence by concentrating their efforts on those families and addresses where the greatest potential problems cluster.

Community Policing's Strengths

One reason for the lengthy analysis of the dynamics involved in crime is to show the tremendous difficulty the police face in making a positive difference. The police as *currently* structured and organized can do little about obvious root causes of crime, such as poverty and unemployment, nor can they do much to influence policy concerning people's access to guns, social support for single parents, or any of the other factors that may play a role in the overall matrix of crime. The police can play only a limited role in controlling crimes of passion, and society's emphasis on the acquisition of material possessions as a yardstick of success is an attitude that the police can do little to alter. Crime encompasses such a broad range of human activity and unpredictability that no single agency in a democratic society, no matter how powerful, can be expected to provide all the answers. Of importance as well is the recognition that the police are only one element in the overall criminal justice system. Yet, police can play a powerful role in the development of social policy by becoming the public's educators on issues of crime and its "root" causes.

Yet what this analysis is also designed to demonstrate is that the traditional police approach holds little promise of doing a better job than it already does. There is good reason to suppose that tinkering with the traditional approach in the hope of dramatically improving police departments' ability to solve the riddle of serious crime is like rearranging the deck chairs on the *Titanic*—too little, too late. What has become glaringly apparent is that the traditional system focuses the vast bulk of its resources on only one of three times that police action can influence the ultimate outcome of a potentially criminal act.

Current efforts target most sworn personnel, the department's first line of defense, toward maintaining the overall ability to respond immediately to those relatively few times where a quick response is vital. One obvious problem with the traditional system therefore is that proactive and follow-up efforts often suffer from lack of resources as a result. Yet an even more serious problem is that the rationale for relying primarily on motor patrol rested on the assumption that encouraging these officers to use their free patrol time on preventive patrol would make a substantial contribution in the fight against serious crime. Unfortunately, this appears to have little, if any, practical value in reducing or controlling crime. Though it rattles the foundations of traditional thinking, research tends to confirm that traditional preventive motor patrol efforts are often no more than an expensive waste of time.

While that may overstate the case, the fact remains that history fails to show that the traditional approach can cope effectively with serious crime. Admittedly, the rates of serious crime in recent years have continued to decline, but these may have as much to do with the maturing of the baby boomers out of their most crime-prone years and the unprecedented strength of the sustained economic boom, as to the contribution the police have made in quadrupling the number of people behind bars in recent years. The fact remains that this society continues to suffer rates of serious crime that would be considered intolerable in other industrialized Western nations. This reality has sparked and continues to fuel a radical re-assessment concerning whether police departments might find better ways to approach the challenge posed by crime.

What community policing proposes is that the riddle of crime requires understanding that crime incidents cannot be solved in isolation—separate from each other and separate from their relationship to the social context. Though it may sound illogical on the surface, the community policing philosophy suggests that only by broadening the police mandate beyond a narrow focus on serious crime incidents as they occur can the police provide short- and long-term answers to the dilemma posed by serious crime.

The subtle and sophisticated community policing approach rests on recognizing that coping with serious crime demands approaching it in context. It is possible that anyone in the United States may at some point in life be swept away by the passion of the moment to commit an irrational act totally out of character, an act that ends up as a crime statistic. In such cases, the police can often do little more than to make sure that they will arrive on the scene as soon as reasonably possible after receiving the call, and both the traditional police approach and community policing guarantee that. But an important flaw in the traditional approach is that it is not much of an exaggeration to suggest the prevailing system supposes a world in which it is equally likely that President Clinton may one day bludgeon Hillary in a fight as that this will happen at an address where domestic disputes routinely escalate into violence.

The traditional approach only superficially recognizes that many criminal acts follow their own internal logic, that they have a context within community and family life. Households with a history of domestic disputes often end up as places where aggravated assaults and even murders are more likely to occur.

The traditional response to this obvious reality is simply to add more patrol cars in problem areas, at problem times. Since the sight of a patrol car whizzing by is rarely much of a deterrent, this simply makes it more likely a car will be available to respond rapidly to the flow of calls for service. This reactive mode means the police do not accomplish much until the call is placed, and most people either cannot or will not call fast enough so that speed of arrival ends up making much difference in the final outcome. More often than not, by the time a citizen calls the police, a crime has already occurred. Therefore, this can hardly be viewed as prevention. As David Carter notes, *random patrol* produces *random results*.

Bicycle Patrol and Community Policing

Steve Cambron, Officer
Louisville Division of Police
Bike Patrol Unit

If you want to improve police/community relations, increase police visibility, and discourage crime, put some officers on mountain bikes.

Cambron, a police mountain bike instructor with the Louisville Police Department, said the city began the bike patrol in 1993 because the city had a new river walk that needed patrolling. The police considered using golf carts, scooters, mopeds, or horses. But the motorized equipment is noisy and needs maintenance, and horses need a lot of attention and care. Cambron said bikes need a minimum of maintenance and are quiet; they provide officers with the advantage of the element of surprise.

Cambron said mountain bike police officers are probably the most mentally and physically disciplined officers in a police department. Officers ride in all kinds of weather and go through rigorous physical training.

"The advantages of having an officer on a mountain bike is that you are getting an all around better officer," Cambron said. "It takes a certain officer to put on a bike patrol. You have to be particular. This bike is one of the most advantageous things that any police department can use. It's the way to go as far as community oriented policing. I can't tell you how much this is going to put you back in touch with your community."

Officers should be screened carefully. Officers need to enjoy talking with citizens and being out in the community. Bike police officers are more approachable; being on a bike puts them in close contact with the community. While foot beats are good, Cambron said a bike officer can cover twice the area of a foot patrol officer in one-third of the time. In addition, bikes can go where cars can't; in heavy traffic, officers on bikes can ride between cars. During events that draw large crowds, bikes make it easy to travel around and through the crowd area.

Cambron said working on the bike unit has changed him as an officer. "This bike unit has really opened me up, it's opened my mind to a brand new form of policing called community oriented policing."

"This bike patrol is here to stay, it's not going anywhere. This is not a fad, it's not going to go away tomorrow, it's not going to go away next week, because it works," Cambron said.

Source: *Technology for Community Policing* (1997). P. 69.

What community policing does is open up the thinking of the department, so that the police learn to see crime in a broader context. The first challenge is to infuse all officers with the community policing approach, so that they learn to look beyond isolated crime incidents, at the underlying dynamics where creative interventions might help solve the problem in ways that need not require arrest. In many cases, this requires looking at the context of crime in a new way.

Yet community policing goes beyond adopting problem-solving police techniques (1) by broadening the police mandate beyond a narrow focus on crime, and (2) by restructuring the department to carry out this expanded mission more effectively. Though it would seem sensible that the best way to reduce and control serious crime is for the police to focus even more attention on just these crimes alone, community policing approaches the problem from a different direction.

This means the police must educate people about what they can do to combat crime. Then the department's community outreach specialists, its CPOs, must go further by involving people in efforts to deal with the social problems that promote neighborhood conditions—fixing potholes in the street, helping the homeless find shelter, providing meaningful activities for idle teens, and helping people with the persistent, nagging problems such as unrelenting noise that escalate the underlying tensions.

Critics contend that community policing detracts from a proper focus on crime, by dissipating the energies of the department in efforts that have nothing to do with serious crime. They argue that this broadening of the police mandate squanders resources better spent addressing the serious crime problems that this society faces. One problem lies in thinking that serious crime occurs in a vacuum, whereas it is instead part of the fabric of the community and family, which cannot be separated from its cultural context. Another problem is that this argument supposes that the traditional approach focuses more time and energy on serious crime than the community policing approach does, whereas the reverse may well be true.

Because it is basically reactive, the traditional approach usually requires a call for service to trigger action—the dispatcher receives a call that a serious crime is in progress and sends a motor patrol officer in response. A department that adopts community policing does the same. The next level of priority is a call about a serious crime that has already occurred—someone discovers a body, the bank robbers have fled, a rape victim arrives at the emergency ward. Again, regardless of whether the call comes into a traditional department or one that has adopted community policing, a motor patrol officer is dispatched to the scene. The major difference here concerns what happens before and after the officer arrives, since a department infused with the community policing philosophy asks the officers to look beyond the individual incidents to see whether there are underlying pressure points that could influence the likelihood of similar problems in the future.

The question then becomes how the department uses its resources beyond fulfilling these most basic functions. In traditional departments, motor patrol officers spend their time between calls involving serious crime on answering relatively minor calls and on preventive patrol. Those calls can include a so-called petty theft, helping people who are locked out of their cars or homes, tagging an abandoned vehicle, issuing a traffic ticket, or responding to a call about a loud party in progress. Most motor patrol officers see those kinds of calls as *nuisance calls,* trivial matters that occupy their time until the *real* business of policing—a call about serious crime—comes over the radio. If they have the luxury of time between even these kinds of nuisance calls, a motor patrol officer may cruise areas, knowing full well that the activity heats up again once their taillights disappear around the corner. As this shows, the traditional approach may well squander precious resources in efforts that hold little promise of addressing the challenge posed by crime.

While it is obviously true that violent crime deserves priority, the existing system often fails to recognize the importance of taking personal and social problems equally seriously. People sense something is askew with police priorities when the department insists it cannot afford to send an officer when a person calls to report that his car has been stolen, yet that same driver knows the police always seem to find the time to write a traffic ticket. And even departments that send officers to take a report on a stolen car may send the wrong message when they refuse to do the same for that 12-year-old whose bike was stolen.

The point is not that the police department must be at the immediate beck and call of each person who asks for service, but community policing allows the department to use the CPO's free patrol time to follow up on reports about property crime. A dispatcher who grasps how community policing works explains to the caller that the CPO will stop by in the next day or so to discuss the problem, since dispatching a motor patrol officer immediately holds no promise of altering the outcome. During that follow-up visit, the CPO has a chance to find out whether there has been a rash of similar incidents in the neighborhood, and whether the person has any ideas concerning who might be involved. Perhaps that stolen bike was one of five that have disappeared, but only this family placed a call to the police.

If nothing else, making that home visit provides the CPO a hook to attempt to involve that family in the police process. This could mean challenging them to recruit five other neighbors for an organizing meeting where the CPO can explain Neighborhood Watch and offer some crime prevention tips. It could mean the CPO succeeds in enlisting various family members for new community-based initiatives, whether that means recruiting a coach for the new softball league or someone in the family to handle calls at the CPO's local office.

Maybe that visit allows the family to share concerns about other problems in the community, as well as their insights and suggestions about possible solutions. Perhaps that casual visit elicits information about the teenager down the street that is rumored to commit thefts, the unexplained bruises on the child next door that they can hear screaming in the night, the group of teenagers they heard shouting racial epithets at passersby. Unlike motor patrol officers whose focus is on handling this call as quickly as possible so that they can move on to the next, the purpose in freeing CPOs from those constraints is so that CPOs have the time and opportunity to use informal interchanges to find out valuable information about the community context of crime, including serious crime.

Freeing CPOs to act as the department's community outreach specialists also allows the department to involve itself in efforts to enhance the quality of community life. Again, critics of community policing see this as distracting from a proper focus on serious crime, because they fail to see the community context. Unless the department educates everyone about the contribution that CPOs make in carrying out the community policing mandate, motor patrol officers in particular may see what CPOs do as unimportant—or even stupid. On the surface, it seems ridiculous to suggest that a CPO is helping the department and its motor patrol officers by haranguing the city sanitation department to pick up the garbage on time. Traditionalists suggest it is tantamount to insanity to allow officers to waste their time on such trivial problems, especially in a neighborhood notorious for violent crime.

Yet that CPO probably stands a better chance of getting timely garbage service for the area than a barrage of calls from people whose address verifies they carry little clout with City Hall. And that achievement can help the CPO gain credibility and inspire confidence among the people whose support is vital in organizing efforts targeted at reducing crime. An enterprising CPO may also be able to capitalize on that initial first step by recruiting kids in the neighborhood to begin picking up litter in exchange for which they receive a donated toy. Perhaps the local shop teacher could involve students in fixing broken benches in the park. The next step might be to involve area businesses in donating paint and shrubs to help spruce up the facility. The park might be a good place to host Neighborhood Watch meetings.

The process of revitalizing the community produces other positive spin-offs. When CPOs involve young people in such efforts, they learn about responsibility, hard work, and doing things for others. Properly structured, they also have the opportunity to learn skills that can enhance their ability to land a part-time job. It also provides CPOs informal opportunities to reinforce positive values. These opportunities demonstrate that the police are not uniformed thugs who thrive on giving kids a hard time, but caring human beings who are willing to help make the community a better and safer place to live.

Involving the police in efforts aimed at juveniles also holds the promise of breaking down the barriers between the police and the adults in the community. Jowanne Barnes-Coney, a foot patrol officer in the Flint experiment, said that by working first on programs aimed at the young people in her beat area, she was able to make in-roads with the parents. Kids are basically more open and trusting, so once she had them on her side, they provided her access to their parents.

Admittedly, the link between community policing's proactive focus and any potential impact on serious crime in the future seems tenuous. Fix a few potholes and someday the murder rate will decline? Teach a kid to plant flowers today and he won't rob someone five years from now? The first thing to remember is that the traditional system does far less. An officer whizzing by in a patrol car on preventive patrol accomplishes little. Investing scarce resources in a new radar gun and patrol car to catch a few more speeders will do virtually nothing to cut tomorrow's rates of serious crime.

Given the choice, does it make better sense to confine two educated and highly trained police officers into one patrol car, where they spend most of their time talking to each other, or should departments consider freeing some of those officers so that they can talk to people in the community instead?

History reveals that serious crime is a stubborn problem, not given to easy or quick solutions. Community policing suggests that creativity and innovation are required to approach serious crime from new angles, making incremental improvements that hold the promise of making long-term substantive improvement. It recognizes the importance of treating all social problems, *including property crime*, as serious police business. It says arrests alone are not the cure and crime rates are not the measure of success. It focuses special attention on those at risk of becoming offenders and victims. It involves people in efforts to make their communities more crime-resistant, including participating in projects to reduce neighborhood problems. It involves CPOs as community outreach specialists, allowing them to function as the community's ombudsman to other agencies that can help. Community policing pays particular attention to juveniles, not only because young people commit crime, but because of the hope that positive police intervention at an early age holds a greater promise of discouraging problems in the future.

For some, such efforts still sound more like social work than police work. Traditionalists sincerely believe that the proper police response to serious crime is embodied in the "tough cop" (Crank, 1998) rolling up to the scene, sirens blaring, even though that may only account for a fraction of the time spent on the job. Faced with this ambitious list of other duties that community policing demands, traditionalists ask, why the police? Proponents of community policing argue instead, who better?

References

Alpert, G.P & M.H. Moore (1993). "Measuring Police Performance in the New Paradigm of Policing." In *Performance Measures for the Criminal Justice System*. Washington, DC: U.S. Department of Justice.

Braiden, C. (1987). Remarks delivered during the National Neighborhood Foot Patrol Training Seminars, Michigan State University, East Lansing, MI.

Brandl, S. & J. Frank (1994). "The Relationship Between Evidence, Detective Effort, and the Dispositions of Burglary and Robbery Investigations." *American Journal of Police*, 13(3):149-168.

Brott, A. (1995). "Major Reworking of Child Abuse Law." *Chicago Tribune*, (Feb. 1):10.

Clinard, M. & P. Yeager (1980). *Corporate Crime*. New York, NY: Macmillan.

Coleman, J. (1984). *The Criminal Elite*, Third Edition. New York, NY: St. Martin's Press.

Cordner, G. & R. Trojanowicz (1992). "Patrol." In G. Cordner & D. Hale (eds.) *What Works in Policing? Operations and Administration Examined.* Cincinnati, OH: Anderson Publishing Co.

Crank, J.P. (1998). *Understanding Police Culture.* Cincinnati, OH: Anderson Publishing Co.

Dunford, F.W., D. Huizinga & D.S. Elliott (1986). "The Role of Arrest in Domestic Assault: The Omaha Experiment." *Criminology*, 28(2):183-206.

Eck, J. (1983). "Solving Crimes: The Investigation of Burglary and Robbery." Washington, DC: Police Executive Research Forum.

Eck, J. & G. Williams (1991). "Criminal Investigations." In W. Geller (ed.) *Local Government Police Management*, pp. 131-158. Washington, DC: ICMA.

Gaines, L., B. Lewis & R. Swanagin (1983). "Case Screening in Criminal Investigations: A Case Study of Robbery." *Police Studies*, 6:22-29.

Goulden, J.C. (1989). *Fit to Print: A.M. Rosenthal and His Times.* New York, NY: Lyle Stuart.

Greenwood, P., J. Chaiken & J. Petersilia (1977). *The Investigative Process.* Lexington, MA: Lexington Books.

Kansas City (Missouri) Police Department (1977). *Response Time Analysis Report.* Kansas City: Board of Police Commissions.

Kappeler, V.E., M. Blumberg & G.W. Potter (1996). *The Mythology of Crime and Criminal Justice,* Second Edition. Prospect Heights, IL: Waveland Press.

Kappeler, V.E., R. Sluder & G.P. Alpert (1998). *Forces of Deviance: Understanding the Dark Side of the Force,* Second Edition. Prospect Heights, IL: Waveland Press.

Kelling, G. (1997). "The Assault on Effective Policing." *The Wall Street Journal*, (August 26):11.

Kelling, G. (1981). *The Newark Foot Patrol Experiment.* Washington, DC: The Police Foundation.

Kelling, G., T. Pate, D. Dieckman & C. Brown (1974). *The Kansas City Preventive Patrol Experiment: A Summary Report.* Washington, DC: The Police Foundation.

Klockars, C. (1993, 1995). "The Legacy of Conservative Ideology and Police." In V.E. Kappeler (ed.) *The Police & Society: Touch Stone Readings.* Prospect Heights, IL: Waveland Press.

Krajick, K. (1980). "Evidence Favors Aggressive Patrol." *Police Magazine*, 3(5):30.

Larson, R.C. & M.F. Cahn (1995). *Synthesizing and Extending the Results of Police Patrol Studies.* Washington, DC: National Institute of Justice.

Manning, P.K. (1992, 1995a). "Economic Rhetoric and Policing Reform." In V.E. Kappeler (ed.) *The Police & Society: Touch Stone Readings.* Prospect Heights, IL: Waveland Press.

Manning, P.K. (1977, 1995). "The Police; Mandate, Strategies, and Appearances." In V.E. Kappeler (ed.) *The Police & Society: Touch Stone Readings.* Prospect Heights, IL: Waveland Press.

Mastrofski, S.D. & R.R. Ritti (1996). "Police Training and the Effects of Organization on Drunk Driving Enforcement." *Justice Quarterly*, 13(2):291-320.

Mastrofski, S.D. & R.R. Ritti (1992). "You Can Lead a Horse to Water . . . : A Case Study of a Police Department's Response to Stricter Drunk-Driving Laws." *Justice Quarterly*, 9(3):465-491.

Pate, T., R. Bowers & R. Parks (1976). *Three Approaches to Criminal Apprehension in Kansas City: An Evaluation Report.* Washington, DC: The Police Foundation.

Pate, T., A. Ferrara, R. Bowers & J. Lorence (1976). *Police Response Time: Its Determinants and Effects.* Washington, DC: The Police Foundation.

Percy, S. (1980). "Response Time and Citizen Evaluation of Police." *Journal of Police Science and Administration*, 8(1):75-86.

Potter, G.W. & V.E. Kappeler (1998). *Constructing Crime.* Prospect Heights, IL: Waveland Press.

Rosenbaum, D.P. (1988, 1996). "Community Crime Prevention: A Review and Synthesis of the Literature." In G. Cordner, L. Gaines & V.E. Kappeler *Police Operations: Analysis and Evaluation.* Cincinnati, OH: Anderson Publishing Co.

Sherman, L.W. & R.A. Berk (1984). *The Minneapolis Domestic Violence Experiment.* Washington, DC: The Police Foundation.

Skogan, W.G. & A.C. Gordon (1982). "A Review of Detective Division Reporting Practices." In *Crime in Illinois 1982.* Springfield, IL: Illinois Department of Law Enforcement.

Skogan, W. G. & S.M. Hartnett (1997). *Community Policing, Chicago Style.* New York, NY: Oxford Press.

Spelman, W. & D. Brown (1984). *Calling the Police: Citizen Reporting of Serious Crime.* Washington, DC: U.S. Government Printing Office.

Strecher, V.G. (1997). *Planning Community Policing. Goal Specific Cases and Exercises.* Prospect Heights, IL: Waveland Press.

Trojanowicz, R.C. (1984). "Foot Patrol: Some Problem Areas." *The Police Chief*, 51(6) (June):47-49.

Trojanowicz, R.C. (1982). *An Evaluation of the Neighborhood Foot Patrol Program in Flint, Michigan.* East Lansing, MI: Michigan State University.

Twain, M. (1972). *The International Thesaurus of Quotations,* compiled by Rhoda Thomas Tripp. New York, NY: Perennial Library, Harper & Row.

Wilson, O.W. & B. McLaren (1977). *Police Administration*, Fourth Edition. New York, NY: McGraw-Hill.

CHAPTER 5
Community Policing and Fear of Crime

*Fear itself carries with it its own danger;
because when fear is excessive it can
make many a man despair.*
                                    —*St. Thomas Aquinas*

Traditional Policing and Fear of Crime

- A woman turns down a promotion because it would mean making sales calls at night and memories of her sister's brutal rape make her too fearful to drive alone after dark.

- An elderly couple no longer feels safe walking to local stores, even during daylight, so they now wait for their daughter to take them with her when she shops. Not only do they worry about what they will do if she cannot take them, they miss the outings they used to take together, stopping at local shops where everyone knew them.

- A sixth-grader begins feigning illness, as an excuse to stay home from school, because a classmate was attacked by older boys, and he is afraid he will be next.

- A man and wife have watched their middle-class neighborhood decline, but they vowed to stay—until there was a rash of burglaries and muggings nearby. To their shock, they find their home is worth less than it was a few years ago, but they sell and move to the suburbs, though it means additional time and expense to commute to their jobs.

In each of these scenarios, no one was the victim of a particular crime, though all were victimized by crime's insidious shadow—fear of crime. The damage that each person suffered was very real and as serious as what many crime victims endure. What we must not forget is that whenever one person is victimized by crime, that individual's family, friends, co-workers, and acquaintances are also victimized. Even reading about crimes in the newspaper or seeing victims on television reinforces the mythic message that no one can be completely safe (Potter & Kappeler, 1998). Anyone can become a victim.

The economic and social damage done to us, as individuals and as a society, as a result of fear of crime has become as important an issue. We must also remember that the damage done by the corrosive fear of crime extends beyond individuals and families, to businesses and to our communities as well. The downtown business districts in many cities today are places that people avoid or flee as soon as they leave work. The large department stores and other retail businesses that once pervaded central business districts have long left for the suburbs. They basically followed economic patterns and the people who have left the cities in growing numbers because of their fear of crime and other social problems. Many businesses that could not afford to make the transition or that waited too long to try have simply disappeared— the family-owned drug store, the ethnic bakery, the corner grocery, the shoe repair shop—taking local jobs with them. They, too, have been absorbed by the corporatizing of America.

In many of our major cities, the damage seems rather dramatic. There are so many stores and homes that have been abandoned and destroyed that entire areas look as if they had been abandoned. In faltering northern industrial cities like Detroit or Chicago, even many comfortable homes now stand empty, a cruel irony in an era when the ranks of the homeless have been expanded drastically, including families with children. In many cases, parts or sections of our cities appear completely disjointed from mainstream society. Fear of crime is not the sole source of the exodus from our cities, but it certainly is a primary contributing factor.

Historically, fear of crime was not a prime concern to the police, and it was not until the 1970s that fear of crime was an issue in the American criminal justice arena. The police, into the 1960s saw law enforcement or crook catching as their most important role in society (Gaines, Kappeler & Vaughn, 1997). This vision of policing is rooted in the depression and prohibition where the police increasingly began to emphasize law enforcement over the provision of services and order maintenance. Indeed, service and order maintenance were seen not only as peripheral, but in some cases, as antithetical to the primary mission of law enforcement. This position dictated that the police see themselves in one-on-one conflicts with the criminal adversaries. The citizen, victim or casual observer, was omitted from the equation.

Simultaneously, police administrators were attempting to implement major reforms in American policing. The depression and prohibition not only caused the police to focus on law enforcement, they also contributed substantially to corrupting the police. Police corruption was a national problem into the 1950s. In an effort to reduce corruption, police administrators moved to a professional model of policing. They implemented training programs and policies that emphasized distancing the police from the citizens they served. The police began to adopt a detached, professional demeanor when dealing with citizens. They tended to behave as automatons as opposed to public servants. This behavior steadily became ingrained in the individual officer's psyche, and it dominated police practices for several decades. Consequently, the police were not overly concerned with the public or their feelings about criminal justice matters.

The 1960s experienced a burgeoning crime problem. The period witnessed unprecedented civil unrest as a result of the civil rights movement and the Vietnam War. Riots in many of our major cities resulted in substantial numbers of deaths and injuries. The riots also caused millions of dollars of destruction, all of which was covered in detail by the nightly news. Crime increased geometrically while America for the first time had an open, widespread drug problem. Crime, drugs, and disorder became central issues in public and political debate. Presidential and congressional elections, as well as state and local elections, were won and lost on candidates' ability to convince the American people of their effectiveness in controlling the crime problem. Fueled by the news media and political agendas, the American public became concerned with crime. Many of the political polls of the time showed crime to be the most important political issue.

Additionally, the victims' movement began in the 1960s (Doerner & Lab, 1995). Although there was interest in victims prior to the 1960s, the bulk of this interest centered around how victims contributed to their own victimization (Schafer, 1968). For example, Amir (1971) published a study of rape in Philadelphia in which he maintained that 19 percent of the rapes between 1958 and 1960 were victim-precipitated. Studies such as Amir's outraged victims and conservatives. The high crime rates, the drug problem, and the widespread disorder contributed to legislators and representatives from the criminal justice system becoming concerned with the treatment of victims and their rights. Conservative members of Congress were concerned over the "coddling" of criminals, so they began to fund programs to assist victims (Weed, 1995). For the most part, the victim's movement was buttressed by the women's and children's rights movements (Kappeler & Kraska, 1998a). These two movements witnessed a genuine concern of how women and children victims were treated. It represented a time when society finally recognized that crimes were being committed against people as well as against the state.

The message to mainstream criminal justice from the victim's movement was that victims were being treated shoddily. Victimization was discussed in terms of primary and secondary victimization. Primary victimization occurred when a criminal act was committed against the victim. Here, the victim suffered financial and sometimes injurious losses as a result of the criminal act. Secondary victimization came with the treatment of the victim by the criminal justice system. For the most part, the police and prosecutors were only interested in victims as witnesses to assist in convicting the criminal perpetrators. They really were not concerned with health or welfare of the victims (Weed, 1995). The treatment of victims by the criminal justice system outraged victims and victims' advocates, and this outrage translated into pressure for the police and prosecutors to intervene in private lives. An ancillary change as a result of the victim's movement was that the police became more concerned with citizens' attitudes about police services. Thus, fear of crime became an issue.

Discovering the "Fear of Crime"

During the 1960s and 1970s, crime became the most important issue to many Americans. It cut through the very fiber of American society. Although there was an increasing number of crime victims and society was finally becoming concerned with their treatment, there was only a general concern within society or the criminal justice arena about citizens' impressions and fear of crime and its consequences. Two events seemed to solidify fear of crime as a mainstream law enforcement and criminal justice concern: victimization surveys (specifically, the Figgie Report) and the Flint, Michigan foot patrol experiment.

The Figgie Report

Published in 1980, the Figgie Report was one of the first national studies to examine the level of fear of crime in the United States. Although the national victimization surveys had been initiated in the mid-1970s, there had been only sporadic efforts to collect information about the fear of crime. The Figgie Report established two barometers of fear, *concrete fear* and *formless fear.* Concrete fear refers to fears about specific crimes, in this case the violent Index crimes, while formless fear relates to a diffuse feeling of being unsafe as a result of crime and disorder in the immediate environment. The research showed four of every 10 people felt a high level of each kind of fear, but that only 40 percent overlapped and showed high degrees of both kinds of fear. While rates of crime have declined overall since the Figgie Report was published in 1980, what the report showed about the dynamics of fear remains valid, though we have reason to hope their overall numbers would be lower today.

The Figgie barometer of concrete fear that looked at fear of murder, rape, robbery, and assault combined showed 55 percent of women fear being raped, 24 percent of both sexes fear they will be beaten up, 23 percent worry they will be robbed, and 17 percent fear they will be murdered. The study also showed the five groups that exhibit the greatest concrete fear:

- people in large cities;
- the young;

INDEX

- women;

- those with more formal education; and

- African-Americans.

While we expect to see the members of high-risk groups and women included, the surprise is that people with more formal education rank among those most afraid of these specific crimes. Apparently, information is the key. The assumption is that education makes people more aware of the threat crime poses, even in places where these people are less likely to be victimized.

The Figgie research also controlled for the effects of social disadvantage and isolation, and the authors admitted surprise that people in these categories did not exhibit high levels of concrete fear. This may confirm how important access to information about crime is, since people in these two categories would probably be less likely to have access to newspapers, magazines, and books, and other sources of information.

To study formless fear, the Figgie research posed questions about six diffuse threats related to how safe people felt at home, out shopping, and in their neighborhoods, during the day and at night. The groups showing the highest rates of formless fear included:

- those with the lowest incomes;

- blue-collar workers;

INDEX

- those with the least education;

- those who do not work full time;

- those who experienced a marital loss; and

- the elderly.

To understand these findings, the researchers suggest they relate strongly to four predictors: victimization, information exposure, social disadvantage, and isolation. Of note as well is that those who showed relatively high levels of both kinds of fear are people in large cities, women, and African-Americans. Those who live in big cities do, in fact, have more to fear of crime, since people who live in the central city or cities with overall populations of 500,000 or more fall victim to crimes of violence roughly 1.5 times more often than people in the suburbs and twice as often as those who live in rural areas (U.S. Department of Justice, 1988).

Many of the findings of the Figgie Report remain true today and are explored in more detail in later sections of this chapter. Of importance is that the Figgie Report was the first comprehensive effort to study fear of crime in the United States. It served to help focus attention on fear of crime and to serve as a barometer with which to compare future studies.

The Flint Foot Patrol Experiment

The Flint foot patrol program began in January 1979, as the result of a $2.6 million grant from the Mott Foundation to Michigan State University. The project was the result of two law enforcement related problems. First, in many parts of Flint, there were no crime prevention programs or programs to help the neighborhood control crime and other problems. Second, police officers were fairly detached from the citizens. Up until the foot patrol experiments, the department had relied on traditional police motorized patrols to respond to calls for service and deal with other citizen problems. The project covered 14 diverse neighborhoods containing approximately 20 percent of the city's total population. This format allowed researchers to gauge foot patrols' success across the complete socio-economic spectrum.

At the time when the program was first initiated, the Flint Police Department was engrossed in substantial controversy. Three separate incidents served as the foundation for the internal problems. First, two officers—a white male and an African-American female officer—got into an argument behind police headquarters over who would drive the patrol car. The dispute escalated to the point that other officers became involved. The argument culminated in gun fire where 14 shots were fired and the female officer was wounded. Second, police officers fired a shotgun and killed a 15-year-old juvenile who was attempting to escape the police by climbing over a fence. The newspaper reporting on the incident showed a photograph of the juvenile at a much younger age than when the incident occurred, resulting in hostile animosity toward the police. Finally, a Michigan State Trooper was killed in a joint undercover operation with the Flint Police Department. These incidents, coming in a relatively short time, caused many citizens to question the capability of their police.

At the same time, the City of Flint was experiencing a number of setbacks. Flint was the birthplace of General Motors (GM), and the City had long depended on GM as a primary employer. Downsizing by GM moved Flint's unemployment rate from single digits to 25 percent, the highest in the country. The economic downturn contributed to one-fourth of Flint's citizens moving away. Flint became riddled with violent crime. It had sixth highest homicide rate in the country. Racial tensions were high, and there were all sorts of recriminations about what had happened to the once prosperous city.

The project began with the employment of 22 officers who were assigned to the foot patrol beats. The objectives of the program were:

- To decrease the amount of actual or perceived criminal activity;

- To increase the citizens' perception of personal safety;

- To deliver to Flint residents a type of law enforcement consistent with community needs and the ideals of modern police practice;

- To create a community awareness of crime problems and methods of increasing law enforcement's ability to deal with actual or potential criminal activity effectively;

- To develop citizen volunteer action in support of and under direction of the police department aimed at various target crimes;

- To eliminate citizen apathy about reporting crimes to the police; and

- To increase protection for women, children, and the elderly.

At the end of the third year of the program, roughly 70 percent of the citizens surveyed reported feeling safer as a result of the foot patrols. Many of the respondents qualified their answer by saying that they felt especially safe when their foot patrol officer was well known and highly visible. This perception of safety increased each year during the three years of the experiment, despite the progressive expansion and increased turnover among foot patrol officers, the result of layoffs and excessive rotations. When the people surveyed in the third year of the program were asked if they felt crime was a more serious problem in their neighborhoods, as compared to other neighborhoods, only 14 percent stated that it was true. Nearly one-half (49%) said their area had fewer crime problems, while another 26 percent rated the crime problem in their area as average.

The Flint study was one of the first police experiments to include fear of crime as a factor. Theretofore, the police adhered to the professional model of policing which not only meant that fear of crime was not important, but that citizen opinions in general were of little use. The Flint study also nudged policing much closer to a general philosophy of community policing. Flint showed that fear of crime was just as, if not more, dehabilitating as crime itself. Fear of crime affects many more people than being victimized, and it has been just as powerful in restricting or changing people's behavior and lifestyle.

What is Fear of Crime?

The preceding sections of this chapter detail how fear of crime came to be recognized as a public safety issue. The Flint foot patrol experiment not only helped law enforcement to focus on fear of crime, but with the inclusion of fear of crime as a mainstream police objective, it helped to usher in the community policing era. Community policing goes beyond traditional policing and focuses on a broad array of problems including fear of crime. Given the importance of fear of crime, it then is important to understand what it is and its causes. What is fear of crime? Garofalo (1981:840) defines it as,

. . . . an emotional reaction characterized by a sense of danger and anxiety. We restrict our definition to the sense of danger and anxiety produced by the threat of physical harm. Furthermore, to constitute fear of crime, the fear must be elicited by perceived cues in the environment that relate to some aspect of crime for the person.

Garofalo's definition implies that fear of crime has a number of implications that center around environmental ques as well as firsthand knowledge and behavioral and psychological reactions to those ques and experiences. Levels of fear are determined by our information about crime and our subsequent impressions of its extent, the amount of risk we incur in our daily lives, and the options we have to avoid or cope with potential victimization. In other words, although simplistic on its face, fear of crime is an extremely complex social phenomenon.

Most of the research into fear of crime shows that there is some degree of irrationality associated with it. That is, fear of crime is not consistent with victimization or levels of crime. Taylor and Hale (1986) discuss three such inconsistencies. First, the ordering of fear of crime by age or gender results in the exact opposite of victimization rates. For example, young males are most likely to be victimized, but are the less fearful. Second, larger numbers of people are fearful than are victimized, even when unreported crime is considered. It appears there are social forces at work that spread the affects of crime over the larger population. Many more people are affected indirectly by crime than are affected directly. Finally, fear patterns within the general population do not match victimization patterns. It seems that actual crime may only play a small role in fear of crime.

It appears that people become fearful of crime in a variety of ways. For example, Thompson and her colleagues (1992) investigated global fear, fear of property crime, and fear of violent crime. Global fear referred to one's general sense of fear from crime, while the other two measures focus on specific categories of crime. Their research indicated that global fear was perhaps the best way to measure or understand people's fear of crime. They also found that all three measures were associated with "perceived seriousness of crime in the community."

In a similar study, Covington and Taylor (1991) examined fear of crime in terms of indirect victimization, community concern, and incivilities. Indirect victimization refers to an individual's indirect knowledge of crime such as that gained by watching television, reading a newspaper, or hearing of a friend or relative being victimized. Community concern is where an individual observes conditions within his or her neighborhood and some level of fear may be generated as a result of concern over the level of disintegration within the neighborhood or overall community. Covington and Taylor explored a fourth model called subcultural diversity (Merry, 1981), whereby people develop fear of crime as a result of the level of cultural heterogeneity within one's immediate environment. They found that all four models contributed to one's fear of crime.

These researchers provide ample evidence that fear of crime is the result of numerous factors interacting with the individual. It also indicates that victimization does not necessarily predict fear of crime, and indeed, direct victimization may only play a minor role in most people's perception of crime and fear of crime. The research also shows that community concern, people's impressions of their neighborhood in terms of incivilities, disorder, and disintegration are key to one's level of fear of crime.

Fear of crime does not necessarily have any direct consequences. In fact, the majority of Americans experience some measure of fear of crime, but it does not necessarily mean that they will take any direct actions. Fear of crime, however, does affect the quality of life of a number of Americans. Hale (1996) has identified six areas that are the indirect costs of fear of crime in our society:

- Fear destroys the sense of community that is necessary for a healthy environment. It causes some public areas to be seen as being dangerous. Once an area has achieved this status, people are much less likely to venture into it;

- It results in more prosperous citizens taking protective actions to safeguard themselves, their homes, and their property, or they may even move out of the neighborhood or city. This enhances the social and crime problems that already plague the poor;

- Fear of crime hardens our attitudes toward criminals, the poor, and generally those who are different. This reduces the likelihood of finding workable solutions;

- Fear of crime potentially can undermine citizens' faith in the police and courts' ability to deal with crime. This can lead to vigilante justice and other measures outside the criminal justice system;

- Fear of crime has detrimental psychological effects on people. This is especially true when fear is coupled with cues and patterns of disorder and decay; and

- People who are victimized by fear of crime change their lifestyle and habits. They stay home at night; they refuse to walk in their own neighborhoods; and they tend to purchase protective devices such as burglar alarms, locks, and expansive lighting. They also may purchase firearms which can result in accidents and additional victimization.

Extent of Fear of Crime

Generally, fear of crime is determined by asking people questions about their fear and activities. In other cases, researchers have attempted to observe behavior such as people's willingness to visit an area, to make a determination about fear. It is difficult to accurately measure fear of crime since there are a number of questions that one can possibly ask. Therefore, researchers have approached measuring the fear of crime differently. The Bureau of Justice Statistics regularly publishes information about fear of crime. These studies are from a national sample and represent fairly accurately people's fear of crime.

In 1995, the *Sourcebook for Criminal Justice Statistics* provided information on several common questions that have been used to measure fear of crime. One question posed to respondents was, "How concerned are you, if at all . . . about becoming a victim of crime?" The results are contained in Table 5.1.

Table 5.1
Respondents' Concern About Becoming a Victim of Crime

By demographic characteristics, United States, 1995

Question: "How concerned are you, if at all . . . about becoming a victim of crime?"

	Very concerned	Somewhat concerned	Not too concerned	Not at all concerned
National	50.6%	29.4%	15.3%	4.4%
Sex				
Male	43.5	28.4	21.8	6.2
Female	57.0	30.4	9.4	2.7
Race				
White	46.6	32.0	16.6	4.4
Nonwhite	74.8	15.0	6.1	4.2
Age				
18 to 29 years	46.5	30.2	16.5	6.7
30 to 49 years	51.3	28.8	16.1	3.8
50 to 64 years	50.7	31.2	13.6	3.4
65 years and older	54.3	28.1	13.3	3.5
Education				
College graduate	35.7	40.5	19.2	4.3
Some college	40.6	35.1	20.5	3.4
High school graduate	60.3	24.0	9.9	5.8
Less than high school graduate	61.2	20.0	15.0	2.6
Family income				
$75,000 and over	33.2	34.1	26.3	6.4
$50,000 to $74,999	39.2	37.2	19.7	3.8
$30,000 to $49,999	50.3	31.1	14.2	4.4
$20,000 to $29,999	54.9	26.5	14.2	4.0
Under $20,000	59.2	23.8	12.3	3.9
Region				
East	58.1	24.0	15.2	2.4
Midwest	45.2	34.4	15.0	5.4
South	52.2	27.8	14.8	4.6
West	46.9	31.5	16.5	4.8

Note: These data are derived from telephone interviews of a nationwide sample of 979 adults, 18 years of age and older. The interviews were conducted Oct. 25-30, 1995 by Princeton Survey Research Associates for the Times Mirror Center for The People & The Press. The "does not apply" and "don't know/refused" categories have been omitted; therefore percents may not sum to 100. For a discussion of public opinion survey sampling procedures, see Appendix 6.

Source: Data provided by The Pew Research Center for The People & The Press, formerly the Times Mirror Center for The People & The Press.

First, as noted in the table in Table 5.1, slightly more than one-half of the Americans surveyed were very concerned about becoming a victim of crime. As discussed, females were more fearful of becoming victims of crime than were males. More than 57 percent of the females stated that they were very concerned while only 43.5 percent of the males were concerned at the same level. The survey shows that non-whites are much more fearful of victimization than whites. Almost 74.8 percent of the non-whites stated they were very concerned, while only 46.6 percent of the white respondents answered similarly. In terms of age, it seems that older Americans are only slightly more fearful than their younger counterparts. They expressed higher levels of fear only by a few percentage points. People with higher levels of education and income where less fearful. People in the East and South voiced higher levels of fear than the respondents from the Midwest and West.

Another way to examine people's fear of crime is to ask them about their impressions regarding the safeness of their own neighborhoods. The Survey Research Program in the College of Criminal Justice at Sam Houston State University asked a sample of respondents, "In the past year do you feel that the crime rate in your neighborhood has increased, decreased, or stayed the same?" The interesting aspect of this issue is that for the past several years, crime has decreased significantly. Thus nationally and in many neighborhoods, crime has decreased.

First, an examination of Table 5.2 reveals that although crime has actually decreased, there were more respondents who thought that crime had increased than decreased. This, to some extent, shows that people's impressions of crime and disorder are related to other factors as well as actual crime (see Potter & Kappeler, 1998). Even the more educated people, those who most likely watch the news or read various news reports and should have a better idea of the actual crime rates, felt that criminality had increased in their neighborhoods. Even the affluent who live in neighborhoods with little crime reported that they believed crime had increased.

The information contained in the above two figures indicate that fear of crime continues to escalate in the face of decreasing crime rates. Of course these findings may be media depictions of America's crime problem. Also, fear of crime is associated with a number of factors. Some of these factors are explored in more detail in the following sections.

Victimization and Fear of Crime

Heretofore, the research has been inconclusive regarding the relationship between victimization and fear of crime. Hale (1996) notes that victimization may make one more cautious or wary, but it will not necessarily contribute to fear of crime. The research on prior victimization, however, is rather mixed. For example, Miethe and Lee (1984) found that direct experience as a victim had an impact on fear from acts of violence, but it did not affect people's fear as a result of property crime. Warr (1984) argues that women who

Table 5.2

Respondents' Feelings of Safety on Streets in Own Neighborhood in Past Year

By demographic characteristics, United States, 1995			
Question: "In the past year do you feel safer, not as safe or about the same on the streets in your neighborhood?"			
	Safer	Not as safe	About the same
National	9.6%	18.1%	70.3%
Sex			
Male	10.6	16.8	70.1
Female	8.6	19.4	70.4
Race			
White	9.1	17.2	71.7
African-American	10.5	21.9	66.7
Hispanic	16.2	18.9	60.8
Age			
18 to 29 years	10.8	18.4	67.7
30 to 39 years	9.0	17.3	73.4
40 to 59 years	10.4	18.2	69.2
60 years and older	9.2	20.7	66.7
Education			
College graduate	8.3	17.6	71.9
Some college	7.7	17.2	73.0
High school graduate	10.8	18.8	69.2
Less than high school graduate	15.7	20.6	59.8
Income			
More than $60,000	8.6	13.4	75.8
Between $30,000 and $60,000	8.9	17.5	72.3
Between $15,000 and $29,999	9.6	19.2	70.0
Less than $15,000	13.6	22.9	58.5
Community			
Urban	12.1	21.7	63.7
Suburban	8.7	14.1	73.4
Small city	9.5	22.8	67.2
Rural/small town	9.1	17.2	72.3
Region			
Northeast	8.5	14.1	76.8
Midwest	10.5	17.3	67.9
South	8.9	21.4	68.3
West	10.7	17.4	70.2
Politics			
Republican	5.4	17.3	75.2
Democrat	9.6	21.8	67.9
Independent/other	13.3	17.0	67.1
Note: See Note, table 2.21. The "don't know" category has been omitted; therefore percents may not sum to 100.			

Source: Survey Research Program, College of Criminal Justice, Sam Houston State University.

have been sexually assaulted or raped tend to be fearful of a host of other criminal acts. Agnew (1985) notes that direct victimization may not affect long-term levels of fear of crime because victims tend to neutralize their victimization. They may blame themselves, disregard the extent of their injuries (physical or economic), or contribute their victimization to helping a friend or acquaintance. Although direct victimization increases people's level of victimization, direct victimization coupled with other factors usually determine the extent of their fear. When an individual has direct experience with victimization, the effect of other cues, such as crime and disorder in the environment, may be substantially increased relative to people who had not been victimized.

Not all people are affected the same by fear of crime. That is, some people are more prone to be afraid, while others tend to disregard the potential consequences of crime regardless of its magnitude. There is substantial research indicating that age, gender, and race play a key role in fear of crime. Since community policing attempts to target fear of crime, it is important to understand the behavioral dynamics related to fear of crime.

Gender and Fear of Crime

A substantial body of research shows that females are more fearful of being victimized than males. A Gallup Report (1989) showed that almost 60 percent of the women surveyed, as compared to only 25 percent of the males, reported being fearful of crime. In fact, gender appears to be the best predictor of fear of crime (Hale, 1996). Given that females are more fearful is uniquely interesting given that young males constitute the group which is victimized most frequently. In fact, young males tend to act irrationally more often and expose themselves to greater victimization risks. Perhaps, women's fear of crime is directly linked to their vulnerability in our society. Rape and sexual assaults constitute a significant category of crime for females but it does not affect males. Also, it is very likely that sexual harassment, a common problem in the American workplace and public places, plays a key role in women's higher levels of fear.

Many feminists maintain that women's fear of crime is generated by significant levels of victimization. They maintain that victimization studies as well as the Uniform Crime Reports substantially under-report female victimization. For example, women are more likely to be sexually assaulted by nonstrangers, which contributes to their not reporting substantial numbers of crimes (Young, 1992). Women are also exposed to substantial levels of unreported hidden violence in the form of domestic violence. It is unlikely that all or even a majority of the domestic violence assaults are ever reported. Thus, the feminists argue that female fear of crime may not necessarily be inconsistent with victimization rates (Walklate, 1994; Hale, 1996).

Another consideration when examining women's fear of crime is children. Their fear for the safety of their children transcends everyday life and constantly is a concern for most mothers. Fear for the safety of others, altruistic fear, is a common phenomenon. Indeed, Warr (1994) found it to be just as prevalent as personal fear. Warr also found that women are most likely to fear for their children. Nonetheless, women experience substantial levels of fear for their children even when they live in relatively safe neighborhoods.

This research shows that community police programming must address several specific areas if the police are to reduce the levels of fear among women. First and foremost, the police must continue their efforts to more effectively deal with crimes that target women: rape, sexual assaults, and domestic violence. These crimes cast a pall over women's lives to the point that many become somewhat fearful anytime they venture into public spaces. Secondly, the police must ensure that there are ample safe public recreational areas for children; all too often the police take the safety of ball fields and parks for granted. A police presence should reduce altruistic fear on the part of parents. Third, it appears that a substantial portion of women's fear of crime is generated from their vulnerability. Police-citizen academies and other training for women should emphasize self-defense, how to respond to victimization, community safety, and support for victims of crime. Such training may increase womens' feelings of safety and reduce their fear of crime.

Age and Fear of Crime

Age is only second to gender in predicting one's level of fear of crime (Hale, 1996). Generally, as people grow older, they become more wary of crime. Indeed, it is commonly believed that the elderly, because of their fear of crime, tend to isolate themselves from larger society. The elderly, to some extent, become captives in their own homes. This heightened level of fear is quite problematic since the elderly tend to be victimized less than any other group in our society.

However, an objective examination on the fear of crime and the elderly produces a number of revealing anecdotal facts that help explain their elevated levels of fear. First, the elderly display heightened levels of fear in high-crime areas, but their levels of fear in non-high-crime areas are consistent with other groups (Jaycox, 1978). Similarly, Clemente and Kleiman (1976) found that age as a predictor of fear was strongest in inner-cities and weakest in rural areas and small towns. Akers and his colleagues (1987) found that areas where there were higher concentrations of elderly, as opposed to a mix of ages, produced lower levels of fear. Also, older persons may not venture out of their homes because of health and money rather than because of their fear of crime (Clarke & Lewis, 1982). It seems that older Americans' view of crime and their environment may be no different when they are in normal or relatively safe environments, but they may react or have heightened levels of fear relative to younger persons when confronted with indicators that alert them to danger. This is understandable since the elderly are less able to protect themselves.

The police have long recognized a need to work with the elderly regarding fear of crime. For example, the International Association of Chiefs of Police, the National Sheriffs' Association, and the American Association for Retired Persons developed a national Triad Program designed to reduce crime and fear of crime among the elderly. Additionally, many local departments have community policing programs that focus on the elderly. Based on the research, it appears that CPOs should focus on the elderly who reside in areas where there are high crime and disorder rates. The police should emphasize to urban planners that elderly-exclusive housing should be made available through the jurisdiction. Finally, the police should attack disorder problems, especially where the elderly reside, since the elderly tend to interpret ques such as disorder as a greater threat.

Race and Fear of Crime

No group of people have a higher rate of victimization from violent crime, particularly homicide, than young, male African-Americans. In fact, homicide is the leading cause of death for this group of people. Also, African-Americans constitute one of the most impoverished categories of people in the United States. Their poverty forces them to live in some of the most crime-ridden neighborhoods that exist. Given where they reside and their victimization rates, there is no question that African-Americans should have a high level of fear of crime.

It is interesting to study the dynamics of race and fear of crime. First, research tends to indicate that younger African-Americans do not have a fear of crime. Young African-American males because of the street culture, more often must project an image of toughness or machismo (Miller, 1958). In the streets, the slightest indication of weakness or fear may very well lead to victimization resulting in young African-American males totally avoiding any inclination whatsoever toward fear.

Older African-Americans, on the other hand, exhibit higher levels of fear of crime. Younger African-American males have significantly higher rates of victimization and criminal perpetration resulting in older African-Americans being exposed to increasingly higher rates of violence. Some have advocated that elderly African-Americans are caught in a double jeopardy (Ortega & Myles, 1987). On the one hand, they are exposed to higher levels of violence while on the other, they have the least amount of resources to escape the violence. Also, older African-Americans because of a lack of resources find it more difficult to recover or cope with criminal victimization.

Historically, the police have under-enforced the law in poorer sections of the cities where African-Americans reside in high numbers. The police have had poor relations with the people, did not understand their problems, and generally attempted to avoid them. Walker (1992) notes that this under-enforcement, as opposed to over-enforcement, generates the largest number of complaints from the African-American community. Indeed, the police frequently come under fire from some segments of the African-American community when they increase their presence and enforcement levels, but they also receive substantial support from a number of residents, especially the elderly, who are in favor of stricter enforcement. Community policing dictates better relations with the community by working with citizens on common problems. CPOs must assure citizens in high-crime areas that the police are there to help and support them.

The Media and Fear of Crime

Crime, especially sensational or unusual crime, is of significant interest to reporters and the general public. Graber (1980), in a study of newspapers, found that 22 to 28 percent of the news stories were devoted to crime, and 12 to 13 percent of the television news was devoted to crime. Harry Marsh (1991) found similar patterns in his examination of newpaper coverage of crime. More importantly, however, is the fact that the media tends to distort such coverage. Gorelick (1989) found that journalistic accounts of crime were distorted, emphasizing pathological individuals who commit bizarre acts. Such coverage tends to bias the public and promote fear of victimization that is diametrically opposed to police purposes. The public comes to develop a convoluted view of crime. Citizens tend to believe that there are many more rapes, murders, assaults, and violent crimes than actually occur. Skogan and Maxfield (1981) noted that news coverage can create an impression of higher crime rates by reporting on criminal acts in other jurisdictions without clearly specifying where the crime took place. For example, what purposes are served when a Kentucky television station reports on a series of homicides or sexual assaults in California or Florida? Indeed, even though news journalists do not admit it, newspaper and television news reporting too often imitates that of supermarket tabloids.

It has long been postulated that the media plays a key role in the fear of crime. The media as a result of their slanted coverage of the news tend to start what some may call "moral panics." The media as a result of their coverage may cause an overreaction to a crime problem that did not exist. For example, Williams and Dickinson (1993) found that those newspapers that report crime, especially crimes involving personal violence, and in the most pronounced form, generally have readers who are the most fearful of victimization. Jurin and Fields (1995) examined newspaper articles about crime and found that sensational nature of the crime, public interest in the victim or perpetrator, or humorous nature of the crime contributed to it being reported. These practices substantially affect the public's fear of crime.

Although the reporting of news, especially violent and sensational crime, serves to heighten fear of crime, the relationship between the two factors is not straightforward. Liska and Baccaglini (1990) identify three factors that serve to predict the influence of news reporting on fear of crime: (1) locale, (2) degree of randomness, and (3) the bizarreness or violence associated with the act. In terms of locale, when crime was reported from other cities or states, it tended not to increase fear of crime. Reporting on crime in one's neighborhood or hometown, however, did increase fear. If the crime was a random act of violence, as opposed to where the perpetrator and victim knew each other or had some pre-existing relationship, resulted in greater levels of fear of crime. Finally, the violent or bizarre crimes tended to increase fear.

The law enforcement community has also contributed to the public's unrealistic fear of crime. In many cases police officials became active in the media process and in providing misleading information to the public. During 1980s and 1990s, a new form of television programming emerged following the format of information commercials, television crime programs began to blend entertainment and government-sponsored messages. These shows used government officials, well-known relatives of crime victims, and law enforcement officers to inform the public about crime. These television programs were broadcast from local stations across the nation under various names like "Crime Solvers," "Secret Witness," and "Crime Line." These programs encourage viewers to report crime and criminals in exchange for monetary rewards. They were predecessors to the government's national media campaign, *Taking a Bite Out of Crime*, which mustered citizen participation in support of crime prevention, citizen self-protection, and neighborhood cooperation (Kappeler, Blumberg & Potter, 1996).

Using police officials as spokespersons gave viewers the impression of official credibility. Television shows like "Unsolved Mysteries," "Rescue 911," "48 Hours," "America's Most Wanted," "Cops," and "Top Cops" reenacted crimes accompanied by narratives from law enforcement officials. "Unsolved Mysteries" had a segment in the show called "FBI Alert." The segment was hosted by FBI director William Sessions and spent its time describing American fugitives (Tunnell, 1992). "Bad Girls" and "Gangs, Cops, and Drugs," both broadcast by the National Broadcasting Company (NBC), featured drug czar William Bennett who "eschewed any social-structural explanation for drug-related crime . . . As mindless as these depictions were, "Gangs, Cops, and Drugs" aired two nights during prime time, evidently cashing in on a recent crime fad" (Tunnell, 1992:299). These shows and their spin-offs contributed to an unprecedented level of fear of crime in American society (Cavender & Bond-Maupin, 1993) and draw upon the believability of police officials. Viewers who rely on such information ended up with a distorted view of the world as more dangerous than it really was (Kappeler, Blumberg & Potter, 1996).

The media contribute to feelings of fear of crime through the reporting of violent, bizarre crimes, and the use of sensational law enforcement shows (Kappeler, Blumberg & Potter, 1996). Much of this reporting is of crimes that

Media Partnership Helps Capture Rutland's Most Wanted

Rutland County, a beautiful 983-square-mile area consisting of 25 towns, boasts two of the country's most popular ski resorts—Killington and Pico. Approximately 77,000 people live in Rutland County year round, a number that increases by one third during the winter months when ski enthusiasts converge from all over the United States.

Even without the seasonal increase in population, the state's continuing economic decline and rising crime rate make it difficult for the county's law enforcement agencies to keep up with the demand for services. After hearing Rutland County State Attorney James P. Mongeon report that his list of outstanding arrest warrants had ballooned to 30 pages in length, two resourceful community policing officers were motivated to implement a new crime-fighting strategy.

The two officers, representing the Rutland County Sheriff's Department and the Rutland City Police Department, believed that one way their law enforcement agencies could impact the ever-increasing list of outstanding warrants was through good working relationships. Several months earlier, the two

officers read that network executives had canceled the nationally-televised program "America's Most Wanted" despite its success in apprehending hardened criminals. Knowing that today's law enforcement agencies readily need the assistance of citizens to reduce and deter crime, the two officers were later delighted to hear that the public outcry for the program's return had resulted in it being reinstated. The officers believed that the local media, just as the national media, could be an excellent resource and partner, especially for agencies like theirs with limited financial and staffing resources.

The two officers solicited the help of their local television station and began working with Station Manager Mike Valentine and Production Coordinator Tom Leypoldt to develop and coordinate their own version of "America's Most Wanted." Aptly renamed "Rutland's Most Wanted," the program, a year old this past June, is proving itself to be a valuable tool to local law enforcement. The program, which airs photos and descriptions of Rutland's wanted criminals, is shown seven days a week in a community bulletin-board format. The

law enforcement agencies update the show as new "wanted" profiles come in and remove ones that don't garner leads after a few runs. Within its first three months, leads from citizens resulted in 15 arrests. The Rutland County law enforcement agencies are very pleased with the program's performance, as are outside agencies, which have also benefited from citizen tips.

The program's viewing audience continues to increase and has been a catalyst for community mobilization throughout the county. Not surprisingly, when the Rutland community saw the level of cooperation between their law enforcement agencies and the media, they too wanted to get involved and show their support.

The success of "Rutland's Most Wanted" is a byproduct of what can happen when state, county and local law enforcement agencies dispense with territorial battles and join together with the business community and citizens in partnership. In Rutland County, law enforcement and the media not only get along, they get the job done.

By Sergeant William Skeens

Source: Community Policing Exchange (1997). July/August, p. 8.

occur in other cities or states. Nonetheless, such reporting has a chilling effect on people's sense of security. Community policing dictates that the police appeal to the news media for more balanced reporting and that the police participate more carefully in media productions. Although crime news is extremely popular, the police should attempt to have the media include more human interest stories about the police and the community. These types of stories may foster a greater sense of security and help reduce the fear of crime.

Community Policing, Disorder, and Fear of Crime

The traditional police response to fear of crime has been to disregard it as a legitimate police objective. The police saw themselves as crime fighters whose primary objective was to attack crime. The reduction of crime was seen as the essence of police work. If fear of crime was reduced, it was a corollary benefit. Reducing the fear of crime did not fit within the scheme of things for policing. Since traditional policing relied primarily on routine patrol, which is basically reactive, there are obvious structural limitations that make it difficult to provide an effective means for confronting the fear of crime separately and directly. Though crime prevention and police-community relations programs have helped broaden the traditional police response in ways that impinge on fear of crime, these peripheral attempts tended to only marginally affect the host of crime and criminal justice concerns facing many citizens, and they were not intended to have an impact on fear.

It is also important to note that routine preventive patrol activities have little impact on citizens' perception of the police and their feelings of safety. The Kansas City Patrol Study conducted in the early 1970s demonstrated this point (Kelling, Pate, Diekman & Brown, 1974). Essentially, the study demonstrated that variances in levels of patrols did not affect crime nor citizens' perceptions of crime and safety. The Kansas City Patrol Study demonstrated that people pay little attention to the police who ride the streets as a function of routine patrol. It appeared that the public's perception of the police was based on direct contacts and the quality of those contacts.

Whereas traditional policing attacks direct sources of fear of crime by attempting to reduce victimization through suppressive tactics, community policing goes beyond this limited perspective by advancing fear of crime as a legitimate police concern or objective. Indeed, departments have implemented programs specifically designed to reduce fear of crime (Ramsey, 1991; Brown & Wycoff, 1987; Williams & Pate, 1987). By addressing property crime, petty crime, and the causes of disorder in neighborhoods, community policing inspires confidence in people that further contribute to crime and fear reduction. And by expanding the police mission to embrace proactive efforts to address social and physical disorder, community policing directly addresses the indirect fears associated with community problems.

In some ways, community policing provides elements of *community action* and *community development,* but as part of a decentralized police approach. It addresses both people problems and problems of neighborhood conditions without launching an expensive new bureaucracy, but as part of restructuring the police role. The lesson perhaps that should be learned by comparing the success of programs such as the G.I. Bill and the failure of the War on Poverty is that the greatest gains appear to be made when opportunity is enhanced as a by-product of addressing a basic need rather than as the primary goal. Redefining and expanding the police role to include fear of crime as part of this new way of delivering decentralized, personalized police service may be the key to addressing the role that opportunity may play in crime.

Because the job demands learning about the various sources of help available, CPOs can also address fear by linking people with emotional problems to affordable and appropriate counseling and helping the homeless find shelter. If the area is plagued by panhandlers, the CPO can tailor the response to local needs and local resources. It might mean linking people to employment opportunities in the area, with the CPO's office as a clearinghouse. In other cases, it might mean involving juveniles in after-school activities so that they make more constructive use of their time. The virtue of the community policing approach is that the officers understand the nature of the challenge, have the opportunity to work with people on developing new solutions, and the CPO's sustained presence provides an opportunity to monitor the results. If it does not work, the CPO can work with people on trying new ideas. If it is successful, the CPO is there to make sure that it keeps working, altering, and refining the initiative to fit changing needs.

Such efforts also demonstrate to people that they can regain control of their communities, and helplessness is an important element of fear. One of the biggest challenges that a CPO faces is the apathy that too much fear can spawn. A healthy dose of fear of crime can inspire positive action, but too much can paralyze people so that they will not take part. Once initial efforts targeted at community conditions begin to make a visible difference, that can galvanize more people to get involved. Community policing can also help channel the vigilante impulse into legitimate and positive efforts. In this regard, a number of police departments have experimented with a variety of programs to reduce fear of crime.

Police Programming and Fear of Crime

As fear began to become an objective for policing, a number of departments developed programs to deal with it. In some cases, fear of crime was the primary objective, while in others, it was one of several law enforcement objectives. Nonetheless, the police began to view fear of crime as an important objective.

Fear Reduction in Newark, New Jersey

Newark is the country's third oldest city, founded in 1666. In 1980, the city had a population of 329,000 residents, and it had one of the highest crime rates in the country. The department, as a result of budget reductions, had lost almost one-third of its officers. Given the crime problem and shortage of officers, Newark represented a city in dire need of a reduction in crime and the fear of crime.

As the result of an extensive planning process, the police department identified three basic sources of fear that should be addressed:

- The lack of local, relevant information about crime and ways to prevent it;

- The presence of social disorder and physical deterioration in a neighborhood; and

- The limited quantity and quality of contacts between police officers and the public (Williams & Wycoff, 1986:56).

The department implemented a three-prong approach to attack the problem. First, the department began publishing a monthly newsletter, which was mailed to a randomly selected set of households. The newsletter contained information about the neighborhood, police efforts in the area, crime prevention and other safety tips, neighborhood meetings, and other positive news about the neighborhood. The purpose of the newsletter was to provide residents with information about the crime problem and the measures that were taken to address it. Second, efforts were made to reduce the signs of crime. This consisted of two distinct strategies: directed patrols and neighborhood cleanup. The directed patrols conducted high visibility law enforcement to include radar, foot patrols to strictly enforce ordinances to reduce disorder, and road checks to enforce a host of motor vehicle codes. The neighborhood cleanup consisted of coordinating efforts with a number of city departments to cleanup trash, repair streets, collect garbage, and improve lighting in the area. The police also worked with the courts to have juveniles provide community service hours to assist in the cleanup. The third prong was community policing, which was coordinated from a storefront police office in the targeted area. Here, officers attempted to implement a number of crime prevention programs including block watches, door-to-door activities, walk-in crime reporting, and referral of citizens to other agencies to assist citizens with problems. Additionally, police officers were assigned to visit individual citizens and citizen groups to further enhance the program.

An evaluation of the program found that the community newsletter had no profound effect on crime or fear problems. Although residents voiced an appreciation for receiving the newsletter, few could recall its contents or receiving it. The evaluators attributed this to most people not reading it once they received it. In terms of reducing the signs of crime, the evaluation found that they had very limited effects on crime or fear of crime. Prior victims of crime were even less affected by the program than non-victims. The community policing program, however, did yield significant effects in several areas. The program resulted in reductions in perceived social disorder problems, reductions in the level of concern about property crime, reductions in actual property crime, and citizens had improved perceptions of the police.

The Newark program demonstrates that community policing efforts can reduce the amount of fear in a community. It also shows that the police must implement the "right" programs. That is, not all police efforts will yield positive results, and the police must be judicious in selecting programs.

Fear Reduction in Houston, Texas

In 1983, Houston had a population of 1.8 million and a significant crime problem. The police department had 3,357 officers distributed across 565 square miles. The primary strategy for dealing with problems was routine preventive patrols. This resulted in citizens having little contact with the police, and in many cases, seldom seeing them involved in law enforcement activities. The department decided to implement a strategy to deal with the fear-of-crime problem as well as citizens' feelings of isolation from their police department and city government.

A task force was formed to examine the problem and recommend strategies. The task force eventually decided upon five strategies. First, the department implemented a victim re-contact program where officers re-contacted recent crime victims to express the department's concern over their loss and to offer additional assistance. Prior to contacting the victim, officers would study the case to determine what possible actions the police could take to help the victim. Unfortunately, the department's paperwork flow resulted in many victims not being contacted until several weeks had passed. Second, as in Newark, the Houston police mailed newsletters to keep citizens abreast of crime news and police activities. Third, the department implemented citizen contact patrols. Here, officers were instructed to get out of their patrol cars while on patrol and meet with citizens. Generally, these contacts lasted for several minutes. Fourth, the department opened a storefront office where they held community meetings and implemented after-school programs for juveniles and service programs for adults and the elderly. Finally, a Community Organizing Response Team (CORT) was dispatched to create organization in the community by working with community leaders. Organizing was accomplished through block meetings and other means of citizen contact.

Brown and Wycoff's (1986) evaluation of the program found that the victim re-contact program did not produce any desirable results. The evaluators surmised that the officer's contacts were too late. Most of the victims had found services long before the officers contacted them. The citizen contact patrols resulted in less fear of crime, perceived declines in disorder, and better feelings about the police. The researchers report the African-Americans and renters perceptions about crime and disorder did not change while whites and Hispanics' attitudes changed. The community police station yielded results similar to the contact patrols. Whites and Hispanics' attitudes were affected positively, while African-Americans did not register the benefits of the program. Finally, the CORT program resulted in reduced perceptions of disorder and improved evaluations of the police. African-Americans registered marginal improvements in their perceptions as a result of the program.

The COPE Project in Baltimore County, Maryland

An effort to reduce fear of crime occurred in Baltimore County, Maryland (Cordner, 1986). The department's Citizen Oriented Police Enforcement (COPE) project was implemented in 1982 with the assignment of 45 officers to the COPE unit. The unit had the specific responsibility of reducing fear of crime. Baltimore county did not have the crime problems facing the City of Baltimore, but high levels of fear were bleeding over into the county as a result of the city's crime problem.

The COPE project consisted of three phases. First, officers would select an area to target and conduct saturated patrols. In some cases, officers would conduct citizen surveys to get feedback and identify problems, but for the most part, the objective was to have a sustained presence. Once a visible, sustained presence had been accomplished, phase two began. Here, officers intensified their contacts with citizens in the area. A host of programs were used. A more personal presence was maintained through foot patrols and door-to-door surveying. Also, crime prevention activities were intensified through business and home security surveys, public meetings, and neighborhood watch programs. In phase two the police moved from a visible presence to a working relationship. During phase three, the COPE officers began to focus their efforts in the targeted areas through problem solving. The COPE officers collected information from a variety of sources and used a combination of traditional and non-traditional methods to attack them. Using Goldstein's (1990) problem-solving approach, it seemed that a combination of approaches would be most effective in dealing with specific community problems.

Evaluations of the program during all three phases showed a marked increase in support for the police and a reduction in the levels of fear of crime. Cordner (1986:232) notes that perhaps the strength of the COPE program was, "the sustained attention to specific, manageable, down-to-earth neighborhood problems." Some of the problems Cordner mentioned included aggressive panhandlers, neighborhood bullies, blatant paint-huffers, open drug trafficking, and noisy and aggravating dirt bikes. Although not significant crimes themselves, these problems in combination contributed to a per-

ception that the neighborhood was experiencing a significant crime problem. By attending to these visible problems, the police were able to assure
the public that their concerns were being addressed and that the neighborhood was indeed safer.

Curbing Incivilities to Reduce Fear of Crime

Fear of crime is not confined to the United States. Other countries have
also experienced problems with it. In England, the City of Coventry had a significant disorder and fear of crime problem. The police attacked the problem
by passing a city ordinance banning the public consumption of alcoholic beverages. Here, "public" meant outside on the streets. Citizens were still able to
drink in their pubs, but they could not carry their drinks into the streets
where they often became rowdy while drinking. The rowdiness led to disorders and the commission of crimes. It was hoped that the law would keep
most of the drinkers inside and out of trouble.

The police minimally enforced the law. They only cited drinkers after they
had been previously warned. Ramsay (1991) reports that the law did not have
an impact on crime, but it did reduce citizens fear of crime and perception of
disorder as a problem. Specifically, citizens reported a drop in the number of
incivilities toward the non-drinking public. There was also a small drop in the
perception that juveniles were a problem, while there was a massive reduction
in the percentage of citizens viewing public drinkers as a problem.

The programs highlighted in this section demonstrate that there are a
variety of tactics that the police can deploy to reduce fear of crime. The evaluations of the programs also demonstrate that not all of them are successful.
It seems that those programs that rely on direct, positive contact with citizens
most likely will positively affect a host of citizen perceptions, while those that
focus on indirect contact such as information sharing will have little if any
impact. The research also shows that fear of crime is only one of several problems that can be addressed. For example, many of the programs not only
reduced fear of crime, but also had positive benefits in areas such as the public perception of the police.

Summary

Without question, fear of crime is a legitimate police concern. Although
it does not register in the Uniform Crime Reports, it does have a substantial
impact on individuals and communities. Our democratic values dictate that
citizens should be able to walk the streets and other public places without
fear of being victimized. Citizens should be safe in their homes without fear
of being burglarized or robbed. Fear directly affects people's quality of life,
and government, primarily the police, have an obligation not only to ensure

that citizens are safe, but that they feel safe. Therefore, it can be inferred that fear of crime is a direct responsibility of the police.

Research shows that women, elderly, and African-Americans have the greatest levels of fear. This same research shows that fear does not exist in uniform levels within each of these groups of people. A number of socioeconomic variables mediate and affect how fear affects people. The police should understand how fear is distributed across populations and use this understanding to formulate programs to assure citizens that they are safe. Reducing fear of crime is just as legitimate as reducing crime itself. In fact, fear may have more detrimental affects on larger numbers of citizens than crime itself.

Police departments have attempted to reduce citizen fear of crime through a variety of programs. These programs have centered around providing citizens with information about the police and crime, decentralized operations through storefronts and mini-police stations, and working more closely with citizens through walking and bicycle patrols, victim re-contact programs, and other programs that emphasize higher quality contacts with citizens. Community policing, as a direct result of its emphasis on the citizen, ensures that the police reduce fear. Police managers must continue this trend by developing strategies that focus on specific problems and fear issues within the community. This brand of community policing will assist the police in their pursuit of crime reduction and enhancement of quality of life.

References

Agnew, R.S. (1985). "Neutralizing the Impact of Crime." *Criminal Justice and Behavior*, 12:221-239.

Akers, R.L., C. Sellers & J. Cochran (1987). "Fear of Crime and Victimization Among the Elderly in Different Types of Communities." *Criminology*, 25(3):487-505.

Amir, M. (1971). *Patterns of Forcible Rape*. Chicago, IL: University of Chicago.

Brown, L.P. & M.A. Wycoff (1986). "Policing Houston: Reducing Fear and Improving Service." *Crime & Delinquency*, 33(1):71-89.

Cavender, G. & L. Bond-Maupin (1998). "Fear and Loathing on Reality Television: An Analysis of 'America's Most Wanted' and 'Unsolved Mysteries'." In G.W. Potter & V.E. Kappeler (eds.) *Constructing Crime*. Prospect Heights, IL: Waveland Press.

Clarke, A.H. & M. Lewis (1982). "Fear of Crime Among the Elderly." *British Journal of Criminology*, 22(1):49-62.

Clemente, F. & M.B. Kleiman (1976). "Fear of Crime Amongst the Aged." *Gerontologist*, 16:207-210.

Cordner, G. (1986). "Fear of Crime and the Police: An Evaluation of a Fear-Reduction Strategy." *Journal of Police Science and Administration*, 14(3):223-233.

Covington, J. & R.B. Taylor (1991). "Fear of Crime in Urban Neighborhoods: Implications of Between and Within Neighborhood Sources for Current Models." *Sociological Quarterly*, 32(2):231-249.

Doerner, W.G. & S.P. Lab (1995). *Victimology*. Cincinnati, OH: Anderson Publishing Co.

Gaines, L.K., V.E. Kappeler & J. Vaughn (1997). *Policing in America*, Second Edition. Cincinnati, OH: Anderson Publishing Co.

Gallup Report (1989). *Sourcebook*. (March/April):185.

Garofalo, J. (1981). "The Fear of Crime: Causes and Consequences." *The Journal of Criminal Law & Criminology*, 72(2):839-857.

Goldstein, H. (1990). *Problem-Oriented Policing*. New York, NY: McGraw-Hill.

Gorelick, S.M. (1989). "Join Our War: The Construction of Ideology in a Newspaper Crime Fighting Campaign." *Crime & Delinquency*, 35(3):421-436.

Graber, D. (1980). *Crime News and the Public*. New York, NY: Praeger.

Hale, C. (1996). "Fear of Crime: A Review of the Literature." *International Review of Victimology*, (4):79-150.

Jaycox, V. (1978). "The Elderly's Fear of Crime: Rational or Irrational." *Victimology*, 3:329-334.

Jurin, R.A. & C. Fields (1994). "Murder and Mayhem in *USA Today*: A Quantitative Analysis of the National Reporting of States' News." In G. Barak (ed.) *Media, Process, and the Social Construction of Crime*, pp. 187-202. New York, NY: Garland Publishing, Inc.

Kappeler, V.E., M. Blumberg & G.W. Potter (1996). *The Mythology of Crime and Criminal Justice*, Second Edition. Prospect Heights, IL: Waveland Press.

Kasinsky, R.G. (1994). "Patrolling the Facts: Media, Cops, and Crime." In G. Barak (ed.) *Media, Process, and the Social Construction of Crime*, pp. 203-236. New York, NY: Garland Publishing, Inc.

Liska, A.E. & W. Baccaglini (1990). "Feeling Safe by Comparison: Crime in the Newspapers." *Social Problems*, 37(3):360-374.

Marsh, H. (1991). "A Comparative Analysis of Crime Coverage in Newspapers in the United States and Other Countries from 1960-1989." *Journal of Criminal Justice*, 19(4):67-79.

Merry, S.E. (1981). *Urban Danger*. Philadelphia, PA: Temple University Press.

Miethe, T. & G.R. Lee (1987). "Fear of Crime Among Older People: A Reassessment of the Predictive Power of Crime Related Factors." *Sociological Quarterly*, 25:397-415.

Miller, W. (1958). "Lower Class Culture as a Generating Milieu of Gang Delinquency." *Journal of Social Issues*, 14:5-19.

Ortega, S.T. & J.L. Myles (1987). "Race and Gender Effects on Fear of Crime: An Interactive Model with Age." *Criminology*, 25(1):133-152.

Potter, G.W. & V.E. Kappeler (1998). *Constructing Crime*. Prospect Heights, IL: Waveland Press.

Ramsay, M. (1991). "A British Experiment in Curbing Incivilities and Fear of Crime." *Security Journal*, 2(2):120-125.

Schafer, S. (1968). *The Victim and His Criminal: A Study in Functional Responsibility*. New York, NY: Random House.

Skogan, W.G. & M.G. Maxfield (1981). *Coping with Crime: Individual and Neighborhood Reactions*. Beverly Hills, CA: Sage Publications.

Taylor, R.B. & M. Hale (1986). "Testing Alternative Models of Fear of Crime." *The Journal of Criminal Law & Criminology*, 77(1):151-189.

Thompson, C., W. Bankston & R.L. St. Pierre (1992). "Parity and Disparity Among Three Measures of Fear of Crime: A Research Note." *Deviant Behavior*, 13(4):373-389.

Tunnel, K, (1992). "Film at Eleven: Recent Developments in the Commodification of Crime." *Sociological Spectrum*, 12:293-313.

U.S. Department of Justice (1988). *Report to the Nation on Crime and Justice*, Second Edition. Washington, DC: Bureau of Justice Statistics.

Walker, S. (1992). *The Police in America*, Second Edition. New York, NY: McGraw-Hill.

Walklate, S. (1994). "Risk and Criminal Victimization: A Modernist Dilemma?" Paper presented at the annual conference of the American Society of Criminology, Miami.

Warr, M. (1994). "Altruistic Fear of Victimization in Households?" *Social Science Quarterly*, 73(4):723-736.

Warr, M. (1984). "Fear of Victimization: Why are Women and the Elderly More Afraid?" *Social Science Quarterly*, 65:681-702.

Weed, F.J. (1995). *Certainty of Justice: Reform in the Crime Victim Movement*. New York, NY: Aldine De Gruyter.

Williams, H. & A.M. Pate (1986). "Returning to First Principles: Reducing the Fear of Crime in Newark." *Crime & Delinquency*, 33(1):53-70.

Williams, P. & J. Dickinson (1993). "Fear of Crime: Read All About It." *British Journal of Criminology*, 33(1):33-56.

Wilson, J.Q. & G. Kelling (1982). "Broken Windows: The Police and Neighborhood Safety." *The Atlantic Monthly*, (March):29-38.

Young, V.D. (1992). "Fear of Victimization and Victimization Rates Among Women: A Paradox?" *Justice Quarterly*, 9(3):419-441.

CHAPTER 6
Managing Community Policing

Do we shrink from change? Why, what
can come into being save change?
—*Marcus Aurelius*

Organizing the Police

Community policing, in its ideal form, represents a significant departure from the way American police departments have operated throughout the better part of the twentieth century. It is a philosophy that substantially broadens the role of police in our society. Community policing is people-based as opposed to being bureaucratic or militaristic. It is about improving citizens' quality of life. CPOs must recognize that their primary function in our society is to serve the public, not law enforcement. Although law enforcement is important, it is recognized that it is only one part of the over-all responsibility of the police.

The people-orientation for the police is not new. For example, a number of researchers have documented how the police during the first part of the nineteenth century were heavily involved in providing services to citizens. For example, the Boston police during the 1800s provided a number of social services. They were involved in public health; in 1834 they visited every house in the city to check whether residents had cholera. In 1853, they provided more than 1,000 homeless people with lodging (Whitehouse, 1973). New York Police Department records show that there were some years in which the department provided as many homeless persons with lodging as they lodged arrestees. In 1916, the NYPD entertained 40,000 children during Christmas. In 1917, the Department created "welfare officers" who were charged with looking after wayward youths. Thus, it seems that community policing is returning American policing to its service roots. This, of course, is not to say that American policing was not fraught with problems during its early development, as the history of policing shows.

During the decades of the 1920s and 1930s, the police began to alter their role from providing miscellaneous services to a role that concentrated primarily on law enforcement. Moore (1978) and Douthit (1975) advise that this change was due to the Great Depression and passage of the Volstead Act, which prohibited the manufacture and sale of alcoholic beverages. The Great Depression witnessed a number of high profile gangsters, such as Baby Face Nelson, Bonnie Parker and Clyde Barrow, and John Dillinger, who robbed and killed at will. These killers became folk heroes in many quarters. Their exploits forced the American policing establishment to take stock of itself and refocus its efforts on bringing the gangsters to justice. Concurrently, prohibition overnight resulted in a massive enforcement orientation for the police. American law enforcement essentially set out to eliminate a vice that had widespread acceptance since this country's existence. The Great Depression and its crime waves, and Prohibition, resulted in the police abandoning their service role for an enforcement role.

Also, during this period American law enforcement began a reform effort that culminated in the 1950s. The shift to the law enforcement role in the 1920s and 1930s resulted in numerous political and corruption problems for the police. Police departments were controlled by local politicians who dictated whom officers arrested and what laws were enforced. Corruption became institutionalized in many departments where large numbers of officers openly cooperated with prostitutes, gamblers, and establishments that illegally sold alcoholic beverages (Kappeler, Sluder & Alpert, 1998). The move to the enforcement role provided officers ample opportunities to take bribes and look the other way.

Police reformers like as O.W. Wilson in Chicago and August Vollmer in Berkeley began to aggressively implement the military model of management as a means of controlling the police. Police administrators attempted to use strict discipline, rules, and structured supervision as means to control the corruption problem. They also attempted to distance the police from the public as a means of reducing politics and corruption. The police became very businesslike and official in their dealings with citizens. By the 1950s, the military or bureaucratic model was fully installed in most American police departments.

Principles of Organization and Police Administration

The military or bureaucratic model of police administration has its roots in the London Metropolitan Police Force in London. Sir Robert Peel created a police force organized along military lines when he established the force in 1829. At the time, the military was the best example of how to administer large organizations. This military orientation was later adopted in the United

States, and elements of this bureaucratic model remain a central part of police administration for many police departments today.

The tenets of the military organization are found in classical organization theory. Although numerous newer organizational variations such as community policing, decentralization, participative management, quality circles, and total quality management have been discussed and attempted in policing, classical organization or bureaucracy remains the foundation from which these innovations are attempted. The principles of classical organization are enumerated below.

Classical Organization Principles

The German sociologist Max Weber, the founder of modern sociology, was the first to outline the principles of organization. Weber studied the church and army to understand why complex organizations were effective. It should be remembered that these early organizations were successful because they had a measure of order or organization to them. As a result of his study, Weber delineated six principles that have become the foundation of classical organizational theory and are used in many police departments today:

- The organization follows the principle of hierarchy—each lower officer is under the control and supervision of a higher one;

- Specialization or division of labor exists whereby individuals are assigned a limited number of job tasks and responsibilities;

- Official policies and procedures guide the activities of the organization;

- Administrative acts, decisions, and rules are recorded in writing;

- Authority within the organization is associated with one's position; and

- Candidates are appointed on the basis of their qualifications, and training is a necessary part of the selection process.

These principles provide organizations a high degree of structure. They are based on the military, to an extent, and sometimes result in employees behaving as bureaucrats. They also can result in a high level of control that is useful in reducing corruption and other problems. Burns and Stalker (1961) have referred to organizations that strictly adhere to these principles as mechanistic because of their centralized authority and rigidity. In other words, early police organizations were designed to create a great deal of conformity by employees.

Community policing, on the other hand, requires what Stalker refers to as an organic organization. Organic organizations are more open and delegate higher levels of responsibility to subordinates at the operational levels of the organization. Community policing dictates that police officers develop a cooperative or personal, rather than a bureaucratic, relationship with citizens. Community policing entails allowing officers a great deal of discretion in handling calls for service and citizen problems. Therefore, the military model is totally inappropriate for community policing (Brown, 1989). It requires that officers be given latitude in choosing options to solve problems rather than relying on standard departmental procedures which may not meet the needs of the problem. In other words, police officers must be released from the shackles of close supervision so that they can adequately perform their jobs.

It should be remembered that all organizations possess some measure of the above principles. They are at the heart of organizing large numbers of employees and work. The degree to which these principles are followed determines the type of organization.

Types of Organizations

Organizational structure is dependent upon what the organization does. For example, the Ford Motor Company has adopted a certain organizational structure because of the nature of its business. It is very likely that Ford will have a structure substantially different from Humana Hospitals. These two companies are in different businesses which means they deliver different types of products or services, interact differently with their customers or clients, and produce their products and services using different technologies and means. The structure of an organization is dependent upon its clients, production processes, and external environment. This basically means that organizations can take a variety of forms, and the appropriate form for a particular organization is dependent on these factors.

Mintzberg (1983) examined organizations and developed a classification based on types of structures. He found that organizations are composed of similar parts, and the part of the organization that dominates its operations dictates its type. Figure 6.1 shows the relative placement and relationship of these strategic parts as they relate to the total police organization. Mitzberg found that organizations consist of the following primary parts:

- The *operating core* which consists of the people who actually perform the organization's work. Police officers would constitute the bulk of the operating core of police departments;

- The *strategic apex* is represented by top management. In a police organization the chief, immediate commanders, assistant chiefs, and majors would constitute the strategic apex;

- The *middle managers* are those individuals who report to the people within the strategic apex. In a police department, unit commanders and precinct commanders and their immediate sub-

ordinates and first-line supervisors constitute middle management in most police departments;

• The *techno-structure* consists of the people who control an organization's activities. In industry, the techno-structure consists of
research, accounting, computer operators, and quality control
people. Some of these same functions exist in the police organization and support operational personnel; and

• The *support staff* are the technicians who advise the strategic
apex on how to proceed. Support staff includes attorneys and
consultants who provide advise and support.

Figure 6.1
Strategic Parts of a Police Organization

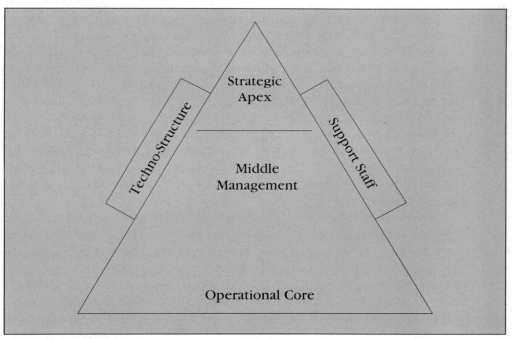

One of these five groups dominates in every organization. For example,
the support staff dominate in engineering and architectural firms, while the
strategic apex typically rules in a governmental bureaucracy. Industries that
utilize assembly lines usually are managed by a techno-structure. Some large
organizations have components which are dominated by different structures.
For example, large corporations such as General Electric, Microsoft, and Coca-
Cola have various components structured differently. Their assembly lines are
very likely controlled by a techno-structure, while their research and development components are organized as support staff.

In the traditional police organization, authority for policies and decision-making is vested with the strategic apex primarily and with middle management secondarily. The people in these two areas of the department dictate approximately how officers will respond to calls and citizen concerns. Officers are controlled through an elaborate system of policies and procedures that specify what should be done in various situations. Supervisors directly observe officers as they perform their duties to ensure that they conform to policies and procedures.

Today, however, it is truly questionable whether police organizations adhere to the traditional organizational model (Gaines & Swanson, 1997; Toch, 1997). While the traditional model of police administration dominated in the 1950s and into the 1960s, there is substantial evidence that police management has evolved into a hybrid or mixed model. For example, narcotics units in large police departments have substantial latitude in enforcement tactics and targets. Top management generally is only interested in whether the drug problem is being adequately addressed. Patrol officers have substantial discretion in how they respond to calls for service (Brooks, 1997; Walker, 1993). Indeed, it is questionable how much direct or indirect effect top administration has on officers' behavior, especially in large departments. Likewise we are beginning to realize that even the most traditional form of police organization does not provide the type of supervision required to insure control of police deviance and corruption (Kappeler, Sluder & Alpert, 1998). Although there are a number of critics of police organization who note that they are too centralized (Brown, 1989; Kuykendall & Roberg, 1997; Gray, Bodnar & Lovrich, 1997), some departments may already be adequately decentralized to the point that officers may have substantial discretion to perform community policing.

As discussed in Chapter 1, community policing is said to have been implemented in a large number of departments throughout the United States. Current research on community policing and organizational structure presents a paradox. One the one hand, if organizational structure was a major hindrance, to the implementation of community policing, those departments reporting to have implemented community policing would have had to alter their organizational structure. On the other hand, if change in organizational structure is a necessary requirement of community policing, departments reporting that they have implemented community policing would also have to report changing their organizational structures. Maguire (1997) examined the organizational structures of departments that reported that they have implemented community policing and found that they essentially retained the structures that were in place before community policing. This suggests that police departments are not fully embracing the spirit of community policing especially considering that while community policing can be successfully implemented in a traditionally organized police department, it would be difficult. The research tends to indicate that organizational structure is a primary, but not the sole, determinant of successful community policing programs. Indeed, successful community policing may be predicated on organizational culture, philosophical orientation, strategies, and tactics when coupled with appropriate structure. To this end, it seems that total quality management provides a good platform to successfully implement community policing, and total quality management can be implemented in just about any structure.

Total Quality Management

Total quality management is rooted in the Japanese industrial revolution which occurred some years after World War II. Through the 1950s and into the 1960s, Japanese exports were viewed as substantially inferior to the products of other industrialized nations. Comparatively, their quality was similar to products exported from many of today's less developed countries. Beginning with the 1970s, Japanese business and industry turned this around, and "Made in Japan" took a connotation of being high quality. Indeed, Japanese automobiles and electronics were recognized as being superior to those made in the United States. The Japanese, in a relatively short time, were able to move from a low-tech, substandard industrial nation to one of the world's foremost economic leaders.

This turnabout, in large part, has been credited to the development and institution of a management philosophy which is superior to all other forms of enterprise. Known as total quality management (TQM), it essentially moves from a focus on production, and attempts to change an organization's culture to encompass workers, cooperative teamwork, feedback, and customers as important considerations in organizational enterprise. As Hradesky (1995:2) notes, "TQM is a philosophy, a set of tools, and a process whose output yields customer satisfaction and continues improvement. TQM is truly a management system because it not only focuses on the management or organizational structures themselves, but it moves beyond and focuses on how work is accomplished and outputs (goods and services) are received by consumers."

Hoover (1996) advises that TQM essentially encompasses three primary areas: culture, customers, and counting. Culture refers to the internal operating philosophy of the organization and its employees; customers are those citizens who consume an organization's product or receive its services; and counting refers to increasing the element of accountability and understanding within an organization in terms of how it operates and provides goods and services to its constituents. These three areas, when a part of a management philosophy, result in a much more powerful organization in terms of efficiency, effectiveness, and responsiveness. TQM has profound consequences for police administration.

Table 6.1
What Total Quality Management Is and Is Not

IT IS	IT IS NOT
A structured approach to solving problems	"Fighting fires"
A systematic way to improve products and services	A new program
Long term	Short term
Conveyed by management's actions	Conveyed by slogans
Supported by statistical quality control	Driven by statistical quality control
Practiced by everyone	Delegated to subordinates

Source: Federal Bureau of Investigation, Administrative Services Division (October 1990). *Total Quality Management*. Washington, DC: U.S. Department of Justice.

Organizational Culture

An organization's culture can hinder or assist with the implementation of a change strategy such as community policing. From this perspective, culture refers to the sum of the matrix of values that exist within an organization. It is a matrix because as an organization becomes larger, so does the number of constituent groups within the organization, and each group, along with each individual, has its own set of beliefs and values. Many of these values overlap with the values of other groups, but nonetheless there are unique values among work groups. For example, detectives and patrol officers often have different viewpoints about what is important, and business leaders and minority residents within a city often disagree about what the police should be doing. Thus, the police organization is pulled in a number of directions as different values compete for dominance. Collectively, these values form a world-view or a culture, which defines what the environment is and how the police should respond to it. Culture also prepares and guides the police officer in defining what activities and behaviors are appropriate or inappropriate (Kappeler, Sluder & Alpert, 1998).

Historically, a department's organizational culture has evolved around how its constituents defined their role. The police are involved in a variety of activities that can be classified as crime, order maintenance, or service (Gaines, Kappeler & Vaughn, 1997). Over the years, there has been substantial debate as to what constitutes the core police role (see Wilson, 1968; Manning, 1997). The police typically envision their role as law enforcement; police officers tend to view making arrests, especially for serious crimes, as being paramount. Likewise, they tend to see all other activities, especially the delivery of miscellaneous services, as being unimportant and a hindrance on their ability to apprehend criminals. This view results in officers attempting to avoid tasks that are perceived as non-essential, or to provide inferior performance when they are assigned by a supervisor.

Research, however, tends to show that law enforcement or "crook catching" constitutes only a minor part of the police's enacted role (Bercal, 1970; Webster, 1970; Whitaker, 1982). "In fact the average cop on television probably sees more action in a half-hour than most officers witness in an entire career. As a general rule, most police work is quite mundane." (Kappeler, Blumberg & Potter, 1996:212). The bulk of police encounters with citizens focuses primarily on order maintenance and service. If a police department is to successfully implement community policing, its officers must come to recognize the importance of non-crime activities. The police culture must move from a traditional police culture to one that consists of values of a social work or social service orientation. Key components of community policing require the police to build stronger relations with citizens and to work with citizens in building better communities. This can only occur when officers accept this as a primary role.

The police organizational value system has focused on efficiency and effectiveness. Police executives attempted to ensure that problems were resolved on a timely basis. Patrol was organized to minimize response time and arrive at calls as soon as possible. The police took special care in making written reports to thoroughly document activities. Detectives attempted to re-contact victims without delay and keep them appraised of any progress made on their cases. However, this emphasis on efficiency and effectiveness was, to a great extent, superficial. The police came to concentrate on procedures rather than outcomes. As Goldstein (1990) aptly pointed out, the police came to concentrate on responding to problems rather than solving problems.

The police culture has also emphasized police superiority over citizens. That is, the police knew best and citizens should always abide by the decisions of the police. This philosophy resulted in a wall separating the police from the public. The police typically responded to citizen concerns bureaucratically, and citizens could do little when the response was inadequate. The police would exert extraordinary efforts toward problems that they considered to be important, but tended to give little consideration to those that they perceived as being minor. Skogan and Hartnett's (1997) study of community policing in Chicago, for example, found great diversity between police and citizens' views of what constituted community problems. In fact, citizens often cited a variety of behaviors of police officers as community problems. The police on the other hand viewed serious crime as the community's most pressing problems. Unfortunately, a number of the problems the police perceived as being minor were very major to the citizens who experienced them.

TQM, as a philosophy, attempts to reverse this trend. Under TQM, the citizen or consumer of police services is most important, followed by the work force, and lastly, management. To accomplish this reversal, the department must change management practices so that everyone from the patrol officer to the chief's staff emphasize serving the citizenry. This means that the traditional organizational culture in most police departments must be altered so that citizen satisfaction and the quality of services rendered to citizens dominates both management and line officers' thinking.

Police management must not only refocus on citizens, but it must also empower employees with the ability to better respond to citizen needs. In the past, police leadership was defined as establishing goals and work standards for employees. Once work standards were established, management undertook to ensure that employees complied with them. Under TQM, leadership is seen as giving officers and first-line supervisors the authority to make decisions that traditionally were reserved for higher-ranking officers. Management must vest line officers and units with the authority to do their jobs. Second, management is seen as a mechanism to facilitate, rather than control, the activities of officers and units. Here, management must ensure that officers have the resources and support to do the job. This requires that officers be allowed to network and work with officers from a variety of line police units as well as other units of government and private agencies. TQM means that officers are able to pursue a wide variety of alternatives when attempting to solve problems.

If management gives line officers more latitude in responding to calls for service, then management must also hold officers and units accountable for getting the job done. All too often, accountability is seen as authoritarianism, but indeed, management has an obligation to ensure that citizens' needs are satisfied. This entails follow-up whereby managers evaluate the police response to ensure that it was adequate. When responses were not adequate, then management must take action to ensure that future responses do meet citizen needs. Too often, accountability is forgotten when empowerment and delegation are discussed. Accountability ultimately means total quality.

Customer Service

Fairly recently, starting with Goldstein, we have begun to recognize that the police have failed to provide the best possible services to the public. Indeed, it may be said that in many instances, law enforcement's response to citizen needs has been inadequate (Goldstein, 1987; 1990). The police's overemphasis on efficiency and rapid response has in many departments turned officers into nothing more than glorified call-takers. That is, officers respond as quickly as possible to calls for service and crimes, but once on the scene, they routinely provide a minimum level of service to the citizen. That is, officers focus on answering calls, rather than solving problems or providing service. They often feel that they cannot devote much time to individual calls, because they must return to their patrol cars and prepare to respond to the next call. Consequently, the police in many jurisdictions concentrated on sufficiency of service, rather than citizen satisfaction. TQM mandates that the citizen comes first. The police must ensure that citizens receive the best possible police service. This should be a police department's highest priority.

Along these same lines, the police must form partnerships with citizens to address their perceptions of problems in the community, not just those of the police. Brown (1989:5) summarizes this position, "Community policing also relies heavily on articulation of policing values that directly incorporate citizen involvement in matters that directly affect the safety and quality of neighborhood life." Oettmeier and Brown (1988:13) explains how this affected line police officers in Houston,

> In moving towards NOP [Neighborhood-Oriented Policing] as a managerial philosophy, a shift in emphasis in the role of the Houston patrol officer will occur. This shift in emphasis will, in general, deemphasize the role of the officers as being primarily 'an enforcer' in the neighborhood beats. The more desired perception is for the officer to be viewed as someone that can provide help and assistance, someone that cares about people and shares their concern for safety, someone that expresses compassion through empathizing and sympathizing with victims of crime, and someone that can organize community groups, inspire and motivate community groups, and facilitate and coordinate the collective efforts and endeavors of others.

Counting Crime

Counting refers to the fact that police organizations must focus on the important, rather than the mundane. Historically, police officers were evaluated by the number of arrests made, citations issued, cases cleared, or stolen property recovered. At best, such measures are only rough estimates of police behavior, and they are inadequate when attempting to measure adequacy of performance. Statistics can be easily manipulated. All officers know where they can write large numbers of citations in a short period of time, or where they can go to observe for violations to make easy misdemeanor arrests. But, such activities do not result in "good" law enforcement. Indeed, sometimes there may be little relationship between numbers of police activities and good police service (Stephens, 1996; Bayley, 1996).

An increasingly larger number of police agencies are attempting to counter this problem with citizen surveys and meetings. For example, Skogan (1994) provides a number of examples of the police collecting direct feedback from citizens as a method of evaluating police effectiveness. Officers in Oakland and Houston used a series of home visits by officers to gather information about crime and drug problems as well as feedback on police performance. Baltimore deployed ombudsman police officers in some areas to collect evaluative data. These officers met with citizens and used questionnaires to collect information about problems and citizen satisfaction with the police. Birmingham and Madison, Wisconsin added police substations in an effort to provide citizens more accessibility to the police. Police departments throughout the United States are implementing programs that attempt to provide higher levels of service and measure citizen opinions about the adequacy of the services provided. Further, departments are targeting public housing and other areas that heretofore generally have been disenfranchised from the police.

Other quantitative criteria involve police promotions and performance evaluations. Police departments must revise their promotion and performance evaluation systems so that they reward officers who successfully perform community policing activities. Skogan and Hartnett (1996:74) note that, "A lack of clarity about new roles and goals also makes it difficult for transitioning departments to develop performance measures that meaningfully represent their aspirations. . . . Developing performance indicators that reflect either the activities or outcomes associated with community policing is a difficult task—one which few departments have successfully faced up to."

These systems are fairly bureaucratic in many departments and do little to modify behavior. When community policing activities are emphasized in promotion and performance evaluation systems, then police will be better CPOs.

TQM as a management philosophy is an ideal vehicle for implementing community policing, and indeed, a number of departments that are implementing community policing already use various elements of TQM. For example, Cordner (1995) describes the elements of community policing in terms of philosophy, strategies, and programmatic dimensions. His description, with only minor changes, could just as easily been a treatise on how to implement TQM. To a great extent, community policing and TQM are to very similar philosophies, and one cannot be considered without the other.

Regardless, it should be noted that TQM is not easily implemented. TQM, like so many other concepts, is easily described, but implementation is much more complex. Swiss (1992) notes that governmental service organizations, such as the police, have much more difficulty in implementing TQM than private enterprise. A profit motive makes it much easier to implement and measure TQM as compared to service organizations. Moreover, government has a number of operational constraints that private enterprise lacks. For example, government cannot always select or refuse the clients it serves. Political necessity often places parameters on what a public agency can or cannot do. Civil service and other personnel laws confine administrators and they cannot adequately reward employees or sufficiently empower them. Finally, public bureaucracies do not have the flexibility to shift direction as service needs or requirements change. Many bureaucratic constraints are not a function of the organization itself, but are mandated by law or tradition. A great deal of what police departments do is dictated by law and government as opposed to police chiefs.

Resource Center Assists Rural Agencies in Establishing New Policies

Many rural criminal justice practitioners don't have enough time in the day to handle routine activities, much less spend hours researching, reviewing and developing new agency policies. Five rural law enforcement executives in Northwest Ohio voiced this concern—an act that led to the creation of the Rural Law Enforcement Policy Center (RLEPC).

The RLEPC, created in 1996 through a Byrne Memorial Grant and funds from the five agencies, was integrated into Defiance College's criminal justice program. The RLEPC has three primary objectives. The first is offering its supporting agencies the most current law enforcement policy information available. To accomplish this, the RLEPC contracted with an Internet service designed for criminal justice administrators. The on-line service provides current research in all facets of policy law and technology. Additionally, the RLEPC obtained policy manuals from several Ohio law enforcement agencies, the Buckeye Sheriffs' Association and a CALEA accredited agency. The RLEPC uses these resources and others to provide practitioners with contemporary information from which new policies can be formulated.

The RLEPC is currently reviewing and composing new policy manuals for each of the participating agencies. The manuals will be tailored to each agency's specific needs, and when finalized, will be submitted for approval and adoption by each agency's legal officer and executive leader.

Educational Opportunities

The RLEPC's second objective is to provide criminal justice majors at Defiance College the opportunity to work on the project and learn policy-making firsthand. Last fall, two students were invited to participate in the RLEPC project. Both also enrolled in a field experience course that places them in an agency where they can observe and participate in day-to-day law enforcement activities. The students were required to work a minimum of 120 hours for the RLEPC, for which they obtained three or more hours of academic credit. The students conducted electronic research, drafted policies and made presentations to the participating agencies. Their RLEPC experience enabled them to couple classroom time with research and technical experience to gain a more comprehensive understanding of rural policing.

Both of the RLEPC students considered the opportunity challenging and educational. One of the students, Isaac Shelton, Jr., completed policy research in the areas of evidence collection, blood-borne pathogens and canines. Shelton said that, "Before participating in the RLEPC, I had little contact or knowledge of how a law enforcement agency operates. The research I did at the RLEPC provided me with a better understanding of the functions and duties of law enforcement officers."

Building a Repository

The RLEPC's third goal is to develop a repository of rural criminal justice information. To date, the RLEPC has obtained a multitude of written policies from law enforcement agencies throughout the state of Ohio, and found a wealth of information through the computer on-line service and journals reporting on rural policing issues. The five supporting agencies also contributed documents, articles and policies they had collected to the repository at Defiance College.

The Rural Law Enforcement Policy Center is a coalition of talent that is working to meet the needs of the understaffed and financially strapped rural criminal justice practitioners. The RLEPC's dedicated research personnel and collection of contemporary resources is already helping to remedy the research and development deficiencies existing in the participating departments.

Nationally, many professors and students are actively engaged in research addressing issues most pressing to the rural criminal justice practitioner. Local agencies should not overlook these potential resources at nearby colleges and universities.

Source: S.J. Sondergaard (1997). *Sheriff Times*, p. 3.

Nonetheless, various TQM attributes have been implemented. Hoover (1996) surveyed 200 Texas police managers and found that they were doing reasonably well applying TQM culture principles, moderately well in focusing on customers or clients, and little effort was being exerted in measuring how well departments were responding to citizen needs. Although the implementation of TQM is somewhat hampered in law enforcement, there are several areas on which police administrators can focus. They include: developing better mechanisms for gathering information about citizen satisfaction, doing a better job of tracking and evaluating performance, work toward continuous improvement rather than reacting to crises, and attempt to implement higher levels of participative management throughout the police organization. As Hoover found, the police now only use moderate levels of TQM, but the philosophy has great potential to improve American policing.

Implementing Community Policing as Change

Change in an organization can be radical where large amounts of change are introduced rather quickly, or it can be planned incremental change. Some changes can be controlled or introduced while other forms of change are a product of the environment external to policing. Given political and organizational realities, perhaps, the best way to approach community policing implementation is as planned incremental change, especially considering that it is tantamount to being impossible to implement radical change in large organizations. One must, however, be mindful that the introduction of change is complex and can result in unintended consequences. Strecher (1997:43-44) explains that change involves one or more of the following: "physical environments or habitats of daily life, technologies, institutions or organizations, beliefs or social values, social functions, knowledge base of the culture, economy, social structure and social roles." Strecher (1997:45) goes on to note that,

> Deliberate change by the police (planning) is acted out within these variables. Each new plan introduces change in one or more of these categories, changes which may then ripple outward into others. If it is a very small plan, confined to a single operational unit of the department, it may not escape the agency and may cause no external ripples at all (for example, a new scheduling method for a unit). A large plan—affecting more of the department and perhaps the community, as well—with a long time-frame may set in motion huge waves of social change rolling outward from the department (a field interrogation program, a new policy on traffic enforcement, or an effort to organize the community against residential burglary).

Planned incremental change is less disruptive to the organization. Even though the change is piecemeal, it nonetheless can be comprehensive. Comprehensive change must focus on: (1) goals and strategy, (2) people, (3) services, and (4) technology (Hodge, Anthony & Gales, 1996).

Goals and Strategy

Two essential elements of community policing are community partnership and problem solving (McEwen, 1994). These two elements represent a move whereby the police respond to the community more effectively when providing services, maintaining order, and enforcing the law. For the most part, community policing programs have not changed law enforcement goals, only repackaged them (Kappeler & Kraska, 1998; 1998a). It has caused police administrators to scrutinize what their officers are doing and attempt to make improvements, especially in terms of quality of services and order maintenance. The police still are engaged in services, order, and enforcement, but the two principle vehicles for doing so are community partnerships and problem solving.

Administrators must ensure that all levels of the department understand and respond to changes in strategies and philosophy. For example, a police administrator cannot expect officers to engage in community policing activities if they do not understand what it is. This problem is remedied through direction and policy formulation. Direction and policies set the tone for the organization and are extremely critical when change is first initiated. That is, when change is first initiated, people in lower levels of the organization often experience role ambiguity and confusion. Skogan and Hartnett's (1997:74) study of community policing in Chicago that role ambiguity "clouds officers' understanding of what they believe to be the real goals of the organization, as opposed to the paperwork involved. Police everywhere spend a great deal of time (a lot of it while on the job) debating what they think is going on amid the shifting power alliances downtown. . ." Administrators must ensure that mechanisms are in place that provide subordinates adequate guidance. Once the change is fully incorporated in the organization, this direction and policies become less important.

A constant criticism of traditional police administration has been that it relies too heavily on policies and procedures to the point that officers are not allowed to use their discretion in resolving citizen's problems. Policies and procedures should not be so restrictive that they bind an officer's judgment and discretion in handling calls for service, but at the same time, a department should have policies in place that adequately describe the department's mission, goals, and objectives. Officers must know what the department's priorities are, and these priorities should center around the delivery of community policing services. If officers are not given adequate information about the department's mission and goals, they will tend to revert to the law enforcement orientation.

People

If community policing is to succeed, traditional human resource systems must be altered to ensure that the proper personnel are recruited and selected, that they are properly trained, and that they receive the support necessary to do the job once hired and deployed. For example, Himelfarb (1997) completely restructured the training regime for the Royal Canadian Mounted Police (RCMP) so that Mounties would give greater consideration to citizens and more comprehensively address problems. The Houston Police Department took this a step further and developed a cascading training program for each rank level within the department to provide everyone a better idea of how community policing affects performance and responsibilities (Kelling & Bratton, 1993). Officers must be exposed to a comprehensive training program that informs them of their responsibilities and authority. Unfortunately, community policing has been discussed in general terms in many training programs, which is of little utility to most officers. Training and direction must be grounded in the realities and techniques of the new job.

Also, CPOs must have a commitment to community policing. For example, McElroy, Cosgrove, and Sadd (1993) investigated the reasons why police officers in New York City volunteered for the department's community policing program. The two most common reasons were flexible hours (68.1%) and fixed days off (56.5%). Only 34.8 percent of the officers responded that they volunteered so that they could be more involved in the community. These results indicated that officers who become CPOs may require substantial redirecting. CPOs should be involved in community policing not because of benefits or better working conditions, but because they are truly committed to community policing as a policing philosophy and strategy.

Services

Community policing drastically alters how the police should view responding to the community. As discussed above, problem solving requires that the police treat and resolve problems rather than superficially attending to citizen calls and requests. Many departments have adopted the SARA model for accomplishing this task: scanning, analysis, response, and assessment (Eck & Spelman, 1987). The important point is, the police must go beyond answering calls and substantively address pertinent activities or problems. This will necessitate officers spending more time at calls, obtaining support from other units within the department, and in some cases, using other governmental agencies as well as private agencies to solve problems.

Whereas problem solving describes how the police should provide services, the idea of community partnerships gives service delivery the correct contextual foundation. Traditional police departments operated as a closed system (Cordner, 1978) whereby the police, not citizens, determined goals and objectives. Over time, the police have come to recognize that citizens have a legitimate right to have direct input into police goals and objectives, and indeed, the police are constituted to serve the public. This has operational meaning at two levels. First, the police must recognize that the community and constituent groups within the community have different needs, and the police must respond to these differential needs. Second, in actuality, citizens who call the police are clients, and they should be treated accordingly. Quality should not be measured by the number of calls answered by the police, but rather quality should be measured by the level of service and citizen satisfaction.

Technology

Perhaps, there is no other governmental agency that collects more information than the police. The police are masters at taking reports. Unfortunately, these data are seldom used to their fullest extent for strategic and tactical purposes. The police, through their computer information systems, must search for problem areas in terms of trends and relationships. Police information systems are one of the best mechanisms to scan the environment for problems. Once problems are identified, the data can be used to assist in tailoring police tactics. These information systems can also be used in assessing whether tactics successfully addressed a problem. Problem solving is focused police work, and information is necessary to develop the focus.

This essentially means that the police must move from an incident-based system to a community-based system. In the past, police operations were incident based. The police responded to and placed the greatest credence on incidents. They typically placed the greatest emphasis on crimes such as homicide, rape, robbery, drug trafficking, and burglary. They were emphasized because of their violence or potential for violence. They also are the crimes that tend to generate the greatest fear among the public. The police generally did not place a great deal of importance on minor incidents, particularly those that did not involve criminal activities, nor did they adequately address citizens' concerns that their own behavior often constituted a community problem. However, community policing recognizes that minor incidents are important, especially to the complainant. Minor incidents are important when there are large numbers of them in concentrated locations. Thus, community policing requires that the police examine all activities within the jurisdiction and address problem areas as well as crimes and other serious incidents.

Implementing Community-Oriented Policing

One aspect of community policing that has received insufficient attention is implementation. Little is known about how one might successfully get such a program under way. Examining the origins of current programs makes it appear that they have developed rather haphazardly. There have been multiple causes for programs in that police administrators have a variety of reasons for deciding to implement community policing. There have also been various levels of involvement from different police department organizational strata, and a fairly wide range of police responses at the operational level. Each organizational level has different perceptions about what community policing should look like and how it should be operationalized. Thus, implementation of community policing has very likely taken a variety of paths. Perhaps the best way to understand implementation is to examine the literature on change. When an agency implements community policing, it, in fact, is implementing change.

There appear to be eight steps in the change process that should occur or be approximated when implementing or changing to community policing (Gaines, Southerland & Angell, 1991:440-445). These steps provide an excellent framework to analyze community policing and to identify stumbling blocks to its successful implementation.

Step 1—Performance Gap

Performance gap has caused a number of administrators to contemplate community policing projects. Basically, administrators come to realize that what the department is doing does not effectively address problems and needs. For example, police chiefs receive a great deal of pressure from politicians, other governmental agencies, news media, and citizen groups as to what the department should be accomplishing. The chief often uses this input to fashion an idea about where the department is in terms of performance. A performance gap, then, refers to a situation where the department's performance does not match the chief's organizational expectations, or where performance and expectations do not match citizen expectations.

It is extremely important that any performance gap be discussed with some level of specificity. It is not enough to state that crime is a problem or even that homicides are a problem. If homicides are a problem it must be learned where they are occurring, when, and who is involved. General discussions fail to provide information about what direction should be taken, and they fail to completely legitimize the move toward community policing. When performance gaps are specified, it provides more detail about where the department is and what its community policing program should look like.

Step 2—Recognizing a Need for Change

Realizing that the department is not meeting expectations does not necessarily mean that its administrators will support or introduce improvements or make changes. Police managers often realize that their agencies' performance falls short of optimal expectations or even minimum requirements, but they may still fail to act. Police administrators might rely on traditional, reactive responses to problems rather than attempting community policing. Here, the administrators attempt to improve what the department has always done. They tend to focus on service-delivery systems rather than problems or how effectively the service deals with the problem.

One other point needs to be made relative to recognizing the need for change. In many instances where community policing has been implemented, community situations have deteriorated to the point that radical intervention is absolutely necessary, and even then, it is not absolute that conditions can be drastically improved. In other words, a performance gap may exist, but the police administrator may feel that meaningful improvement is beyond the grasp of the department's capabilities. Are police departments likely to change their operational philosophy if it appears that they cannot succeed?

Step 3—Creating a Proper Climate for Change

Creating the proper climate relates to actions whereby administrators prepare and sell the change to departmental constituents and to citizens who will be affected by the new program. Regarding departmental constituents, perceptions, values, and commitments must be changed throughout the chain of command. Not only must program participants such as CPOs be acclimated to the change, but all other members of the department must be addressed and develop an understanding and commitment to community policing. For example, a patrol officer may not be directly involved in the community policing program, but he or she can contribute a great deal to assist or derail the program.

Middle management (Sherman, 1974; Sparrow, Moore & Kennedy, 1990) and first-line supervisors (Weisburd, McElroy & Hardyman, 1988) drastically affect program success, and individuals at these levels must buy into the new strategy before it can be implemented. For example, in the 1970s, a number of police departments implemented team policing, a program very similar to some forms of community policing. It was short lived primarily because of resistance and outright sabotage from middle managers (Sherman, Milton & Kelly, 1973). Middle managers were threatened by the program because it delegated substantial authority to teams of officers and supervisors. The middle managers essentially were left out of the equation. If administrators and program planners had adequately considered the needs of middle managers, the program very likely would have met with greater success. Some community policing efforts are suffering the same consequences as team policing. Skogan and Hartnett's (1997:74) study of community policing in Chicago found,

"New management philosophies will rub salt in the wounds of those who rose to the top when the command-and-control idea was the rule of the day. In many cities, managers near the top of police organizations have mounted an effective rear-guard action against change, making life difficult for those under them who are caught in the cross-fire."

Herein lie a number of problems. First, as was pointed out previously, that the traditional police value system is incongruent with the culture and value system required for community policing. A large part of the police officer's role, as espoused by police officers, most citizens, and many politicians alike, is law enforcement (Van Maanen, 1978; Sykes, 1986), and law enforcement has been the core police role for decades. It likely is very difficult to move a department's values, especially line police officers (Greene, Bergman & McLaughlin, 1994), to come in line with those required for community policing. It would be especially difficult in a large department since so many officers and units would be involved.

Second, when values are in fact changed, do the new values match program needs? We have never addressed the concept of preciseness in value transformation and alignment. There must be some degree of accuracy when changing values, and this issue seems to be omitted from previous experiences with community policing. In other words, we may be able to change officers and the department's culture and values, but can they be moved to where community policing and its various programs are fully accepted?

Third, is a change in values enough to equate to a change in actions? Organizations must be definitive when inducing responsive behaviors from organizational incumbents. Changing values is not definitive; there must be an announced change in departmental goals, reward-punishment systems, management, supervision, personnel practices, and leadership. Sparrow (1988) summarizes the extent to which change must be implemented,

> . . . movement of the most talented and promising personnel into the newly defined jobs; making it clear that the route to promotion lies within such jobs; disbanding those squads that embody and add weight to the traditional values; re-categorizing the crime statistics according to their effect on the community; redesigning the staff evaluation system to take account of contributions to the nature and quality of community life; providing in-service training in problem-solving skills for veteran officers and managers; altering the nature of the training given to new recruits to include problem-solving skills; establishing new communication channels with other public services; and contracting for annual community surveys for a period of years.

A comprehensive, organization-wide change of this nature is extremely difficult. Furthermore, some police departments have the freedom to make the changes that Sparrow suggests. Regardless of whether it is good or bad, most police departments are "rationally bound" (March & Simon, 1958) by civil service regulations, union contracts, political-governmental requirements and expectations, and citizen expectations for traditional responses to crime and disorder. For example, the structure and content most police departments' performance evaluation systems are dictated by a city personnel office. It may be quite difficult to incorporate community policing dimensions within the performance evaluation system.

Also, there is evidence that officers do not always enthusiastically accept community policing. Greene, Bergman, and McLaughlin (1994) examined the implementation of community policing in Philadelphia and found that the union was opposed to it. Lurigo and Skogan (1994) found officers in Chicago to be fairly ambivalent about the new tasks and responsibilities associated with community policing, and Lord (1996) found that officers in Charlotte-Mechlenburg County became stressed as a result of the implementation of community policing. Hoover (1992:23-24) in an assessment of community policing in Houston observed,

> . . . . at least 80 percent of the patrol officers involved remain strong skeptics. Most are outright cynics. Command staff indicate that at best 20 percent of the officers who have been involved in the neighborhood-oriented patrol effort are supporters. Indeed, skeptical managers point out that the 20 percent support may well represent individuals who have decided that the politically correct way to get ahead in the organization is to support the initiatives of central administration. Keep in mind that these are not patrol officers who have merely received a one-hour orientation to community policing. They have had a great deal of training, have been in numerous discussion sessions on neighborhood-oriented patrol, and have been assigned to neighborhood-oriented patrol areas for a number of years.

Collectively, this research indicates that a number of stumbling blocks exist when community policing is implemented and extraordinary efforts must be made to ensure that the proper climate exists. Creating the proper climate for a police department to move toward community policing may be very difficult, but it is possible. It requires a total commitment from the police chief and his or her staff. It also requires that they develop an implementation strategy which addresses every part of the department.

Step 4—Diagnosing the Problem

Police departments are complex organizations. It may be fairly easy to implement community policing in a small police department (Thurman & McGarrell, 1997), but the task is much more complicated for large departments (Silverman, 1995). When implementing a new strategy such as community policing, every officer and unit within the police department must be considered. What problems will exist during implementation? Which groups and individuals will have the greatest resistance to community policing? And most importantly, what should community policing look like or how should it operate? These are all questions which the implementer must address. Community policing should be considered a template of activities that will be over-laid and integrated with the existing police structure. Substantial thought must be given to make it fit.

Along these lines, Brown (1989:5) provides some guidance on how to proceed when implementing community policing. Actions which should prepare a department for community policing include:

- Breaking down barriers to change;

- Educating its leaders and rank-and-file members for community policing;

- Reassuring the rank-and-file members that the community policing concepts being adopted had not been imported from outside the department but instead were an outgrowth of programs already in place; and

- Reducing the likelihood that members for the department would reject the concepts of community policing as "foreign" or not appropriate for the department and the community.

Step 5—Identifying Alternative Strategies

Basically there are two strategies for implementing community policing: piecemeal and comprehensive strategies. The comprehensive model attempts to introduce community policing concepts and techniques throughout the department, while the piecemeal approach introduces it to a specialized unit charged with community policing throughout the jurisdiction or a geographical area where it supplants traditional policing. When geographical implementation is used, it is usually assumed that ultimately it will be implemented throughout the jurisdiction. The piecemeal approach is commonly used in large departments while the comprehensive approach is used in smaller agencies. It is difficult to drastically and quickly change large complex police departments, so an incremental method must sometimes be used.

Piecemeal implementation of community policing posses a particular problem to administrators. The personnel and units involved in the program may become isolated from the main body of personnel and units within the department. Toch and Grant (1991:61) used the term "innovative ghettos" to describe units that were out of the mainstream. In their worst form, such units become ridiculed, criticized, and undermined by other units and personnel. A balance between the CPOs and other personnel must be maintained by administrators if community policing is to succeed.

How to implement community policing is only one part of the identification equation. The implementation of community policing is rooted in the rationale that the department is not reaching its fullest potential. This means that the community policing units and personnel must perform beyond that which was previously accomplished. This may be a tall order, especially for a program that encounters substantial resistance.

Step 6—Selecting the Strategy

Basically, the police executive must determine if implementation initially will be jurisdiction-wide, or if it will be implemented piecemeal. If community policing is to be implemented piecemeal, will it be implemented in a geographical area, or will it be confined to a specialized unit that will apply its precepts throughout the jurisdiction. There are a number of implications for each of these strategies, and the executive must carefully consider the ramifications of each before selecting.

Step 7—Determining and Operationalizing Implementation Strategy

Two points are relevant here regarding community policing. First, since community policing consists of a decentralized structure at the line level, it is most amenable to the development of a flexible, realistic implementation strategy. In many cases, line officers who are constantly involved in daily problems develop the best understanding for what needs to be done and how it should be done. Involvement of line police officers is one of the major advantages of community policing as a strategy.

Second, community policing's benefit in this area is also its greatest liability. It is disadvantageous because it is less structured as compared to traditional arrangements. That is, when it is applied as a philosophy, as Goldstein (1990) and others have suggested, line police officers are not provided adequate guidance on how to respond to problems and how their decisions and actions interact with the activities of other departmental operations strategies. If community policing tactics are to be successful, they must be applied within a structured framework. In this situation, community policing becomes one of several tactics available to the administrator when confronting problems. This is especially true when the response to a problem goes beyond the capabilities of the individual officer who is attempted to resolve the problem.

When implementing community policing, it must have some level of preciseness so that officers and supervisors are to understand what is expected of them. For example, Walsh (1995) found that a lack of support and understanding from patrol supervisors and officers; minimal managerial support; no job descriptions for CP supervisors and CPOs; and no policy or directives regarding community policing program to be major stumbling blocks for officers involved in community policing. Walsh's findings insinuate that implementation was rather haphazard in the department he studied. Administrators must have a thorough, comprehensive implementation plan if they are to successfully implement community policing.

Step 8—Evaluating and Modifying the Strategy

Whenever a program is implemented, there is a need to determine the program's impact on a problem, group of people, or geographical area. In other words, what happened when community policing was implemented? Were the results any different from police operational arrangements and outcomes prior to its implementation? Did community policing accomplish that which was expected? Once implemented, community policing must be evaluated to answer these questions.

There will always be a need to make adjustments or fine tuning in a new program. One of the major errors that police administrators traditionally have made is to assume that their programs were properly and correctly implemented and that the programs were producing desired or anticipated results. Seldom is any new program implemented consistently with its implementation plans. Planners have specific ideas about the roles and responsibilities of people throughout the organization, but they often get shifted around and sometimes not performed at all. Once the program is in operation, seldom does it function according to expectations. Middle and upper management have the responsibility of monitoring and evaluating community policing once it is in place. They must identify any irregularities or problems and ensure that operational corrections are made.

Once community policing is implemented, administration must take measures to ensure that it becomes institutionalized. They must develop a reward and reinforcement structure that continuously encourages officers to use community policing. This means that promotional and performance evaluation criteria must be adjusted to emphasize community policing. In-service and basic training curriculum must be altered to reflect the department's style of community policing. Supervisors must reinforce community policing as they provide direct supervision of officers. Elements opposed to it must be brought into the fold to accept it. Management must do everything in its power to support and improve community policing. If this does not occur, it will very likely fail.

Summary

Administrators have a tall order when deciding to implement community policing. For the most part, every element within the police department must be changed. It is not always easy to move a police department given history, size, and resistance to change. However, there is substantial evidence proving that traditional policing is not as effective as community policing. Therefore, there is ample justification for the effort.

The first step in successfully implementing is to evaluate the department's organizational structure and make changes if necessary. Authority must be decentralized to the point that unit commanders, supervisors, and officers have authority to the solve problems they confront. Police officers' responses to problems must not be confined to a limited number of options, but officers must have the discretion to decide on the best approach to a problem. Once officers are given the proper authority to make decisions, they must be held accountable for solving problems at the beat level. At the same time, commanders must be held accountable for resolving problems in district or precinct areas. It appears that total quality management is perhaps the best vehicle to accomplish this task.

Second, the department's values must be changed. Law enforcement and crook catching have always been at the core of the police role. Community policing dictates that the police must substantially expand their role to include problem solver and concerned citizen. Police officers must be concerned with any situation or problem that causes citizens distress. The police have a broad, overarching responsibility to attempt to improve the quality of life of its residents. The department's management structure should be fashioned so as to constantly reinforce these expanded responsibilities. As total quality management dictates, citizens must be considered as valued clients or customers and treated accordingly.

Third, internal processes in the department must be modified to reinforce community policing. This means that the selection process should emphasize selecting candidates who have a strong commitment to helping others. The training process should not only provide officers with the skills to be CPOs, it should constantly reinforce its importance. Performance evaluations and promotion processes should focus on community policing attributes. Finally, the department's management and supervision processes should constantly reinforce community policing.

Fourth, the police must recognize that they cannot do it alone. The police must develop partnerships with citizens, citizen groups, and other governmental agencies. Alleviation of many community problems requires a cooperative effort among different groups of people. For example, when dealing with a drug or crime problem in public housing, the police must work with community leaders, public housing officials, and other social service agencies to devise comprehensive solutions to very complex problems. The police working by themselves do not have the resources to effectively deal with the problem.

Police administrators have a key role to play in community policing. It is not an easy or simple matter to implement it. It requires everyone working together to change the department's course and move it toward a philosophy that provides citizens with a higher quality of service. Police administrators must be dedicated to this principle.

References

Bayley, D.H. (1996). "Measuring Overall Effectiveness." In L. Hoover (ed.) *Quantifying Quality in Policing*, pp. 37-54. Washington, DC: PERF.

Bercal, T. (1970). "Calls for Police Assistance." *American Behavioral Scientist*, 13:681-691.

Brooks, L. (1997). "Police Discretionary Behavior: A Study of Style." In R. Dunham & G. Alpert (eds.) *Critical Issues in Policing: Contemporary Readings*, pp. 149-166. Prospect Heights, IL: Waveland Press.

Brown, L.P. (1989). *Community Policing: A Practical Guide for Police Officers*. Perspectives on Policing, No. 12. Washington, DC: National Institute of Justice.

Burns, T. & G. Stalker (1961). *The Management of Innovation*. London, England: Tavistock.

Cordner, G. (1995). "Community Policing: Elements and Effects." *Police Forum*, 5(3):1-7.

Cordner, G. (1978). "Open and Closed Models of Police Organizations: Traditions, Dilemmas, and Practical Considerations." *Journal of Police Science and Administration*, 6:22-34.

Douthit, N. (1975). "Enforcement and Nonenforcement Roles in Policing: A Historical Inquiry." *Journal of Police Science and Administration*, 3(3):336-345.

Eck, J.E. & W. Spelman (1987). "Who Ya Gonna Call? The Police as Problem-Busters." *Crime & Delinquency*, 33(1):31-52.

Gaines, L.K., V. Kappeler & J. Vaughn (1997). *Policing in America*, Second Edition. Cincinnati, OH: Anderson Publishing Co.

Gaines, L.K., M. Southerland & J. Angell (1991). *Police Administration*. New York, NY: McGraw-Hill.

Gaines, L.K. & C.R. Swanson (1997). "Empowering Police Officers: A Tarnished Silver Bullet?" *Police Forum*, forthcoming.

Goldstein, H. (1990). *Problem-Oriented Policing*. New York, NY: McGraw-Hill.

Goldstein, H. (1987). "Toward Community-Oriented Policing: Potential, Basic Requirements, and Threshold Questions." *Crime & Delinquency*, 33(1):6-30.

Gray, K., J. Bodnar & N.P. Lovrich (1997). "Community Policing and Organizational Change Dynamics." In Q. Thurman & E.F. McGarrell (eds.) *Community Policing in a Rural Setting*, pp. 41-48. Cincinnati, OH: Anderson Publishing Co.

Greene, J., W. Bergman & E. McLaughlin (1994). "Implementing Community Policing: Cultural and Structural Change in Police Organizations." In D. Rosenbaum (ed.) *The Challenge of Community Policing: Testing the Promises*, pp. 92-109. Thousand Oaks, CA: Sage Publications.

Himelfarb, F. (1997). "RCMP Learning and Renewal: Building on Strengths." In Q. Thurman & E.F. McGarrell (eds.) *Community Policing in a Rural Setting*, pp. 33-39. Cincinnati, OH: Anderson Publishing Co.

Hodge, B., W. Anthony & L. Gales (1996). *Organization Theory: A Strategic Approach*. Upper Saddle River, NJ: Prentice-Hall.

Hoover, L. (1996). "Translating Total Quality Management from the Private Sector to Policing." In L. Hoover (ed.) *Quantifying Quality in Policing*, pp. 1-22. Washington, DC: PERF.

Hoover, L. (1992). "Police Mission: An Era of Debate." In L. Hoover (ed.) *Police Management: Issues and Perspectives*. Washington, DC: PERF.

Hradesky, J.L. (1995). *Total Quality Management Handbook*. New York, NY: McGraw-Hill.

Kappeler, V.E., M. Blumberg & G.W. Potter (1996). *The Mythology of Crime and Criminal Justice*, Second Edition. Prospect Heights, IL: Waveland Press.

Kappeler, V.E. & P.B. Kraska (1998). "Police Adapting to High Modernity: A Textual Critique of Community Policing." *Policing: An International Journal of Police Strategies and Management*.

Kappeler, V.E. & P.B. Kraska (1998a). "Police Modernity: Scientific and Community Based Violence on Symbolic Playing Fields." In S. Henry & D. Milovanovic (eds.) *Constitutive Criminology at Work*. Albany, NY: SUNY Press.

Kappeler, V.E., R.D. Sluder & G. Alpert (1998). *Forces of Deviance: Understanding the Dark Side of Policing*, Second Edition. Prospect Heights, IL: Waveland Press.

Kelling, G. & W. Bratton (1993). *Implementing Community Policing: The Administrative Problem*. Perspectives on Policing, No. 17. Washington, DC: National Institute of Justice.

Kraska, P.B. & V.E. Kappeler (1997). "Militarizing American Police: The Rise and Normalization of Paramilitary Units." *Social Problems*, 44(1):1-18.

Lord, V. (1996). "An Impact of Community Policing: Reported Stressors, Social Support, and Strain Among Police Officers in a Changing Police Department." *Journal of Criminal Justice*, 24(6):503-522.

Lurigio, A. & W. Skogan (1994). "Winning the Hearts and Minds of Police Officers: An Assessment of Staff Perceptions of Community Policing in Chicago." *Crime & Delinquency*, 40(3):315-330.

Maguire, E.R. (1997). "Structural Change in Large Municipal Police Organizations During the Community Policing Era." *Justice Quarterly*, forthcoming.

Manning, P.K. (1997). *Police Work*, Second Edition. Prospect Heights, IL: Waveland Press.

March, S. & H. Simon (1958). *Organizations*. New York, NY: John Wiley and Sons.

McElroy, J.E., C.A. Cosgrove & S. Sadd (1993). *Community Policing: The CPOP in New York*. Newbury Park, CA: Sage Publications.

McEwen, T. (1994). *National Assessment Program: 1994 Survey Results*. Washington, DC: National Institute of Justice.

Mintzberg, H. (1983). *Structure in Fives: Designing Effective Organizations*. Englewood Cliffs, NJ: Prentice Hall.

Moore, M.D. (1978). "The Police in Search of Direction." In L. Gaines & T. Ricks (eds.) *Managing the Police Organization*. St. Paul, MN: West.

Oettmeier, T.N. & L.P. Brown (1988). "Role Expectations and the Concept of Neighborhood-Oriented Policing." In IACP (ed.) *Developing Neighborhood Oriented Policing*. Arlington, VA: IACP.

Roberg, R.R. & J. Kuykendall (1997). *Police Management*. Los Angeles, CA: Roxbury.

Sherman, L. (1974). "Middle Management and Team Policing." *Criminology*, 11:363-377.

Sherman, L., C. Milton & T. Kelly (1973). *Team Policing: Seven Case Studies*. Washington, DC: The Police Foundation.

Silverman, E.B. (1995). "Community Policing: The Implementation Gap." In P. Kratcoski & D. Dukes (eds.) *Issues in Community Policing*, pp. 35-47. Cincinnati, OH: Anderson Publishing Co.

Skogan, W. (1994). "The Impact of Community Policing on Neighborhood Residents: a Cross-Site Analysis." In D. Rosenbaum (ed.) *The Challenge of Community Policing: Testing the Promises*. Thousand Oaks, CA: Sage Publications.

Skogan, W.G. & S.M. Hartnett (1997). *Community Policing, Chicago Style*. New York, NY: Oxford University Press.

Sparrow, M.K. (1988). *Implementing Community Policing*. Perspectives in Policing, No. 9. Washington, DC: National Institute of Justice.

Sparrow, M.K., M.H. Moore & D.M. Kennedy (1990). *Beyond 911: A New Era for Policing*. New York, NY: Basic Books.

Stephens, D. (1996). "Community Problem-Oriented Policing: Measuring Impacts." In L. Hoover (ed.) *Quantifying Quality in Policing*, pp. 95-130. Washington, DC: PERF.

Strecher, V.G. (1997). *Planning Community Policing*. Prospect Heights, IL: Waveland Press.

Swiss, J.E. (1992). "Adapting Total Quality Management (TQM) to Government." *Public Administration Review*, 52(4):356-362.

Sykes, G. (1986). "Street Justice: A Moral Defense of Order Maintenance Policing." In V.E. Kappeler (ed.) *The Police & Society: Touch Stone Readings*. Prospect Heights, IL: Waveland Press.

Thurman, Q.C. & E.F. McGarrell (1997). *Community Policing in a Rural Setting*. Cincinnati, OH: Anderson Publishing Co.

Toch, H. (1997). "The Democratization of Policing in the United States: 1895-1973." *Police Forum*, 7(2):1-8.

Toch, H. & J.D. Grant (1991). *Police as Problem Solvers*. New York, NY: Plenum Press.

Van Maanen, J. (1978, 1995). "The Asshole." In V.E. Kappeler (ed.). *The Police & Society: Touch Stone Readings*. Prospect Heights, IL: Waveland Press.

Walker, S. (1993). *Taming the System*. New York, NY: Oxford.

Walsh, W.F. (1995). "Analysis of the Police Supervisor's Role in Community Policing." In P. Kratcoski & D. Dukes (eds.) *Issues in Community Policing*, pp. 141-151 Cincinnati, OH: Anderson Publishing Co.

Webster, J. (1970). "Police Task and Time Study." *Journal of Criminal Law, Criminology, and Police Science*, 61:94-100.

Weisburd, D., J. McElroy & P. Hardyman (1988). "Challenges to Supervision in Community Policing: Observations on a Pilot Project." *American Journal of Police*, 7(2):29-50.

Whitaker, G.P. (1982). "What is Police Work?" *Police Studies*, 4(1):13-22.

Whitehouse, J. (1973). "Historical Perspectives on the Police Community Service Function." *Journal of Police Science and Administration*, 1(1):87-92.

Wilson, J.Q. (1968). "Dilemmas of Police Administration." *Public Administration Review*, (Sept./Oct.):407-416.

CHAPTER 7
Sitting Ducks, Ravenous Wolves, and Helping Hands: New Approaches to Urban Policing[*]

I have often heard that the outstanding man is he who deeply thinks about a problem

—Livy

Drug dealers have taken over a park. Neighborhood residents, afraid to use the park, feel helpless. Foot patrols and drug raids fail to roust the dealers.

A city is hit with a rash of convenience store robberies. Stakeouts, fast response to robbery calls, and enhanced investigations lead to some arrests—but do not solve the robbery problem.

Disorderly kids invade a peaceful residential neighborhood. Although they have committed no serious crimes, they are noisy and unpredictable; some acts of vandalism have been reported. The kids are black and the residents white—and the police fear a racial incident.

Problems like these plague cities everywhere. Social incivilities, drug dealing and abuse, and violent crime hurt more than the immediate victims: they create fears among the rest of us. We wonder who will be next, but feel incapable of taking action.

[*]Source: William Spelman and John E. Eck (1989). "Sitting Ducks, Ravenous Wolves, and New Approaches to Urban Policing." *Public Affairs Comment,* XXXV (2):1-9. Reprinted by permission of The University of Texas at Austin, Lyndon B. Johnson School of Public Affairs.

Until recently, there was little the criminal justice system could do to help. Police continued to respond to calls for service, and attempted (usually without success) to arrest and punish the most serious criminals. Sometimes they tried to organize a neighborhood watch. But research conducted in the 1970s and early 1980s showed repeatedly that these strategies were severely limited in their effectiveness.

Since the mid-1980s, some innovative police departments have begun to test a new approach to these problems. This "problem-oriented" approach differs from the traditional methods in several ways:

- Police actively seek ways to prevent crime and better the quality of neighborhood life rather than simply react to calls for service and reported crimes;

- Police recognize that crime and disorder problems arise from a variety of conditions and that thorough analysis is needed before they can tailor effective responses to these conditions; and

- Police understand that many crime and disorder problems stem from factors beyond the control of any single public or private agency. If these problems are to be solved, they must be attacked on many different fronts, with the police, other agencies, and the public "coproducing" neighborhood security.

Recent research shows that when police adopt a proactive stance, analyze local conditions, and recognize the value of coproduction in framing and implementing a response, they can reduce crime and fear of crime. This new approach has profound implications for the management and operations of police agencies, and for the relationship between the police and the communities they serve.

The Problem: The Incident-Driven Approach

Problem-oriented policing is the culmination of more than two decades of research into the nature of crime and the effectiveness of police response. Many strands of research led to the new approach, but three basic findings were particularly important:

- Additional police resources, if applied in response to individual incidents of crime and disorder, will be ineffective at controlling crime;

- Few incidents are isolated; most are symptoms of some recurring, underlying problem. Problem analysis can help police develop effective, proactive tactics; and

- Crime problems are integrally linked to other urban problems, and so the most effective responses require coordinating the activities of private citizens, the business sector, and government agencies outside the criminal justice system.

In short, "incident-driven policing," the prevailing method of delivering police services, consistently treats symptoms, not diseases. By working with others to identify, analyze, and treat the diseases, police can hope to make headway against crime and disorder.

Adding Police Resources Will be Ineffective

Most police work is reactive—a response to crimes and disorders reported by the public. And current reactive tactics may be effective at controlling crime, to a point. For example, by maintaining some threat of apprehension and punishment, current police actions may deter many would-be offenders.[1]

Nevertheless, twenty years of research into police operations suggest that the marginal value of additional police resources, if applied in the traditional, reactive ways, will be very small.[2] For example, preventive patrol tactics probably will not deter offenders unless the patrol force can be increased dramatically—perhaps by a factor of thirty or more.[3] Only 10 percent of crimes are reported to the police within five minutes of their being committed; thus even the fastest police response to the scene will not result in apprehension of a suspect for the vast majority of crimes.[4] And case solution rates are low because detectives rarely have many leads to work with; even if the number of detectives could be doubled or tripled, it would have virtually no effect on the number of cases solved.[5]

Research has also revealed that alternative deployment methods—split force, investigative case screening, differential response to calls—can succeed in shifting scarce resources to those incidents where they are most needed.[6] In the cases studied, these schemes, often directed by crime analysis, made police operations more efficient and freed up resources for other activities. But they did not make operations more effective.

Crime Analysis Can Lead to More Effective Tactics

Three elements must generally be present before a crime will be committed: someone must be motivated to commit the crime; a suitable target must be present; and the target must be (relatively) unguarded, providing the offender with an opportunity to commit the crime.[7] These elements are more likely to be present at some times and places than at others, forming crime patterns and recurring crime problems. The removal of just one of the elements can alter a crime pattern. Thus, by identifying the elements that are easiest to remove and working to remove them, police can make crime prevention tactics more efficient and effective.

The most obvious crime patterns are spatial. Since the 1930s, researchers have shown that crime types and offender methods of operation—not to mention gross crime rates—differed substantially among neighborhoods.[8] One reason for these differences is that some kinds of neighborhoods have fewer unguarded targets than others. For example, neighborhoods with diverse land uses, single-family houses and garden apartment buildings, and intense street lighting provide criminals with fewer opportunities and incur lower crime rates.[9] Social characteristics such as residential stability, homogeneity of lifestyle, and family orientation empower residents of a neighborhood to "handle" bad actors without calling the police.[10]

Another reason crime rates differ between neighborhoods is that some areas have more potential offenders and victims than others. Adolescents, the poor, and members of minority groups commit property crimes at higher rates. Also, poor youths have few sources of transportation, so it is not surprising that burglary and robbery rates are highest in neighborhoods with many poor African-American and Hispanic youths. Some neighborhoods attract more than their share of offenders because open-air drug markets or bars that cater to the especially rowdy or criminal are located there. Potential victims who have the money to do so can make themselves unattractive to offenders by keeping valuables in safe deposit boxes or safes, garaging their cars, and buying houses with sturdy locks and alarms.

Thus neighborhood crime patterns differ in predictable ways, for comprehensible reasons. The implications for crime prevention policies are obvious: if our aim is to reduce the crime rate in a given neighborhood, it is clearly important to know what crimes are committed there, and what might be done either to reduce the number of available offenders or victims or to increase the number of willing and able guardians. Since neighborhoods differ, the best crime prevention strategies will differ from one neighborhood to the next. Officers assigned to an area must study the social and physical conditions there before developing and implementing strategies.

These strategies are given a focus by one regularity that seems to hold for crime problems in all neighborhoods: crime is concentrated. Suppose we took all the criminals active in a community and lined them up in order of the frequency with which they committed crimes. Those who committed crimes most often would go to the head of the line; those who committed crimes only occasionally would go to the end. If all offenders were alike, then it would not matter much where we lined the offenders up; the offenders at the front of the line would commit about as many crimes as those at the end. For example, the "worst" 10 percent of criminals would account for about 10 percent of all crimes. But if there were significant differences among offenders, those at the head of the line would account for far more than their share of all crimes committed; the worst 10 percent would account for much more than 10 percent of all crimes. Analysis of arrest records and offender interviews shows that offenders differ substantially, and that the worst 10 percent of criminals commit about 55 percent of the crimes (see Figure 7.1).[11]

Figure 7.1
Ducks, Wolves, and Dens: Crime is Concentrated

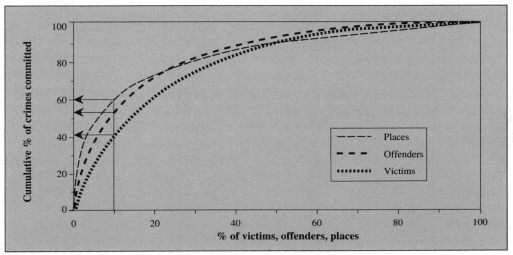

The same principle applies to victims and places. A few particularly vulnerable people run risks of victimization that are much higher than average—the most vulnerable 10 percent of victims are involved in about 40 percent of all crimes.[12] And over 60 percent of crimes are committed at a few particularly dangerous locations.[13] Research suggests that there are usually good reasons why these offenders, victims, and locations account for so many crimes. If something can be done about these "ravenous wolves," "sitting ducks," and "dens of iniquity," the crime problem can, in theory, be reduced dramatically.

This is all the more true because current police policies systematically overlook the most crime-prone people and places. For example, until recently, police gave little attention to cases of family violence—even though abused family members suffer particularly high risks of being abused again.[14] If repeat calls to a single location are made at different times of the day, they will be distributed over several shifts; thus even the beat officers may not recognize the continuing nature of the problem. The most frequent offenders are also the most successful at evading arrest.[15]

These concentrations of crimes among victims, locations, and offenders are important handles for proactive crime-prevention activity. They are the "problems" that are the focus of problem-oriented policing. Government and private agencies have mounted a wide variety of programs aimed at preventing these most predictable of crimes. For example, police, prosecutors, judges, and parole boards have adopted programs and policies aimed at deterrence and incapacitation of frequent, serious offenders.[16] Especially vulnerable people—abused spouses and children, the elderly, the mentally disabled—have been the subject of many recent crime prevention efforts. Through directed patrols[17] and environmental and situational crime prevention,[18] police and other agencies have begun to deal with crime-prone locations as well.

But because the nature of these concentrations is different for every problem, standardized responses will not generally succeed. Previous experience can be a guide, but police must study and create a somewhat different response for each problem they take on.

Neighborhood Problems Are Linked to Other Urban Problems

Knowing whether a given crime or disorder problem results from frequent offenders, high-risk victims, vulnerable locations, or some combination of the three may be helpful, but it is often insufficient to allow the police to identify a workable solution. To solve many problems, the police need the help of outside agencies, the business sector, or the public.

Often this cooperation is necessary because the police lack the authority to remove the offending conditions. If a rowdy bar produces many assaults, it can be closed down—by the state alcoholic beverage control board. If a blind corner produces many automobile accidents, a stop light can be installed—by the city traffic department. If a woman is continually beaten by her husband, she can move out—by her own volition, perhaps with the assistance of a battered women's shelter; the police cannot force her to do so, however.

Perhaps a more important reason for cooperative solutions is that recurring problems have many parts, and no single agency is responsible for all of them. A run-down apartment complex may look like a serious burglary problem to the police. But the fire department sees burnt-out, vacant apartments and a high risk of fire. The housing department sees code violations and the health department sees an abundance of trash and rats. The bank sees a bad risk and refuses to loan the apartment owner the money needed to renovate the vacant apartments taken over by the drug addicts who commit the burglaries. The residents, beset on all sides, see no hope—they cannot afford cleaner and safer housing.

Clearly, no single agency will be able to solve this problem, because the various parts feed off one another. On the other hand, if all the parts could be addressed at the same time, it is possible that the conditions could be removed and the problem solved. This would require the cooperation of the police, fire, housing, and health departments, the bank, and the apartment owner. It might also require the help of the residents, to ensure that the appropriate agencies are notified should the problems start to return.

There is evidence that citizens in particular "coproduce" crime control with public agencies. In addition to cooperating with the police and pressuring public and private agencies to deliver the goods and services the neighborhood needs, citizens sometimes intervene directly in disorderly or criminal incidents. Although some experts maintain that these informal interventions are the most important determinants of a neighborhood's crime rate, they are difficult to maintain in high-crime areas. The physical design of urban neighborhoods—public housing, in particular—discourages surveillance and intervention by neighbors.[19] Often the residents of these poor neighborhoods are fearful of cooperating with the police; they have little in common with one another; they do not expect to stay long; and they do not even recognize one another. These characteristics make it hard for neighbors to control the minor disorders that may contribute to crime. When families are headed by single parents who must work, parents may not even be able to control their own children.[20] On the other hand, the physical and social environment of high-crime neighborhoods can be improved by governments and businesses, in turn increasing the prospects for intervention and cooperation.

All this suggests that crime prevention strategies are incomplete and possibly ineffective unless they recognize the close links between crime, the physical environment, neighborhood culture, and other factors. In general, these links require that the public and outside agencies work with the police to eliminate or ameliorate the conditions that cause the problem.

A Solution: Problem-Oriented Policing

Police could be more effective if they reduced their reliance on traditional methods and instead relied on tailor-made responses that coordinate the activities of people and agencies both inside and outside the criminal justice system. How would such a police department work? How would it be structured? How well would it control crime and disorder? The problem-oriented approach is new, but the experiences of innovative departments suggest some intriguing answers.

Designing Problem-Oriented Policing

The heart of problem-oriented policing is systematic thinking. Although problem solving has been conducted in very different ways in different departments, the most methodical approach has been adopted in Newport News, Virginia.

The Newport News Police Department bases its problem-solving system on three principles. First, officers of all ranks, from all units, should be able to use the procedures as part of their daily routine. Second, the system must encourage officers to collect information from a broad range of sources and not limit themselves to conventional police data. Finally, the system should encourage "coproduction" solutions not limited to the criminal justice process.

After several months of work, a department task force developed a problem-solving process that fit these criteria. It consists of four parts:

- **Scanning.** As part of their daily routine, officers are expected to look for possible problems.

- **Analysis.** Officers then collect information about the problem. They rely on a Problem Analysis Guide, developed by the task force, which directs officers to examine offenders, victims, the social and physical environment, and previous responses to the problem. The goal is to understand the scope, nature, and causes of the problem.

- **Response.** The knowledge gained in the analysis stage is then used to develop and implement solutions. Officers seek the assistance of other police units, public and private organizations, and anyone else who can help.

- **Assessment.** Finally, officers evaluate the effectiveness of their response. They may use the results to revise the response, collect more data, or even redefine the problem.

Newport News's systematic process has since been adopted by other agencies interested in problem solving, including San Diego, Tulsa, Madison, and New York City. Similar approaches have been adopted, although less explicitly, by other police agencies that have experimented with problem-oriented policing.

Problem Solving in Practice

Since the early 1980s, police agencies have applied the problem-solving approach to a wide variety of problems. To illustrate the breadth of problems and solutions that are possible, three case studies are described here. The first two are serious and complex problems—one affecting a residential neighborhood, the other an entire city—that succumbed to careful analysis and comprehensive responses. The third case is an apparently difficult neighborhood problem that was solved in only a few hours through careful observation and a little thought.

New York Retirees Sting Drug Dealers. When out-of-towners think of New York City, they think first of the Empire State Building, Wall Street, and Broadway—the glitz and glitter of Manhattan. But New Yorkers tend to think first of districts like Sunset Park in Brooklyn, a neighborhood of row houses and small businesses peopled by a mix of working- and middle-class Irish, Italians, Puerto Ricans, and African-Americans. Contrary to the national stereotype, Sunset Park is clean. Many streets are lined with trees. The district is dotted with vest-pocket parks containing some amenities as handball and basketball courts for the vigorous, sandboxes and swings for the young, and sunny benches for the relaxed.

Despite these amenities, for years the neighborhood park at the corner of 49th Street and 5th Avenue had lured only drug users looking for a quick score. Respectable residents avoided the park, fearing confrontations with the drug traffickers. The New York Police Department tried to respond to the problem, directing its officers to patrol the park and issue loitering citations to apparent dealers. This dispersed the dealers and users—until the patrol car had turned the corner and disappeared from view. Then business returned to normal. Not surprisingly, the problem persisted.

In May 1986, Officer Vinny Esposito was assigned to the 49th Street beat. As one of the first members of New York's innovative Community Patrol Officer Program (CPOP), Esposito was expected to do more than just handle individual incidents on his beat. His job was to identify and solve recurring problems. The drug-ridden 49th Street park clearly fit the bill, and Esposito went to work.

At first, Esposito used the old tactics. He spent as much time in the park as he could, dispersing dealers and making arrests whenever possible. Unfortunately, his beat was large and the time he could spend in the park was limited. Worse yet, every arrest took him away from the park for an hour or more—and whenever he left, the junkies returned. Weeks passed with no apparent effect on the drug trade. Esposito considered the problem further, and decided to take a different tack.

He began by recognizing that loitering citations and even drug arrests were at worst minor inconveniences to the dealers and users, since few arrests led to jail or prison terms. On the other hand, Esposito reasoned, the threat of losing hundreds or thousands of dollars worth of drugs could be a serious deterrent. Dealers, recognizing their vulnerability in the event of a police field stop, typically hid their stashes in the park. Esposito could seize the dope if he knew where it was hidden—but that required the assistance of local residents.

Esposito held meetings of the tenants in the apartment buildings that overlooked the park. Many tenants were elderly and spent most of their days at home. Esposito asked them to watch the dealers from their windows and report the locations of any drug stashes they saw to the local precinct station. Reassured that their tips would remain completely anonymous, the frustrated tenants readily agreed to help.

Calls began coming in. For each one, a CPOP officer at the precinct station took down the information and radioed the location of the stash to Officer Esposito, who then confiscated the drugs and took them to the station. Within 20 minutes of each time, Esposito was back on the beat and the dealers were a little bit poorer.

This new strategy had several effects. Some dealers found themselves having to explain to unsympathetic suppliers where their goods had gone. Others began keeping their stashes on their person, making them more vulnerable to arrest. Others simply quit the park. Within one month, all the dealers had gotten the message—and the park was free of drugs.

Today, the park is a different place. Children play on the swings, youths play basketball. Many of the older residents who once sat at home, phoning in anonymous tips, now spend their days sunning themselves on the benches of "their" park. They show no signs of giving it back to the dealers.

The actions taken by Officer Esposito and local residents may not work as well anywhere else. But the thinking that led to their actions can. Like the Sunset Park case, many persistent problems affect residents of small neighborhoods the most. As Officer Esposito's actions illustrate, these problems can often be solved with the resident's help. But other such problems are not restricted to small localities—they affect residents throughout the city. For problems like these, citywide changes in policies and practices are necessary. Sometimes there is a citywide "community of interest" that can be relied upon to assist the police in much the same way that the elderly residents of Sunset Park helped clear the drug dealers out of their vest-pocket park. Merchant associations, chain retail stores, and citywide community groups may all be of assistance. Even when these communities are uncooperative, however, the police may still be able to solve the problem.

Gainesville Puts the Brakes on QuikStop Crime. When the university town of Gainesville, Florida, was hit with a rash of convenience store robberies in spring 1985, the police recognized that they were dealing with more than just a series of unrelated incidents. The department's crime analysts expected to find that one or two repeat offenders were responsible for the robberies, but suspect description provided by the victims proved otherwise—many different offenders were responsible. Word had apparently spread that convenience stores were an easy target. Police Chief Wayland Clifton, Jr., wondered why, and detailed several members of his department to find out.[21]

Gainesvillle police officers compared the stores that were robbed to others that were not. Their conclusions were revealing. Many of the stores that had been robbed had posted large advertisements in their front windows, blocking the view from the street. Often, the checkout stand could not be seen by a passing car or pedestrian. Many stores failed to light their parking lots, further limiting visibility. Others kept large sums of money in the cash register, and some provided only one inexperienced employee during the late night hours. The stores that had not been robbed tended to provide better visibility, limit the amount of cash in the register, and train their employees in crime prevention techniques. Thus the criminals seemed to be focusing on the most lucrative and vulnerable targets.

To confirm their findings, the Gainesville Police arranged for a psychologist at a local university to interview sixty-five offenders who were serving sentences for convenience store robberies. This independent analysis provided even clearer results: would-be robbers avoided stores staffed by two clerks. Many of the robbers were simply taking advantage of available opportunities; if they had had trouble finding stores with only one clerk on duty, many of the robberies might never have been committed at all.

The police department presented these findings to an association of local merchants that had been established to develop a response to the problem. The police asked for a commitment to change the conditions that made robberies easy to commit. They were disappointed: the merchants felt that the solution lay in more frequent police patrols, and they refused to agree to voluntary crime prevention standards. In effect, the merchants argued that the costs of convenience store crime prevention should be borne by the public as a whole rather than by the stores themselves.

Chief Clifton knew that he could not stop the robberies with police presence unless he assigned his officers to stand guard at every convenience store in the city. Instead, he directed his officers to search for another way of mandating crime prevention measures. Their research revealed that the cities of Akron, Ohio, and Coral Gables, Florida, had passed ordinances requiring merchants to take certain crime prevention measures, and that these ordinances had reduced the incidence of robbery. Clifton and his officers began drafting such an ordinance for Gainesville.

By the summer of 1986, the department was ready to present its findings to the City Commission. The proposed ordinance would require convenience stores to remove window advertising, place cash registers in full view of the street, install security cameras and outside lighting, and limit the amount of cash available in the register. Most important, it would require two or more employees, trained in crime prevention techniques, to work late at night. In July, the City Commission overruled the objections of the convenience store owners and passed the ordinance.

The stores fought the ordinance in court, arguing that the crime prevention measures would be costly and ineffective. But the judge found the police department's research to be persuasive. The store owners' injunction was denied, and the ordinance took effect on schedule.

The first year after the adoption of the new ordinance brought encouraging results: convenience store robberies were down by 65 percent overall, and by 75 percent at night. Best of all, the robbery rate was reduced far below its pre-1985 levels. Convenience stores continue to do a land-office business in Gainesville, and many store owners now admit—a bit grudgingly—that the police department's city-wide approach has solved a difficult problem.

Persistent problems are natural targets of problem solving. It is easy to see how time-consuming research and complex crime prevention measures can be worth the effort if they will help to remove a longstanding problem. But many crime and disorder problems are temporary and nagging, rather than persistent and severe; they do not merit lengthy analysis and complicated responses. Still, thinking systematically about even a minor problem can often reveal quick solutions that are easy to implement.

Newport News Skates out of Trouble. The quiet nights of a middle-class Newport News neighborhood were spoiled when groups of rowdy teenagers began to frequent the area on Fridays and Saturdays. There had been no violence, and the kids' primary offenses were loud music, horseplay, and occasional vandalism. But residents felt the teenagers were unpredictable, particularly since they came from the city's mostly African-American south-east side, several miles away. The neighborhood became a regular stop for officers working the evening shift.

Sergeant Jim Hogan recognized that responding to these calls took time but accomplished little except to irritate everyone involved. One Friday night he asked the beat officer, Paul Summerfield, to look into the problem and develop a better solution.

Summerfield suspected that the source of the problem might be a roller skating rink. The rink had been trying to increase business by offering reduced rates and transportation on Friday and Saturday nights. As he drove north toward the rink later that night, Summerfield saw several large groups of youths walking south. Other kids were still hanging around the rink, which had closed shortly before. Summerfield talked to several of them and found that they were waiting for a bus. The others, he was told, had become impatient and begun the three-mile walk home. Then Summerfield talked to the rink owner. The owner told him he had leased the bus to pick up and drop off kids who lived far from the rink. But he said there were always more kids needing rides at the end of the night than the bus had picked up earlier.

When Officer Summerfield returned to the skating rink early the next evening, he saw about 50 youngsters get out of the bus rented by the skating rink. But he saw others get out of the public transit buses that stopped running at midnight, and he saw parents in pajamas drop off kids, then turn around and go home. Clearly the rink's bus would be unable to take home all the kids who would be stranded at closing time.

Summerfield consulted Sergeant Hogan. They agreed that the skating rink owner should be asked to bus the kids home. Summerfield returned to the rink Monday and spoke with the owner. When informed of the size of the problem he had unwittingly created, the owner agreed to lease more buses. By the next weekend, the buses were in use and Summerfield and Hogan saw no kids walking home.

Elapsed time from problem identification to problem solution: one week. Resources used: about four hours of an officer's time. Results: fewer calls, happier kids, satisfied homeowners.

Implementing Problem-Oriented Policing

Problem-oriented policing is a state of mind, not a program, technique, or procedure. Problem-solving procedures and analysis guides can be helpful, but only if they encourage clear-headed analysis of problems and an uninhibited search for solutions. Moreover, there are any number of ways of implementing the approach. The New York Police Department established a special unit to focus on neighborhood problems full time; in Newport News, all officers are obliged to spend some of their time identifying and working out problems. There is a place for problem solving in any agency's standard operating procedures. In the long run, however, it is likely that the problem-oriented approach will have its most dramatic impact on the management structure of American policing and on the relationship between the police, other city agencies, and the public.

Changes in Management Structure. As the case studies considered above suggest, crime and disorder problems are fundamentally local and specialized in nature. As a result, they are best analyzed and responded to on a case-by-case basis by the line officers and detectives assigned to the problem neighborhood or crime type. Implementing this approach will require changes in the centralized, control-oriented organizational structure and management style of most police agencies. Command staff and mid-level managers can structure problem-solving efforts by creating standard operating procedures, such as the problem-solving process created in Newport News. They can also encourage effective and innovative efforts by regarding the officers who undertake them. But they cannot make the many individual decisions that are required to identify, analyze, and solve problems.

Inevitably, the changes in structure and style will affect line supervisors—sergeants—the most. Problem solving puts a dual burden on supervisors. On the one hand, they must make many of the tough, operational decisions: setting priorities among different problems, facilitating communication and cooperation with other divisions of the police department and outside agencies, and making sure their officers solve the problems they are assigned. On the other hand, sergeants must also provide leadership, encouraging creative analysis and response. As the sergeant's role shifts from taskmaster to team leader, police agencies must take greater care in selecting, training, and rewarding their line supervisors.

As the structure and style of police agencies change, managers must also shift their focus from internal management problems to the external problems of the public. When a few routine procedures such as preventive patrol, rapid response, and follow-up investigations formed the bulk of an agency's activity, the manager's job was mostly to remove barriers to efficient execution of these routines. Good managers streamlined administrative procedures and reduced paperwork; they implemented new resource deployment

schemes; they structured officer discretion.[22] They did not need to emphasize crime and disorder reduction, since crimes and disorders would pre-
sumably take care of themselves if the routines were implemented properly.

On the other hand, problem-solving activities are inherently nonroutine;
it is far more important to choose the correct response from among many
possibilities—to "do the right thing"—than it is to "do things right." Thus managers must shift their attention from internal efficiency measures to external
effectiveness measures. And they must shift from global, city- and precinct-
wide measures to carefully defined, problem-specific measures. Instead of
city-wide clearance and arrest rates, police must emphasize neighborhood
crime rates; Instead of counting the number of tickets written by all officers,
they must count the number of auto accidents on particular stretches of road.
Implicitly, police must recognize that problem-specific crime rates, accident
rates, and the like are partly within their control. Whereas no agency can be
held accountable for citywide crime and accident rates, police managers and
officers must accept partial responsibility for conditions in their areas.

Changes in Police Role. Of course, crime, disorder, and other evils are only
partly the responsibility of the police. As the three case studies illustrate, police
cannot solve these problems by themselves; they need help from other public
service agencies, the business community, and the public. The need to obtain
cooperation and assistance from these "coproducers" of public safety requires
that the role of the police agency must change.

One fundamental change will be in the autonomy of the police relative to
other public service agencies. Urban bureaucracies are currently structured
along functional lines—public works maintains roads and sewers, codes compliance ensures that building codes are met, and so on. But if urban problems
are interrelated and concentrated, as the research and case studies presented
above suggest, then these functional distinctions begin to blur. The activities
of the public works, codes, and other departments affect (and perhaps wors-
en) the problems of all the other departments, so at a minimum they must
communicate to one another what they are doing about a problem and why.
A more ambitious and effective strategy would be for them to develop and
implement a common response. In the short run, each agency gives up some
of its "turf"; in the long run, each agency saves itself a lot of work.

Problem-oriented police agencies have found that line personnel in other
agencies can be "hidden allies," bending procedures to get the job done. For
example, one police agency attempted to solve a recurring traffic accident
problem at a blind corner by convincing the traffic engineer to install a stop
sign. The engineer refused to comply until he had conducted his own study;
unfortunately, many similar problems were already awaiting study, so the engineer would not be able to consider the corner for several months. Then a
police officer discovered that the public works personnel who actually installed
the signs could replace a missing or deteriorated sign within a few days, and

that the roadworkers would by happy to install the "missing" stop sign. The work order was placed, and the sign was installed within a week. Now police officers in this jurisdiction regularly bypass the traffic engineer and deal directly with public works officials.

Hidden allies may help get the job done, but in the long run turf difficulties are best surmounted when top managers—city managers and department heads—recognize the value of a cooperative, problem-solving approach and urge their managers and line personnel to comply. This puts the onus on problem-oriented police administrators to educate and lobby their colleagues, running interference for their officers. As will be discussed later, such an education effort may ultimately result in substantial changes in the city bureaucracy.

Problem-oriented policing also requires that police take on a different role with regard to the public it serves. At present, police ask little more of citizens than that they report crimes, be good witnesses, and stand aside to let the professionals do their job. As with public service agencies, however, problem solving requires that the police and the public communicate and cooperate more frequently, on a wider variety of issues. In particular, problem-oriented police agencies recognize that sometimes citizens know better what must be done.

This raises many difficult questions. Just as different public service agencies see different aspects of a problem, so do different groups of citizens. If there is no consensus among the community of interest as to the nature of the problem, but public cooperation is necessary to solve it, the police must play a role in forging this consensus. Few police agencies are well equipped for such essentially political activities.

The dilemma is even more serious when the conflict is of values, not just perceptions. Quiet residents of an urban neighborhood may see nothing wrong with police harassment of their rowdier neighbors; the rowdies may legitimately claim that they have the right to be raucous so long as they end their loud parties before midnight and do not threaten other residents. In dealing with such a problem, police must balance the rights and needs of the two groups. This is hardly new—police have always had to balance the goals of serving the majority while guarding the liberties of the minority. Because the problem-oriented approach encourages police to seek such difficult situations, however, they may find themselves making such tough choices more often. On the other hand, problem solving also emphasizes the power of information and cooperative action over the power of formal, unilateral authority. If police can develop a broader repertoire of solutions to conflicts like these, they may find that these tough choices are easier to make.

It remains to be seen how the limits on police authority will be set, but it is certain that problem solving will require a new consensus on the role, authority, and limitations of the police in each jurisdiction that adopts it.[23]

The Future: Beyond Problem-Oriented Policing

Problem-oriented policing is new. Traditional procedures die hard, problem-solving methods are still under development, and no one knows for sure how successful the approach will be. As a result, no police agency has adopted the approach fully, and it will be a long time before many agencies do. On the other hand, problem-oriented policing is a realistic response to the limitations of traditional, incident-driven policing. It relies on our growing knowledge of the nature of crime and disorder, and it has been successful in a wide variety of police agencies, for a wide variety of urban crime and disorder problems. The problem-oriented approach seems to be where police work is going.

It also seems to be where other urban service agencies are going. Problem-oriented approaches have been implemented on an experimental basis in electric utilities,[24] urban transit authorities,[25] and recreation and parks departments.[26] Over the next few years, it makes sense to expect dramatic growth in the use of problem-solving techniques not only in municipal policing but in other areas as well. It is likely, then, that problem-oriented police officers will find problem-oriented firefighters, housing inspectors, and others to work with.

This seems to be the case in Madison, Wisconsin, where city agencies have been working on problem solving since 1984. The city has implemented a program of quality and productivity improvement, a form of problem solving originally developed in the private sector to improve the quality of manufactured goods. Project teams have been established within most city agencies, consisting of line personnel, supervisors, and managers, often working with a statistical consultant. They identify a recurring problem within their agency, usually an administrative bottleneck, and use methods successful in private industry to analyze and solve it.[27] Although most Madison city agencies have concentrated on administrative problems, some—including the Madison Police Department—are beginning to extend the methods to public problems. When Madison police officers take on a public problem, chances are they will find sympathetic and experienced problem solvers to work with in other agencies.

The growing use of problem-oriented approaches should help to reduce turf problems. As standard operating procedures become more flexible and decisionmaking becomes decentralized, line officials may find that they owe as much allegiance to their colleagues from other agencies as they do to their own bureaucracies. One natural method of institutionalizing these developments would be to adopt a matrix organizational structure. Neighborhood teams, consisting of members of the police, fire, public works, and other departments, would work together on a formal basis to deliver urban services. Although full implementation of a matrix is a long way off, the foundation for such a structure has already been laid in New York City. All urban service agencies are decentralized into 88 districts with identical boundaries; citizens participate in agency decisionmaking through community boards, a permanent part of the city government structure.[28]

A central element of problem-oriented policing is that administrative arrangements are less important than the activities that line officers undertake. But just as the centralized, control-oriented police structure helped police administrators to institutionalize incident-driven policing, so might a decentralized, team-based matrix help city managers to institutionalize problem-oriented urban service provision.

Such an interagency team approach would also provide long-term benefits for the relationship between city government and the public. More problem solvers would be available, with different backgrounds, viewpoints, and opportunities for contact with the public; this would improve the chances of early identification and complete analysis of problems. Because they would report to different bureaucracies, members of problem-solving teams would act as a check on one another, reducing many of the potential dangers of community problem solving. Finally, the teams would provide a unified contact point for frustrated citizens who would otherwise be unable to negotiate their way through the city bureaucracy. If problem-solving teams can be linked to community organizations, the opportunities for cooperative efforts would increase dramatically.

Such benefits, like the interagency team or matrix structure, are speculative. Problem-oriented policing is not. It provides a tested, practical approach for police agencies frustrated with putting Band-Aids on symptoms. By responding to recurring problems, and by working with other agencies, businesses, and the public whenever possible, innovative police agencies have begun to develop an effective strategy for reducing crime and other troubling conditions in our cities.

Notes

[1]   Philip J. Cook, "Research in Criminal Deterrence: Laying the Groundwork for the Second Decade," in *Crime and Justice: An Annual Review of Research,* vol. 4, ed. Michael Tonry and Norval Morrris (Chicago: University of Chicago Press, 1980).

[2]   John E. Eck and William Spelman, *Problem Solving: Problem-oriented Policing in Newport News* (Washington, D.C.: Police Executive Research Forum, 1987).

[3]   J. Schnelle, R. Kirchner, J. Casey, P. Uselton, and M. McNees, "Patrol Evaluation Research: A Multiple-Baseline Analysis of Saturation Police Patrolling during Day and Night Hours," *Journal of Applied Behavior Analysis* 10 (1976): 33-40; George L. Kelling, Tony Pate, Duane Dieckman, and Charles E. Brown, *The Kansas City Preventive Patrol Experiment: A Technical Report* (Washington, D.C.: The Police Foundation, 1974).

[4]   William Spelman and Dale K. Brown, *Calling the Police: Citizen Reporting of Serious Crime* (Washington, D.C.: U.S. Government Printing Office, 1984).

[5]   John E. Eck, *Solving Crimes: The Investigation of Burglary and Robbery* (Washington, D.C.: Police Executive Research Forum, 1982); William Spelman, Michael Oshima, and George L. Kelling, *Crime Suppression and Traditional Police Tactics,* final report to the Florence V. Burden Foundation (Cambridge, Mass.: Program in Criminal Justice Policy and Management, Harvard University, 1985).

6   James M. Tien, James A. Simon, and Richard C. Larson, *An Alternative Approach in Police Patrol: The Wilmington Split-Force Experiment* (Washington, D.C.: U.S. Government Printing Office, 1978); John E. Eck, *Managing Case Assignments: The Burglary Investigation Decision Model Replication* (Washington, D.C.: Police Executive Research Forum, 1979); J. Thomas McEwen, Edward F. Connors, and Marcia I. Cohen, *Evaluation of the Differential Police Response Field Test* (Alexandria, Va: Research Management Associates, 1984).

7   Lawrence E. Cohen and Marcus Felson, "Social Change and Crime Rate Trends: A Routine Activity Approach," *American Sociological Review* 44 (August 1979): 588-608.

8   For example, Clifford R. Shaw and Henry E. McKay, *Juvenile Delinquency and Urban Areas* (Chicago: University of Chicago Press, 1942); and Thomas A. Reppetto, *Residential Crime* (Cambridge, Mass.: Ballinger, 1974).

9   Jane Jacobs, *The Death and Life of Great American Cities* (New York: Vintage, 1961); Floyd J. Fowler, Jr., Mary Ellen McCalla, and Thomas W. Mangione, *Reducing Residential Crime and Fear: The Hartford Neighborhood Crime Prevention Program* (Washington, D.C.: U.S. Government Printing Office. 1979).

10   Stephanie W. Greenberg, William M. Rohe, and Jay R. Williams, *Safe and Secure Neighborhoods: Physical Characteristics and Informal Territorial Control in High and Low Crime Neighborhoods* (Washington, D.C.: U.S. Government Printing Office, 1984).

11   Alfred Blumstein, Jacqueline Cohen, Jeffrey A. Roth, and Christy A. Visher, *Criminal Careers and "Career Criminals,"* vol. 1 (Washington, D.C.: National Academy Press, 1986).

12   James F. Nelson, "Multiple Victimization in American Cities: A Statistical Analysis of Rare Events," *American Journal of Sociology* 85 (1980): 870-91.

13   Glenn L. Pierce, Susan Spaar, and LeBaron R. Briggs, *The Character of Police Work: Strategic and Tactical Implications* (Boston: Center for Applied Social Research, Northeastern University, 1986); Lawrence W. Sherman, "Repeat Calls to Police in Minneapolis," in *Crime Control Reports Number 4* (Washington, D.C.: Crime Control Institute, 1987).

14   Albert J. Reiss, Jr., "Victim Proneness in Repeat Victimization by Type of Crime," in *Indicators of Crime and Criminal Justice: Quantitative Studies,* ed. Stephen E. Fienberg and Albert J. Reiss, Jr. (Washington, D.C.: U.S. Government Printing Office, 1980), pp. 41-53.

15   William Spelman, "The Incapacitation Benefits of Selective Criminal Justice Policies," Ph.D. diss., Harvard University, 1988.

16   Mark H. Moore, Susan R. Estrich, Daniel McGillis, and William Spelman, *Dangerous Offenders: The Elusive Target of Justice* (Cambridge, Mass.: Harvard University Press, 1985).

17   Tien, Simon, and Larson, *Alternative Approach.*

18   C. Ray Jeffery, *Crime Prevention through Environmental Design* (Beverly Hills, Cal.: Sage, 1971); Ronald V. Clarke and Derek B. Cornish, "Modeling Offenders' Decisions: A Framework for Research and Policy," in *Crime and Justice: An Annual Review of Research,* vol. 6, ed. Michael Tonry and Norval Morris (Chicago: University of Chicago Press, 1985, pp. 147-85).

19   Oscar Newman, *Defensible Space: Crime Prevention through Urban Design* (New York: Macmillan, 1972).

20   Greenberg, Rohe, and Williams, *Safe and Secure Neighborhoods.*

21   Wayland Clifton, Jr., "Convenience Store Robberies in Gainesville, Florida: An Intervention Strategy by the Gainesville Police Department," reported by the Gainesville Police Department, Gainesville, Florida, 1987.

22   Herman Goldstein, "Improving Policing: A Problem-oriented Approach," *Crime and Delinquency* 25 (April 1979): 236-58.

23   Herman Goldstein, "Toward Community-Oriented Policing: Potential Basic Requirements and Threshold Questions," *Crime and Delinquency* 33 (January 1986): 1-30.

24   John Francis Hird, "An Electric Utility," in *Out of the Crisis,* ed. W. Edwards Deming (Cambridge, Mass.: Center for Advanced Engineering Study, Massachusetts Institute of Technology, 1986).

25   Harvey J. Brightman, *Group Problem Solving: An Improved Managerial Approach* (Atlanta: Business Publishing Division, College of Business Administration, Georgia State University, 1988).

26   Joseph J. Bannon, *Problem Solving in Recreation and Parks* (Englewood Cliffs, N.J.: Prentice-Hall, 1972).

27   William Hunter, Jan O'Neill, and Carol Wallen, *Doing More with Less in the Public Sector: A Progress Report from Madison, Wisconsin,* report no. 13 (Madison: Center for Quality and Productivity Improvement, College of Engineering, University of Wisconsin, 1986).

28   John Mudd, *Neighborhood Services* (New Haven, Conn.: Yale University Press, 1984).

CHAPTER 8
Police Methods for Identifying Community Problems*

Advice is for those contemplating action.
—Seneca

The results of a recent national survey of criminal justice agencies shows a tremendous interest among police chiefs in community and problem-oriented policing. Eighty percent of chiefs report needing technical assistance or research on the subject, and 69 percent are interested in applying problem-solving techniques specifically to drug problems (McEwen et al., 1991).

Technical distinctions can be made between community policing (also known as neighborhood policing) and problem-oriented policing, and police managers often ask about the differences between the two. Both approaches recognize a need to draw the community and the police closer together, and they have several common elements: consultations between police and residents, development of strategies to fit neighborhood needs, and mobilization of community resources (Bayley, 1991). But problem-oriented policing as conceptualized by Herman Goldstein encourages (among other things) a higher level of community problem identification and analysis (Goldstein, 1990a). It represents a "fine-tuning approach" found in "the most advanced community-oriented policing programs" (Goldstein, 1990b). The operational term, then, is leaning toward community policing, with problem-oriented policing viewed as a specific enhancement to community policing.

Community policing is often described as both a philosophy and an organizational strategy. As a philosophy, it broadens the police mandate by placing an increased emphasis on involving community members in identifying

---

*Source: Barbara Webster and Edward F. Connors (1993). "Police Methods for Identifying Community Problems." *American Journal of Police,* 12(1):75-102. Reprinted by permission of MCB University Press Ltd.

problems and exploring creative solutions to them. Problems of interest to both the police and the community include not only crimes but also fear of crime, crime prevention, disorder, and neighborhood deterioration. The community policing philosophy recognizes the apparent link between blighted neighborhood conditions and the level of crime in a community. It suggests that if the police can address the conditions that breed crime, they may be able to reduce crime and fear (Wilson & Kelling, 1989; New York City Police Department and Vera Institute of Justice, 1988).

Within the past few years, the community policing plans devised by many police departments reflect a common philosophy, although it varies somewhat in emphasis. For example, the Portland, Oregon, community policing plan (Portland Police Bureau, 1990) identifies "partnership, empowerment, problem solving, accountability, and service orientation" as key factors. The Montgomery County, Maryland, Police Department echoes Portland's view but concludes that ultimately, the definition of community policing "is what the Department and the Community agree it to be." (Montgomery County Police, 1991). Seattle, Washington, stresses community policing as "an operating philosophy (values and attitudes) rather than specific tactics" and sees it as "a proactive complement to the traditional (reactive) approach of answering emergency calls." Seattle also includes an emphasis on crime prevention; problem solving; and cooperation between the police, the community, and other agencies (Seattle Police Department, 1991). Tempe, Arizona, stresses that community policing is a partnership between the police and citizens to "improve the quality of life in our city by identifying and resolving public safety concerns . . . not a program or addition to traditional policing. It is an umbrella that encompasses a broad range of techniques and resources." (Tempe Police Department, 1991).

There is also considerable agreement on what community policing is *not*—or should not be. It is often discussed as *not* an attempt to turn police officers into social workers; *not* a return to unprofessionalism, payoffs, and political manipulation of police business; and *not* a public relations ploy or a limited community relations unit.

While there seems to be agreement among police practitioners about what a community policing philosophy means, there is a great deal of diversity in how the philosophy is making the leap into action. Departments that have articulated community policing goals may be using any number of tactics in a variety of combinations—long-term assignments of officers to neighborhood beats, special squads of community police officers, neighborhood police offices, foot patrol assignments, training in problem-solving skills, and many others. These tactics may or may not be part of a master plan for organizational change or decentralization.

Some researchers at times seem to straddle a line between a desire to observe, hands-off, the community policing phenomenon, and a need to offer guidelines. Trojanowicz and Bucqueroux (1990) express concern about "pinning it [community policing] down in ways that might inhibit its continued growth," but they also offer specific community policing tenets to introduce a book that is largely prescriptive (Kelling, 1990). Goldstein worries that taking a cookbook approach to instruction in problem solving runs the risk of discouraging innovation and oversimplifying the concept; but he concludes that guidelines are needed and provides some (Goldstein, 1990c).

There are four main steps to the problem-solving process as discussed by Herman Goldstein and others: problem identification or scanning, analysis, response and assessment (Eck & Spelman, 1987). This article focuses on one aspect of this process: identifying community problems. In our experience, this aspect of community policing has proved more difficult than anticipated for some departments new to the problem-solving approach. The intent is not to write a prescription, but to review and expand upon some of the problem identification techniques discussed by Eck and Spelman (1987), Goldstein (1990c), and others.

There is now a considerable body of experience on which to draw. Since the late 1970s, many law enforcement agencies have experimented with special community policing squads or programs, and some have used problem-solving techniques in a structured way. Some of the best known include the foot patrol program in Flint, Michigan (Trojanowicz & Bucqueroux, 1990), and community policing experiments in Madison, Wisconsin (Goldstein, 1990c), Edmonton, Canada (Koller, 1990), and in Houston and Newark (Pate et al., 1986); New York City's Community Patrol Officer Program (CPOP) (Farrell, 1988); and Baltimore County, Maryland's, Citizen Oriented Police Enforcement (COPE) program, which was created to address problems that contributed to fear of crime (Cordner, 1985).

Further, in just the past two years since Goldstein's comprehensive work on problem-oriented policing was published (Goldstein, 1990c), the U.S. Department of Justice has greatly increased its commitment to community-oriented policing. Eight large and medium-sized cities are currently implementing programs with funding from the Bureau of Justice Assistance (BJA) under its Innovative Neighborhood-Oriented Policing (INOP) program, and four rural sites will soon develop demonstration projects under a rural INOP initiative. The BJA-sponsored "Weed and Seed" effort, which includes a strong emphasis on community policing, will soon involve 19 sites in implementing a comprehensive attack on violent crime and drug trafficking. There are an even greater number of law enforcement agencies that have made public commitments to implement a community policing approach without federal funding.

Some of these departments are still contemplating the best ways to put the community policing philosophy into operation. Others, such as Portland, Oregon, have developed detailed, time-phased plans. Still others have implemented special projects, but have not yet made the types of organizational changes needed to support a major shift to community policing. A few departments have gained considerable experience in implementing the concept department-wide. The Newport News, Virginia, Police Department is one of the first police agencies in the country to attempt this (Eck & Spelman,

1987). New York City's community-oriented approach includes eventually integrating CPOP into all precincts.

The Baltimore County, Maryland, Police Department in 1987 introduced problem solving to 350 patrol officers in one patrol area. The department viewed this experiment as a step toward department-wide problem solving (Webster et al., 1989). The Institute for Law and Justice (ILJ) and the Police Executive Research Forum (PERF) evaluated the Baltimore County experiment, making many site visits to observe and discuss the problem-solving process. Thus, this paper draws many of its examples from Baltimore County.

Although the literature contains many accounts of crimes and problems solved through community policing efforts, few, if any, comprehensive community policing efforts have been rigorously evaluated. Many must simply stand the test of time before a meaningful impact evaluation is possible. Nevertheless, patrol officers throughout the country are now being called upon to bear significant responsibilities for identifying, analyzing, and solving community problems. To have any chance at success, they must have meaningful training, strong leadership, and systems throughout the department that support their efforts to identify and solve problems when they are not answering calls.

Issues Involved in Identifying Problems

Identifying problems can be a stumbling block for several reasons. Some of the obstacles relate to officer attitudes about change in general and about community policing in particular. Other difficulties relate to the department's overall readiness to support community policing.

Officer Attitudes

Many officers, including supervisors, may see community policing as yet another program—a fad that will come and go if they can just wait it out. In addition, community policing generally calls for a new emphasis on disorder problems such as juveniles hanging out, or on environmental conditions that facilitate crime (e.g., abandoned buildings). Involvement in projects that deal with these issues may conflict with many officers' views of themselves as crime-busters.

Of course, patrol officers are not the only police employees who may resist change. Personnel who prepare budgets, purchase equipment and supplies, or perform crime analysis, for example, may hold back the support needed for successful problem solving. In short, a shift to community policing is subject to all the considerations inherent in making any major change in a police organization (Sparrow, 1988).

A survey of Baltimore County officers in the experimental patrol area revealed that before the project began, about 25 percent agreed with problem solving and community policing objectives, half were neutral, and 25 percent were opposed. An earlier study compared the attitudes of Baltimore County COPE officers with a control group of officers who had routine patrol duties. The conclusion was that officers implementing community-oriented strategies tend to have more job satisfaction, more positive attitudes toward the community, and a broader view of the police role (Hayeslip & Cordner, 1987).

It is typical, and perhaps easier, for departments to begin community policing with individual programs rather than to introduce the concept department-wide (Brown, 1989). While it makes sense to test a new approach with a limited program, it is also important to foster an understanding of that program among officers in the field. This was demonstrated in Baltimore County, where some commanders were concerned that officers would resist problem solving because it was closely associated with COPE. There was a negative perception of COPE among many patrol officers and supervisors. COPE officers did not respond to calls, provide backups, or work rotating shifts, factors that contributed to officers' low opinion of COPE. Poor communication between COPE and regular patrol was also a problem. Efforts were made to improve communication during the patrol experiment by involving COPE officers in training sessions.

Department Preparation and Support

Other difficulties with problem identification relate to the department's preparation for community policing. This includes ensuring that officers have enough time for problem solving. Time may not be an issue for special squads in which officers have limited call-handling responsibilities and a clear problem-solving mission. Well-staffed departments in low crime areas may also find that there is sufficient patrol down time that can be used for problem solving. But time is an issue for department-wide problem solving in a busy department that is still at the mercy of 911.

Officers who spend more than 40 percent of their available time answering calls are not likely to have the blocks of time needed for problem solving or, for that matter, for many other types of directed patrol activities.[1] This can be expected to affect officers' willingness (although not their ability) to identify problems, since they may believe they will not have enough time to follow up.

Patrol supervisors must assume responsibility for freeing up as much time as possible for problem solving. However, other department systems, resources, and policies must be in place if they are to do this. For example, a review of the department's differential police response (DPR) policies may reveal several types of calls that could be handled by a telephone report unit or some other means. Full use of all available DPR options can free up additional time for problem solving, or at least enable officers to gain more control of their work day (McEwen et al., 1986). Similarly, the department may need to use other methods (e.g., civilian police aides) to reduce officer time spent on certain types of calls, such as minor traffic accidents.

In addition, many patrol supervisors are not accustomed to soliciting information about community problems from patrol officers. The Baltimore County study suggested that few officers would identify problems unless shift supervisors provided leadership and guidance. Officers also needed clear procedures for taking action once problems were identified. Details like forms, resource checklists, and monitoring procedures need to be in place. In addition, crime analysts will need the capability—computer software and hardware, experience, training, and time to handle officers' special requests.

An absence of rewards for problem solving may also inhibit problem identification. If evaluations and pay increases still depend exclusively on traditional performance measures (e.g., number of arrests, traffic tickets issued), officers without a great deal of internal motivation are likely to hold their participation in problem solving to a minimum.

In short, administrators may expect only a limited amount of problem solving to occur by decree. The department must provide the leadership and make the organizational changes needed to support it. In the recent Baltimore County experiment, it appeared that leadership by precinct commanders and shift lieutenants was especially important to successful problem solving. A recent report on the Newport News experience also stresses the significant role that mid-level managers and first-line supervisors play in motivating officers to identify and work on problems (Mitchell, 1990).

Defining Problems: The First Step

Training in problem identification often begins with the following working definition of a problem: *a group of incidents that are similar in one or more ways and are of concern to the police and the public.* Central to this definition is that public concern is paramount (Goldstein, 1979). The problem must be of some concern to a portion of the public, and not just a concern of the police. Thus, the definition eliminates issues that are strictly police administrative matters (e.g., the need for daily briefings). It also eliminates community concerns for which the police clearly do not have responsibility (e.g., the cost of school lunches).

However, if the public *expects* the police to be involved, then the problem becomes a police matter and a candidate for the problem-solving approach. The definition, therefore, does allow inclusion of many community problems that in the past technically have not been the responsibility of the police. These problems are appropriate for police action because they contribute to a crime, disorder, or fear of crime problem, or simply because the public believes the police ought to do something.

For example, a run-down building provides a haven for drug trafficking. Police have observed the activity and citizens have complained about it. A traditional police response might include arresting users and dealers and ordering intensified patrols in the area. If the drug activity persists despite these efforts, it may well be time to consider why. Part of the solution may lie in having the building either fixed up or condemned. The question then arises: is this a police responsibility?

The police are not general contractors, nor do they have the power to condemn buildings. But the community-oriented, problem-oriented view is that the police can, and probably should, inspire the appropriate agencies, groups, or individuals to act. In this instance, action may be required of the health department, zoning department, citizen groups, a private property owner, the housing authority, or some combination of these entities.

Similarly, a lack of sports programs may contribute to a problem with teenagers loitering, or poor lighting may contribute to muggings at an apartment parking lot. While it may not be appropriate for police to organize a team or install new street lights, it would be appropriate for them to pursue these options with others who have a stake in solving the problem.

Ways To Identify Problems

When the Baltimore County experiment began, officers used three main sources of information to identify problems: their own observations, citizen complaints, and police department data. Other methods were used to clarify the scope of these problems (and could also have been used initially to identify problems). These included door-to-door neighborhood surveys, officer participation at community meetings, and consultations with other agencies and police department units. Problem solving in Newport News also relied heavily on these methods (Eck & Spelman, 1987). As a department gains more experience with problem solving, and as crime analysis capabilities improve, many more information sources can be developed. This section discusses a range of options. Some require a considerable expenditure for computer software, data entry, and data analysis. Others are as simple as a conversation over a cup of coffee.

Officer Observation and Experience

One of the easiest and best ways to learn of problems is to listen to patrol officers recount their experiences and observations. Often, they have a greater stake and interest in problems than police officials further removed from the street.

Most officers have responded to, or know about, repeat domestic calls to particular addresses, repeat false alarm calls to commercial establishments, street corners overtaken by drug activity, bars where violence regularly occurs, and many other recurring problems.

Officers on routine patrol can also identify opportunities to prevent crime or accidents. For example, an officer may notice that an elementary school needs a crossing guard, or that political campaign signs are blocking the view at an intersection. Also important are officers' observations of neighborhood deterioration. Graffiti, trash, vandalism, junk cars, and the like can all be signs that a public place is no longer under public control (Wilson & Kelling, 1989).

Officers on foot patrol and officers assigned to neighborhood police offices have additional opportunities to observe neighborhood conditions and activities. New York City CPOP officers, for example, are required to conduct foot patrol of some part of their beats each day, covering the entire beat at least twice a week. They are also expected to talk to residents and merchants, attend community meetings, and make personal observations (Farrell, 1988).

The problem identification task challenges the department to capture officers' information about crime and community problems so that it can be brought to the attention of supervisors and acted upon. The information can be harnessed in a number of ways. Officers may use a special form to report problems for further consideration. A focus group of patrol officers may brainstorm a list of problems, using the general definition noted earlier. An alternative is to form a problem identification task group with representatives from patrol, investigations, crime analysis, crime prevention, community relations, and other units. This type of multi-disciplinary group was used to launch problem solving in Newport News (Eck & Spelman, 1987).

Citizen Complaints

Ideally, problem identification in a community policing department is a proactive, "bottom up" process in which officers, by virtue of their close contact with residents, are able to bring community concerns to the department's attention. Realistically, citizens and elected officials often bring problems directly to the attention of the chief of police, precinct captain, or other command staff. Complaints may be received in the form of phone calls, letters, or comments at public meetings. Many of these problems can be appropriately delegated to patrol officers for follow-up using the problem-solving process.

In Oakland, California, the police department attempted to encourage citizens in the central district to report problems through the RID card program (Report Incidents Directly). The police, private developers, and city officials recognized that "soft crime" was a problem that contributed to fear and discouraged people from living, working, and patronizing businesses in the central district. Soft crime involved many behaviors that people felt threatened their safety, but which received low priority when reported to 911. Included were verbal and physical harassment, panhandling, drug sales, public intoxication, loitering, littering, bizarre and frightening behavior, soliciting, and similar matters.

Many of these incidents were either not reported, or were reported to private security personnel who had no mechanism for passing the information along to the police. The RID cards were intended to give complaints about soft crime higher priority. They took the form of postcard-sized incident reports and were distributed by officers, private security guards, and building managers. Citizens could mail the cards directly to the central district section or hand them to any Oakland police officer or uniformed private guard. Fliers encouraged use of the cards, stating that they were important for identifying crime patterns and potential suspects, and that they would be used to deploy officers and assist investigators.

After the initial promotion, the use of the cards declined, but they appear to have been valuable at least in the short run. They helped focus officers' attention on looking into soft crime issues, and they informed supervisors of the kinds of problems that residents and users of the central district considered important (Reiss, 1985).

Crime Analysis

Crime analysis has the potential to become increasingly useful to police engaged in problem solving. The value of crime analysis will depend, of course, on many factors, including the following:

- Extent and quality of data captured (garbage in, garbage out);
- Availability of software programs to sort and cross-reference data;
- Capacity to produce reports that describe crimes and disorder at the beat or neighborhood level, or by specific addresses;
- Ability to present data in useful formats; and
- Accessibility of data to patrol officers.

Finally, the value of crime analysis to problem solving will depend on the time crime analysts are allotted to respond to individual officer requests and their ability to become problem analysts. This can mean devising new ways to collect and analyze information on disorder problems, and integrating information from concerned citizens with data from official police records.

The techniques discussed in this section include using various police reports to identify problems; using computer-assisted dispatch data to identify hot spots through repeat call analysis; and generating graphs and maps from crime data and information provided by citizen groups.

Police Reports

Police offense reports can be analyzed for suspect characteristics, MOs, victim characteristics, and many other factors. Offense reports are also a potential source of information about high-crime areas and addresses, since they capture exact descriptions of locations. However, there are considerable limitations to their use for this purpose.

First, they may not be programmed to be sorted by address. Second, the picture they present of high crime and disturbance locations will be incomplete, since police do not file offense reports for all crimes and activities reported to them. In a typical police department, patrol officers may write official reports on only about 25 to 30 percent of calls to which they respond.

Third, there may be a considerable lag between the time the officer files a report and the time data entry and analysis are complete. Departments with precinct-based crime analysts generally have an advantage over agencies that rely solely on a centralized crime analysis unit for all data analysis. The precinct analyst usually answers to the precinct commander and has an investment in meeting the needs of the officers assigned there. For example, the precinct analyst may develop special databases on activities of interest using offense reports (e.g., reported garage burglaries by time of day, day of week, patrol beat, and address).

Officers may also conduct manual searches of offense reports, field contact cards, and other records to uncover problems. In Baltimore County, for example, each precinct maintained a notebook of offense reports filed from that precinct. Two officers scanned the reports and found several on runaways from a girls home. Since various officers had responded from various shifts and had not talked about the situation, no one was aware that there was a pattern. Further investigation revealed frequent delays of more than 24 hours between the time a girl was noticed missing and the time the police were called. A problem-solving project was undertaken, resulting in more timely reporting and security improvements at the girls home.

Call for Service Analysis

With the advent of computer-assisted dispatch (CAD) systems, a more reliable source of data on crime and disorder has become available. Call for service data does have limitations, but it is more complete than offense reports, providing the most extensive account available of what the public tells the police about crime. The data captured by CAD systems can be sorted to reveal "hot spots" of crime and disturbances—specific locations from which an unusual number of calls to the police are made (Sherman et al., 1989).

One study on hot spots recently analyzed nearly 324,000 calls for service for a one-year period over all 115,000 addresses and intersections in Minneapolis. The results showed relatively few hot spots accounting for the majority of calls to the police:

- 50 percent of all calls came from 3 percent of places;

- All robbery calls came from 2.2 percent of places;

- All rape calls came from 1.2 percent of places; and

- All auto thefts came from 2.7 percent of places (Sherman et al., 1989).

Using CAD runs for repeat call analysis requires an understanding of the CAD system's limitations. These may vary from department to department, but basic limitations include the following:

- Data may include calls made in error or as intentional lies;

- One event may generate more than one call;

- Information from police at the scene may be recorded as a separate call, rather than replacing the earlier call;

- There is often a considerable lag between the time an event occurs and the time the call is made;

- Some systems may allow entry of the caller's address and the address to which police respond, but not the actual location of the event;

- Hospitals and other public locations (e.g., phone booth in a public housing complex) may account for overreporting; the locations where those crimes occurred will be undercounted; and

- Misspellings, omissions, and variations in the way place names are entered (e.g., Joe E.'s Tavern and Joey's Tavern) will result in undercounting crime at a location.

Many departments have the capability to use CAD data for repeat call analysis. The repeat call locations identified in this way can become targets of directed patrol efforts, including problem solving.

For example, early in the Baltimore County study, the test precincts received printouts of the top 25 call for service areas to review for problem-solving assignments. In a separate effort, the Baltimore County domestic assault unit developed its own list of repeat call locations. After the Minneapolis study noted earlier, the police department formed a five-officer unit to address crime problems at the most crime-ridden locations. In Houston, the police and Hispanic citizens were concerned about violence at cantinas. Through repeat call analysis, police learned that only 3 percent of the cantinas in the city were responsible for 40 percent of the violence. The data narrowed the scope of the problem and enabled a special liquor control squad to better target its efforts (Spelman, 1988).

Repeat alarm calls are another example of how CAD data can be used to support patrol officer problem solving. In fact, when the Baltimore County experiment began, some commanders preferred that officers start with alarm projects. There were several reasons for this. Data documenting repeat alarm calls by address were readily available. Commanders anticipated that solving alarm problems would be relatively simple, and that the benefits compared to the investment of time would be significant.

As in many jurisdictions, alarms were priority calls requiring an immediate response by two officers. At least 90 percent of commercial alarm calls were false alarms, generated by faulty equipment or employee error. Officers used CAD printouts to identify repeat alarm addresses; or, when they had already identified these addresses from their own experience, they requested the CAD printouts to use in their follow-up discussions with merchants. Few alarm problems took more than two hours of any officer's time to resolve, and all merchants contacted either eliminated or greatly reduced the number of false alarm calls from their establishments.

Crime Mapping

Traditional pin maps can aid police work by graphically representing crime locations; but with a high volume of crimes, they are too time-consuming to put together and update. Computer-generated crime maps can now display more information, do it more quickly, and present it in an easy-to-read format.

One sophisticated crime analysis and mapping system was developed by the Illinois Criminal Justice Information Authority under a grant from the Bureau of Justice Statistics. It involves a group of computer programs and analytical methods for detecting community crime patterns, and uses time as well as geographic data. Areas ranging from a city block to an entire town can be examined, and spot maps can be produced seconds after an incident has been entered into the computer (Illinois Criminal Justice Information Authority, 1987).

Another system developed in the Chicago Police Department's 25th district generates graphs, maps, and reports using crime data from both police and citizens. The Microcomputer Assisted Patrol Analysis and Deployment System (MAPADS) was funded by the National Institute of Justice and developed by the Chicago Police Department, University of Illinois, Northwestern University, the Chicago Alliance for Neighborhood Safety (CANS), and Apple Computer, Inc.

Input from citizens is obtained through CANS, a nonprofit organization comprised of many local community groups. CANS collects two types of data from citizens. The first is data on "incivilities" and quality of life concerns that do not usually require police intervention (e.g., youth loitering, abandoned buildings, noisy parties). The second is data on crime concerns about which police often lack good intelligence (e.g., gang and narcotics activity). One of the specific purposes of MAPADS is to "determine target areas for community based/problem oriented policing" (Casey & Muslik, 1988).

Community Groups

Problem solving involves soliciting information from community groups and involving citizens in solving their own problems. Both police and scholars concerned with community organizations are still trying to answer two key questions: How can local organizations be encouraged to adopt a crime-fighting agenda; and how can new anticrime groups be developed in areas that have none? (Skogan, 1989).

One obvious source of information about problems is Neighborhood Watch. However, there are some limitations on this source. Considerable evidence suggests that anticrime groups like Neighborhood Watch are most likely to flourish in middle-class communities with moderate crime problems. In affluent and low-crime areas, citizens see little reason to organize in this way. At the other extreme, fear and distrust among neighbors in crime-ridden neighborhoods may paralyze collective action.

There are many accounts in the community policing literature of officers working closely with other types of citizen groups. These include civic associations, tenant groups in private apartment complexes and public housing areas, business organizations, parent-teacher organizations, churches, and issue-oriented advocacy groups such as Mothers Against Drunk Driving (MADD).

In Dallas, Operation CLEAN (Community and Law Enforcement Against Narcotics) provides one example of how police, public and private agencies, clergy, and community groups can combine efforts to control drug problems. Based on police information and citizen complaints of high-profile drug trafficking, an area as small as one block is targeted. Next, narcotics officers are assigned to the area for about 10 days. A police sweep is then made to provide immediate relief, followed by two weeks of 24-hour, intensified patrol. During the next six weeks, other city agencies begin rehabilitation, code enforcement, and demolition of unsalvageable properties.

Finally, a long-range rehabilitation process begins. This has involved such efforts as calling on ministerial alliances to assist agencies and counsel residents, obtaining corporate sponsors to "adopt a block," pursuing park department funds for after-school programs in a park, and moving church-donated houses into neighborhoods (Vines, 1989).

There are several cautions to keep in mind when working with community groups to identify problems. First, the group's priorities may not be those of the neighborhood as a whole. Second, the group's members are not necessarily representative of all those who would be affected by proposed solutions. Third, police who encourage input from citizens must be careful not to raise expectations that the problems identified will be solved immediately.

Fourth, information provided at citizen group meetings—like a report from a single citizen or an informant—usually needs to be expanded or corroborated. Much of this work may be done during the analysis phase of the problem-solving process. However, some initial information gathering is advisable to determine the scope of the problem. Police may do this by observing problem locations at various times of day and days of the week; using various types of traditional investigative techniques; holding a special neighborhood meeting on the situation; or conducting a survey.

Finally, a department's commitment to community policing suggests that a greater number of patrol officers—not just crime prevention or community relations specialists—will be expected to participate in community meetings. Police may also organize their own ad hoc groups around a particular crime problem. The group may disband when the problem is resolved, or it may continue to bring concerns to police attention. Police departments need to ensure that officers who organize or participate in community meetings are well prepared. Officers may benefit from training to develop skills in group process and facilitation. Experienced community relations, public information, or crime prevention officers may be able to assist, either by providing in-service training sessions, or in less formal ways. For example, in Baltimore County, two officers' efforts to restore an abandoned playground culminated in their having to present their proposal to a recreation department committee. To sharpen their oral presentation, the officers consulted with the precinct's administrative sergeant, who had many years' experience speaking before similar groups.

Surveys

There are a number of ways in which officers may conduct surveys to identify or clarify problems. For example, an officer may canvass all the business proprietors in a strip shopping center on his or her beat. The community policing approach encourages this type of face-to-face, proactive contact with merchants.

A variation on this theme occurred during the Baltimore County experiment. One officer was charged with telephoning businesses to update the department's after-hours business contact cards. Although he did not conduct a formal survey, he used this task to also inquire about problems the owners might want to bring to police attention.

On a somewhat larger scale, a team of officers may survey residents of a housing complex or neighborhood known to have particular crime problems. The survey could be of value in determining residents' priority concerns, gaining specific information about trouble spots, and learning more about residents' expectations of police. The process may also help officers identify allies and community leaders who can aid in solving the problems identified.[2] Residents may be more likely to contact the police about future problems when officers leave their cards and encourage residents to call them directly. A survey can also present a public relations opportunity for the department when officers inform citizens of the agency's new community policing objectives.

Another approach to the survey process involves developing a beat pro-file. In Tempe, Arizona, a special community policing squad began by con-ducting a detailed profile of a target beat. Surveys conducted by squad mem-bers involved both door-to-door surveys of residents and businesses and detailed observations of the environment. A survey instrument was developed and pilot tested, and all survey team members were trained and given a uni-form protocol to follow. The survey instrument included questions about socio-demographic characteristics of residents, observed crime and drug prob-lems, fear of crime, perception of city and police services, willingness to par-ticipate in and support community policing objectives, and other information.

Survey team members also recorded information about the surround-ings—condition of buildings, homes, streets, and yards; presence of aban-doned vehicles; possible zoning and other code violations; and existence of such problems as graffiti, trash, loiterers, gang members, and other signs of disorder. All the information obtained from the surveys and observation reports is being entered into a microcomputer and will be analyzed for trends and patterns. The information will also provide evaluators with "before" data needed to assess the impact of the Tempe community policing project.[3]

As noted earlier, officer surveys can also be conducted to clarify the scope of known problems. For example, in Baltimore County, a business pro-prietor called police about a shoplifting problem. By conducting a brief sur-vey of other merchants in the shopping center, police learned that none of the other businesses had this problem. The solution, therefore, was a simple one that involved advising a single merchant on how to improve security.

In another Baltimore County project, a resident frequently called police about noisy customers at an all-night, self-service car wash. Officers con-ducted a door-to-door survey of other residents adjacent to the business. They learned that the vast majority were also disturbed by the situation. The solution involved several neighbors meeting with police, the business owner, zoning personnel, and others to negotiate construction of a sound barrier.

Finally, in connection with a department-wide shift to community polic-ing, administrators may consider conducting a large-scale community survey to identify specific problems. This effort would differ from surveys that focus on police performance, citizen attitudes about the police, or victimization. A starting point might be to review the work done by the Lansing, Michigan, Police Department in cooperation with the National Neighborhood Foot Patrol Center. The Lansing Police Department Community Survey asks citi-zens to prioritize police services, functions, and responses to crime (Tro-janowicz et al., 1987). The survey has a few drawbacks, however. It is a writ-ten survey that requires a fairly high reading level, and it does not ask about specific concerns. A survey that gathered more specific information about problems could prove useful in developing responsive community policing policies and programs (Patterson & Grant, 1988).

Other Information Sources

There is probably no special unit in a department that could not assist patrol officers to some degree with problem identification. The difficulty lies in tapping into this information. In small departments, the process for doing so may be quite informal. Larger agencies may want to consider developing processes, forms, and referral guidelines. Special units and divisions that contributed to problem identification in Baltimore County and Newport News included the office of the chief, crime analysis, crime prevention, community relations, detectives, vice/narcotics, communications and dispatch, and others.

Television, newspaper, and other media reports can be another source of information about community problems, and can help police identify organizations and individuals who may be allies in efforts to solve them. Letters to the editor, editorials, and op-ed columns should not be overlooked, and media coverage of national or regional events can suggest problems that may be of local concern as well. Some departments may find it useful to maintain a clippings file, which can be used to suggest possible problem-solving projects. Maintaining such a file would be an appropriate task for department volunteers.

In summary, information sources about community problems are virtually unlimited for officers with initiative, creativity, and a commitment to the problem-solving approach. Conducting a formal survey may not be possible for all officers, but most can take advantage of a coffee break to ask a convenience store manager about problems, or stop and talk for a minute with a playground supervisor. In Tempe, some members of the community policing squad have begun to have lunch with schoolteachers on a regular basis. Simply by looking around an elementary school cafeteria, they saw that many new ethnic groups were represented, an observation that may help them anticipate changes in the community. As part of problem-solving training in Baltimore County, COPE officers assisted in preparing a checklist of resources that officers might use to gain information about problems. Such a list might include other law enforcement agencies; schools; churches and church councils; elected officials and other community leaders; local government agencies; nonprofit human service youth and recreation programs; business groups; local service clubs; and many others.

Types of Problems Appropriate for Patrol Problem Solving

There does not appear to be any inherent limit on the types of problems patrol officers can work on successfully. If the problem is identified as being of concern to the community and the police, then it is legitimate to have a patrol officer address the problem (or in some instances, bring it to the attention of a special unit).

Officers can be expected to identify both crime and disorder problems. In Baltimore County, there was an emphasis on disorder problems, perhaps because problem solving was closely linked to community policing. To many of the officers and supervisors interviewed, community policing meant focusing on non-crime concerns. The training for patrol officers also placed considerable emphasis on building links with other agencies, residents, and business people. The applicability of problem solving to major crime problems was not as obvious, and was not emphasized by administrators or supervisors. In addition, Baltimore County has many special units designed to address crime problems.

If disorder and other quality-of-life problems are the most frequent types of problems in an area, and citizens are more concerned about them, then an emphasis on these problems seems well placed. However, this would not preclude applying a problem-solving approach to major crime problems. The list that follows demonstrates the diversity of problems identified and addressed in several jurisdictions.

Examples of Crime and Disturbance Problems

Some of the problems identified in Baltimore County included:

- A series of burglaries from trailers at a construction site;

- Drug activity, drinking, and disorderly conduct at a community park;

- Auto thefts at a shopping plaza;

- Suspected drug activity at a private residence;

- Thefts from autos at a shopping mall;

- Large groups of young people drinking and trespassing at a quarry;

- Juveniles loitering at a shopping center;

- Juveniles loitering near a bar;

- Adults drinking in public outside a tavern;

- Vagrants panhandling at a shopping center;

- Problems with false and faulty alarms at commercial addresses;

- Conflicts within families; and

- Parking and traffic problems.

Early problem-solving projects in Newport News, Virginia, included the following:

- Street prostitution and related robberies in a downtown neighborhood;

- Thefts from autos at a parking lot used by employees of a shipbuilding company;

- A high rate of burglaries at a run-down apartment complex; and

- Repeat domestic assault calls to certain addresses.

In a project conducted by PERF for the Bureau of Justice Assistance, five police departments agreed to apply the problem-solving approach to drug crimes. The following are typical of the drug-related problems identified:

- Abandoned cars on public housing property created an eyesore and were used to stash drugs (Tampa);

- Repeat calls over a period of years involved drugs and violence at a private residence (San Diego);

- The absentee owner of a pool hall allowed drug-related activity and illegal gambling on the premises (San Diego);

- Poor outdoor lighting at a public housing complex facilitated street drug sales (Tampa);

- Juveniles sold drugs at a public housing complex (Tulsa); and

- Repeat thefts from autos by a crack addict (Philadelphia) (Weisel, 1990).

As the list above suggests, few if any crime or disorder problems would be categorically inappropriate for patrol problem solving. Of course, some problems initially identified may need to be screened out for a variety of reasons. For example, the department may be addressing a problem at the administrative level, a special unit may be assigned exclusive responsibility for a particular type of problem, or a reported problem cannot be corroborated. But the experience of many departments suggests that officers, given enough support from the department, can successfully tackle problems ranging from double parking to homicide prevention.

Summary

Community policing has been promoted as both a new approach to police work, and as a return to the good old days when officers knew the people they served. Either way, it involves improving a department's responsiveness to the law enforcement needs of a diverse community. It also involves listening more carefully to how the community defines those needs.

The obvious first step in this process is identifying crime and disorder problems that are of mutual concern to both the police and some portion of the public. On the surface, identifying problems should be an easy task for police. But for many officers, major problem means major crime. Indeed, much of their training involves preparing for the dangerous but relatively rare incident. Understandably, they may distrust the department's community policing approach, with its new emphasis on such citizen concerns as "incivilities" and signs of neighborhood decline.

Police departments vary in the resources they can provide to support problem identification. Large departments like Chicago have developed sophisticated computer-aided crime mapping systems; other departments may work with a university to analyze large call-for-service databases. Yet many sources of information about problems exist in even the smallest departments—officer knowledge and observation, citizen complaints, police reports and call data, surveys, information from community groups, and many others.

In addition to information sources, officers must have sufficient blocks of time to identify and work on problems. Before department-wide community policing can succeed, the agency will need to evaluate whether it is doing all it can to relieve officers of duties that do not require sworn authority. But the problem-solving experiences in Baltimore County and Newport News suggest that leadership—from the top, of course, but particularly at the precinct commander and supervisory levels—is even more important than time for ensuring that officers become actively involved in identifying and solving community problems.

Well-developed efforts to strengthen the police-community partnership must adapt and employ some type of systematic way to identify, analyze, and resolve problems. Comprehensive evaluations of community policing strategies—however necessary they may be—are expensive and lengthy propositions. There are other ways in which researchers might use their expertise to aid and shed light on what appears to qualify as a nationwide movement toward community policing. This article summarizes a range of methods that police can use to identify problems. There is much that remains to be discovered and communicated about the pros and cons of these methods and how to make them more effective.

Community surveys, for example, are of interest to many police agencies, yet they can be misused as well as useful. Experiences with crime mapping need to be explored more fully. The difficulties involved in using call-for-service data for identifying problems or in obtaining useful information from community groups have only been hinted at here. Exploring these and other problem identification methods in-depth could be of tremendous value to the field as police departments attempt to develop new ways of thinking about crime and community problems.

Notes

1   Recent patrol resource allocation studies by ILJ have concluded that departments committed to community policing should set a goal of having officers spend about 35 to 40 percent of their time on community policing activities, including problem solving. This would allow for sufficient blocks of time to perform meaningful tasks, and would leave about one-third of patrol time for responding to calls and another third for other duties (court appearances, roll call, training, meals, etc.).

2   For an example of this type of survey process, see William H. Lindsey and Bruce Quint, *The Oasis Technique*, Fort Lauderdale, Florida, Florida Atlantic University/Florida International University Joint Center for Environmental and Urban Problems, 1986.

3   ILJ is currently studying the Tempe community policing project for the U.S. Department of Justice, Bureau of Justice Assistance.

References

Bayley, D. (1991). "The Best Defense." *Fresh Perspectives*. Washington, DC: Police Executive Research Forum.

Brown, L. (1989). "Community Policing: A Practical Guide for Police Officials." *Police Chief*. Arlington, VA: International Association of Chiefs of Police (August).

Casey, M. and M. Buslik (1988). *Computerized Decision Support: Innovative Policing in Chicago*. Chicago, IL: Police Department (September).

Cordner, G. (1985). *The Baltimore County Citizen Oriented Police Enforcement (COPE) Project: Final Evaluation*. Baltimore County, MD: Police Department.

Eck, J. and W. Spelman (1987). *Problem-Solving: Problem-Oriented Policing in Newport News*. Washington, DC: National Institute of Justice.

Farrell, M. (1988). "The Development of the Community Patrol Officer Program: Community-Oriented Policing in the New York City Police Department." In J. Greene and S. Mastrofski (eds.), *Community Policing: Rhetoric or Reality?* New York: Praeger Publishers.

Goldstein, H. (1990a). "Remarks." Police Executive Research Forum National Conference on Problem Oriented Policing. San Diego, CA (November).

Goldstein, H. (1990b). "Does Community Policing Work?" *The New York Times*, December 20:E11.

Goldstein, H. (1990c). *Problem-Oriented Policing*. New York: McGraw-Hill, Inc.

Goldstein, H. (1979). "Improving Policing: A Problem-Oriented Approach." *Crime and Delinquency*, 25.

Hayeslip, D. and G. Cordner (1987). "The Effects of Community-Oriented Patrol on Police Officer Attitudes." *American Journal of Police*, 6(1).

Illinois Criminal Justice Information Authority (1987). "Spatial and Temporal Analysis of Crime." *Research Bulletin*, (April).

Koller, K. (1990). *Working the Beat*. Edmonton, Canada: Edmonton Police Service.

McEwen, J. et al. (1991). *1990 National Assessment Survey of Criminal Justice Agencies: Final Report*. Washington, DC: National Institute of Justice.

McEwen, J. et al. (1986). *Evaluation of the Differential Police Response Field Test*. Washington, DC: National Institute of Justice.

Mitchell, W. (1990). "Problem-Oriented Policing and Drug Enforcement in Newport News." *Public Management*. Washington, DC: International City Managers Association (July).

Montgomery County Police, Community Policing Project (1990). *An Overview of Community Policing*. Montgomery County, MD: Police Department.

New York City Police Department and Vera Institute of Justice, (1988). *The Community Patrol Officer Program Problem-Solving Guide*. New York: Police Department (September).

Pate, A. (1986). *Reducing Fear of Crime in Houston and Newark: A Summary Report*. Washington, DC: The Police Foundation.

Patterson, R., Jr. and N. Grant (1988). "Community Mapping: Rationale and Considerations for Implementation." *Journal of Police Science and Administration*, 16(2).

Portland Police Bureau (1990). *Community Policing Transition Plan*. Portland, OR: Police Bureau.

Reiss, A. (1985). *Policing a City's Central District: The Oakland Story*. Washington, DC: National Institute of Justice.

Seattle Police Department, Planning Section (1990). *Community Policing in Seattle: A Descriptive Study of the South Seattle Crime Reduction Project*. Seattle, WA: Police Department.

Sherman, L. (1989). "Hot Spots of Predatory Crime: Routine Activities and the Criminology of Place." *Criminology*, 27(1).

Skogan, W. (1989). "Communities, Crime, and Neighborhood Organization." *Crime and Delinquency*, 35(3).

Sparrow, M. (1988). "Implementing Community Policing." *Perspectives on Policing*. Washington, DC: National Institute of Justice and the John F. Kennedy School of Government, Harvard University.

Spelman, W. (1988). *Beyond Bean Counting: New Approaches for Managing Crime Data*. Washington, DC: Police Executive Research Forum.

Tempe Police Department (1991). *Master Plan for Community Policing*. Tempe, AZ: Police Department.

Trojanowicz, R. (1987). *Community Policing: Community Input into Police Policy-Making*. East Lansing, MI: National Neighborhood Foot Patrol Center.

Trojanowicz, R. and B. Bucqueroux (1990). *Community Policing: A Contemporary Perspective*. Cincinnati, OH: Anderson Publishing Co.

Vines, M. (1989). "City of Dallas Implements Operation CLEAN." *NCTAP News*. Alexandria, VA: Institute for Law and Justice, 3(2): August.

Webster, B. (1989). *Evaluation of Community Crime/Problem Resolution Through Police Directed Patrol*. Final report to the National Institute of Justice.

Weisel, D. (1990). *Tackling Drug Problems in Public Housing: A Guide for Police*. Washington, DC: Police Executive Research Forum.

Wilson, J. and G. Kelling (1989). "Making Neighborhoods Safe." *Atlantic Monthly* (February).

Wilson, J. and G. Kelling (1982). "The Police and Neighborhood Safety: Broken Windows." *Atlantic Monthly* (March).

CHAPTER 9
Community Policing and Drugs

*The wrong that men do can be traced to
those who mistaught them.*

—Sophocles

Since the 1960s, America has been coping with a drug problem. Although drugs have always been present in some form or another, it was not until the 1960s that they were the focus of attention to large segments of our society. This period also witnessed the public use of drugs by those who would flaunt drugs to mainstream society. Drugs remain a problem that concerns many Americans and constantly remains at the forefront of American politics and governmental policymaking. Many see drugs as a stimulant for crime, especially violent crime, while others are concerned with their devastating affects on people, especially family members. The drug problem has so occupied attention that several American presidents, beginning with President Nixon, have declared war on drugs. Talk of war has helped to mobilize support and stir peoples' emotions. It should be noted, however, that we have never had a war against drugs. Although stated as such, our drug wars actually have been aimed at people, and to this end, our war has had no limits. In many instances, it has been a no holds barred, all out assault on those who are associated with drugs or perceived to be associated with drugs.

The war on drugs is cloaked in imagery. In the classic sense, it is good versus evil. There are good people within our society who are being corrupted or harmed by evil drug dealers. The drug war is shrouded in moralism with a disgust, disdain, and fear of drugs, their users, and their sellers (Christie, 1994). The drugs problem causes society to paint with a broad moral brush. Our condemnations and attacks focus on broad categories of persons, sometimes irrespective of the nature or extent of their involvement in the drug problem (Kappeler, 1998). Subsequently, our fears, concerns, and reactions to drugs result in substantial levels of covert as well as overt racism (Lusane, 1990; Kappeler, Blumberg & Potter, 1996; Kappeler, 1998). The drug problem is used by politicians to further disenfranchise the poor and minority groups. Drugs drive a wedge between the poor and other classes within our society. From this perspective, there has been a substantial measure of immorality inherent to our moral drug war.

This moral drug war has placed the police in the middle of a quagmire. On the one hand, drugs have a destructive influence on our society. Drugs can disrupt and destroy people's lives. They tear at the very fiber of the American family. Drugs are associated with crime although the amount of crime as a result of drugs most likely is far less than most predict (McBride & McCoy, 1993). Consequently, drugs are a problem that require an effective police response. On the other hand, community policing dictates that the police develop programs to help the disadvantaged within our society. It dictates that we must work with the disadvantaged to develop solutions to problems. We must empower minorities and the disadvantaged so they can develop their own solutions to community problems. In this sense, it is counterproductive to declare war on whole classes of people, especially when the police must at some point attempt to develop working relationships with them. For example, if you consider the most crime and drug-ridden neighborhood in the United States, it must be remembered that the overwhelming majority of people residing there are law abiding and are being victimized by a small number of criminals and only some are drug dealers.

Community policing requires that we abandon the all-out law enforcement assault on drugs and adopt solutions that center around problem solving. Within this framework, the police should identify practices that effectively counter them. Drug dealers and drug dealing locations should be targeted for problem solving. At the same time, it is ineffective to use tactics that hassle large numbers of people, typically the poor and minorities, who obviously are not involved in drugs. The police, in conjunction with citizens, must work with other public and private agencies and groups to reduce crime and alleviate the conditions that result in crime and drug abuse. The police must utilize a public health approach whereby the "health" of a community is of primary concern, rather than producing numbers of arrests and citations or focusing on one dominant problem.

Nature and Extent of the Drug Problem

The drug problem must be fully understood before effective strategies can be developed to counter the problem. Although everyone is aware of the drug problem and most people have misgivings about it, few have taken the time to try to understand it. That is, how bad is America's drug problem? What toll does it take on our society and our quality of life? The media, politicians, and, to some extent, the police, would have us believe that it is the most important issue facing society today. Certainly, however, there are other problems that are just as pressing. Juvenile crime and violence, poverty and joblessness, treatment of the mentally ill, a lack of quality education in many parts of our country, and discrimination are problems that sorely need addressing. In fact, if many of these problems were alleviated, it is very likely that we would realize a significant reduction in our drug problem. Drug abuse is just one problem within a set of interrelated problems that begs for attention.

In terms of the scope of the drug problem, the Office of National Drug Control Policy (1996) reports that in 1995, 48.4 percent of all high school seniors had used drugs. Along these same lines, it was reported that in 1994, 37.6 percent of people ages 12 and older had used an illicit drug. In other words, approximately 73 million Americans have used an illicit drug. Data from emergency rooms in 1994 indicate that drugs were mentioned in slightly more than 900,000 emergency room cases. Also, data from inmate populations show that approximately 50 percent of prison inmates had used drugs in the month of the offense that resulted in their imprisonment. These data further indicate that illicit drug use is a significant problem in our society.

However, such global figures are of little value to the police in describing or estimating a local drug problem. Although some 73 million Americans have used drugs, to what extent is their drug usage a problem? Most of the drug use relates to marijuana, and for the most part, marijuana has not been associated with crime or police problems other than its illegal consumption and distribution. Certainly, most drug users have not been dehabilitated by their drug usage. Alcohol very likely has had a more negative effect on our society than any illicit drugs (Kappeler, Blumberg & Potter, 1996). If we scan our environment, there are few indications of a drug problem except in a few areas where drugs are used openly and extensively by some people, and these areas often suffer from a host of social problems that have for decades remained unattended. Even the emergency room admissions are misleading. Although drugs were mentioned in almost one million instances, it should be noted that drugs in most cases were not the primary causes for these people being admitted to the hospital, but were only present at the time of admission. This is also true for inmates.

The nature and extent of a particular jurisdiction's drug problem is best understood from a problem-solving perspective. That is, how do drugs adversely affect a community in terms of quality of life, crime, and disorder? Although drug education and drug prevention are important police objectives, the police should focus their primary attention on specific problems, neighborhoods or areas, and people that constitute visible or identifiable problems. The police must concentrate their resources on these real problems if they are to have an impact on community life.

Police Drug Strategies

The drug problem is expansive, cutting across many segments of the population. As such, it is impossible for the police to eliminate drugs. Therefore, the police should make "harm reduction" the criterion by which to guide drug enforcement planning and to evaluate enforcement programming. Since the police will never eliminate drugs as a law enforcement or social problem, so they must expend their energy and resources in such a way that the harm to the community as a result of drugs is minimized. Priority must be given to solving problems that are the most harmful to people and the community. This means the police should target problems as opposed to apprehending offenders without regard to activities and impact. The police should focus on problem solving as opposed to bean counting.

To this end, Moore and Kleiman (1989) have identified six goals that are useful in guiding police decisionmaking when implementing drug elimination strategies. They are:

- Reduce the gang violence associated with drug trafficking and prevent the emergence of powerful organized criminal groups;

- Control the street crimes committed by drug users;

- Improve the health and economic and social well-being of drug users;

- Restore the quality of life in urban communities by ending street-level drug dealing;

- Help prevent children from experimenting with drugs; and

- Protect the integrity of criminal justice institutions.

The first two goals identified by Moore and Kleiman relate to law enforcement, the next three establish objectives for community partnerships and community building, while the final goal causes us to realize that drugs have long had a corrupting influence on the police and others within the criminal justice system (Kappeler, Sluder & Alpert, 1998). If corruption is not controlled, then it is virtually impossible for any kind of enforcement to be effective.

Moore and Kleiman's two law enforcement goals connote a hierarchy of drug dealing. At the top of the hierarchy are the so-called drug kingpins who are responsible for smuggling and distributing drugs to street dealers. At the bottom are the street dealers who receive drugs from low level wholesalers and then sell small quantities of drugs to individual customers or users. If law enforcement could successfully disrupt the flow of drugs at any level of this hierarchy, then the problem could be substantially reduced. However, law enforcement for the past 30 years or so has not been able to accomplish this objective. Thus, it is useful to examine the drug trafficking hierarchy relative to how law enforcement may address the problem.

High-Level Enforcement

High-level enforcement is designed to attack the drug problem at the top of the drug trafficking hierarchy. High-level enforcement is designed to arrest those individuals who are involved in smuggling large quantities of drugs into the United States, manufacture large quantities of drugs, or distribute drugs to large, expansive drug networks. The reasoning behind high-level enforcement is that if a drug kingpin is eliminated, his whole network will be rendered useless, and it will cause a large gap in street drug supplies. If enough drug networks can be rendered inoperable, then the supply of drugs to the street will be substantially disrupted.

The responsibility for high-level enforcement has fallen on the shoulders of federal enforcement agencies: the Drug Enforcement Agency; Federal Bureau of Investigation; Bureau of Alcohol, Tobacco, and Firearms; and U.S. Customs Service. The Drug Enforcement Agency is responsible for stopping drugs from coming into the United States. They do this by working with foreign governments in obtaining drug smuggling intelligence and seizing the drugs as they are smuggled into the country. The Federal Bureau of Investigation is responsible for attacking the criminal organizations that are responsible for distributing large quantities of drugs. The FBI targets organized crime and other criminal syndicates that are involved in distributing drugs. The Bureau of Alcohol, Tobacco, and Firearms works closely with state and local police agencies in attempting to target mid-level drug wholesalers and dealers. The U.S. Customs Service has the responsibility of interdicting drugs that are intermingled with exports coming into the United States. The U.S. Customs Service inspects goods as they are imported into the United States.

Federal agents use a variety of tactics to apprehend drug dealers and to seize drugs. Kleiman and Smith (1990:82-83) summarize how federal law officers approach the problem:

> . . . long term, high level undercover operations: developing informants, often by making cases against low-level dealers which can then be bargained away in return for their help against their suppliers ("working up the chain"); searching through police files, financial records, telephone logs, and the like to demonstrate connections; and, most powerful but most expensive, electronic surveillance (wiretaps and less frequently, bugs).

Drug enforcement against high-level smugglers and wholesalers is expensive and time consuming. Indeed, some high-level investigations take years before an arrest is made. Federal agencies with their vast resources are best equipped to handle high-level investigations. Local law enforcement agencies, on the other hand, do not have the resources to devote to long-term investigations. Local law enforcement also has the primary responsibility of controlling street drug dealing.

The economics of supply and demand dictate that anything that substantially reduces supply should result in a price increase. The price of coffee in the United States jumped dramatically a number of years ago when a drought in Colombia reduced the supply. If either nature or law enforcement interfered sufficiently with the amount of Colombian cocaine reaching city streets, we would expect to see a similar rise in price. The United States has continually increased its enforcement efforts since the early 1980s, especially in terms of interdicting drugs coming into the United States from foreign countries. Indeed, there are approximately 3,000 agents assigned to the Drug Enforcement Agency (DEA) whose primary responsibility is to cut off drugs coming into the United States. Even though the DEA and local and state law enforcement agencies have successfully interdicted large quantities of drugs, the price of cocaine has steadily dropped and the number of users has steadily increased. These disheartening statistics indicate that increasingly larger quantities of drugs have been smuggled into the United States despite enhanced enforcement efforts.

An unfortunate consequence of high-level enforcement is that the high-level dealers that the police catch may well be the sloppiest or weakest, so that law enforcement is inadvertently toughening the remaining drug dealing organizations (Kleiman & Smith, 1990). Also, high-level enforcement assumes that a void will occur when the head of a drug dealing organization is arrested. However, there are often many lieutenants willing to take their boss' place, and there are other organizations who would quickly fill any void in market territory. Of concern as well is that, since one of the primary goals of any police strategy is to reduce the violence and health consequences associated with drug trafficking, arresting high-level dealers risks triggering a round of violence, as lieutenants and other drug trafficking organizations battle for the vacated territory. Such violence tends to undermine enforcement efforts and create public hysteria which is counterproductive to community policing and law enforcement in general. This type of enforcement does little to effectively negate health consequences of drugs to the community.

Reuter, Crawford, and Cace (1988) examined the impact of drug interdiction for the Pentagon. The purpose of the study was to determine how military interdiction may affect drug trafficking within our borders. The Pentagon proposed to use military ships and aircraft to seal our borders from drugs. Members of Congress, as well as many other politicians, have long advocated militarizing the war on drugs. Some have even suggested that we shoot down airplanes suspected of carrying illegal drugs. Regardless, Reuter and his colleagues found that increased interdiction was futile. They concluded that 75 percent of the money spent on cocaine went to street dealers and their immediate suppliers. Only 10 percent of the price of cocaine went to drug production and smuggling. At the time, the Coast Guard found drugs on only one in eight boats it boarded. Even if the Navy were to double the number of boats being inspected, it would only have a minimal impact on smuggling. Reuter suggested that, at best, the volume of cocaine would be reduced from 120 metric tons of cocaine per year to 90 metric tons per year.

The supply would not be reduced significantly or to the point that street supplies would be appreciably disrupted.

In the end, high-level enforcement has little impact on the availability and price of drugs on the street. At best, high-level enforcement keeps smugglers from being too blatant, and it serves to discourage more people from becoming involved in smuggling. Large seizures of drugs serve as a public relations tool. The public sees such police actions as victories in the war on drugs even though they effectively are meaningless in terms of supply. The real war on drugs, for any community, remains at the retail level.

Retail-Level Enforcement

If police strategies that aim upward in the drug distribution hierarchy have failed, what about those that focus downward, at the street level? Retail-level enforcement strategies attempt to reduce "discreet" and "indiscreet" drug dealing, with the latter more susceptible to control. Indiscreet drug dealing includes open street dealing, as well as crack houses and shooting galleries used exclusively to sell drugs to large numbers of customers. Transactions that take place in people's homes, offices, nightclubs, and other locations where drug dealing is not the facility's sole reason for being are considered relatively discreet and are much more difficult to attack.

Generally, when a city or area within a city has a substantial amount of indiscreet drug trafficking, it indicates that the problem is out of control. For example, Zimmer (1990:48) described such an area in the Lower East Side of Manhattan:

> . . . the area gained a local reputation as a "drug supermarket" and a national reputation as "the most open heroin market in the nation. Police videotapes . . . . show long lines of double-parked cars, hundreds of people milling around waiting to purchase heroin and cocaine, sellers shouting out the "brand names" and prices of their drugs, and others openly advertising "works"—hypodermic needles—guaranteed clean for two or three dollars. Enterprising young men and women sometimes searched the crowd looking for novice customers who might be willing to pay to have someone else "score" for them. When long lines formed behind dealers, waiting buyers at the end of the line were sometimes offered "express service," for a fee. On some blocks, vendors set up their carts, selling hot dogs and sodas to the crowd; portable radios competed with the shouting. The unaware might have thought for a moment that they had stumbled upon a block party or street festival.

Indiscriminate drug trafficking also means the police have failed to protect citizens who reside in those neighborhoods where drug dealers work.

Indiscreet drug trafficking usually results in increased collateral crime and disorder. Unchecked, the problem will eventually spread into surrounding areas and the quality of life in the affected neighborhoods will continue to deteriorate. Thus, the police should make indiscreet drug trafficking their first priority. Attacking indiscreet drug trafficking will ultimately result in the greatest harm reduction in the community.

Discreet drug trafficking, on the other hand, presents a different problem. First, since it is discreet and very likely widespread in many communities, it is virtually impossible for the police to stop. Police undercover operations and buy-busts will result in a few arrests, but such arrests are costly in terms of the amount of time and effort devoted to making each arrest. Second, discreet drug dealing seldom results in collateral crime and disorder problems. People discreetly purchase their drugs and then consume them out of public view. When the police concentrate their efforts on indiscreet drug trafficking, it generally results in larger numbers of minority arrests and subsequent charges of discrimination on the part of the police (Lusane, 1990).

Tactics such as "street-sweeping" and "focused crackdowns" target indiscreet dealing in the hope that this will at least drive it underground or make drug dealing more difficult. These tactics consist of identifying areas where there is a large amount of open drug dealing and making as many arrests as possible regardless of charges. By making large numbers of arrests for such minor offenses as drinking in public or alcohol intoxication, the police are also able to make a number of drug and weapons charges. Critics suggest that street-sweeping and focused crackdowns are only temporary remedies (Kappeler, Blumberg & Potter, 1996). Once the police leave the area, dealers return and status quo is maintained. Sherman (1990), however, argues that crackdowns have residual effects. The status quo is not immediately achieved when the police discontinue high levels of enforcement in an area. The drug dealers will wait to ensure that the police have left and are not returning before they begin to blatantly sell drugs. Sherman suggests that for crackdowns to be successful, they should occur intermittently. Periodic, random crackdowns may result in far greater levels of deterrence, but drug dealers are quick to modify their operations to meet enforcement challenges.

Other forms of drug enforcement for use in areas where there are high levels of drug trafficking are buy-bust operations and reverse stings. Whereas crackdowns entail officers making large numbers of indiscriminate arrests, buy-busts are where officers target an area, pose as drug buyers, and once a transaction is made, arrest the seller. Reverse stings, on the other hand, are where undercover officers pose as drug dealers, sell drugs to customers, and then arrest the customers. Buy-busts and reverse stings usually include undercover officers and a chase team who arrests suspects once the transaction has been completed. These types of operations allow the police to focus on drug dealing and get a number of street dealers off the street. They are methods of making indiscreet drug trafficking more discreet and fewer in number.

If nothing else, concentrated enforcement should increase drug buyers' search time, which should reduce the total amount of drugs sold and the number of crimes committed to buy drugs. It may also reduce the overall pool of users, by frustrating or scaring some casual and first-time users. These benefits can also improve the quality of life in the community, and there is also obvious virtue in reducing or eliminating open dealing, since it sends a message that the police care about drugs and the quality of life in a community.

Efforts Aimed at Juveniles

The police should place a high priority on reducing the drug problem among juveniles. These efforts should focus on prevention, as well as enforcement. As noted above, statistics point out that increasingly larger numbers of younger people are using drugs. Hopefully, it is experimental in nature rather than long-term, heavy usage. Nonetheless, the police should make special efforts to reduce juvenile drug usage.

These means that the police should have an increased presence at places and events that draw juveniles. The police should patrol areas where juveniles congregate. This may mean having officers check skating rinks, drive-in restaurants, and similar businesses on a regular basis. It also means having officers check more closely adults who loiter in these areas. For the most part, the police tend to avoid such places unless they are dispatched there on a call. The lack of attention to such areas may allow a drug problem to develop.

Cumberland Police Ask for Parents' OK to Bust Teen House Parties

The party could be over for Cumberland, R.I., teens who plan to roll in the kegs when their parents roll out of town, police said May 7.

In what's believed a first-of-its-kind initiative, parents may sign a form allowing police to search their homes when they're away. The intent is to curb underage drinking at house parties, Police Chief Anthony Silva said.

"It's time to say enough is enough," Silva said. "We're not going to tolerate this kind of thing anymore."

The "Parents Consent to Search" form is available at the police station and will be mailed to parents of the 283 seniors at Cumberland High School. It stipulates the "sole purpose" is to allow police "to make visual searches for alcoholic beverages." The permission expires after a year.

"We're not going to be going into cupboards and digging into bedroom draw-

ers," Silva said. "We're not talking about a full-blown search of someone's home."

The state chapter of the American Civil Liberties Union opposes the form, but acknowledged there is little it can do about it.

"People do have the ability to waive their constitutional rights, though it's something they may end up regretting," executive director Steven Brown said. "It's a tremendous overreaction to a problem that can be addressed in more moderate and reasonable ways."

Silva stressed even if police suspect underage drinking, they cannot search a home unless the wrongdoing is in plain view.

"If we see 50 or 60 cars parked at a house, hear the noise and know there's a party going on inside, there's nothing we can do if the shades are down and the kid won't let us in," Silva said. "Kids have these parties when their parents are away and can't control the situation."

Local police decided to look for a new way to combat teen drinking after a sophomore at a school dance was hospitalized with alcohol poisoning earlier this year, Silva said.

Other communities have come up with different ways to try to stop underage drinking. In the Massachusetts border town of Rehoboth, school officials last month required students at the Dighton-Rehoboth High School prom to pass a Breathalyzer test before being allowed in.

Cumberland School Superintendent Joseph Nasif Jr. said the consent form is less intrusive than such a test.

"Who can argue with something that gives parents peace of mind and can protect kids?" Nasif asked. "You do something like this out of love for your kids and out of concern for other people."

Nasif would not allow a reporter to interview students about the form, but parents were willing to talk. Donna Bergeron, whose son is a high school senior, said the form is a good idea.

"There are lots of single parents who work two jobs and can't keep an eye on their kids 24 hours a day, seven days a week," she said.

Sally Field, also the mother of a high school senior, said she would never sign a consent form. "Parents, not police, should be taking responsibility for their children," she said. "My son's 18 and when we go away, he has a baby sitter."

Silva said he is not encouraging parents to mistrust their children, "but they have to remember that they're kids and do the things kids do these days."

"Maybe we're taking away the rights of some teenagers—that remains to be seen," Silva said. "But are we giving parents more rights? Absolutely."

Source: *Community Policing Digest* (1997). May 22, pp. 5-6.

Involving police officers in drug education is fairly common, and many departments have adopted the model provided by the Drug Abuse Resistance Education (DARE) project in Los Angeles. DARE began in 1983 when the Los Angeles Police Department began sending officers into the schools to teach children about drugs. The questionable rationale behind DARE is that police officers have more credibility and expertise on drug issues than most teachers, so generally they can make a lasting impact on children's future attitudes and behavior. More comprehensive than simply urging kids to *Just Say No,* the program is based on the assumption that most kids experiment with drugs because of an inability to withstand peer pressure, problems with low self-esteem, and lack of training in values clarification. DARE was first implemented in a few grades in elementary school; now however, there is a curriculum for all levels of elementary and secondary education (Carter, 1995).

Unfortunately, research on DARE indicates that it is not successful in reducing drug usage by juveniles (Wysong, Aniskiewicz & Wright, 1994; Rosenbaum et al., 1994). Juveniles exposed to the program have similar usage rates and attitudes toward drugs as those who were not enrolled in the program. Obviously, these results are discouraging, but they point to a need to further examine curriculum and program activities. It means that we should continue to experiment and attempt to develop a program that will reduce future drug usage.

Community Policing and the Drug Problem

It may well prove to be a mistake for the police to treat drugs as the exclusive province of a special unit within the department. Perhaps an important lesson to be learned from the Drug Usage Forecast data, which showed that drugs are involved in as many as four of every five people arrested in some cities, is that drugs are deeply woven into the total fabric of police work, from child abuse to homicides. Though drugs are not the cause of all the problems the police face, the Drug Usage Forecast data shows that they play some immediate role in the lives of the vast majority of people arrested in our major cities.

Furthermore, the police cannot be expected to do the job alone. A three-pronged approach, involving law enforcement, drug education, and drug treatment, appears to hold the best promise of making a long-term difference, but it also implies a tug-of-war among the three perspectives for scarce resources. While it is vital to educate young people about the threats drugs pose and help them learn how to resist drugs, and it seems tantamount to scandal that many who seek drug treatment must wait months before it is available, people are beginning to question whether too much money has been devoted to enforcement and not enough to prevention and treatment (Skolnick, 1990).

Because of the vast number of different kinds of problems that drugs create, a community problem-solving approach obviously makes better sense than simply responding to individual incidents. Community policing also allows the department to fashion responses tailored to local problems and needs, without focusing exclusively on arrest, which often engages the rest of the expensive criminal justice system with little effect. As a department's community outreach specialists, CPOs have a particularly vital role to play in controlling crime and improving relations between the department and the community.

Former DARE Student Says Police Forced Her to Inform on Parents

The police officer giving Crystal Grendell and her fellow Searsport, Maine, sixth graders a DARE course on the dangers of drug abuse confused her. Crystal had seen her parents smoke marijuana at home for years, but she says, "They didn't act any different."

In a set of circumstances still in dispute, officer James Gillway later questioned the 11-year-old girl, Crystal says, assuring her nobody would be arrested if she cooperated. He warned her not to tell mom and dad because "often parents beat their children after the children talk to the police," Crystal recalls him saying.

Soon afterwards, state narcotics agents raided her house, her parents were arrested on her birthday, and the soft-spoken girl with hazel eyes was left to pick up the pieces of a life she says has been torn asunder by guilt and anger.

"It makes it hard for me to trust anybody," says Grendell, now 18. "People I thought I could trust let me down."

A lot is unclear about what exactly happened that spring of 1991 in this once prominent ship-building town. Grendell has gone to Federal court to sue Gillway, now Searsport police chief, accusing him of violating her constitutional rights.

Meanwhile, civil libertarians portray the case as an example of what they have long claimed: The nationwide program known as DARE (Drug Abuse Resistance Education) is not only ineffective, it encourages children to rat on their parents.

"How strange that we're spending all this time and money trying to get our 10- and 11-year-olds to worship uniformed officers of the state," said Gary Peterson of Fort Collins, Colo., head of Parents Against DARE. "Gee, where did that happen in history before?"

Los Angeles-based DARE America, Inc. boasts that 33 million school children around the world—25 million in the United States—will take its course this year in skills to resist drugs, gangs and violence.

DARE, which started in 1983 and trains local police officers, denies charges it seeks to recruit child informants. The program's boosters say its goal is to bring families together and point out there have been very few incidents where police officers have had to act on tips given them by pupils.

"If the children know that if they're going to that DARE officer and tell that officer something that's going to cause problems in their homes, quite honestly, I don't think it would be very good for the relationship," said Frank Pegueros, a former Los Angeles Police commander who now helps train DARE officers.

How everything started is a bit of a mystery. Grendell says a guidance counselor called her out of English class one day to tell her she knew her parents grew marijuana. Grendell insisted in an interview she didn't know how the counselor found out, since she hadn't told anyone since second grade about the drugs.

But Gillway's attorney, Edward Benjamin disputes that: "This kid Crystal had been telling anyone that would listen to her for three years about her parents and drugs." Grendell's own lawyer, Jed Davis, says, "this girl came forward because of what she heard in the DARE class."

After a few meetings, the counselor suggested the girl talk to police, Grendell said.

Gillway, then a sergeant, interviewed Grendell, who told him her parents were growing marijuana plants under grow lights in a closet, according to court documents. She also answered the officer's questions about her parents' schedules, where they worked, and the layout of their house.

Grendell contends Gillway warned her parents would be arrested if she didn't cooperate, and, later that day, kept the girl in his office against her will when Grendell's mother arrived at the police station, sobbing. The mother, Gail Grendell, had just refused to let state drug agents search her house.

Gillway, through his attorney, says Grendell gave the information voluntarily and denies holding her. Since Searsport only has a two-member police force, it was just a coincidence the DARE officer also was the one to question Grendell, he says.

"I did not have any conversations with Crystal as part of the DARE program and did not consider this conversation to be related to DARE activities," Gillway said in an affidavit, adding Grendell had told him in 1987 her parents smoked marijuana, but the district attorney's office did not pursue it.

Grendell said the DARE program confused her, but she doesn't think it had anything to do with her troubles. Davis claims the case demonstrates "an abuse of the DARE program."

Police confiscated 49 marijuana plants from the Grendell residence, including several bags of dried marijuana, a police scanner and a pistol, Gillway said.

Grendell says her parents never shared their marijuana with her, although she did experiment with it after the DARE program outside of her house.

Grendell's father, Preston Grendell, pleaded guilty to cultivating marijuana and got a year's probation in exchange for charges against Mrs. Grendell being dropped. Gail Grendell lost her jobs as a bus driver and teacher's assistant at the school district.

"If the cops had come to me, then I would've dealt with it," said Mrs. Grendell. "Don't bring my daughter into it; she wasn't involved in it, so why get her involved?"

Crystal Grendell said she needed counseling after the incident, and her grades suffered. She dropped out of high school and now lives with her boyfriend in nearby Bucksport. They just found out they're going to have a second child.

The family has appeared on several talk shows. Grendell said her family wanted her to wait until she was 18 to file a lawsuit, which originally also named the town, the school district and the guidance counselor. A Federal judge said in July that only Gillway had to face the suit.

The case is expected to get under way in U.S. District Court in Bangor next month.

"It still bothers me that it happened, that it happened that way," Grendell said. "But I don't blame myself anymore."

Source: *Community Policing Digest* (1997). September 18, pp. 5-7.

Davis and Lurigio (1996) have provided perhaps the best taxonomy by which to understand how the police interact with the public in the war on drugs. They analyze the interaction in terms of citizen and government involvement. Figure 9.1 depicts this relationship. Please note that maximum involvement comes from indigenous community anti-drug activities. These activities have occurred when citizens have become frustrated with the drug and crime problems in their neighborhood and have taken action on their own. Davis, Smith, Lurigio, and Skogan (1991) found that three factors that generally contributed to citizen initiatives: (1) they occur in less affluent, high-crime neighborhoods, (2) activism is strongly related to a neighborhood's capacity to initiate marches, rallies, and citizen patrols, and (3) the existence of a "community" leader to initiate and sustain activities. Thus, some neighborhoods are more capable of initiating problem solving than others. If a neighborhood has not or is not capable of such action, the police should implant programs. Cook and Roehl (1993) note that the more successful programs are those that consist of partnerships among large numbers of agencies and constituent groups. Thus, when the police attempt to transplant a program, they must attempt to secure a number of commitments.

Drug house abatement, community policing, and traditional policing represent a gamut of enforcement where tactics are designed to meet specific problems. Drug house abatement refers to where the police address a specific drug outlet. They may use buy-busts, civil actions, or raids. Regardless, the aim is to remove the problem from the neighborhood. Community policing tactics refer to those where the police use enhanced enforcement coupled with community relations. For example, the police when attempting to abate drugs in an area should initiate and maintain contact with residents to garner their support for the efforts. Finally, the police can continue with traditional enforcement, which by itself, has remained fairly ineffective.

Figure 9.1
Police-Citizen Responses to Neighborhood Drug Problems

Citizen Anti-Drug Initiatives	Implemented Anti-Drug Initiatives	Drug House Abatement	Community Policing	Traditional Methods

Citizen Involvement				Government Involvement

Adopted from: R.C. Davis & A.J. Lurigio. (1996). *Fighting Back: Neighborhood Antidrug Strategies.* Thousand Oaks, CA: Sage Publications.

The following should be considered a partial list of what community policing can do and a blueprint for how it might be used to accomplish more in the future:

- **Community policing directly addresses the problems of discreet and indiscreet retail-level drug dealing.** If the police are to maintain public confidence, they must find new ways to address retail drug dealing. Retail drug dealing, especially when it is indiscreet, occurs in the neighborhoods and in the streets where people live. This type of trafficking directly threatens citizen perception of the community; it may result in higher levels of collateral crime and disorder; and it can destroy community life when left unchecked. A sense of fairness would seem to dictate that both indiscreet and discreet dealing should receive equal police attention, but open dealing is even more pernicious because it reinforces the public perception that drugs have careened out of control, a singularly dangerous message to send to citizens, especially young people. Open dealing also makes it far too easy for casual and first-time users as well as addicts to find a ready supply of drugs.

Community policing can provide the department's first line of defense against both indiscreet and discreet dealing. The shift from focusing on responding to calls and making arrests to solving community problems reorders overall department priorities to a proper emphasis on helping people feel safer from the threats drugs pose. Through its CPOs, community policing provides a permanent, citywide, neighborhood-based approach to drug problems. When CPOs are permanently assigned to beats or areas of the city, they can build bridges between the police and the people whose support and participation are crucial in bringing retail-level dealing under control.

Enlisting CPOs directly in addressing retail-level dealing may require a shift in thinking or a change in policy. Traditionally, the police have been call-oriented as opposed to neighborhood-oriented. That is, the police would respond to each call, and once they had responded to a call, they would wait for the next. Community policing dictates that the police not only take care of calls for service, but that CPOs survey their beat or neighborhood, identify crime and disorder problems, and respond to them. In many instances, the responses are non-traditional and may require the cooperation of the community or other elements of government.

In North Miami Beach, CPO Charles Reynolds was assigned to a low-income neighborhood notorious as a supermarket for drugs. Once Reynolds gained the trust of the people in the area, he tackled problems personally by warning low-level dealers that he would make it his business to arrest them if they persisted—but that if they wanted help in finding a job, he would provide that as well. Reynolds then proceeded to back up both his threat and his promise. He made cases against those who continued to sell drugs and commit other crimes, and he also provided individualized and broad-based assistance to help people find work.

Each week Reynolds posted in his office a list of jobs available in the community, and he referred specific people to companies that he knew were hiring people requiring their skills. Reynolds also worked with business and professional leaders to host a Job Fair in the community policing office. That event provided classes on a wide range of topic including how to dress for an interview, how to write a resume, and it involved people in role-playing so that they could assess their performance in mock job interviews. By tailoring the police response to community needs, Reynolds was able to bring open dealing under control without mass arrests that might have resulted in resentment and distrust toward the police on the part of the neighborhood citizens. Positive action often is more meaningful than negative action.

In Lansing, Michigan, Lt. James Rapp reported success with using foot patrol officers to make repeated visits each day to knock on the door of known dope houses. Sometimes the officers just stood outside and watched and talked with people who attempted to go to the drug house. Having officers appear in front of drug houses meant a disruption of business, and in some cases the traffickers inside flushed their drugs since they never knew when the officer's arrival might signal a bust. The officer's visible presence also helped drive customers away, which reduced profits even further. The officers also signaled to the neighborhood residents that the police cared about their problems and were doing something about it.

Metropolitan areas plagued by widespread, open dealing requires more drastic actions. For example, the department may have to implement an aggressive enforcement program such as a sweep or crackdown. Since such tactics often are seen as harassment and create resentment in the community, the department could use its CPOs to prepare the affected citizens. This could be accomplished by talking with community leaders and individual citizens, explaining the situation, and requesting their support. Such actions should reduce the negative police-community relations once the tactic is implemented. One or more sweeps might be enough to sufficiently disrupt and reduce the open dealing (Sherman, 1990). Once the problem has ebbed somewhat, CPOs could enter the area and implement community-based programs to maintain control. In other cases, it might prove necessary to increase the number of CPOs so that there are ample personnel to attend to the most severe drug problems. Not only would they be able to sustain gains made by coordinating their efforts with the drug sweeps, but they would be free to pursue new initiatives aimed at a broad range of community concerns, including crime, fear of crime, and disorder.

Community Transforms Crack Houses into Family Homes

Police Chief Al Bosse invited the community to help restore a sense of safety to Covington's inner-city neighborhoods by turning the boarded-up homes used by crack dealers into homes for hard-working families. The community responded to the chief's invitation, and commitments from local government officials, social service agencies and community members poured in.

Complementary Goals

One company that offered its assistance renovates abandoned buildings to make low-cost housing available to people with minimal financial resources. The organization's mission perfectly blended with Bosse's vision to fight crime by reviving abandoned buildings.

The new partners chose an old building located in a police-targeted neighborhood to renovate and use as shared space for offices and community meetings. They planned to use the refurbished space as a central location to host support training, meetings and youth forums for the residents who would soon occupy the surrounding rehabilitated crack houses.

A Strategic Plan

With their operation base established, the partners began their thrust to achieve neighborhood stabilization and improvement. An important facet of the partners' collective goal was to maintain interactive relationships with residents and foster a comfortable atmosphere of cooperation and increased communication. The plan also included making property and tenant lists available to the Covington Police Department as the renovated buildings became occupied. The lists serve a dual purpose: they help officers become acquainted with residents, and also assist them in separating residents from nonresidents when it's necessary to disperse crowds from a property. Through this arrangement, officers have the authority to arrest nonresidents who refuse to leave when asked.

Rules to Live By

Tenants who want to live in the renovated units have to agree to tough house rules to get approved. The standard lease states that tenants are obligated to cooperate with the police. Tenants also must consent to be held accountable for the actions of their guests and are aware that they will be evicted from their apartment should they in any way contribute to a neighborhood problem. These conditions lay the groundwork for neighborhood integrity and improvement and also further the goal to provide safe housing for many of the city's low-income single mothers.

The department's effort to make officers more accessible in the troubled neighborhoods has largely been accomplished by establishing a centrally located satellite resource office. Covington's police officers assist residents in identifying security improvements and serve as a visible and approachable support system. Beyond meeting emergency needs, the officers also help residents locate social services and educational opportunities that can give them direction and help them gain control of their lives.

Conclusion

The Covington Police Department continues to actively solicit involvement from residents in the targeted areas and uses all available resources to address community concerns and accomplish common goals. The department encourages the Covington community to take an active role in implementing programs that help identify problems and find solutions through effective partnerships.

By Specialist Ann Haegele

Source: *Community Policing Exchange* (1997). July/August, p.7.

The problem with relying on sweeps and focused crackdowns that are not part of a community policing approach is that these tactics often alienate the people the police are trying to protect. Community policing coupled with limited enforcement results in citizens accepting and, to some extent, cooperating with the police. Community policing recognizes that people must accept their responsibility to become involved in efforts to address problems in their own neighborhoods.

In a notoriously drug-infested area of the District of Columbia, members of the Nation of Islam have achieved notable success by working with residents directly to develop initiatives to eliminate open dealing. Their success demonstrates what a relatively small but dedicated group of citizens can do to develop grassroots community support and attack community problems. The goal of the police should be to use CPOs as the initiators and supervisors in community-based efforts, because this model offers the opportunity for success (Davis & Lurigio, 1996).

Once the immediate priority of controlling open dealing has been achieved, community policing can then address indiscreet dealing in new ways. A single mother with two sons who was studying at Hunter College moved into a housing project on the Lower East Side of New York City. She soon found that the complex was dominated by a major crack and marijuana dealer operating from an apartment in the building. Although no fan of the police, the woman felt she had no choice but to ask for their help. She contacted the community patrol officer program (CPOP) team in her area. Together they developed a strategy that included making *vertical patrols* of the apartment building; offering to escort customers inside, which scared many of them away; and making arrests on a variety of charges, including disorderly conduct and other minor violations. The sustained pressure ultimately resulted in the police arresting the drug dealer and effectively ridding the building of its drug problem.

- **Community policing can often gather more and better information about retail-level and even high-level drug dealing with less danger and expense than traditional undercover operations.** It bears repeating that two groups of people have information about crime, criminals and the citizens who are unwillingly exposed to their criminal operations. Traditional police efforts focus on getting the criminals to "roll over," or provide information on their associates in exchange for money or deference on some criminal charge (see Kappeler, Sluder & Alpert, 1998). Community policing instead works on developing the trust between the police and citizens so that citizens will provide information about crime and suspicious activities that occur in their neighborhoods. CPOs, as a result of the positive relationships they develop with citizens, often are in a position to gather intelligence about drug dealing beyond that which can be obtained using traditional methods.

Bruce Benson, a member of the Flint, Michigan, Police Department found that narcotics officers were routinely frustrated because people would call with a tip, but they rarely provided more than an address before hanging up. The officers would try to follow up, but often found little to go on. The caller often would call again to complain that the police were not doing their job. Once the Flint foot patrol program began, citizens began to personally provide officers with information. Community policing resulted in citizens providing in-depth information about drug operations, not just the address, but the names or license plate numbers of the dealers and customers, hours of operation, kinds of drugs sold, and physical descriptions of the drug houses. Even if the people did not know the details, they were often willing to work with the officer to find out what the police needed to know. The foot patrol officers would then transmit the information to the narcotics squad, so that they had enough information to secure a warrant to make a successful investigation and arrest.

Flint was not an isolated case. When a new community policing effort was launched in Morristown, New Jersey, the officers and the administration were amazed at how much information people would pass on about drug dealing during routine visits with citizens. One woman was able to provide police enough detailed information to break up a broad-based drug dealing ring shortly after the new program started, the result of an unrelated home visit.

CPOs say that the answer often lies in finding someone in the neighborhood who is interested or concerned about the neighborhood. For example, retired people often keep track of neighborhood activities, including the neighborhood's drug problems. The inherent drawback in the traditional approach is that a motor patrol officer rarely has the time or opportunity to develop the level of trust necessary for people to divulge information, or the officer is there for other reasons and does not have time to devote to cultivating contacts and collecting information.

Another reason that community policing often elicits information that traditional police cannot obtain stems from the fact that home visits and chats on the street are routine. Criminals and drug dealers are not able to identify who in the neighborhood is providing information to the police. A CPO on foot, a bike, or even on horseback is more approachable than officers in patrol cars. When people see CPOs walking the same streets as them, they know that the officers have good reason to care about what goes on in the neighborhood. This also can inspire people to venture out of their homes, provide officers with information, and participate in police-sponsored programs.

In Tulsa, Oklahoma, CPOs assigned to a public housing complex patrolled on horseback. The horse acted as an icebreaker, especially with kids. This allowed both adults and children the opportunity of petting the horse as they provided the CPOs information about problems, including drug dealing, in the neighborhood. The horses allowed the citizens to cooperate with the police without drawing attention to themselves. In one instance, the COPs were able to rescue a mother who literally was being held captive by cocaine dealers who had taken over her apartment.

- **Community policing addresses street-level dealing in ways that need not always engage or overwhelm the rest of the criminal justice system.** In the District of Columbia during a two-year period, police sweeps succeeded in arresting roughly 45,000 people without making any dent in the drug-related violence or the amount of open dealing visible on the streets. Meanwhile, the rest of the criminal justice system has been overwhelmed, prison costs alone have increased 400 percent during an eight-year period (Pooley, 1989).

  Similarly, the tally on Detroit's crack problem showed that 144 (more than 10%) of the 1,041 people arrested on felony drug charges during a three-month period never appeared after they had been released on bond or freed because of jail overcrowding. A report prepared by Detroit Recorder's Court seeking more funds to add more judges said that 86.7 percent of all people arrested on drug charges go free on bond because of backlogged dockets and jail overcrowding.

  Instead of sending the message that the system has the ability to deal with drug traffickers, the criminal justice response instead seems to ensure that the dealer arrested today will be back in business tomorrow—hustling even harder to pay for legal fees. Community policing approaches the overall problem from a different perspective, by employing arrest as only one of the tools in its arsenal. The traditional police response to a problem often stresses the number of arrests made as a measure of success, but particularly with the problem of open dealing, this yardstick may not always be the best solution. In some cases, actions and outcomes other than arrest may benefit the community.

  The account of the CPOP efforts in New York City highlights the importance of solving the problem without focusing on felony drug busts as the primary goal. In that case, using misdemeanor disorderly conduct charges discouraged users from making buys, as did having CPOs and tenants offer to escort them inside. In Wisconsin, an enterprising neighborhood watch group boldly held its meetings across the street from open dealing, thereby driving customers and eventually the dealers away.

  The hallmark of the community policing approach is its ability to generate creative, new, community-based, police-supervised approaches. It recognizes that generating arrests beyond what the criminal justice system can handle risks creating bottlenecks that can undermine confidence in the entire system. Community policing shifts the focus from arrest as the primary means of achieving solutions to one that recognizes it as an expensive and time-consuming option.

- **Community policing can make the best use of police presence to reduce open dealing.** One way for the police to address open dealing without always engaging the rest of the criminal justice system involves the judicious and lawful use of presence. A neighborhood group, with a CPO in the lead, making periodic sweeps of streets infested with open drug dealing can have the same effect as those vertical sweeps floor-by-floor that the CPOP officers used in apartment houses. Perhaps one of the best examples of citizens harassing drug dealers occurred in Houston. There, approximately 100 residents from the Acres Homes neighborhood banded together and literally chased drug dealers out of the neighborhood (Phillips, 1989).

Creative CPOs and neighborhood residents working together can also employ a host of other tactics to make dealers nervous enough to dispose of their drugs and drive customers away, such as visibly taking down license plate numbers of potential buyers or clicking cameras (without film) at people making dope deals on the street. The purpose is not to assemble lists, but to make buyers and sellers think that they are under surveillance. One CPO even posted signs in his beat area saying that drug dealing would not be tolerated. The goal is to turn up the heat as much as possible, so that the police and people together demonstrate that they will not let up.

- **Community policing develops and bolsters community participation in anti-drug efforts.** Areas overwhelmed with drug problems promote apathy and despair because people feel there is nothing they can do that will make a difference. Community policing sometimes requires that only one committed person spark an effort that can achieve a measure of success, and that, in turn, can result in others becoming directly involved in recovering their neighborhoods. The CPO's job is to be a catalyst or motivator to get people involved. Once people are involved, the CPO must constantly expand community efforts.

  If a focused crackdown achieves success, but the officers are then removed, only to have the drug dealers return, people can rightfully feel abandoned and betrayed. Many people have expressed concern that traditional efforts ignore them—their needs and concerns and their potential support and participation as well. Community policing pays attention to average citizens, allowing them a voice in setting priorities and fashioning solutions tailored to their concerns. The community policing alternative to flooding an area with a lot of police for a short time is to substitute a smaller number of CPOs who are stationed in the community permanently, so that they can recruit people in the community to help themselves.

  Most often, the first goal in many areas is to reduce open dealing, to stabilize the neighborhood, then focus on indiscreet dealing to maintain the pressure. As the area begins to improve, the CPO can brainstorm with people in the community about new ways to address the broader spectrum of drug problems. This might mean linking addicts to proper treatment. Or it could include working with area businesses to provide jobs for recovering addicts. Community policing provides a way for the police to link arms with people who understand that they must become part of the answer if drug problems are to be brought under control.

- **Community policing can harness the vigilante impulse and channel it in positive directions.** If the police fail to find a way to tap into and control the frustration people feel when they are inundated with drug, crime, and disorder problems in their neighborhoods, this positive energy can erupt into corrosive vigilantism, which only serves to undermine respect for the law even further. Several years ago a jury in Detroit acquitted self-admitted arsonists who burned down a crack house. The arsonists actions signify the danger in ignoring people's desire to do something concrete about their concerns. Violence begets violence, and the police must not only stop the cycle of violence that can erupt in a community, but they must also harness the community energy and turn it toward positive objectives.

  One major problem with traditional police efforts is that police officers do not spend enough time in the community talking to people and cultivating their support. Indeed, traditional preventive patrol dictates that officers respond to calls as quickly as possible and then return to their cars so that they can take another call. Traditional preventive patrol basically prohibits the police from developing meaningful relations with citizens. CPOs can work with people on developing effective and lawful ways to address their problems. An effective CPO can transmute the dangerous impulse to vigilantism into efforts that maintain respect for the law, efforts that do not endanger either the civil rights or physical safety of innocent bystanders. Because CPOs are stationed in beat areas, they not only recruit citizens to work with them on neighborhood problems, but they also provide continuous and personalized supervision of citizen participation in efforts that might otherwise become destructive or counterproductive.

- **Community policing provides the best way to involve the entire department in anti-drug efforts with the least risk of corruption and abuse of authority.** Historically, much of the reluctance by many police departments to involve line officers in street-level anti-drug initiatives stems from the unwarranted fear that it would promote corruption and abuse. Many of the police reforms beginning in the 1950s stem from efforts to thwart police corruption. Even today, there are periodic police corruption scandals that revolve around drug enforcement. For example, the Mollen Commission in New York City found officers who were openly involved in drug abuse and corruption. Many police managers fear the potential corrupting influence that drugs and drug money has on law enforcement.

  The dynamic most likely to promote widespread corruption and abuse appears to be when an elite unit is put on the task, especially a unit cloaked in secrecy (Kappeler, Sluder & Alpert, 1998). A system that also focuses on the number of arrests as the sole or primary measure of success can pressure police to cross the into abuse, entrapment, and fraud. The structure can promote an "if you can't beat 'em, join 'em" mind-set. The officers involved in the drug corruption scandal in the 77th Precinct in New York, where narcotics officers allegedly robbed dealers and resold the drugs, apparently thought of themselves as modern-day equivalents of Robin Hood even after they were exposed.

Yet police administrators still worry that putting an officer into a beat in a drug-ridden neighborhood invites corruption or abuse of authority. No doubt this stems from concern that when officers band together and begin to see themselves as part of a cohesive brotherhood (Crank, 1998), they can also adopt an unofficial code of silence that demands that they refuse to report a fellow officer's transgressions (Kappeler, Sluder & Alpert, 1998). This bonding is why departments plagued by problems with officers using excessive force often find the situation difficult to reverse.

Ironically, one of community policing's supposed drawbacks may actually be one of its greatest strengths. Because CPOs spend so much time working with citizens rather than with their fellow officers, they are more likely to identify with the needs of the people they serve. CPOs are less likely to adopt the traditional police mind-set of us (the police) against them (everybody else) (see Skolnick, 1966). Since CPOs are community based, they sometimes are viewed as a breed apart by their traditional fellow officers. While that can cause problems of internal dissension, it also makes CPOs less likely than their traditional counterparts to indulge in abuse of authority.

- **Community policing can help reduce the overall profitability of drug dealing.** As explained before, strategies that target high-level drug smugglers and dealers have not had much impact on reducing the drug problem. Every time a high-level dealer is arrested, there is another to take his or her place. By focusing the bulk of its attention on disrupting and reducing retail-level dealing, community policing reduces the overall profits of the drug trade in ways that do not threaten a price increase. Street-level drug enforcement attempts to reduce the demand by arresting or otherwise frightening drug buyers. Demand reduction will harm drug dealers and their profitability much more than interdicting the drug supply.

- **Community policing can best employ problem-solving tactics aimed at drug dealing.** Problem solving has become the centerpiece for modern police work. As discussed in Chapter 1, it basically asks officers to look beyond individual incidents and analyze and come to understand underlying crime patterns and dynamics. The purpose is to identify possible pressure points where police intervention can have an impact on a specific problem. CPOs, because of their intense and sustained community involvement, are often the best candidates to identify, launch, and supervise problem-solving initiatives, adjusting them as needed based on their evaluation of the results.

Low-level dealing and user crime can both lend themselves to problem-solving techniques. Perhaps it means having the CPO persuade the city to install high-intensity streetlights in areas where open dealing takes place at night. In North Miami Beach, Florida, the city officials in charge of code enforcement have actually been moved into the department, in part because of the hope that CPOs can work with them to use the regulations as a means to close dope houses. In Lexington, Kentucky, police officers used cutting torches to remove several basketball goals in a city park. The goals were located next to the street, and drug dealers were using basketball games to disguise drug dealing. The police made sure that there were ample goals in the park to handle all of the legitimate sports activities.

Problem-solving tactics can also prove useful in addressing drug-related crime. Research tends to indicate that drug users often commit most of their crimes within a close radius of their homes. CPOs could counter this problem by working with citizens to implement crime prevention programs in high-crime and drug-usage areas. CPOs could help develop strategies to reduce robberies, burglaries, and other property crimes by improving outdoor lighting and clipping back bushes where muggers can hide. Such efforts to alter the environment potentially can have a substantial impact on crime (Felson, 1994). It could mean working with the manager of an apartment complex on a system to issue identification cards and visitor passes or a no-trespass system in public housing to discourage outsiders from coming in to make buys—and robbing residents to pay for the drugs. Problem solving means that the police must use imaginative, non-traditional ways to address old problems.

- **Community policing can focus on youth gangs for special attention.**
  As discussed in the next chapter, the police have the opportunity to play an expanded role in addressing the problem of youth gangs, not only in targeting existing gangs for special attention, but by providing lawful alternatives. The problem with many youth gangs today is that they have discovered the potential profits available in drug dealing, and laws aimed at protecting juveniles can also inadvertently serve as a shield to protect young operatives from harsh penalties. Also, traditional enforcement aimed at youth gangs largely has been ineffective. Community policing can play a unique and important role in working with youth gangs, to reduce open warfare, to gather intelligence, and to help prevent wanna-be's or potential recruits from becoming hard-core gangbangers.

  Kids join gangs for identity, for the recreational activities they provide, and for protection, including protection from the gangs themselves. Community policing focuses on juveniles for special attention, an important part of its overall mandate, and many CPOs have been instrumental in working with individuals and business people to organize alternative activities for young people. Involving CPOs in youth clubs and sports and recreational activities for young people also adds that vital element of protection, and CPOs can also enlist adults willing to provide additional security for youngsters who need a lawful alternative. For example, a number of police departments, as a part of their community policing efforts, have created Police Athletic Leagues for the purpose of organizing sports activities in disadvantaged neighborhoods. A number of departments have also helped to establish after-school tutoring programs to assist disadvantaged kids to assimilate into mainstream activities.

- **Community policing can focus on juveniles, particularly high-risk youngsters, with efforts to reduce the likelihood that they will become drug abusers or dealers.** For example, in Flint, foot patrol officer Jowanne Barnes-Coney took the proactive approach of trying to identify high-risk youngsters, so that she could work with them and discourage them from experimenting with or selling drugs. Her rapport with the youngsters in her beat area allowed her to gather a list of young people at risk—those kids whose friends said they worried about them because they were either dabbling in drug use or they had talked about wanting to become a dealer someday. Barnes-Coney first visited the parents of these youngsters potentially at risk, explaining her concerns and offering to work with them on ways to intervene, including involving teachers in the effort.

  In the role of community liaison, Barnes-Coney attempted to link families to appropriate community counseling. She developed a program that rewarded young people for arriving home by the curfew set by their parents. She also worked with people in the community to host broad-based efforts, such as a drug-free rally where each child who participated received a T-shirt. Barnes-Coney became persuaded that many of the youngsters she saw turned to drugs because they did not feel good about themselves. As a result, she organized teen self-esteem clubs designed to boost a positive self-image. Barnes-Coney's efforts demonstrate how the police can initiate a number of grassroots programs that attack the drug problem. Since CPOs have close relationships with people and neighborhoods, they are best qualified to identify those programs with the greatest potential and elicit the highest level of support and participation on the part of those who are in need.

  The police have an important role to play in drug education, and community policing can go beyond programs like DARE, by reaching out beyond schools, to the truants and dropouts who may well be at greatest risk. CPOs make presentations in classrooms, and many work within schools. But they also initiate community-based initiatives and activities designed to include youngsters in positive activities as an alternative to drug use. Because they have the opportunity to work with youngsters over time, CPOs can develop informal, one-on-one relationships with youngsters who need special attention. They can also reinforce the anti-drug message in group activities, whether that includes a summer softball league or classes on child care for teen mothers.

  The problem with many well-meaning educational approaches is that they find their warmest acceptance among those at least risk, whereas the challenge lies in developing a wide range of approaches in the hope of reaching a broad spectrum of young people with different problems and needs. CPOs have the opportunity to serve as positive role models themselves in a variety of initiatives aimed at young people, so that they can transmit and reinforce the anti-drug message directly and indirectly. Though they remain adult authority figures, their personal relationship with the juveniles in their beat areas holds some promise that CPOs can breach the problem of teenage rebellion. Their sustained presence in the community as a trusted adult also allows them to identify new drug and crime problems and assist in launching countermeasure efforts.

As the example above demonstrates, community policing allows the police to employ proactive strategies designed to support families in their anti-drug efforts. All too often, the only time that many families see the police is when they arrive as adversaries, seeking information or to make an arrest. Community policing allows youngsters and adults to enjoy positive interactions with the police, so that they are not simply authority figures who "will take you away if you are bad."

A hotly debated law in Los Angeles led to the arrest of a mother who was charged with failing to stop her son from becoming involved in gang activity. Parental responsibility is an important component in juvenile drug abuse and drug dealing. The police must not only sanction youths transgressions and crimes, but they must also provide families the support they need in controlling their youngsters.

Another problem the police must begin to contend with more directly is abuse within families. Unfortunately officials at all levels in the United States are only beginning to grapple with the high levels of child abuse, child sexual abuse, and neglect that occurs in many families, and no one would argue that our efforts thus far have been less than adequate. This is an area where CPOs can have a real impact. CPOs can link families to appropriate help, and they can work to initiate community-based efforts to provide support to troubled families. They could encourage an alcoholic parent to obtain counseling or otherwise help protect family members who are being abused by another family member who is substance dependent. But most importantly, CPOs can work with social service organizations to provide direct intervention where necessary. When CPOs identify homes with abuse and neglect, they should demand direct social service intervention. If these kinds of family problems go unattended, it substantially increases the probability that the children will later encounter problems.

- **Community policing can serve as the link to public and private agencies that can help.** The above example shows that there are some public and private agencies that are more capable than the police to intervene into social problems. In the past, police departments worked with or otherwise cooperated with other agencies. They saw their roles simply as referral agents. That is, if the police encountered a problem they believed was in the domain of another agency, they referred the citizen to the other agency, effectively washing their hands of it. Community policing dictates that the police understand that they have a vested interested in devising effective responses to community problems, and the most effective responses sometimes involve working with a myriad of other public and private agencies.

Police departments must make concerted efforts in developing working relationships, as opposed to mutually exclusive relationships, with a variety of other agencies. When the police team up with other agencies, they can have a profound impact on problems. This can occur only after the department identifies agencies and establishes a liaison with them. Furthermore, officers must be trained to identify problems that can be handled by or in conjunction with those agencies, and they must be taught to call on them for help. Supervisors must constantly reinforce these efforts. As a part of the supervision process, first-line supervisors should attempt to determine if other agencies could be effective in providing assistance.

- **Community policing provides a logical mechanism for disseminating information on AIDS and other diseases related to IV drug use.** Failure to involve the police in efforts to reduce the potential number of AIDS victims is short-sighted. Not only are the police one of the most logical candidates for the job, because they come in contact with many IV drug users, it is in their enlightened self-interest to do all they can to reduce the spread of these disease. AIDS not only imposes an expensive financial toll on society, it results in substantial human misery. The disease creates a street population desperately in need of police and social services.

  CPOs should be encouraged to use their local offices as a clearinghouse for information on preventing AIDS and other diseases such as hepatitis-B caused by sharing infected drug needles. They can also enlist community support in informational efforts, such as how to use bleach to clean and disinfect needles. CPOs can also disseminate information about agencies that offer assistance to those already afflicted. Educating the community about the threat of AIDS can also enlist cooperation and support for efforts aimed at closing down so-called shooting galleries, where addicts often share infected needles. AIDS, perhaps, is the best example of a community problem that demands everyone's attention.

- **Community policing adds both scope and continuity to the overall police effort, providing sustained, citywide retail-drug enforcement without under-utilizing scarce resources.** By using CPOs as the backbone of the department's anti-drug efforts, police departments automatically extend their anti-drug efforts beyond what any special unit, such as a narcotics division, can provide. In essence, considering and further exploiting the ability of community policing to fashion short and long-term solutions to the entire spectrum of problems associated with drugs is a way to make drugs the top police priority overall, as it is with most citizens.

  The mistake in talking about the drug crisis is that the traditional police response to a crisis is to look for ways to make massive, short-term interventions to bring the emergency under control, but without any coordinated follow-up—or prevention. It can be argued that drugs have reached emergency status in some areas of our cities, in part, because of the failure to provide sustained, proactive police efforts in the past. Street-sweeps and focused crackdowns allow the police to have a temporary impact on the drug problem, but the problem floods back once the massive police intervention is withdrawn. An important prescription that community policing fills best, because it is not a single-purpose approach, is that it consists of effective, creative ways of providing basic police services.

- **Community policing may help reduce the risk of civil disturbances and rioting that could be triggered by aggressive anti-drug initiatives.** Frustration with open dealing has increased the pressure to take drastic action. A number of departments have deployed militarized police units to patrol high-crime and drug areas (Kraska & Kappeler, 1997). Such units do not have problem solving as their primary objective, but for the most part, they are there to send a message to the community and to produce numbers of arrests. Their primary function is to make a statement for the police. Unfortunately, the message is unsound and random arrests seldom accomplish little in terms of improving the quality of life for citizens or reducing the drug problem. Also, aggressive police actions alienate the public and ultimately lead to direct confrontations with citizens. Historically, if we examine most of the major riots in the United States, they were touched off by some police incident (National Advisory Commission on Civil Disorders, 1968).

A community policing approach may offer substantially more than a militarized movement in areas with high levels of drugs and crime. Not only can community policing help reduce tensions between the police department and the community, particularly in the area of race relations, it can also be used to address a number of problems that contribute to crime and drug abuse.

Summary

It also seems increasingly urgent to explore what community policing can offer in solving the drug problem. For the past quarter of a century our police and our criminal justice system have responded to drugs with a tough, aggressive response. Unfortunately, it does not appear that this response has had much of an impact on the problem. Indeed, the drug problem does not appear to have subsided one iota. The drug problem results in mounting frustration within our society. This frustration has led to a continuation of the same old draconian solutions. Their failure should suggest that something else must be attempted.

Another problem with traditional methods of controlling drugs is that they erode our cherished civil rights. The courts on a number of occasions have rendered decisions that substantially limit or reduce citizens' rights. Traditional police may applaud such actions; however, such support is short-sited. The constitutional rights guaranteed American citizens under the Bill of Rights are what generally distinguishes our legal system from others. An erosion of our rights eventually places unrealistic expectations on the police and generally will be counterproductive for our society.

Community policing offers a commonsense approach to the drug and crime problems. Community policing is more than the weed-and-seed programs of a decade ago. Those programs were designed to couple enforcement with community building. Roehl (1995) evaluated the programs and found that the police concentrated on weeding (enforcement) and gave little consideration to seeding (community building). As history has proven, the police will not be successful in ridding society of drug and crime problems by focusing singularly on enforcement; the police also must be actively involved in community building. Perhaps a positive example of this is where the Chicago police implemented a drug eradication program in two public housing areas. The police combined enforcement with education, prevention, and treatment (Popkin et al., 1995). Such a comprehensive program has much more promise than enforcement.

References

Carter, D. (1995). "Community Policing and DARE: A Practitioner's Perspective." *BJA Bulletin*. Washington, DC: Bureau of Justice Administration.

Christie, N. (1994). *Crime Control as Industry: Toward Gulags, Western Style.* New York, NY: Routlege.

Cook, R. & J. Roehl (1993). "National Evaluation of the Community Partnership Program: Preliminary Findings." In R. Davis, A. Lurigio & D. Rosenbaum (eds.) *Drugs and the Community*, pp. 225-250. Springfield, IL: Charles C Thomas.

Crank, J.P. (1998). *Understanding Police Culture*. Cincinnati, OH: Anderson Publishing Co.

Davis, R.C. & A.J. Lurigio (1996). *Fighting Back: Neighborhood Antidrug Strategies*. Thousand Oaks, CA: Sage Publications.

Davis, R.C., B.E. Smith, A.J. Lurigio & W.G. Skogan (1991). "Community Response to Crack: Grassroots Anti-Drug Programs." Report of the Victim Services Agency, New York, to the National Institute of Justice.

Kappeler, V.E. (1998). "Can We Continue to Incarcerate Non-Violent Drug Offenders?" In C.B. Fields (ed.) *Issues in Corrections*. New York, NY: Allyn & Bacon.

Kappeler, V.E., M. Blumberg & G.W. Potter (1996). *The Mythology of Crime and Criminal Justice*, Second Edition. Prospect Heights, IL: Waveland Press.

Kappeler, V.E., R. Sluder & G.P. Alpert (1998). *Forces of Deviance: Understanding the Dark Side of Policing*, Second Edition. Prospect Heights, IL: Waveland Press.

Kleiman, M. & K. Smith (1990). "State and Local Drug Enforcement: In Search of a Strategy." In M. Tonry & J. Wilson (eds.) *Drugs and Crime*, pp. 69-108. Chicago, IL: University of Chicago Press.

Kraska, P.B. & V.E. Kappeler (1997). "Militarizing American Police: The Rise and Normalization of Paramilitary Units." *Social Problems*, 44(1):1-18.

Lusane, C. (1990). *Pipe Dream Blues*. Boston, MA: Beacon Press.

McBride, D.C. & C.B. McCoy (1994). "The Drugs-Crime Relationship: An Analytical Framework." *The Prison Journal*, 73(3&4):257-278.

Moore, M. & M. Kleiman (1989). *The Police and Drugs*. Perspectives on Policing. Washington, DC: National Institute of Justice and the Program in Criminal Justice Policy and Management, Harvard University.

National Commission on Civil Disorders (1968). *Report of the National Advisory Commission on Civil Disorders*. New York, NY: Bantam Books.

Office of National Drug Control Policy (1996). *Drugs & Crime Data Fact Sheet*. Washington, DC: Author.

Phillips, C. (1989, September 6). "Houston Group Battles, Reclaims Park." *The Wall Street Journal*, Sec. A, pp. 10-11.

Pooley, E. (1989, January 12). "Fighting Back Against Crack." *New York Magazine*, p. 39.

Popkin, S., L. Olson, A. Lurigio, V. Gwiasda & R. Carter (1995). "Sweeping Out Drugs and Crime: Residents' Views of the Chicago Housing Authority's Public Housing Drug Elimination Program." *Crime & Delinquency*, 41(1):73-99.

Reuter, P., G. Crawford & J. Cace (1988). *Sealing the Borders: The Effects of Increased Military Participation in Drug Interdiction*. (R-3594-USDP) Santa Monica, CA: The RAND Corporation.

Roehl, J. (1995). *National Evaluation of the Weed and Seed Initiative*. Washington, DC: National Institute of Justice.

Rosenbaum, D., R.L. Flewelling, S.L. Bailey, C.L. Ringwalt & D.L. Wilkinson (1994). "Cops in the Classroom: A Longitudinal Evaluation of Drug Abuse Resistance Education (DARE)." *Journal of Research in Crime and Delinquency*, 31(1):3-31.

Sherman, L. (1990). *Police Crackdowns*. (NIJ Reports, March/April). Washington, DC: National Institute of Justice.

Skolnick, J.H. (1990). "A Critical Look at the National Drug Control Strategy." *Yale Law and Policy Review*, 8(1):75-116.

Skolnick, J. (1966). *Justice Without Trial*. New York, NY: John Wiley & Sons.

Wysong, E., R. Aniskiewicz & D. Wright (1994). "Truth and DARE: Tracking Drug Education to Graduation and as Symbolic Politics." *Social Problems*, 41(3):448-471.

Zimmer, L. (1966). "Proactive Policing Against Street-Level Drug Trafficking." *American Journal of Police*, 9(1):43-74.

CHAPTER 10
Community Policing
and Special Populations

*Non-violence is an unchangeable creed.
It has to be pursued in the face of violence raging around you. The path of
true non-violence requires much more
courage than violence.*

—Gandhi

By counterbalancing the emphasis on reacting to calls for service with a proactive focus on solving problems, community policing addresses many needs that would otherwise be left unmet as a result of traditional law enforcement tactics. Community policing requires that the police extend personalized services to many groups whose concerns historically have been overlooked. Traditional policing tends to limit the department's response to crimes and those who commit them. Community policing broadens the police mission, sending CPOs into the community as outreach specialists, so that they can learn about community problems related to crime, fear of crime, and disorder and provide a measure of services to a wide variety of constituent populations.

Even as early as the latter part of the nineteenth century, the police singled out special groups for special attention. The police worked with the infirmed and sick, the homeless, juveniles, criminals, and women (Douthit, 1975; Whitehouse, 1973). During this period, the police were very service oriented. Local politicians knew that they could garner more votes and support from citizens when their police officers helped people as opposed to arresting them or issuing them citations. In fact, in many instances, the police totally neglected their law enforcement duties. This philosophy resulted in the police providing a wide variety of services to the public.

This orientation disappeared in the 1950s as professional policing came to dominate police thinking. During the professional era, the police implemented a bureaucratic, monolithic organization and concentrated on law enforcement and crook catching. Providing services to citizens was seen as being outside the purview of police duties. This remained the case into the 1960s when large-scale urban and campus rioting caused the police to rethink its position. The human relations problems of the 1960s made the police realize that law enforcement alone was not adequate in serving citizens. Since the 1960s, the police have adopted a service orientation that continues today with community policing. Community policing provides a new organizational model that encourages the police to address the problems of groups who have not routinely turned to the police for help. Community policing also fosters the idea that the police cannot handle complex crime and drug problems alone. The police must engage the public in a partnership and cooperatively address crime, drug, and disorder problems.

Community policing, without a question, has caused the police to be more attentive to citizen needs and concerns. In the past, the police relied on the political process to help guide policy decisions. That is, citizens would contact governmental officials such as city council persons who then would discuss problems with the police. Unfortunately, many groups such as the poor, elderly, minorities, and youth were neglected as a result of the process, because they have little or no clout or access into government. Community policing results in direct communication between the police and the public in an effort to ensure that all constituent groups are considered and serviced. Essentially, policing becomes people-oriented, whereby the police favor no singular group and attempt to meet everyone's needs.

Critics of the police working more closely with citizens note that it may very well contribute to renewed police corruption (Bracey, 1992). Part of the impetus for the professional movement was to separate the police from the public and reduce police corruption (Gaines, Kappeler & Vaughn, 1997). During the 1950s, insulating the police from the public, along with closer supervision and better management practices, resulted in a decrease in police corruption. It is feared that community policing may indeed result in a renewed cycle of corruption or in civil liability (Kappeler, 1997) as the police are better able to forge closer working relationships with a variety of people, some of which have unwholesome designs.

The potential benefits from community policing far outweigh its potential problems. Many groups, often those who suffer the highest rates of victimization, are literally disenfranchised from the American political system, and community policing is the most appropriate way for the police to identify these individuals and groups and attempt to bring them back into the system. For example, the homeless do not have a fixed address so they generally are not represented in the political system. Juveniles are too young and many immigrants and undocumented aliens have no vote and are too fearful to become involved in our political process. Residents of many of the highest-crime areas are also among the groups least likely to exercise their franchise. Many such groups also fail to organize, they lack the money to lobby for their concerns, and their relative lack of social standing means they are unlikely to gain formal and informal access to those who hold power. Community policing as a political modality allows such individuals to have input into government and receive some measure of service.

Community policing's ability to involve the disenfranchised and to reach out to other groups who are reluctant to contact the police offers everyone in the community grass-roots input into the police process. The following is a discussion of specific groups that are likely to benefit from community policing.

Juveniles

Juveniles represent a special problem for community policing. On the one hand, juvenile crime, especially violent crime, is portrayed as increasing. It is politicized to the point that many legislative bodies are passing stricter laws in terms of penalties and how juveniles are processed in the criminal justice system (Donziger, 1996). On the other hand, juveniles remain one of the most victimized groups in our society. Advocates claim that child abuse, neglect, and abandonment have substantially increased over the last several years. For example, it has been estimated that there are four to five million children neglected or physically or sexually abused each year (Drowns & Hess, 1995). One study found that as many as 190,000 juveniles are "thrown away" each year by their parents (U.S. Attorney General's Advisory Board on Missing Children, 1986). On any given night, there are between 68,000 and one-half million children who are homeless. Of those who end up homeless, 80 percent report being the victim of sexual abuse at home (Taylor, 1986). Mounting evidence also suggests a link between childhood sexual victimization and adult sex offenses. Of the 255 sex offenders in the Massachusetts Treatment Center, 90 percent reported they were sexually abused as children (Brand, 1987). While these estimates are most certainly inflated (Kappeler, Blumberg & Potter, 1996), children represent a special population as well as a distinctive victim population. Community policing must address both problems within the juvenile population.

In terms of juvenile victims, Fleisher (1995) in a study in Seattle found that on some nights there were more children on the streets at 2:00 a.m. than there were at 4:00 p.m. Many of these children were runaways, castaways, or out on the streets because their parents did not want them or care about them. Introduction to the street life generally meant that they eventually became criminals who were in and out of jails and prison all their lives as the path to survival consists of panhandling and crime. When a juvenile is encountered at 2:00 a.m., the police should make sure that something is done. An investigation by the police and social agencies should be initiated and action should be taken to ensure that the juvenile is cared for. Not only is it an indictment on the police, but it is also telling of our society when we have children walking the streets in the early hours of the day.

In terms of abused children, the police must take an active role in discovering, investigating, and prosecuting such cases. They must come to see themselves as the first line of defense in protecting our nation's children. The police can deploy three general strategies to accomplish this objective. First, the police must become more active in attempting to identify abused and exploited children. For example, how often do police officers check on children when they answer calls at a residence? Since child abuse is more common in homes where other forms of domestic violence occurs, the police should always check on the well-being of any children, even though they may not be a part of the original complaint. The same holds true for those homes where problems of alcoholism and drug abuse are apparent. When there are suspicions circumstances, the police should thoroughly investigate them. When the police otherwise come into contact with children, they should take the opportunity to talk with them and inquire into the possibilities of abuse.

Parents with alcohol or drug problems can have a devastating effect on young lives. Membership in Alcoholics Anonymous has grown from 96,000 in 1950 to nearly one million today. A study of 155,000 pregnant women nationwide showed 11 percent admitted taking an illegal drug during their pregnancy, with cocaine cited most often. This is of great concern because evidence is emerging that the fetus or breast-fed newborn can suffer when the mother uses crack cocaine even one time. Police officers should be trained to recognize signs of abuse, and they should know how to respond to it.

Second, it is also important for the police to cooperate with the social agencies that are directly involved in investigating child abuse and neglect. In the past, the police and social workers functioned independently of each other. Realistically, both agencies have similar goals, the welfare of children. The Louisville, Kentucky Police Department has developed a working relationship with the Kentucky Department of Social Services whereby officers and social workers meet to discuss cases, and in some cases, perform joint investigations. This not only leads to a more effective investigations, but officers are able to fairly quickly provide services to children in need. Close working relationships between the police and social workers can result in less bureaucratic red tape as cases and problems arise.

Third, in the role of community liaison, a CPO can also link families to public and private agencies who can help, whether that is in the form of affordable counseling for the juvenile or perhaps a substance abuse program for one or both of the parents. CPOs intense involvement with the community allows them to reach out to families who need assistance, at the same time it increases the likelihood that people will trust them enough to ask for help. CPOs, when appropriate, should act as family counselors and encourage adults to get help for problems that lead to abuse and delinquency. When they fail to seek help on their own, the CPO should bring in social workers to appraise the situation and take action if necessary.

Juvenile Crime and Violence

Substantial attention to juvenile violent crime began in the 1980s and continues today. If the trend continues, it is estimated that arrests for juveniles will double by the year 2010 (Snyder & Sickmund, 1995). Although juveniles commit approximately 3,000 homicides annually, the media focus on the brutal and spectacular results in national attention to only select acts. For example, in 1993, England and the world was shocked when two 10-year-old boys kidnapped and killed two-year-old James Bolger. Around the same time, national attention was focused on Madison, Indiana, where 12-year-old Shanda Renee Sharer was brutally beaten, sodomized, tortured, doused with gasoline, and set afire. The culprits were four teenage girls. The motive appeared to have been jealousies (see Potter & Kappeler, 1998). Such incidents are not commonplace, but as a result of their sensationalism, they receive national attention resulting in the semblance of widespread youthful violence.

There appear to be a number of causes of violence among young people. The National Coalition of State Juvenile Justice Advisory Groups (1992) report the following to be causal factors:

- Abuse and neglect;

- Economic, social, and educational conditions;

- Gangs; and

- Accessibility of weapons.

Martin (1994) suggests other causes:

- Hopelessness and exposure to violence;

- Weakening of the family unit;

- Media celebration of violence; and

- Drug culture leading to a gun culture.

The causes of violence have direct implications for community policing. First, and perhaps most importantly, it seems that violence begets violence. Many of the teens who are committing violent acts are themselves victims of violence or are subjected to it on a fairly regular basis (Potter & Kappeler, 1998). The police must survey their jurisdiction and identify those areas which have elevated levels of violence. This violence can be interpersonal such as that commonly found around schools or it can be collective violence which is generally associated with gangs. The police must identify the pockets of violence and reduce its levels through enforcement, education, and community action. The police must help organize neighborhoods to help fight those elements which are directly and indirectly associated with violent acts. This can include neighborhood rallies, block watches, citizen patrols, and an increased police presence. Citizens and the police both must understand that the problem cannot be solved without cooperation.

The police must also become involved in providing recreational, civic, and cultural services to the area. The Lexington, Kentucky Police Department, with the support of the Public Housing Authority and the Parks and Recreation Department, operates a police athletic league (PAL) to provide a variety of services to disadvantaged youth. The program offers youth a variety of sports including football and basketball. The department attempts to have sporting programs in place most of the year. The PAL centers are equipped with computers that are used to provide classes to both youth and adults. The computers are also equipped with a variety of game and entertainment software to provide meaningful recreation to area youth. The department has a mentoring program whereby local celebrities such as University of Kentucky basketball players make appearances and give talks. The Public Housing Authority sponsors a number of cultural events including ballet, modern dance, and self-esteem and pride training.

The police must also work with school systems to reduce the levels of crime and violence. Zawitz et al. (1993) report that 22 percent of public school children fear attack. They also found that 16 percent of the respondents in their study reported that a student had attacked or threatened a teacher within the last six months. A recent study by the University of Michigan estimates that there are about 270,000 guns in schools on an average day, and about nine percent of eighth-graders carry a weapon such as a gun, knife, or club to school at least once a month (Martin, 1994). The Bureau of Justice Statistics reports that 24 percent of victimizations of children and teenagers occur in school (Crowe, 1991). These statistics clearly indicate that some of America's schools are an integral part of the juvenile violence picture.

Felson (1994) attributes a great deal of the problem to the fact that school systems for the past several decades have been merging smaller high schools into larger, cost-efficient high schools. Many high schools now have in excess of 1,000 students. These larger schools remove the intimacy where in the past principals, teachers, and staff knew or, at least, recognized all the students. Now students are able to blend into the unknown crowd when they commit assaults and other criminal acts. School staff now control crowds rather than individual students. Felson also notes that routes to these larger schools are where a great deal of crime occurs. Large groups of teenagers are able to congregate unsupervised, which can lead to disorder, vandalism, and other criminal acts.

Youth gangs are a particular problem in some schools. Although many gang members abhor school, they still see schools as a part of their turf. They recruit members from within schools, assault and intimidate students, and deface schools with their graffiti. School administrators must recognize the existence of such problems and act on them when they occur. The Office of Juvenile Justice and Delinquency Prevention (1994) has identified three components of an effective school-based gang control strategy:

- The development of a school gang code, with guidelines specifying an appropriate response by teachers and staff to different kinds of gang behavior, including a mechanism for dealing with serious gang delinquency; and

- The application of these rules and regulations within a context of positive relationships and open communication by school personnel with parents, community agencies, and students.

Denver School Cop Riles Parents

There's one less police officer assigned to Denver schools this year, after a parents' group protested the continued operation of a police substation at a middle school located in a gang-plagued neighborhood, which they said contributed to a "prison-like atmosphere" at the school.

During the 1996-97 school year, the Police Department assigned an officer to the Horace Mann Middle School, which is located in a predominantly Latino neighborhood that police say has seen its share of gang activity.

The pilot effort, which was initiated by then-Principal Miguel Elias, was supposed to improve relations between police and students, as well as keep criminal activity in and near the school to a minimum.

A room at the school was set aside for the officer, and officers working in the district also were encouraged to stop by and do their paperwork there. The officer posted at Horace Mann visited classrooms and interacted with students.

But when members of Concerned Parents of Horace Mann Middle School got wind of the program, they protested, saying the police were not needed there. They petitioned for the removal of the substation, demanding an end to the "prison-like atmosphere" the officer's presence allegedly conjured, The Denver Post reported recently.

The outcry led to the officer being removed and the room closed. Elias later resigned, although he said controversies surrounding his programs, which included a strict dress code, were not factors in his decision.

Police and school officials apparently have not ruled out restarting the program, which was supposed to become permanent starting this academic year. Horace Mann principal Jim Treviño told the newspaper he was planning a series of town hall meetings with parents to gauge possible support for the return of a police officer to the school. In the meantime, police say, offi-

cers will continue to maintain a patrol presence in the area.

Treviño did not return calls from Law Enforcement News for comment on the current status of the issue. But a police spokeswoman, Det. Virginia Lopez, who herself served two years as a school resource officer, told LEN that no officer had yet been assigned to the school as of Sept. 30.

Currently, the Police Department assigns 11 officers to teach Drug Abuse and Resistance Education programs in city elementary schools, and some of them also do double-duty as middle school resource officers. "They're there mostly to improve relations with students, but the program also leans toward enforcement," Lopez said.

High schools will be covered after Jan. 1, the starting date for a new program to assign officers to each of the district's 10 high schools, she added.

Source: *Law Enforcement News* (1997). November 15, p. 5.

- A clear distinction between gang and non-gang-related activity so as not to exaggerate the scope of the problem (1994:18).

CPOs should be assigned to schools to work with school officials in developing programs within the schools to reduce drug abuse, crime, and violence. The police should take a more active role in investigating drug and crime problems on school property. In the past, the schools have unfortunately attempted to handle such problems internally and cover them up effectively. When the schools did take action, it usually was in the form of suspensions which, for the most part, are ineffective in dealing with problem students. School officials must understand and accept that in some cases the juvenile justice system is better equipped to deal with problems. A number of states have now passed laws that require schools to report criminal violations to the police. Recently, the Louisville Police Department charged a school official for failing to report a crime to the police. The police action is said to have resulted in greater cooperation afterwards.

Conversely, the police should cooperate with the schools. A number of departments now have programs where they provide the school system with information on arrests of juveniles who are charged with drug or weapons offenses. Although the schools do not necessarily take any action, it does alert the school staff to the problems, and it may allow teachers and staff to monitor these students' activities more closely. Such information also may assist individual teachers in protecting themselves by carefully monitoring potentially violent students who are in their classes. There are, however, many issues, such as privacy and labeling of juveniles, that make this practice problematic.

Community policing substantially expands the police role regarding juveniles. In the past, the police merely monitored trouble areas and detained juveniles who committed criminal acts. Community policing requires that the police work with a variety of public and private agencies throughout the community in identifying problems and developing solutions to them.

Urban Youth Gangs

Urban youth gangs have become one of law enforcement's most difficult problems. Gangs not only exist in our major cities, they now have spread to medium-sized cities. A national survey found gangs present in 110 jurisdictions with an estimated 4,881 gangs with about 249,300 gang members (Curry, Ball & Fox, 1994). The gangs are substantially involved in drug trafficking and indiscriminate violence. Curry and his colleagues found that gangs were responsible for 1,072 homicides and 46,359 crimes within a 12-month period. More importantly, their violent nature has resulted in numerous deaths of innocent bystanders which has caused public rage and massive fear. Urban youth gangs represent a problem that the police must make every effort to effectively handle.

Given the public attention provided to gangs, it would appear that they are a relatively new phenomenon. However, gangs have existed throughout our history. A number of the organized crime groups that dominated American crime in the early and middle decades of the twentieth century began as gangs. Movies such as *Blackboard Jungle* and *West Side Story* focused public attention on the problem decades ago, but for the most part, up until the 1980s, gangs existed almost exclusively on the east and west coasts and in Chicago (Miller, 1991). The spread of gangs into America's heartland has been attributed to drug trafficking. As the crack markets in the larger cities became saturated, the gangs moved into other cities or markets where there was little or no competition. The gangs also found that the police were inexperienced in dealing with them, which made it much easier for them to become entrenched in the community.

Given the public concern, and in some cases hysteria, associated with gangs, it is important to fully understand what a gang is. Too often the public and officials tend to label any group of young African-Americans, Hispanics, and in some cases, Asian-Americans, as gangs when in fact they do not constitute a gang. Indeed, Decker and Kempf-Leonard (1991) find substantial disagreement among criminal justice officials and academics in terms of what constitutes a gang. No one definition is totally accurate, but there are several worth examining. First, Dart (1992) notes that street gangs have the following characteristics:

- A gang name and recognizable symbols;

- A geographic territory;

- A regular meeting pattern; and

- An organized, continuous course of criminality (1992:96).

Miller (1980) offers a more comprehensive definition,

- A youth gang is a self-forming association of peers, bound together by mutual interests, with identifiable leadership, well-developed lines of authority, and other organizational features, who act in concert to achieve a specific purpose or purposes which generally include the conduct of illegal activity and control over a particular territory, facility or type of enterprise (1980:121).

Both of the definitions presented here offer a number of points, and it is clear that gangs are difficult to concretely define. The problem comes when attempting to calculate the amount of crime and violence associated with gangs. Regoli and Hewitt (1994) note that the Chicago Police Department has a more restrictive definition of gang-related crimes as compared to the Los Angeles Police Department, which results in Los Angeles reporting far more gang-related criminal activity. There is a propensity for the police to over-report gang activities. For example, Bursik and Grasmick (1993) report that a Frederick, Oklahoma police chief warned the community that the city was being invaded by urban youth gangs. His evidence of the gang problem was graffiti, increase in auto thefts, cases of shoplifting, drug trafficking, and notes left on cars attributed to the Crips. The evidence presented by the chief, basically, is unconvincing. However, the police must be able to determine fairly accurately whether gangs are present, and if they are present, what their nature is? This is critical in devising an effective police response.

It is just as important for the police to accurately identify who gang members are. Typically, some departments label any minority youth who gives them problems as a gang member. Such a practice tends to exaggerate the problem and prevent the police from developing meaningful solutions. Sanders (1994) has perhaps developed the best criteria to be used by the police in identifying gang members:

- Admits to being a member of a gang;

- Has tattoos, clothing, or other paraphernalia which is associated with a particular gang;

- Police records or observations confirm association with other known gang members;

- Has been arrested with gang members while committing a gang-related crime; and

- A reliable informant confirms membership in a gang.

It should be noted that all sorts of gangs exist, but here we are more concerned with the urban youth gangs that have spread across the country. Skolnick et al. (1990) point out that urban youth gangs are cultural or entrepreneurial in nature. The cultural gangs are those which evolve in a particular neighborhood. They seem to originate as a result of social needs. Their members band together as a result of their familiarity with one another and the need for self-protection. Some have discussed the cultural gang in terms of the extended family where the gang serves to provide some of the belonging and nurturing functions that are often absent in many inner-city homes. They tend to establish a turf area and protect it from intrusion from other youth gangs. The entrepreneurial gangs tend to form as a result of the pecuniary benefits associated with drug trafficking. They band together to form a business enterprise. This does not mean that cultural gangs are not involved in drug trafficking. They also deal in drugs as a result of the lucrative profits, but their primary objective is to fulfill a variety of social and cultural needs.

Some gangs have a distinctive organization. Gangs are organized into sets. A set represents particular neighborhood. For example, there are several thousand Bloods in Los Angeles. They are organized into sets, and each set is fairly independent from the other sets. In some cases, sets within the same gang may go to war with each other. Also, each set has an organization:

The sets are structured along lines of seniority and function. They have caste-like sub-divisions within each set, notably (1) original gang members (O.G.); (2) gangsters, the hard-core members, whose ages range from 16 to 22; (3) baby gangsters, who are between nine and 12; and (4) in some cases, tiny gangsters, who are even younger. While some age groups go the late 20s and early 30s, the most violent and active members are those between 14 and 18, many of the them "wantabees" who want to prove themselves in order to be accepted by other gang members and who are precisely the ones most useful as soldiers in gang activities (Attorney General, 1989:33).

Gangs can develop throughout a city. For example, Figure 10.1 shows the organization of gangs for a section of Chicago. Chicago has three primary gangs and a host of other, smaller gangs with approximately 40,000 total gang members. The map also depicts the patterns of violence. Note the areas are fairly evenly divided between turf-related violence and drug-related violence. There are also a number of areas that are relatively free of violence.

Figure 10.1
Street Gang-Motivated Homicide, Other Violence, and Drug Crime, 1987-1990

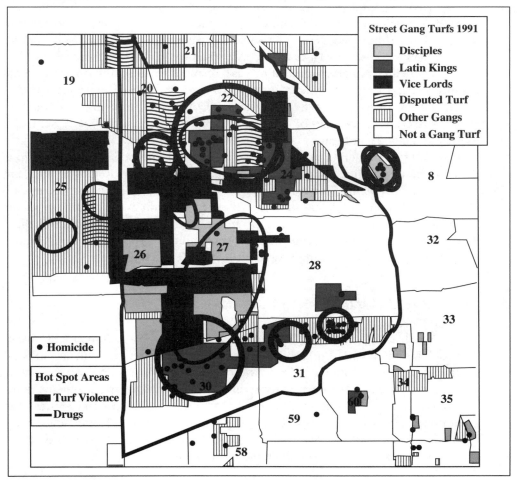

Source: Chicago Police Department.

Between 1987 and 1990, there were 288 street gang-motivated homicides in Chicago. Only eight were drug-related. The data seem to indicate that the relationship between drugs, gangs, and homicide is rather weak and over-stated. Most of the lethal gang violence occurred in areas where turf, rather than drugs, was being disputed. Also, 51 percent of the city's gang-related homicides and 35 percent of nonlethal gang violence occurred in ten community areas. There was some level of variation in gang activities in the various community areas. In some cases, gangs were selling heroin, while gangs in other areas were concentrating on crack cocaine. All the gangs were engaged in a variety of criminal activities (Block & Block, 1993).

There seems to be some agreement about why kids are attracted to and join gangs. Thrasher (1928) postulated that gangs fill the void of social disorganization that exists in lower-class communities. Fleisher (1995) agrees by noting, "Neighborhoods in that informal social control mechanisms have deteriorated are left with a gaping hole in their social fabric. This tear is filled by gangs acting as self-help groups (1995:150). Along these same lines, Cloward and Ohlin (1960) saw gangs form as a result of sparse access to legitimate means for accomplishing traditional goals or attaining success. Gangs represent an illegitimate means to accomplish goals such as wealth, power, and societal or neighborhood recognition. Also, once gangs exist, they actively recruit members and force juveniles to join as a result of fear tactics (Sanders, 1994).

There are a number implications as a result of the research on gangs. First and perhaps foremost, is that gangs form as a result of disorganization and disintegration that occur in neighborhoods. Community policing is a comprehensive strategy that can be used to rehabilitate neighborhoods. Essentially, neighborhoods, not gangs, are the problem. Improvements in neighborhoods can lead to a reduction in gang problems. Second, the police must develop a keen understanding of any gang problems and develop strategies tailored for individual problems. The research shows that a variety of gang problems can develop, and no individual strategy will be effective in every case. The police must collect data and information on problems, diagnose them, and then deploy their resources accordingly. Perhaps most importantly, police must refrain from using the gang problem to generate citizens' fear.

COP Intervention Programs

Youth gangs represent a complex problem for law enforcement. Gang problems intertwine themselves throughout a community, which results in the opening of a number of fronts which require police action. All too often, police strategies have been reactive and fail to address gang problems comprehensively. The police must develop a host of strategies and tactics that address all aspects of the problem. The Office of Juvenile Justice and Delinquency Prevention (1994) has identified a package of tactics which on their face have the potential to reduce gang problems:

- Targeting, arresting, and incarcerating gang leaders and repeat violent gang offenders;

- Referring fringe members and their parents to youth services for counseling and guidance;

- Providing preventative services for youth who are clearly at risk;

- Crisis intervention or mediation of gang fights; and

- Patrols of community [gang] hot spots.

An excellent example of how a department developed a comprehensive community policing approach to its gang problems is Reno, Nevada (Weston, 1993). The department established a Community Action Team (CAT) to deal with the expanding gang problem. The first step the CAT team took was to gather intelligence about the gangs and their membership. The team was issued gang kits that consisted of cameras, field interview cards, and tape recorders. Police officers, suspects, and informants were interviewed in an effort to develop information about gang activities and membership. CAT members routinely visited the jail and interviewed prisoners to gather additional information. Once collected, the information was collected in a gang-related database.

CAT members then attempted to identify the most violent gang members and the ones most involved in criminal activities. A majority of the gang-related crime was found to be committed by 10 to 15 percent of the city's gang members. Five local departments and the Federal Bureau of Investigation created a Violent Crime Task Force to target the gang members who were involved in the greatest amount of criminal activities.

The CAT team then implemented a community awareness program. The team had a brochure printed that provided parents information about gangs and community services in dealing with the gang problem. When officers encountered gang members, the officers would speak with the parents and provide them a copy of the brochure. It was hoped that the parents would seek help from the counseling services provided in the brochure. At the same time, the department initiated a number of neighborhood advisory boards to provide feedback to the department relative to its gang-related programs. By emphasizing assistance and cooperation, the police were able to garner higher levels of public support for the program.

The CAT team also initiated an intervention program. CAT officers operated a bicycle shop that employed gang members to repair bicycles. The repaired bikes were then donated to needy children in the area. CAT officers also established a job apprenticeship program for gang members. Here a number of construction companies, body shops, and other businesses provided employment opportunities to gang members as a result of police referral. The intervention program focused on getting the neophyte gang members out of the gang milieu. It also showed other gang members that opportunities other than gang membership existed.

Finally, the department was instrumental in creating the Gang Alternatives Partnership (GAP). GAP was created to coordinate the efforts of the many private and public agencies who were involved in the gang problem. Agencies included: police departments, the district attorney's office, juvenile probation, the school district, private agencies, and private businesses. Members of the group recognized that singularly they had little impact, but collectively, they could perhaps make some significant inroads. GAP began to serve as a single source of information to the community as well as to coordinate agencies' efforts. Ultimately, a full-time executive director was hired, which helped to sustain the group's efforts.

In summary, gangs represent a unique challenge for law enforcement and communities. The very existence of gangs evidences traditional law enforcement's failure. Community policing appears to be the only viable way to confront the gang problem. Even then, departments must develop comprehensive programs that cut across a variety of fronts.

Policing the Homeless

It is virtually impossible to obtain an accurate count of the homeless people in a given jurisdiction, let alone for the nation. However, anytime one visits a major city in the United States, he or she is likely to encounter homeless people. It is a problem that appears to have been growing in magnitude for several decades. Snyder and Hombs (1986) note that the homeless population is somewhere between two and three million with less than 100,000 shelter beds available to them. They attribute the growing numbers to several problems:

- A shortage of affordable housing. The last decade has witnessed a substantial decrease in the amount of federal spending for subsidized housing, and the trend continues;

- The careless and wholesale depopulation of the nation's mental hospitals. When non-dangerous mental patients were de-institutionalized, many of them ended up on the streets. The American Psychiatric Association estimates that there are one million homeless who are in need of mental health services;

- The cumulative effects of cuts to a variety of federal programs have resulted in many people becoming homeless. When recent changes in the welfare system come to fruition, there will be an additional round of homeless;

- Although unemployment is the lowest it has been for several decades, the unskilled remain jobless or underemployed. Technology and the business enterprise seem to be bypassing a large number of Americans;

- The minimum wage has not kept pace with the cost of living. Unskilled jobs pay at the bottom of the pay scale, and such wages make it impossible for families to afford any kind of housing; and

- The breakdown of the traditional family has contributed to the homeless problem. In past decades, it was unheard of for families to allow other family members to become homeless.

The homeless constitute a two-fold problem for police. As discussed in the chapter on fear of crime, people are most fearful of potentially menacing strangers loitering. Even though no figures exist concerning how many homeless people commit crimes, their desperate straits make people uneasy. Anyone who has walked past the ragged, homeless people who dot the tunnels in New York City's subways or the streets of any large city's central business district knows that they inspire an anguished mix of feelings that include fear, guilt, revulsion, and shame. Their hand-lettered signs detailing real or embellished horror stories about why they have been reduced to begging constitute a grim litany of modern problems, AIDS, Vietnam vets who cannot find work, pregnant women with nowhere to go, and children who have been evicted from their homes. These conditions can result in the homeless committing a variety of crimes. However, for the most part, their crimes are minor and generally relate to the acquisition of food, shelter, and drugs or alcohol (Fischer, 1988; Solarz, 1985).

The second concern is the alarming rates of victimization that the homeless suffer. There is growing awareness that the children in shelters for the homeless are targets of sexual abuse. Generally, homeless children are with their mother. In some sensational cases, children are bartered for food, alcohol, or drugs by a parent. A study of the elderly homeless in Detroit showed that more than one-half had been beaten, robbed, or raped the preceding year, and many report they do not stay in shelters because of the fear of victimization (Chandler, 1988). These are people whose lack of a permanent address already robs them of their right to vote, which effectively muzzles them from having a direct say in the political process.

The homeless cannot simply pick up a phone to call the police when they are threatened, yet traditional policing depends on a call for service as the primary impetus for taking action. Community policing, in contrast, "goes looking for trouble" before problems erupt into a crisis. Just because the homeless have no votes, no PAC money, and no telephones should not mean they are excluded from police priorities. Their complex dilemma requires more than crisis intervention, and this is yet another niche where community policing offers unique opportunities to make a positive difference.

In the role of community liaison, CPOs can help link homeless people to public and private agencies that can help. CPOs are also the logical candidates to enlist and work with community volunteers on improving security in shelters and on the street. The police response must include more than rousting the homeless whenever their unnerving presence inflames taxpayers to demand visual relief or arresting those homeless people who take over abandoned, federally owned houses. In New York City, the Transit Authority officers have had to balance the rights of the homeless with the rights of the general public. This means protecting the homeless' right to take shelter in the public subway tunnels, free from harm. At the same time it means people must be allowed unobstructed access to the system, and they must be protected from harassment. It took years to create the current crisis, so even a concerted and well-funded effort will no doubt take years to undo. This is an obvious area where community policing can help.

Balancing the needs of the homeless with society's right to not be harassed by the homeless has not been an easy task for the police. Indeed, the police often are caught in the middle between where people desire to have the homeless removed, but the police do not have any place to take them. Plotkin and Narr (1993) found ample examples of the problem. In Santa Cruz, California, the police were bombarded with complaints ranging from citizens' groups to the American Civil Liberties Union over the treatment of the homeless by police officers who were enforcing "no camping" and other anti-homeless ordinances. The Miami Police Department was sued after it stepped up enforcement of "no sleeping in public and loitering in parks after hours" ordinances. At one point, the Santa Monica city prosecutor refused to prosecute "offenses related to economic status" because of the criminal justice system's inability to deal with the problem. Perhaps the most dramatic case came from Santa Ana, California where the police department was required to pay $400,000 after officers chained 64 homeless people to benches and wrote identification numbers on their arms. It becomes extremely frustrating for the police when on the one hand there are demands to deal with the homeless who are making a nuisance of themselves while on the other hand, there are inadequate resources to effectively deal with the problem.

When dealing with the homeless, CPOs must realize that there are different types of homeless. For example, the police in Kansas City have devised a typology consisting of four groups:

- *Socio-economic Homeless* who are homeless as a result of losing a job, being under-employed, spouse abuse, or a divorce. People in this classification were a part of society, but they became homeless as a result of some economic or social event. They lost their ability to "make it" in the real world;

- *Mentally Ill Homeless* are those who have mental problems but are not institutionalized or have been abandoned or thrown out by their families. These individuals generally are not ill enough for institutionalization, but they are disruptive, angry, or violent to the point that family members and friends are not able to care for them;

- *Homeless Lifestyle* include those individ
  the streets as their lifestyle. They feel co
  lives, and they tend to view a change toward
  threatening; and

- *Undocumented Aliens* represent a sizable homeles
  in a number of cities and small towns. They do not re
  victimized to the police for fear of being deported. I
  cases, they also represent a group who is prone to crime an
  lence (Plotkin & Narr, 1993).

Police officers will encounter all types of homeless, and as such, no si gular program will be adequate in addressing the needs of all four types. Police officers must be adept at recognizing the root cause of homelessness in each case and act accordingly. This is especially true since many homeless suffer from alcohol and drug abuse problems. Along these same lines, police departments must recognize that a variety of programs will be needed to address the homeless problem. When officers encounter homeless persons who require some type of social service or other assistance, the help should be readily available.

Perhaps the most important component of a police response to the homeless is deciding upon the department's goals and policy regarding the problem. The first step here is to come to grips with the scope of the problem itself. For example, Plotkin and Narr (1993) in their national study of homelessness found that almost 50 percent of the police agencies in their survey reported that the homeless was a minor problem, while about 17 percent reported that it was a major problem. It appears that the homeless problem varies from jurisdiction to jurisdiction and perception of the homeless may be more a reflection of available resources. Those departments with adequate resources, a small homeless population, and few complaints about the homeless are more apt to view the homeless as a minor problem. Regardless, the vast majority of large municipalities have a homeless problem.

Many police departments do not have specific written policies to guide police officers when dealing with the homeless. These departments depend on ordinances such as public intoxication, loitering, emergency mental health commitments, and other public disorder ordinances to contend with the homeless problem. Other jurisdictions such as Los Angeles and Santa Monica developed special units to deal with the homeless. However, the units' primary objective was to make enforcement and order maintenance more efficient as opposed to providing the homeless assistance. Most traditionally organized departments depend almost exclusively on enforcement as the way to deal with the homeless. Community policing dictates that the police combine enforcement with the delivery of services as the best approach to the homeless problem.

The first step beyond traditional responses to the homeless is where the department adopts policies for dealing with the homeless in emergency situ-

Department has an inclement
or the homeless. In terms of
ture drops below 32 degrees
ons. Once located they are
Resource Authority which
the numbers of persons
ng force for officers and
e being policed for home-
cold-weather deaths. The
are to handle homeless
ment. In these cases, the
e individuals from shel-
Narr, 1993).

e that departments go
operative relations with a variety
with the problem. Although most communities
resources to adequately handle the homeless, more can be
done in most communities. First, the police must make a special effort to
provide the homeless with adequate police protection. Patrols should periodically check areas where the homeless congregate. And reports of crime
should be taken seriously and investigated thoroughly. The homeless are easily victimized and special efforts should be made to reduce victimization
where possible. Second, the police should serve as referral agents to provide
the homeless with access to food, shelter, and medical care. This is accomplished by ensuring that officers are familiar with facilities and policies
regarding admission or access. Third, the police should avail themselves to
facilitate the homeless access to employment opportunities and job training.
Although not all homeless are interested in services, some, especially those
who are homeless as the result of socio-economic problems very well may be.

There is no panacea when dealing with the homeless. For example, Mac-
Donald (1995) chronicled the Matrix Program in San Francisco where the
police coupled enhanced enforcement with expanded social services. The
police were able to substantially reduce the visible homeless problem, primarily as a result of enforcement, but they and social workers were not able
to substantially increase the homeless participation in social programs.

Minorities and the Police

Historically, a substantial amount of resentment existed between the
police and minorities. For the most part, the police have seen themselves as
the servants of the ruling class and tended to be opposed to cultures outside
the mainstream. Also, minorities tended to be poor and had little if any rep-
resentation in our political system. Only recently have the police made strides

in providing better services to all citizens regardless of their race or culture. This movement began in the 1960s as police departments implemented police-community relations programs to reach out to the underprivileged classes. Today, many police departments have embraced the idea of mult-culturalism and have made substantial efforts to provide all citizens better services. This has become a cornerstone in community policing. However, race remains a volatile police issue because:

- the alarming rates of victimization many minority groups endure;

- the disproportionate number of minorities arrested and incarcerated;

- the debate about how best to promote minority hiring and promotion in police departments;

- the role of race as a common factor in police brutality;

- the concern that racially motivated incidents and attacks are on the rise; and

- the worrisome emergence and growth of new militant groups, such as the skinheads, who openly advocate violence against minorities.

The police will no doubt face even greater pressure to deal with these issues as the racial balance in the United States continues to shift. According to a recent report by the Census Bureau, America will become dramatically less white over the next century. In a study projecting population trends 100 years into the future, the Census Bureau projected that by 2080, white, non-Hispanic Americans will be close to losing majority status to today's three major minority groups—African-Americans, Asian-Americans, and Hispanics (Scanlan, 1989). As America moves toward greater diversity, the police must be ready and equipped to protect all citizens when conflict occurs.

As Williams and Murphy (1988) have written, African-Americans in particular among minorities were long excluded completely from political power. When the reform era substituted the law for politics as the source of police power, this made a difference for the white mainstream, but not for African-Americans. "For those who lacked both political power and equal protection under the law, however, such a transformation could have little significance." The concern even now is that the politically powerful will influence the allocation of police resources so that community policing will be implemented in strong communities where community or business organizations have access to the political leadership, rather than to disintegrating minority neighborhoods with less political influence. This is the avenue that crime prevention took in the late 1970s and early 1980s. It was not until community policing was accepted by law enforcement did the police begin to respond to many minority community needs.

Even today, a number of problems remain. In many instances police departments have failed to adequately address minority relations or have given them a low priority. Minorities have continue to voice a number of complaints against the police. Radelet and Carter (1994) summarize the complaints:

- Substandard or poor police protection;

- Substandard or poor service to minorities, especially inner-city residents;

- The expectation that the police will not treat them fairly;

- Numerous incidents of verbal abuse and harassment;

- Stereotyping of minorities as criminals, particularly in "stop and frisk incidents;"

- Police use of excessive force; and

- Discrimination in police personnel administration.

The Rodney King Incident

A number of incidents illustrate the problems between the police and minorities. Perhaps the Rodney King incident in Los Angeles which received national attention best characterizes the problem and minority sentiment toward the police. The King incident is significant because of the brutality of the incident and the fact that it was videotaped and shown on national television. The incident was the highlight of national news broadcasts for several days.

The incident began at 12:40 a.m. when a California Highway Patrol (CHIP) unit began following King who was driving a white Hyundai. After observing King speeding, the CHIP officers signaled him to stop by activating their emergency equipment, but he failed to do so. King continued to drive for several more miles, allegedly reaching speeds of 110 to 115 m.p.h., running several stop signs and stop lights during the chase. In the meantime, two Los Angeles Police units and a cruiser from the Los Angeles Unified School District Police joined in the chase.

When King finally pulled over he was ordered out of the car. In the meantime, eleven additional LAPD units including a helicopter with 21 officers arrived at the scene (Christopher Commission, 1991). Two passengers, Bryant Allen and Freddie Helms, both African-Americans, complied with police orders to exit the vehicle and were taken into custody without incident. However, King refused to exit the vehicle. When he did exit the vehicle, he was shocked twice with a 50,000 volt taser by LAPD Sergeant Stacy Koon. LAPD officers Powell and Wind began hitting King with their nightsticks, and he was repeatedly kicked by Officer Briseno. Officers hit King at least 56 times, while 21 to 27 officers stood by and watched. When it was over, King suffered 11 skull fractures, a broken cheekbone, a fractured eye socket, a broken ankle, missing teeth, kidney damage, external burns, and permanent brain damage (Kappeler, Sluder & Alpert, 1994). He remained in jail for four days until prosecutors decided there was not enough evidence to charge him for attempting to evade the police.

At the root of the problem in Los Angeles was a police culture that not only sanctioned police violence, but encouraged it. For example, Kappeler, Sluder, and Alpert (1994:151) provide a number of public examples where Chief Daryl F. Gates was insensitive to the treatment of minorities by his police officers,

> . . . . after becoming chief, Gates attended a luncheon of the Coalition of Mexicanos/Latinos Against Defamation and was asked about the LAPD's failure to employ and promote appropriate numbers of Hispanic officers; Gates simply replied that Hispanics are "lazy" and told a story to illustrate the point. Four years later when besieged with questions about police use of a controversial choke hold that resulted in the deaths of at least sixteen citizens-most of whom were African-American, Gates responded that "the veins or arteries [of African-Americans] do not open up as fast as they do on normal people" [citations omitted].

Police officers were encouraged to be aggressive. Aggressiveness, not problem solving or community partnerships and empowerment, was the department's primary strategy for dealing with all problems. The Christopher Commission (1991:2-3) noted,

> While the overall rate of violent crime in the United States increased three and one-half times between 1960 and 1989, the rate in Los Angeles during the same period was more than twice the national average. According to the 1986 data recently published by the Police Foundation, the Los Angeles police were the busiest among the officers in the nation's largest six cities. . . . Of the police departments of the six largest United States cities, the LAPD has the fewest officers per resident and the fewest officers per square mile. Yet the LAPD boasts more arrests per officer than other forces.

The Christopher Commission also examined complaints of excessive force. There were complaints filed against 1,800 officers from 1986 to 1990. More than 1,400 officers had only one or two complaints, but 183 officers had four or more allegations. Forty-four officers had six or more complaints, 16 had eight or more, and one officer had 16 complaints. Similar patterns emerged for use of force reports which were filed each time an officer used force against a citizen. Nearly 6,000 officers filed use of force report from January 1987 to March 1991. Four thousand of the officers had fewer than five such reports each. There were 63 officers who had 20 or more reports, and the top five percent of the officers accounted for 20 percent of all the use of force reports filed.

It is important to note that LAPD's top administrators did little to control or investigate officers' use of force. A number of assistant chiefs blamed the problem on first-line supervisors who did little to control officers or report excessive force cases to higher authorities. It seems that managers and supervisors abdicated their responsibility to control excessive use of force and willingly contributed to the department's subculture of violence.

The police aggressiveness was also evidenced by the number of civil rights claims filed against the Los Angeles Police Department. In a five-year period, there were 3,716 non-traffic-related claims filed. The department litigated more than 300 excessive force cases in just four years. The cost of the judgments, settlements, and jury verdicts was in excess of $20 million in four years (Christopher Commission, 1991). Police aggression cost the City of Los Angeles substantially. Apparently, the City was willing to pay the price for the department to use arrests as the primary mechanism for dealing with crime and other problems (Kappeler, Sluder & Alpert, 1994).

While community policing is no panacea that can erase all minority concerns, it can make valuable contributions toward easing racial tensions and addressing minority crime concerns. Not only does community policing differ from traditional policing because it takes all crime and disorder problems seriously, it does so in ways that empower rather than alienate members of the community. This is especially important for minorities who often have felt their needs and concerns did not receive the priority they deserved. By improving police-community relations as a by-product of delivering personalized police service, instead of as its primary focus, community policing does not suffer from the ineffectiveness problems of programs from the past. Community police attempts to focus on real problems, whereas traditional policing generally attended to symptoms of problems.

If community policing is to be successful in reducing minority tensions within a community, the philosophy must be embraced by everyone in the department. Whereas the Los Angeles Police Department operated under a philosophy of aggression and traditionalism, community policing dictates that the police first view its citizens as customers. All citizens are customers who should be shown a measure of respect and afforded a commitment to service. This philosophy dictates that the police defuse situations, not incite them. It means that police officers must engage in problem solving and attempt to identify solutions that meet the needs of constituents and situations. This philosophy also applies to persons who are being investigated or arrested. Police officers must rise above the fray and treat people impartially, fairly, and show them the respect they deserve.

Undocumented Aliens

Precise figures regarding undocumented aliens are obviously difficult to obtain. The best estimate is that there are now approximately five million undocumented aliens or nearly two percent of the total United States population. It is also estimated that this number increases by approximately 275,000 each year (McDonald, 1997). Within the ranks of new arrivals are those who have some hope of remaining legally, if they can prove they fled political repression and face retaliation if returned home. Those who left their homes because of economic problems are routinely deported, and Mexican nationals automatically fall into this category, as do Canadians and citizens of most European and Asian countries. Haitians have also had notable difficulty in establishing political grounds. Table 10.1 provides a breakdown of the top five countries with undocumented aliens in the United States.

Table 10.1
Where Do Most Undocumented Aliens Come From?

Undocumented Aliens enter the United States from every part of the globe, but as of 1992, the top five coutries of origin were:	
Originating Country	**Number of Undocumented Aliens in the United States**
Mexico	1,321,000
El Salvador	327,000
Guatemala	129,000
Canada	97,000
Poland	91,000

Source: U.S. Immigration and Naturalization Service (1996). *Statistical Yearbook of the Immigration and Naturalization Service, 1994.* Washington, DC: U.S. Government Printing Office.

Undocumented aliens pose a difficult challenge for police, because fear of deportation often makes them reluctant to report crimes committed against them—which also makes them easy prey. They can also fall victim to crimes related to their vulnerability—scams include extortion, fees for phony documentation, supposed bribes to judges, and other creative cons. Without legal status, many take jobs in the *grey economy,* and employers often exploit their status by underpaying them or refusing to pay them at all. Because so many arrive with little or no money and have difficulty making a living, undocumented aliens often cluster in low-income, high-crime areas.

Although some politicians have inferred that undocumented aliens are involved in crime, it appears that they are not overrepresented in the criminal population. For example, a 1994 study estimated that there were 21,395 undocumented aliens in prisons in seven states with California holding more than 70 percent of them and New York next with 10 percent (Clark, Passel, Zimmermann & Fix, 1994). Studies in San Diego and El Paso, two cities with large undocumented alien populations, showed that undocumented aliens constituted 12 and 15 percent respectively for serious crime (McDonald, 1997). These statistics indicate that undocumented aliens are not overly represented in criminality.

The smuggling of immigrants has mushroomed into a major crime problem in the United States. For example, in 1993, gangs in New York City were charging residents of China between $15,000 and $50,000 to be smuggled into the United States. It was estimated that the Chinese smuggling market alone was worth approximately $3.5 billion. Most of the immigrants would pay a down payment of about $1,500 and rest upon arrival. In many cases, the immigrants would be required to work much like an indentured slave to pay the remainder of the fee. In 1995, Central America became a free trade zone which allowed government officials to sell visas and passports to the Chinese. This allowed the Chinese to leave for the United States by plane, which was far safer than other arrangements. It is estimated that 10,000 undocumented aliens per month were being moved to the United States (McDonald, 1997). The transporting of undocumented aliens very likely is far safer and more lucrative than smuggling drugs, at least for the smugglers.

Undocumented aliens place the police in a rather precarious position. On the one hand, they are violating federal laws, while on the other, they are often in need of police protection and services. In order to deal with this problem, the San Diego County Sheriff's Department issued the following policy:

> The primary responsibility for the enforcement of immigration laws rests with Federal authorities. Nonetheless, the Sheriff's Department has a responsibility to guarantee the safety and well-being of all people living within this county. The scope of this responsibility includes the enforcement of applicable Federal and State statutes concerned with illegal immigration into the United States and the County of San Diego to ensure the safety and well-being of illegal immigrants of this county.

Although the department recognizes its responsibility for enforcing immigration laws, it seems that the department's priority rests with providing all persons within the county with a reasonable level of services. This philosophy seems to be spreading to non-border states. For example, the State Attorney's office in Montgomery County, Maryland, recently started a "theft of services" unit whose primary objective is to obtain justice for undocumented aliens who are cheated by employers. Undocumented aliens are a challenge to community policing. However, it seems logical that the plight of people often outweigh the need for strict enforcement.

Tourists and Transients

Many summer and winter resort communities as well as cities that are popular entertainment centers face problems because of the influx of tourists and part-time residents who swell the population at different seasons of the year. An obvious concern is that people who have no long-range stake in the community adopt the conventioneer syndrome where they behave recklessly and irresponsibly. They exhibit drunkenness, vandalism, or skipping out on bills. They tend to victimize the community they visit. The reverse of this problem is where tourists such as those in some of the gambling cities of Atlantic City or Las Vegas are targeted as victims by local robbers, prostitutes, or even local merchants. Without a doubt, tourists and transient populations create problems for the police, and the police must develop strategies for dealing with them. Community policing is the ideal solution to many problems associated with tourists and transients.

A number of resort cities have specialized problems. For example, cities such as Daytona Beach, Ft. Lauderdale, and Panama City, Florida, are inundated with students during spring break. These cities are literally overwhelmed with partying college students. Similarly, Louisville has the Kentucky Derby, New Orleans has its Mardi Gras, and Indianapolis has the Indianapolis 500 race. Such activities require the police to apply the precepts of community policing, especially if they are to maintain some semblance of order. The police must control the situation while allowing the visitors to enjoy themselves and engage the local businesses. Such a process requires large numbers of police officers with exceptional personal skills. It requires that the police department develop operational plans that assist in controlling crowds while at the same time allowing the tourists to enjoy themselves.

Victimization of tourists has evolved into a major problem for some jurisdictions. Over the last several years there have been several tourists, including foreign nationals, who have been robbed and murdered in south Florida, which has resulted in world-wide publicity. Florida has developed an extensive tourist information program to educate tourists about some of the dangerous areas in south Florida and how to protect themselves. Law enforcement officials have stepped up patrols and enforcement at interstate highway rest stops where some of the crimes have occurred. In some cases, the police have stopped tourists to warn them of the dangers of certain areas. Although the cases of murdered tourists are rare, the problem is not unique to Florida. Several rest areas on interstate highways in Kentucky were closed because of robberies. A number of states have developed state plans to educate tourists and provide them with better protection.

The protection of tourists is a major concern in a number of convention cities, especially in those areas with reputed vice districts. Tourists are seen as a viable, rich market for prostitution, escort services, adult entertainment, and drugs. Too often tourists or convention-goers seek out vice areas and become victimized because of their unfamiliarity with the dangers associated with vice activities. This poses a special problem for the police as they attempt to protect somewhat naive people who wander into dangerous areas. CPOs must actively solicit the assistance of hotels and other business establishments in providing tourists with information about how to safely navigate through the city. In some instances, this includes advising people to avoid certain areas of the city. Officers patrolling in dangerous areas should be watchful of people who appear to be out of their environment.

Summary

This chapter cannot explore all the potential benefits that particular groups may derive from community policing, but it is obvious that community policing has profound changes on the police in terms of their treatment of various groups. As noted in previous chapters, community policing necessitates philosophical, strategical, and tactical changes in the way police departments do business. The foremost change is that the police begin to view citizens as customers who are to be "satisfied" as opposed to viewing them as hindrances or as the enemies. It also means that the police should emphasize quality of service as opposed to bean counting where the department measures productivity in terms of numbers of arrests, numbers of citations issued, or response time.

Policing must come to grips with the fact that we live in a culturally diverse society. For example, 10 years ago Kentucky had a fairly homogeneous society. However, this has changed substantially in the last decade. Toyota built a major automobile manufacturing plant in Kentucky, and dozens of other Japanese plants followed. Kentucky farmers now use thousands of migrant workers, many of whom have remained in the state. Add to this an African-American population of approximately 12 percent, the state is seeing a number of cultural changes. For example, several Kentucky police departments are now recruiting officers who are bilingual, something that would have been considered absurd 10 years ago.

Police departments and police officers must recognize the existence of diverging cultures. Police officers must be trained in understanding and dealing with different types of people. This may include training on customs as well as language. This is not to limit police responsibility to ethnic or national cultures, the poor, the homeless, and other disadvantaged groups represent cultures with distinct sets of values which must be understood by police officers. Police departments must embody the philosophy of multi-culturalism and service throughout the agency.

References

Attorney General of the United States (1989). *Drug Trafficking: A Report to the President of the United States*. Washington, DC: U.S. Department of Justice.

Block, C.R. & R. Block (1993). *Street Gang Crime in Chicago*. Research in Brief. Washington, DC: National Institute of Justice.

Brand, D. (1987). "In Massachusetts: Theater Therapy." *Time*, (November 9).

Bursik, R. & H. Grasmick (1993). *Neighborhoods and Crime: The Dimensions of Effective Community Control*. New York, NY: Lexington Books.

Chandler, M. (1988). "Disturbing Plight of Homeless Elderly Studied." *Detroit Free Press*, (December 22).

Christopher, W. (1991). *Report of the Independent Commission on the Los Angeles Police Department*. Los Angeles, CA: City of Los Angeles.

Clark, R.L., S.J. Passel, W.N. Zimmerman & M.E. Fix (1994). *Fiscal Impacts of Undocumented Aliens: Selected Estimates for Seven States*. Washington, DC: The Urban Institute.

Cloward, R. & L. Ohlin (1960). *Delinquency and Opportunity: A Theory of Delinquent Gangs*. New York, NY: The Free Press.

Crowe, T. (1991). *Habitual Juvenile Offenders: Guidelines for Citizen Action and Public Responses*. Washington, DC: Office of Juvenile Justice and Delinquency Prevention.

Curry, G.D., R. Ball & R. Fox (1994). *Gang Crime and Law Enforcement Recordkeeping*. Research in Brief. Washington, DC: National Institute of Justice.

Dart, R. (1992). "Chicago's Flying Squad Tackles Street Gangs." *Police Chief*, (October):96-104.

Decker, S. & K. Kempf-Leonard (1991). "Constructing Gangs: The Social Definition of Youth Activities." *Criminal Justice Policy Review*, 5(3):271-291.

Donziger, S.R. (1996). *The Real War on Crime: The Report of the National Criminal Justice Commission*. New York, NY: Harper Collins.

Douthit, N. (1975). "Enforcement and Non-Enforcement Roles in Policing: A Historical Inquiry." *Journal of Police Science and Administration*, 3(3):336-345.

Drowns, R. & K. Hess (1995). *Juvenile Justice*. St. Paul, MN: West.

Felson, M. (1994). *Crime and Everyday Life: Insights and Implications for Society*. Thousand Oaks, CA: Pine Forge Press.

Fischer, P.J. (1988). "Criminal Activity Among the Homeless: A Study of Arrests in Baltimore." *Hospital and Community Psychiatry*, 39(1):46-51.

Fleisher, M. (1995). *Beggars & Thieves: Lives of Urban Street Criminals*. Madison, WI: University of Wisconsin Press.

Hatchett, G. (1987). "Ripping Off Immigrants." *Newsweek*, (September, 7):21.

Kappeler, V.E. (1997). *Critical Issues in Police Civil Liability*, Second Edition. Prospect Heights, IL: Waveland Press.

Kappeler, V.E., M. Blumberg & G.W. Potter (1996). *The Mythology of Crime and Criminal Justice*, Second Edition. Prospect Heights, IL: Waveland Press.

Kappeler, V., R. Sluder & G. Alpert (1994). *Forces of Deviance: Understanding the Dark Side of Policing*. Prospect Heights, IL: Waveland Press.

MacDonald, H. (1995). "San Francisco's Matrix Program for the Homeless." *Criminal Justice Ethics*, 14(1):2, 79-80.

Martin, D. (1994). "Teen Violence: Why It's on the Rise and How to Stem its Tide." *Law Enforcement Technology*, 36-42.

McDonald, W.F. (1997). "Crime and Illegal Immigration." *National Institute of Justice Journal*, (June):2-10.

Miller, W. (1980). "Gangs, Groups, and Serious Youth Crime." In D. Shichor & D. Kelly (eds.) *Critical Issues in Juvenile Delinquency*, pp. 115-138. Lexington, MA: D.C. Heath.

National Coalition of State Juvenile Justice Advisory Groups (1992). *Myths and Realities: Meeting the Challenge of Serious, Violent, and Chronic Juvenile Offenders*. Washington, DC: Author.

Office of Juvenile Justice and Delinquency Prevention (1994). *Gang Suppression and Intervention: Community Models*. Washington, DC: Author.

Plotkin, M. & O. Narr (1993). *The Police Response to the Homeless: A Status Report*. Washington, DC: PERF.

Potter, G.W. & V.E. Kappeler (1998). *Constructing Crime*. Prospect Heights, IL: Waveland Press.

Radelet, L. & D. Carter (1994). *The Police and the Community*, Fifth Edition. New York, NY: Macmillan.

Regoli, R. & J. Hewitt (1994). *Delinquency & Society*, Second Edition. New York, NY: McGraw-Hill.

Sanders, W.B. (1994). *Gangbangs and Drive-Bys*. New York, NY: Aldine De Gruyter.

Scanlan, C. (1989). "An Older, Less White America Predicted." *Detroit Free Press*, (February 1).

Snyder, H. & M. Sickmund (1995). *Juvenile Offenders and Victims: A Focus on Violence*. Washington, DC: Office of Juvenile Justice and Delinquency Prevention.

Snyder, M. & M. Hombs (1986). "Sheltering the Homeless: An American Imperative." *State Government: The Journal of State Affairs*, (Nov./Dec.).

Solarz, A. (1985). "An Examination of Criminal Behavior Among the Homeless." Paper presented at the annual conference of the American Society of Criminology.

Taylor, C. (1986). "Black Urban Youth Gangs: Analysis of Contemporary Issues." Paper presented at the annual conference of the American Society of Criminology.

Thrasher, F. (1928). *The Gang: A Study of 1,303 Gangs in Chicago*. Chicago, IL: University of Chicago Press.

U.S. Attorney General's Advisory Board on Missing Children (1986). *America's Missing and Exploited Children: Their Safety and Their Future*. Washington, DC: Office of Juvenile Justice and Delinquency Prevention.

Whitehouse, J. (1973). "Historical Perspectives on the Police Community Service Function." *Journal of Police Science and Administration*, 1(1):87-92.

Williams, H. & P. Murphy (1988). *The Evolving Strategy of Police: A Minority View*. Washington, DC: National Institute of Justice.

Zawitz, M. et al. (1993). *Highlights from 20 Years of Surveying Crime Victims: The National Crime Victimization Survey, 1973-1992*. Washington, DC: U.S. Department of Justice.

CHAPTER 11
Toward a New Breed of Police Officer

*Every society gets the kind of criminal it
deserves. What is equally true is that
every community gets the kind of law
enforcement it insists on.*
                              —*Robert F. Kennedy*

Images and Impressions

What image comes to mind when someone says police officer? Some people conjure up Norman Rockwell's vision of the friendly cop offering a lost child an ice cream cone at the station house. For others, it is Dirty Harry looking down the barrel of his .357, begging some scumbag to "make my day." Some of us grew up being told that police officers are our friends, someone to turn to whenever we are in trouble. Others were raised with the warning to be good or "the police will take you away." Many of us remember the disturbing TV images of the police decades ago loosing dogs and firehoses on civil rights protesters, then a few years later clubbing protesters outside the Democratic Convention in Chicago. Younger generations are more likely to recall the graphic images of Los Angeles burning after the senseless police beating of motorist Rodney King. Still others may see the police as battling drug gangs or trying to protect school children under siege from gun-wielding lunatics. Or perhaps, we recall gun-wielding citizens and police officers at Ruby Ridge or Waco, Texas. Maybe our most vivid memory is the police officer who gave us a speeding ticket or arrested a family member.

Police officers, peace officers, law enforcement officers, cops. No matter what term we attach to the job, most people have a vivid, if not always accurate, image of what police work entails, one that might blend awe, respect, disdain, and fear. Our personalized picture is the end result of our cumulative exposure to the police in real life and reel life—the officers we have met, the ones we have seen in the theater, and the ones we learn about from the media.

In a democratic society, where there is great tension between our desire to allow police the power to protect us and, at the same time, our fear that we must circumscribe their role to protect our civil rights, the police have always played an ambiguous role. In *Policing in a Free Society,* Herman Goldstein (1977:3) wrote about the "basic pervasive conflict between crime-fighting and constitutional due process which is inherent in the police function in a free society." Kappeler has remarked, "This means the police may be seen by the public in paradoxical roles. To many segments of society, the police represent what has been termed the 'thin blue line' that separates anarchy from order. Seen in this light, the police represent a governmental body whose ultimate mission is to protect the civil liberties of citizens. This responsibility is paradoxical in the sense that police also represent one of the greatest threats to these liberties" (Kappeler, Sluder & Alpert, 1994:2). This is especially true when police officers abuse the authority of their office.

The police have the power to "put us away." The police are also the only agents of formal social control with the right to use force, including deadly force. By emphasizing their role as crime-fighters, we see them as the thin blue line protecting the forces of light from the powers of evil. Not only does this narrow view ignore the complexity of policing, it reinforces the perception of society as divided into the Good Guys in the White Hats versus a smaller pool of Bad Guys in Black Hats. Though it provides a convenient shorthand, for both the police and the community, when referring to crime situations to divide the world into the law-abiding people who must remain vigilant against predators, the real world is blessed with only a handful of saints above reproach and an equally small number of unregenerate monsters. In between is the vast majority of people.

The danger in oversimplification is that we can fall victim to the temptation to *demonize* those who break the law or glorify those who enforce it, thereby robbing both of their humanity. How many of us can say with absolute certainty where we would draw the line, if we had a sick, hungry child and no money? We must also remember that many people who would never think of committing crimes as adults wince at things they did when they were younger. Many youngsters who threw a rock through a window at school, shoplifted something from a store, or even went joyriding in a "borrowed" car grew up to become valuable members of the community. The line between law-abiding and law-breaking can shift and change at different times and in different circumstances. While there is great nobility in the notion that the police provide a thin blue line of uniformed officers who can protect good people from evil, real life also requires confronting vast and shifting shades of gray. In fact, many behaviors of police officers fall within this area of gray; somewhere between right and wrong (see Kappeler, Sluder & Alpert, 1994; Crank, 1998).

The goal in this chapter is to examine traditional police culture and the police role, to separate myth from reality, to see what it takes to have "the right stuff" for the real job of policing. We will begin by exploring what the job involves in a traditional department, to see the kind of people who are attracted to this career field, and what they find once they are on the job. Then we will look at what a shift to a community policing approach portends. Does it mean departments must find ways to attract and hire candidates with different qualities, skills, and abilities? Does the job of being a CPO require attributes that differ from what we have traditionally associated with being a police officer? Do we need a new breed of police officer to handle the challenges of the job as we approach the twenty-first century? Can such a dramatic change in the very culture of policing be achieved?

Traditional Police Culture

Patrol officers are the backbone of the traditional police approach. They are the *grunts* in the trenches, the individuals in the department who must deal directly with the community every day (Crank, 1998). In that sense, they are the traditional department's bridge to the saints, sinners, and average citizens who constitute the real world. Therefore, to understand what the real job of policing entails in a traditional department, it is important to explore what incoming candidates expect from the job—and what they find once they arrive.

Many candidates say that they are drawn to police work as a career because of a desire to help others. While police departments must always be alert to the danger that some people will be attracted to the job because of an unhealthy desire to wield power over others, many of the men and women who seek careers in policing are inspired by idealism and altruism. Yet, many of the people who have entered police work also exhibit a tendency toward conformity and authoritarianism. Authoritarianism is characterized by conservative, aggressive, cynical, and rigid behaviors. Authoritarian have a limited view of the world and see issues in terms of black and white (Adorno, 1950). For the authoritarian there is little room for the shades of gray that exist in most aspects of life. People are either good or bad, likable or unlikable, friends or enemies. These people are said to be conservative, often having "knee jerk" reactions to social issues. Some have labeled these people as "reactionary conservatives" because they are said to instinctively react in a conservative manner regardless of the merit of their position and often without reflecting upon the consequences of their acts (Kappeler, Sluder & Alpert, 1994). John J. Broderick (1987:31) has done an excellent job of capturing how the term authoritarian is used in discussions of police.

> Those who . . . use it are usually referring to a person who has great respect for power and authority and strongly adheres to the demands of his or her own group. This person is also submissive to higher authority and hostile toward outsiders who do not conform to conventional standards of behavior. The characteristics of willingness to

follow orders and respect for authority might seem to be virtues when possessed by police officers, but in the sense used here, the term authoritarian means an extreme, unquestioning willingness to do what one is told and an extremely hostile attitude toward people who are different than oneself.

Carpenter and Raza (1987:16) found that police applicants differ from other occupational groups in several significant ways. First, these researchers found that police applicants, as a group, are psychologically healthy, "less depressed and anxious, and more assertive in making and maintaining social contacts." Second, their findings indicated that police are a more homogeneous group of people and that this "greater homogeneity is probably due to the sharing of personality characteristics which lead one to desire becoming a police officer." Finally, they found that police were more like military personnel in their conformance to authority.

It would seem that the people who have traditionally entered police work share the qualities of idealism and those of authoritarianism. They view the unique power conferred on them as a tool they can use to make a valid contribution in making society a conventional place to live. Unfortunately, the same people attracted to policing often do not understand the shades of gray we just mentioned, they see the world in terms of good and evil. They, also tend to view police work as an exciting, danger-filled occupation.

If these idealistic candidates succeed in becoming motor patrol officers, many are often surprised to find much of the job involves waiting for something to happen rather than making something happen. "In fact, the average cop on television probably sees more action in a half-hour than most officers witness in an entire career. As a general rule, most police work is quite mundane" (Kappeler, Blumberg & Potter, 1996:212). A variety of research techniques have been employed to study police activities (Greene & Klockars, 1991). Radio calls from dispatchers to patrol cars (Bercal, 1970), telephone calls by citizens to the police (Cumming, Cumming & Edell, 1965), dispatch records (Reiss, 1971), observational data (Kelling et al., 1974), self-reports from police officers (O'Neill & Bloom, 1972) and telephone interviews of citizens (Mafstrofski, 1983). What all these studies show is that relatively little of a police officer's day is taken up responding to crime. Jack Greene and Carl Klockars (1991:283) perhaps said it best noting that research, "findings in no way lend support to the headline news vision of police work as a violent running battle between police and criminals." There is far less fighting evil than police recruits might anticipate or even hope for.

Police patrol time is also poorly structured. As most research attests, motor patrol officers spend most of their time on patrol, waiting for a call (Payne & Trojanowicz, 1985). While cruising around on patrol, the officers are, in essence, waiting to spot some sign of trouble, whether it's a traffic violation or some suspicious activity on the street. The opportunities to initiate positive action are limited by the need to remain available to handle the next call. The second most time-consuming aspect of the job is handling complaints—and that term can seem particularly apt, since one of the surprises many fledgling officers face is realizing the amount of friction with the community that they encounter on the job. As James Q. Wilson (1970) noted, we often equate crime-fighters with fire-fighters, as if the jobs were pretty much alike. Yet police officers often feel far more alienated from the community, because they are far more likely to find themselves in adversarial situations where they are perceived as the antagonist.

That feeling of being separate and apart from society at large explains why police officers so often band together for mutual support. The job contains an element of danger, which means officers must rely on each other for their mutual safety. As Skolnick (1966) has observed, danger is one of the most important facets in the development of a police working personality. The relationship between the "real" dangers associated with police work and the police perception of the job as hazardous is complex. While police officers perceive their work as dangerous, they realize that the chances of being injured are not as great as their preoccupation with the idea of danger (Cullen, Link, Travis & Lemming, 1983). The disjuncture between the potential for injury and the exaggerated sense of danger found among police officers is best explained in the remarks of David Bayley (1976:171) who observes:

> The possibility of armed confrontation shapes training, patrol preoccupations, and operating procedures. It also shapes the relationship between citizen and policeman by generating mutual apprehension. The policeman can never forget that the individual he contacts may be armed and dangerous; the citizen can never forget that the policeman is armed and may consider the citizen dangerous.

Such occupational conceptions foster isolation and antagonism and also encourage police to pull together into a separate subculture of their own. Isolation is an emotional and physical condition that makes it difficult for members of one social group to have relationships and interact with members of another group. This feeling of separateness from the surrounding community is a frequently noted attribute of police subculture (Westley, 1953, 1956, 1970; Skolnick, 1966; Reiss & Bordua, 1967; Manning, 1971; Harris, 1973; Sherman, 1982). The self-imposed social isolation of the police from the surrounding community is well documented (Baldwin, 1962; Clark, 1965; Skolnick, 1966; Cain, 1973; Swanton, 1981). Social isolation reinforces the notion that people outside the police subculture are to be viewed warily as potential threats to the members' physical or emotional well-being, as well as challenges to the officer's authority and autonomy. According to Baldwin (1962) and Skolnick (1966), police impose social isolation upon themselves as a means of protection against real and perceived dangers, loss of personal and professional autonomy, and social rejection. Rejection by the community stems, in part, from the resentment that sometimes arises when laws are enforced (Clark, 1965). As no one enjoys receiving a traffic ticket or being arrested and no one enjoys being disliked, the police tend to look inward to their own members for validity and support (Kappeler, Sluder & Alpert, 1994).

Even the uniform, badge, and gun serve as symbols of being different from the "civilian" on the street. The police, by virtue of their social role, are granted a unique position in the law. Police have a legal monopoly on the sanctioned use of violence (Westley, 1953; Bordua & Reiss, 1967; Reiss, 1971) and coercion (Westley, 1953; Bittner, 1970) against other members of society. The police are, therefore, set apart from the community because of their unique position in the law and their ability to use violence legally and invoke the force of law. This legal distinction between citizens and police sets officers apart from the larger culture and other occupations.

That sense of being separate and apart from the rest of the community is also heightened by the fact that police officers see things that other people do not see. Most people are spared the sight of mangled bodies crushed in cars, battered children, women who have been raped, decaying corpses, yet this is a small part of what police work entails. The job also requires peeking into people's private lives in ways no other job does, which means the police tend to see people at their worst, not their best. People do not call the police to come share their triumphs and joys, but when they are hurt, angry, frightened, and upset.

The need to pull together is also reinforced in traditional departments where those at the bottom of the police pyramid can feel thwarted by the restrictions imposed by working in a paramilitary bureaucracy. Those altruistic candidates who chose police work so that they could make a positive difference can feel frustrated at finding themselves inhibited by a structure where the emphasis on avoiding mistakes seems to overshadow the opportunities to take creative action. Paramilitary bureaucracy stifles innovation and breeds immature personalities (Angell, 1971), two characteristics that are antithetical to community policing. Police work has been called the most unprofessional profession, because traditional departments often seem to expend more energy in defining the limits of the job than in supporting autonomy and innovation.

The power of traditional police culture can serve as an unhealthy lure for those who want to dominate and abuse others (Kappeler, Sluder & Alpert, 1994). Yet, even the most altruistic candidates can find the job sometimes dangerous and often tedious, one in which they see the horrors that people inflict on each other, horrors they often appear powerless to prevent. Compounding the problem, many find themselves trapped in a system and culture where they receive little support from superiors for taking any initiative. In some departments, turning to their peers for support requires embracing a macho ethic that puts the highest premium on acting tough and aggressive, regardless of the situation. No matter how well their education and prior experience may have prepared them to understand the full range of human dynamics that impel people to act as they do, that knowledge can be *washed out* by the combination of the ugliness they see and the callous indifference that their seasoned peers insist is the only way to survive the rigors of the job. Thwarted idealists may struggle against becoming cynics, but cynicism toward the community and toward the police hierarchy may be so potent that few can resist.

Rewarding the Officers

Most police departments provide incentives for their officers. These include traditional promotions, merit increases, and "officer-of-the-month" recognition. Many departments offer several opportunities for their officers to receive or earn rewards. Traditionally, these rewards have been based upon aggressive actions that led to arrest(s), the capture of a dangerous felon, or some other heroic activity. These criteria for rewarding police officers are important and serve to encourage similar actions from others. Yet other types of police behavior deserve recognition but remain lost and hidden behind the visible, aggressive activities of police officers. Activities that should receive more attention include exemplary service to the community and the reduction or diffusion of violence. Those who provide meritorious service may be recognized but often their actions are lost behind the brave shooting incident or heroic rescue. The local community needs to recognize officers who serve their "beat" or neighborhood in an exemplary fashion. A "Best Cop on the Block" recognition would be an important reward, if provided by local residents or merchants. When an officer avoids a shooting or talks a suspect into custody, his or her superiors may not find out; if they do, the officer may be labeled as a "chicken" or one who cannot provide needed back-up to his fellow officers. Nonaggressive behavior that reduces violence needs to be reinforced, rewarded, and established as the model for other officers to copy.

An institutional reward system should be established for officers who avoid or reduce violent situations and who avoid the use of force, especially deadly force, when avoidance is justifiable. When command officers, from the chief to the sergeants, support and reward violence reduction, private business and service groups can be enlisted to provide symbolic and monetary rewards for such behavior. The institutional support for the effective policing of a neighborhood can only encourage others to consider a change in priorities and style. While this is only one aspect of a neighborhood intervention and community evaluation model, it could serve as a successful step toward meeting the joint needs of the citizens and the police.

Data on these activities should be collected, assessed and evaluated to help determine police departments' performance to do justice and promote secure communities.

Source: G.P. Alpert & M.H. Moore (1993). "Measuring Police Performance in the New Paradigm of Policing." In *Performance Measures for the Criminal Justice System*. Washington, DC: U.S. Department of Justice, Bureau of Justice Statistics.

Left unchallenged and unaddressed, such pressures can make officers feel that their superiors use them as pawns in a cat-and-mouse game in which they must follow rules, but their opponents do not. Especially today, an exaggerated sense of the menace posed by drugs, motor patrol officers can see themselves as outmanned, outgunned, underpaid, and bound by rigid rules that the "predators" exploit. The intellectual and emotional leap required to adopt the view that police officers are trapped between an ungrateful community and unthinking superiors can seem small, especially when peers insist that it is emotional suicide to do otherwise.

Resistance to Community Policing

There are reasons that people inside and outside policing will never become fans of community policing. Some resistance stems from a general reluctance to embrace change, no matter how positive. Others have philosophical concerns that have led them to reach an honest difference of opinion. Those who think they fare better under the existing system and culture also have reason to resist change. Part of the internal resistance to a new community policing effort will stem from the normal human tendency of individuals and organizations to resist change. Part of the resistance stems from the fact that police departments are conservative, paramilitary organizations that view change with skepticism. And some resistance will come from traditionalists who disagree with the effort on philosophical grounds, primarily those who feel that the police department's plate is already full enough dealing with "serious crime," and that the police should not broaden their mandate to include problems where they may not have sufficient expertise. Added to them are people inside the department who are the *winners* under the existing system, those who may see themselves as relative *losers* under the community policing approach.

Regardless of their assignment, anyone who has loudly championed or defended the existing system and culture risks becoming a loser, since the change implies a rejection of the system and culture they probably continue to believe in, one they probably worked hard to make succeed, and one that supports the traditional view of the occupation and their place in it. The change may be viewed not only as a betrayal, but as an insult as well. After all, if the existing system was working well, there would be no need to make any change, especially one as dramatic, fundamental, and far-reaching as community policing.

People who currently hold particular positions within the department can perceive themselves as becoming losers as a result of the change. Yet for the most part, though the police in general may have been reluctant to change, once educated to the benefits of community policing, many police chiefs were at least numbered among the primary proponents responsible for making the shift. But the chief often has the most to lose if the new approach appears to fail or produces embarrassing mistakes. One of the ways in which the traditional system makes the chief a winner is that it promotes predictability. By rewarding those who follow rules and procedures closely, the system emphasizes avoiding mistakes. As long as no one challenges whether those rules and procedures do as much to produce the results that people want as community policing, the traditional system often hums along relatively smoothly, causing little unexpected grief for the person at the top, though there have obviously been many examples where this has not been true (see, Kappeler, Sluder & Alpert, 1994).

The traditional system also provides at least some "protective cover" when problems erupt. Many times the chief can deflect criticism by pointing out that the mistake occurred because the officers involved violated or ignored the rules and procedures. This also allows administrators to cast abuses by police officers as isolated and aberrant behaviors rather than problems that follow directly from the existing system and culture (Kappeler, Sluder & Alpert, 1994). When a police officer abuses a citizen, when criminal violence erupts, an area suffers a dramatic rise in property crimes, or people complain about new drug problems, the chief in a traditional department can hope to deflect responsibility by pointing to the underlying social problems. Though the traditional approach emphasizes the role of the police as the community's crime-fighters, the chief can usually elicit at least some sympathy by saying that police cannot do anything about the *slum* or *ghetto* conditions under which people live, the places that breed crime and drug problems. In a traditional police department, the chief can rail about how his officers are doing all they can to help, but the blame for decaying neighborhoods lies with city fathers who allow garbage to rot uncollected on the street and who fail to provide idle teens enough summer activities to keep them out of mischief.

Community policing puts the chief on the hook for many problems that the traditional system does not. The rotten apple metaphor that is often used to explain away police corruption and deviance is less acceptable when the department has cleaned the barrel by adopting community policing. So too are excuses for the use of unnecessary force by police officers since community policing does not rely on the use of force to solve community problems. Other excuse mechanisms also become problematic and negative behaviors less defensible by the adoption of community policing. It says the department has a valid role to play in making sure that garbage is picked up and kids have something worthwhile to do. In granting the responsibility to line officers to tackle a broader range of community problems, it also provides them the authority and power to do more—which means more opportunities for mistakes. There was the embarrassing incident in Flint, in which a well-meaning officer inadvertently took a group of area youngsters to an X-rated movie.

Not only will some creative solutions fail totally, even if they help reduce overall severity or frequency, some people will still take potshots at involving the police in anything that does not focus on arresting the bad guys and putting them away. Doing anything else seems to them to ignore getting tough on the people who break the law.

By granting officers greater autonomy, some officers will potentially put the chief on the spot by abusing their new freedom. In one case, a person called the department to report that a male CPO and his female counterpart appeared to be sneaking away to an apartment for an afternoon tryst every day. The bad news was that an investigation proved the allegations were true, but the good news was that this shows people become so involved in the police process as a result of community policing that they not only act as unofficial supervisors, but trust their department well enough to call and complain.

The same problems the chief faces extend to the people in top command, as well as middle managers and especially supervisors. Supervisors, who usually feel caught in the middle regardless of which system is in place, have reason to worry about becoming big losers with a shift to community policing, because the worst part of their job is carrying any bad news to the boss. Middle managers can also feel threatened by a loss of status and control, because community policing requires them to share decision-making with officers beneath them in the hierarchy. In the traditional police department supervisors have a vested interest in both detecting minor problems by officers for sanction as well as ignoring major behavioral problems that would cast their supervision in unfavorable light (Kappeler, Sluder & Alpert, 1994). It is also demonstrably more difficult to supervise CPOs, since a true assessment of their performance requires making personal visits to the beat areas to see firsthand how well the CPO is doing. The ability of supervisors to argue effectively that they did not know about a particular problem officer of behavior is less if supervisors are expected to make these personal contacts rather than just check-up on officers over the radio.

It would seem that all line officers would benefit under a community policing approach, because of the greater responsibility, authority, and freedom to explore new ways to solve problems. Yet experience shows that much of the resistance to community policing comes from motor patrol officers. This was often more true in the past, when community policing was adopted piecemeal. This often meant that the ranks of the department's motor patrol officers were thinned to field the new CPOs required. Instead of educating and energizing everyone in the department about how to become community problem-solvers, many departments focused first on using CPOs as their new, creative thinkers, while motor patrol officers were pretty much told to keep doing the same old thing, with fewer officers.

Eager, open-minded CPOs enthusiastic about their new opportunity to work with people directly on a host of challenging new initiatives are obvious winners, yet it is easy to see why their motor patrol peers resented their greater autonomy—especially since CPOs may not work nights or weekends, and they often have additional flexibility in setting their schedules. Motor patrol officers who take great pride in their role as crime-fighters, and who see themselves as potentially risking their lives daily for people in the community they often perceive as ungrateful, can see themselves as losers if the department begins to emphasize broader goals. The cultural divide between line officers and administrators (Reuss-Ianni, 1983) can widen if a significant number of line officers do not embrace community policing when the administration has full-heartedly endorsed it. Many openly resent the social work approach of community policing, dismissing CPOs as *lollicops* or the *grin-and-wave squad*. Victor G. Strecher (1995:77-78) has commented that, "When officers assigned in the COP mode are asked what they do, they paw the ground, shrug, and give answers such as, 'walk and talk,' 'gin and chin,' 'chat and charm,' 'schmooze,' and often, 'maybe the brass will let us know.'" Part of the reasons behind these responses are, of course, not because of a failure of direction or because of a genuine concern with the manner in which the community policing philosophy is operationalized but rather expresses of resistance to a philosophy that directly challenges the traditional police culture as well as the professional identity these officers have developed over years of culturalization into an ethos of crime fighting.

Motor patrol officers pose a thorny problem, since many automatically resent the fact that some CPOs may inappropriately keep bankers' hours, with weekends off, and they can also benefit from more flexible schedules. If the motor patrol officers share a commitment to community problem solving as a valid goal and understand how their CPOs can help them, that will help. But many motor patrol officers will at least take time to grasp the benefits. Until or unless this happens, there exists the risk that resentment could become outright hostility.

Many motor patrol officers who believe bravery and toughness are "the right stuff" can rankle when they see people treat their CPOs as heroes. The macho myth says that people should not like police officers, but respect them, as if the two were mutually exclusive. Even though CPOs still use force, when appropriate, many motor patrol officers feel this new kind of officer is just not a real cop.

Community policing requires supervisors to share power with underlings, at the same time they must be willing to work harder to find out if CPOs are doing a good job. The loss of status and control, as well as the new challenge imposed by finding new ways to assess performance, both make the job tougher and challenge the balance of power between line officers and supervisors. Supervisors who see the wisdom of the effort, at first or over time, find the change invigorating, while those who do not like what community policing entails find the new demands draining and perhaps stressful.

Changing Traditional Police Culture

Dramatically altering the educational, cultural, racial, ethnic, and sexual mix of the police officers within police departments implies a tremendous change, even if there has been no change in the organizational structure. It means that modern police departments can no longer be dominated by white males. Not only does this militate against the danger that the department will adopt an ethnocentric, macho ethic, an influx of college-educated officers also implies that the officers will demand greater autonomy and flexibility. The job has long attracted idealists who want to make a positive difference, but now that the job increasingly attracts less authoritarian and more innovative college-educated candidates armed with the values and skills of professionals, this increases the pressure on police managers to allow them to function more as professionals within the community.

Yet there are limits inherent in the traditional approach that no doubt have contributed to the concern that the police risk losing these most valued employees to other careers. In a traditional department, the system can only be bent so much before it risks falling apart entirely. The cultural strings that have held policing together—danger, isolation, control, authority—must be severed if community policing is to make a meaningful foothold in the police institution. Yet, there are inherent limits on how much freedom officers can be given, considering the restrictions of the traditional mandate as crime fighters and the reliance on violence and traditional police tactics as the best means of achieving that mission.

Many traditional departments have responded to the challenge posed by these dramatic changes in the overall make-up of their line officers by making at least tentative steps toward broadening the police mandate from crime-fighting to community problem solving. Officially and unofficially, police officers have been exploring ways to employ problem-solving techniques. Many departments still restrict their application primarily to crime incidents, insisting that other problems are beyond the proper purview of the police. This plays into the hands of traditional police culture because it allows the institution to maintain its unrealistic crime fighting orientation and further solidifies the negative aspects of traditional police culture. Others have broadened their mandate to include involving officers in efforts to control social and physical disorder, but often without allowing officers the time and the sustained presence in one area to develop a feel for the underlying dynamics and the continued presence in the community that may be required to enhance the likelihood of success. This, however, is a limited attempt at community policing because it allows the structuring of police work to limit the full acceptance of the spirit of community policing. Without modifications, which few police departments have made, to organizational structure, community policing runs the risk of being little more than lip service. Traditional police culture and organizational structure represent formidable barriers to a full conversation to community policing.

Even so, there has been increasing pressure from below on police officials to grant line officers greater professional autonomy, responsibility, and authority. Those idealistic candidates seeking to change their communities for the better through a career in policing have been a major force in promoting experimentation with new ideas. Basically, they are more likely to reject the simplistic notion that communities can become safer and better places to live if line officers embrace an unwritten code that the solution lies in tough cops cracking more heads and making more arrests. Such officers are obviously more likely to think that brains are even more important than brawn and bullets in most situations. The police will always have to exercise the use of force in discharging their duty, but college-educated officers probably tend to generate fewer citizen complaints because they may be more likely to explore other options first, whenever possible (Kappeler, Sapp & Carter, 1992). In general as well, these officers have a greater grasp of the complexity and diversity in the real world, which implies a greater appreciation of those shifting shades of gray.

Controversial Homicide Squad Aimed at Public Housing Murders

A police unit that successfully solved several murders in the city's public housing projects—though not without criticism for alleged heavy-handed tactics—is disbanding.

Homicide inspectors handpicked the seven-member Crime Response Unit to Stop Homicide (CRUSH) nearly two years ago after a rash of killings in San Francisco's predominantly black southeastern neighborhoods.

Public defender Jeff Brown called the unit's officers the "cowboys of the police department. In lots of the neighborhoods, these guys were the terror unit," Brown said. "They were the goon squad. The fought fire with fire. They would break down doors, search cars, and the niceties of the Fourth Amendment didn't bother them."

However, police chief Fred Lau said the unit was not being dropped because of the criticism. "This is in response to our new focus on community policing. This was meant to be a temporary program," Lau said March 24. "The good things that CRUSH does will continue."

Inspector Napoleon Hendrix, who was one of CRUSH's founding inspectors, has been promoted to assistant chief. Meanwhile, five of the seven members are being reassigned to the new Bayview station. One is in a desk job pending resolution of departmental misconduct charges, and another is returning to the robbery detail.

Unit Formed In 1995

The unit was formed in May 1995, days after four black men were killed in a single week. The unit's mission was to solve a series of 32 homicides, mainly in Hunters Point and in several other housing projects.

The squad quickly developed a reputation for being streetwise and aggressive, which sometimes made them the object of citizen complaints. The racially diverse group also injected some new blood into the mostly white homicide unit.

Lt. David Robinson, of the department's homicide unit, praised CRUSH for not only solving killings but also preventing violence in an historically high crime area. "People know they are out there—they are more careful," Robinson said in December.

But Brown, the public defender, said the unit went overboard by treating everyone as a suspect. "There's a place for tough in-your-face enforcement at times," he said. "But to make it your day-to-day, hour-to-hour mode is excessive."

Lau said there had been no sustained complaints against any CRUSH members relating to their investigative techniques or on-duty activities.

"We want them to become teachers," Lau said. "It makes sense that we not just have four or five people who know how to respond to these types of crimes. It makes more sense to have eight or 12 or 16."

Source: *Community Policing Digest* (1997). April 3, p. 6.

Part of the problem CPOs face on the job in a traditional department stems from the reality that the traditional model attempts to make sense of the world and make the officer's job *easier* by casting the police in the role of the tough cops who protect the forces of light from the forces of evil—that thin blue line. Sophisticated and educated police officers often do not find that narrow view comforting, but confining. Instead of being overwhelmed or frustrated by the ambiguities of the real world, they are more likely to find the challenge a stimulating opportunity to see how much they can achieve. This can make the limitations and periods of inactivity that are often part of the traditional approach seem like obstacles that prevent them from accomplishing the goal of making communities safer and better places to live.

What Community Policing Offers

While there may be other theoretical models that might do a better job of capitalizing on some of the attributes, talents, and aspirations of this new breed of police officer who is beginning to permeate the ranks of departments nationwide, community policing comprehensively addresses all of the important issues raised. By broadening the police mandate and making substantive changes that provide organizational support and encouragement for innovation, community policing provides all officers within the department the cultural ethos and structural underpinnings necessary to do more toward that altruistic and idealistic goal of improving the overall quality of life in the community.

By expanding police work to include addressing the full range of community concerns, including crime, fear of crime, and community conditions, community policing gives police officers an expanded agenda that allows fuller expression of their full range of talents, skills, and abilities. And by making that all-important shift from seeing the police officer primarily as a crime-fighter to enlarging their role to that of community problem-solver, this not only opens up the scope of the job, but it changes the basic nature of the police response from an emphasis on dealing with individual crime incidents to attacking the underlying dynamics that detract from the overall quality of life in the community.

If this new breed of college-educated officers is perceived as being more professional, better able to grasp *the big picture,* and more attuned to community needs, they should therefore be more likely to thrive in a system and culture that grants them more freedom and autonomy to explore proactive solutions to community problems. The police have faced tremendous pressure from college-educated officers to grant them additional responsibility and authority. To attract and retain the best candidates for the job required rethinking a system and culture that focused more on ensuring control and distributing the use of force (Bittner, 1970) than supporting innovation.

Implications for the Future

Putting all the pieces together, it appears that the community policing approach overall, and the CPO's job in particular, demands a new breed of police officer. It means that police departments must recruit a broad mix of individuals so that they can more closely mirror the sexual, racial, and ethnic composition of the communities they serve, and it also means those candidates should be sensitive to, and tolerant of, diversity.

In particular as well, the focus on community problem solving that is an integral part of all officers' jobs in a department that has adopted community policing demands recruiting candidates who can think for themselves. Because the community policing philosophy means a shift from focusing on individual crime incidents and the use of force to address them to exploring creative ways to address the underlying dynamics that create an environment where problems can persist, the best candidates must also be creative and innovative. This is not found among the authoritarian and conformists that have traditionally entered police service or the veteran officers who insist on transmitting the negative cultural aspects of policing to every new generation of officers.

Because community policing grants more freedom and autonomy to line officers, the best candidates will be individuals who can function as true professionals. This means they must be able to act responsibly, without constant supervision, and they must be able to exercise good judgment, consistent with the values and goals of society. This also implies the ability to develop and execute plans aimed at accomplishing realistic and achievable goals. To be professional also implies the capacity to use time wisely and to exercise self-discipline.

The new job of CPO in particular requires all this and more. It appears that the most critical determinant of future success as a CPO is superior communication skills. A good CPO must be able to communicate well with people from all walks of life, one-on-one and in groups. The ability to prepare and deliver speeches and write articles for publication is another obvious plus.

And because the research tends to show that the officers who function in this capacity tend to internalize the orientation and goals of the people they serve, rather than to turn to their fellow officers for guidance and approval, the job perhaps demands an even higher degree of professionalism than almost any other police role. While this is part of the reason for friction between motor patrol officers and CPOs, it is also part of the key in resisting the tendency of the traditional system and its culture to foster an internal climate dominated by the macho ethic of the tough cop.

The day-to-day job of being a CPO also means the best officers will strive to stay abreast of all the various kinds of help that public and private agencies can provide. This implies that the best candidates have experience in seeking out new information, individuals who know how to find what they need on their own. This also means that police departments must restructure themselves and police work to allow officers the time to develop the talents and collect the information necessary to do community policing.

As even this cursory analysis verifies, community policing demands a new breed of police officer, one who possesses specific attributes, qualities, and skills. As this analysis also shows, the college-educated men and women of diverse ethnic and racial backgrounds would have the "right stuff" for the job.

The major problem that police managers will have had to contend with is how to hold onto these most highly prized new employees and how to insulate them from the negative effects of police culture. Not only do such candidates tend to chafe under the restrictions and narrowness implicit in the police officer's role in the traditional system, they usually have other options available to them to enter jobs where their attributes and skills might be allowed fuller expression—and where, in addition, the monetary rewards are greater.

Yet true professionals worry as much or more about their opportunity to make a valid contribution through their work as they do about the size of their income. The idealists attracted to police work because of the altruistic desire to make communities better and safer places in which to live and work find the community policing approach offers more opportunities for job enrichment, job enhancement, job enlargement, and overall job satisfaction.

In particular, the new position as the department's outreach specialist, the CPO, not only provides the best candidates a worthwhile new option, but the job provides the autonomy and freedom to allow the most talented individuals a new and unique opportunity to make the most of themselves. The job challenges individuals to see how much they can accomplish, because the boundaries of what can be achieved have yet to be fully defined. Each day, CPOs are discovering and developing new ways to make a positive difference, and the standard of excellence goes up yet another notch as creative and innovative officers find out how they can do even more.

The shift also has implications concerning how criminal justice education must change to meet these new demands. As the PERF study showed, many police managers suggest that future candidates for police work should be encouraged to take college classes beyond those that directly relate to the "nuts-and-bolts" of police work (Carter, Sapp & Stephens, 1989). A curriculum that emphasizes exposure to the social sciences—psychology, sociology, anthropology—as well as disciplines such as economics and business administration would enhance an individual's overall knowledge about how the real world works, at the same time it would provide future police officers skills in areas that are becoming increasingly important in the job.

The new breed of police officer whose emergence into the field has already changed the composition of police departments will help shape the future of community policing. The basic job description emphasizes the ability to think, act, and communicate. No one knows for sure precisely how community policing will evolve in years to come. What is clear, however, is that the officers who capitalize on the flexibility and autonomy that are the hallmarks of this new approach will help define and refine what it can and cannot do in practice. Not only will they be able to help police departments find new ways to meet the challenge of helping communities cope with the problems that they face as they approach the twenty-first century, this new breed of officer, armed with those enhanced communication skills, will be able to tell us what it will take to do the job well.

References

Adlam, K.R. (1982). "The Police Personality: Psychological Consequences of Becoming a Police Officer." *The Journal of Police Science and Administration*, 10(3):347-348.

Adorno, T.W. (1950). *The Authoritarian Personality*. New York, NY: Harper & Row, Publishers.

Angell, J.E. (1977). "Toward an Alternative to the Classical Police Organizational Arrangements: A Democratic Model." In L.K. Gaines & T.A. Ricks (eds.) *Managing the Police Organization*. St. Paul, MN: West.

Baldwin, J. (1962). *Nobody Knows My Name*. New York, NY: Dell Publishing Company.

Bayley, D. (1976). *Forces of Order: Police Behavior in Japan and the United States*. Berkeley, CA: University of California Press.

Bercal, T. (1970). "Calls for Police Assistance." *American Behavioral Scientist*, 13:681-691.

Bittner, E. (1970). *The Functions of Police in Modern Society*. Chevy Chase, MD: National Clearinghouse for Mental Health.

Broderick, J.J. (1987). *Police in a Time of Change*, Second Edition. Prospect Heights, IL: Waveland Press.

Brown, M.K. (1981). *Working the Street: Police Discretion and the Dilemmas of Reform*. New York, NY: Russell Sage Foundation.

Cain, M.E. (1973). *Society and the Policeman's Role*. London, England: Routledge and Kegal Paul.

Carpenter, B.N. & S.M. Raza (1987). "Personality Characteristics of Police Applicants: Comparisons Across Subgroups and with Other Populations." *Journal of Police Science and Administration*, 15(1):10-17.

Carter, D.L., A.D. Sapp & D.W. Stephens (1989). *The State of Police Education*. Washington, DC: PERF.

Clark, J.P. (1965). "Isolation of the Police: A Comparison of the British and American Situations." *Journal of Criminal Law, Criminology and Police Science*, 56:307-319.

Crank, J.P. (1998). *Understanding Police Culture*. Cincinnati, OH: Anderson Publishing Co.

Cullen, F.T., B.G. Link, L.F. Travis & T. Lemming (1983). "Paradox in Policing: A Note on Perceptions of Danger." *Journal of Police Science and Administration*, 11(4):457-462.

Cumming, E., I. Cumming & L. Edell (1965). "Policeman as Philosopher, Friend and Guide." *Social Problems*, 12:14-49.

Goldstein, H. (1977). *Policing in a Free Society*. Cambridge, MA: Ballinger.

Greene J. & C. Klockars (1991). "What Police Do." In C. Klockars & S. Mafstrofski (eds.) *Thinking About Police: Contemporary Readings*, Second Edition. New York, NY: McGraw-Hill.

Harris, R. (1973). *The Police Academy: An Insider's View*. New York, NY: John Wiley and Sons.

Kappeler, V.E., M. Blumberg & G.W. Potter (1996). *The Mythology of Crime and Criminal Justice*, Second Edition. Prospect Heights, IL: Waveland Press.

Kappeler, V.E., A. Sapp & D. Carter (1992). "Police Officer Higher Education, Citizen Complaints and Departmental Rule Violations." *American Journal of Police*, 11(2):37-54.

Kappeler, V.E., R. Sluder & G.P. Alpert (1994). *Force of Deviance: Understanding the Dark Side of the Force*. Prospect Heights, IL: Waveland Press.

Kelling, G., T. Pate, D. Diekman & C.E. Brown (1974). *The Kansas City Preventive Patrol Experiment: A Summary Report*. Washington, DC: The Police Foundation.

Manning. P.K. (1997). *Police Work: The Social Organization of Policing*, Second Edition. Prospect Heights, IL: Waveland Press.

Manning, P.K. (1978). "The Police: Mandate, Strategies and Appearances." In L.K. Gaines & T.A. Ricks (eds.) *Managing The Police Organization*. St. Paul, MN: West.

Mastrofski, S. (1983). "The Police and Non-Crime Services." In G. Whitaker & C. Phillips (eds.) *Evaluating Performance of Criminal Justice Agencies*. Beverly Hills, CA: Sage Publications.

O'Neill, M. & C. Bloom (1972). "The Field Officer: Is He Really Fighting Crime?" *Police Chief*, 39:30-32.

Payne, D.M. & R.C. Trojanowicz (1985). "Performance Profiles of Foot Verses Motor Officers." *Community Policing Series*, 6. East Lansing, MI: Michigan State University.

Reiss, A.J. (1971). *The Police and the Public*. New Haven, CT: Yale University Press.

Reiss, A.J. & D.J. Bordua (1967). "Environment and Organization: A Perspective on the Police." In D.J. Bordua (ed.) *The Police: Six Sociological Essays*. New York, NY: John Wiley and Sons.

Reuss-Ianni, E. (1983). *Two Cultures of Policing*. New Brunswick, NJ: Transaction Books.

Rubinstein, J. (1973). *City Police*. New York, NY: Farrar, Strauss and Giroux.

Sherman, L. (1982). "Learning Police Ethics." *Criminal Justice Ethics*, 1(1):10-19.

Skolnick, J.H. (1966). *Justice Without Trial: Law Enforcement in a Democratic Society.* New York, NY: John Wiley and Sons.

Strecher, V. (1995). "Revising the Histories and Futures of Policing." In V.E. Kappeler (ed.) *The Police & Society: Touch Stone Readings*, pp. 69-82. Prospect Heights, IL: Waveland Press.

Swanton, B. (1981). "Social Isolation of Police: Structural Determinants and Remedies." *Police Studies*, 3:14-21.

Van Maanen, J. (1978a). "On Becoming a Policeman." In V.E. Kappeler (ed.) *Police & Society: Touch Stone Readings*. Prospect Heights, IL: Waveland Press.

Van Maanen, J. (1978b). "The Asshole." In P.K. Manning & J. Van Maanen (eds.) *Policing: A View From The Street*. Santa Monica, CA: Goodyear.

Westley, W.A. (1970). *Violence And the Police: A Sociological Study of Law, Custom and Morality.* Cambridge, MA: The MIT Press.

Westley, W.A. (1956). "Secrecy and the Police." *Social Forces*, 34(3):254-257.

Westley, W.A. (1953). "Violence and the Police." *American Journal of Sociology*, 59:34-41.

Wilson, J.Q. (1970). "The Police and Their Problems." In A. Neiderhoffer & A.S. Blumberg (eds.). *The Ambivalent Force: Perspectives on the Police*. Waltham, MA: Ginn and Company.

CHAPTER 12
Community Policing at the Crossroads

Every image should be confronted with another image.

—*Paul Eluard*

Community Policing: From Theory to Practice

The past two decades have seen exponential growth in the research and literature on community policing. The philosophy has come under close scrutiny by both scholars and police executives. Although community policing has been criticized for lack of continuity with history (Kappeler, 1996), flaws in its parent doctrines (Walker, 1983), and for serving as a legitimating tactic (Crank, 1994), police academicians have mostly played the role of community policing advocates. While many scholars and reformers have attempted to make distinctions between the philosophy of community policing and the many and varied strategies and tactics loosely associated with the philosophy, the phrase has become an umbrella term for almost any innovation in policing. Police chiefs, politicians, and even members of the community now invoke the phrase whenever problems associated with policing or communities surface. For too many people, community policing has become a buzz phrase and a panacea for almost all social problems facing the police and society.

It has been a decade since Robert Trojanowicz sat down to write *Community Policing: A Contemporary Perspective*. As we read *Community Policing* today it is clear that Trojanowicz approached the project in a hopeful, but cautious manner. While, community policing has come to mean many things to many people, the spirit of Trojanowicz's community policing was something quite specific, not nearly the catchall phrase it has become today. Whether community policing is described as a philosophy, a paradigm shift, a new model for policing, or a collection of strategies and tactics, community policing was a vehicle for the articulation of values that should guide policing.

In this chapter, with the benefit of hindsight, we will briefly appraise the social context that gave rise to community policing, discuss the ideal form of community policing, and raise issues and questions about the current state of policing and its relationship to the community policing movement. But before we embark on an assessment of the present and possible futures of community policing it is helpful to revisit Trojanowicz's vision to demonstrate the depth of that vision, what changes that vision entails, and the difficulties of making it a reality.

A Restatement of the Philosophy of Community Policing

The idea of community policing is a radical departure from traditional notions of policing. Community policing is a paradigm shift that challenges long-standing conceptualizations of the police and fundamental assumptions about doing police work. As a philosophy, community policing is grounded in a defined set of values that serve as its ethical and moral foundation, values that sought to change both the nature of the tasks police perform and the number of people responsible for determining the desired means and ends associated with policing. The assumptions upon which community policing rest represent a dramatic departure from the past that threatens the values and beliefs embraced by the traditional system and culture of policing.

Ideally, community policing values people and their concerns thereby relegating the police and its law enforcement agenda to a secondary concern. By paying attention to human and social problems and by tailoring police service to those problems, communities might be transformed into safer places with an improved quality of life for all people. Solving human problems and making communities safer places in which to live are accomplished by giving average people control over the police agenda. This means a radical redistribution of the power that has traditionally marked the divide between government, police, and citizens. From this perspective people are no longer passive actors in the policing process, they are active participants in determining both what constitutes a social problem and how best to address it.

By transforming the values of the police institution, community policing seeks to inject an ethos of service into a culture that has historically focused solely on crime rather than social problems. The traditional police institution's obsession with law enforcement based tactics is supplanted with an ethos of service and a problem-solving orientation. By retooling policing, the social isolation and inequities inherent in the traditional system are broken down and police form a new partnership with the people they are sworn to serve. By allowing line officers and average people, not just police executives and political elites, the power to set immediate priorities and launch new initiatives, police become responsive to community needs.

Community policing, therefore, implies a reduction in the power and control of local political officials and the rich and powerful in the community—the beneficiaries of traditional policing. Conversely, this also meant increased empowerment of those groups that had less access and clout in the current system. Community policing allows new groups direct input into the police process, broadening the base of community involvement. Powerful interests in the community are not ignored but harnessed, keeping them from dominating the social agenda. For example, a powerful business person may want the police to do something about the homeless who "scare" customers away from a store front, but community policing might focus on creating shelters for the homeless and offer new ways to protect the homeless from victimization, which is not what the business owner might have had in mind initially. Rather than relying on enforcement tactics that have a limited impact on social problems, like conducting street sweeps, arresting or displacing the homeless, community policing efforts are directed at solving some of the problems associated with homelessness.

Within police departments, community policing redefined power, control, and accountability, allowing those at the base of the organizational pyramid more autonomy and freedom to act independently in achieving the goal of becoming community servants. This means that police officers become educated in the social and community contexts of crime rather than just the rule of law and the tactics of law enforcement. Community policing recognizes that crime, like poverty, is a problem that has so far defied easy answers, and that despite their best efforts, the police will never be able to control it alone. Many of the social problems facing our urban centers today are the direct result of poor policy decisions of decades past, not inherent pathologies of our cities and their inhabitants. While the police do not dictate the social policies that give rise to the conditions found in American cities, they can make better use of resources, so that they can do a better job of reducing and controlling social problems, by focusing more attention on their underlying dynamics. Understanding social problems and interacting more closely with the community allows the police to become better advocates of sound public policy. In this way police do not merely respond to public policy and social problems but they inform policy and mitigate the negative effects of poor social policies. A community policing approach allows the police to expand beyond a narrow focus on crime, to address a broader spectrum of community concerns, such as fear of crime, quality of life issues, and neighborhood needs. This allows the police the ability to become advocates for their communities and hopefully effect pubic policy.

We can recount the basic values of community policing in the following changes it calls for:

- All people deserve a say in how they are policed, regardless of who they are or what position they hold in society. People have a right to decide both the means and objectives of the police;

- People—and not the police—have the ultimate power to control crime, enhance their own safety, and help improve the overall quality of life in the community. Community policing must empower groups that previously had less power and control;

- People are not only a vital police resource, they are the reason for policing. To do their job, the police must have access to average people. Average people are no longer the passive recipients of police service, but important partners in the policing process;

- People in the community become important arbiters in determining the relative success or failure of local initiatives, and they have a new role to play in supervising and assessing police performance;

- Police officers must be educated to see themselves as community problem-solvers, not just as crime-fighters. Within realistic limits, they must move beyond responding to calls as isolated incidents, to identifying and altering the underlying dynamics that create social problems;

- Police executives must actively demonstrate their commitment to this new philosophy, by delegating power and control to the community; and

- Police executives must shift to emphasizing trust while maintaining accountability, allowing all officers within the department the freedom and autonomy to move beyond responding to calls as isolated incidents to managing social problems.

The philosophy of community policing is not only a shift in the values that underpins policing but entails restructuring the police organization and rethinking of the organization of police work and police agencies. Community policing is a radical shift in the way police departments view and handle police work. It implies both a broader mandate that focuses on community and a structural shift to deliver decentralized and personalized service to the community. Community policing calls for the decentralization of police organizations in a manner that police officers on the street have greater organizational power, as well as a working environment that is structured to allow them to engage the community.

Community policing means departments are to downsize the number of motor patrol officers on free patrol at any given time. This allows the department to get greater mileage out of its line officers, by retreading many patrol officers into the department's community outreach specialists. The time wasted on random patrol is to be reclaimed under the community policing philosophy and restructured to allow all officers to participate in the new "business" of policing. This does not mean that police officers are merely redeployed in new tactical variations like directed patrol, street sweeps, split force patrol, or SWAT teams; it means that officers freed from patrol go out directly to the people in need of service, allowing their input to ensure the department does not lose touch with their wants and needs.

Community policing requires a reordering of patrol deployment. Under such a reordering, non-emergency calls do not receive the speediest response, but line officers are freed from motor patrol duty to serve as community outreach specialists. Until a restructuring of organizational power and a reordering in the work of policing takes place for the entire department, the effort is merely an expensive add-on, one that detracted from a proper focus on solving social problems.

Community policing implies changes in the kinds of services the department currently provides. A shift to community policing means that political leaders and community elites no longer have as much police protection as before. Powerful business interests may suffer a cut in the level of service that they had enjoyed. Non-emergency calls no longer demand the fastest possible response. What makes community policing so threatening is that it is not just a new strategy or technique, but a radical new approach to the business of policing, one that implies a reversal of winners and losers under the current system.

The organizational and structural issues associated with community policing are briefly summarized in the following list of changes:

- Community policing requires changes in the way that police resources are spent;

- Community policing requires a reordering of police work to allow time for problem solving;

- Community policing requires the decentralization of organizational power in a manner that allows line officers greater freedom to address human and social problems;

- Community policing requires a flattening of the organizational structure of police departments;

- Community policing requires educating the public on the new nature of police work especially as it relates to changes in police responses to citizens' calls for service; and

- Community policing requires a new system of accountability to the community.

Before we embark on a discussion of how the ideal form of community policing would be transformed into practice it is necessary to briefly revisit the social context in which the ideal of community policing arose. Philosophies, theories, and ideals are not created in a vacuum and understanding the context in which they arise can help inform us of both their meaning and the possibility of transforming them into practice.

The Social Context of the Community Policing Revolution

To understand fully the issues and challenges involved in shifting to community policing requires taking yet another look at the past, to understand the forces that spawned the community policing movement. Much of the resistance to community policing and many of the problems in today's failure to really operationalize the spirit of community policing stems from the fact that the impetus to change came primarily from outside police departments in a time of dramatic social change and institutional crisis. The shift from the professional model of policing to the community policing model was less the product of enlightened reformers than the effect of extreme social pressures on an institution that was facing a crisis in legitimacy. While reformers and advocates of community policing certainly offered the police institution a direction for change, the movement toward community policing was largely the result of social and intellectual pressures outside the police profession.

Like any other conservative institution, the police institution is slow to embrace change. Yet ever since the reform era of the 1930s, the police had little reason to re-examine their basic mission. Reformers helped set the tone for modern policing, by repositioning the police from peace keepers to crime-fighters. This repositioning also allowed the police to partially divorce themselves from direct political control and reattach themselves to the rule of law and the notion of professionalism. As management and police science began to grow, police departments had good reason to identify themselves with that new mission, especially since it seemed they continued to make progress toward that goal. Some police departments might have to address the occasional "crime wave," but there was general optimism that improved police procedures, new crime-fighting technologies, and the continued rise in the overall standard of living might someday mean that crime, like polio, would ultimately be conquered. At this stage in the development of the police institution, the conceptual changes to the meaning of what it meant to be a law enforcement officer and the changes in the language used to characterize that mission might have been more important than any real advances in either science or the actual management of the police.

Then that rosy view of an increasingly brighter future was shattered, seemingly overnight. The police soon found themselves under assault on three fronts. On college campuses nationwide, students and other anti-war protesters screamed at the police across the barricades sometimes spitting on them or hurling rocks. Police more often than not responded with violence. In inner-city, African-American neighborhoods, officers saw themselves as battling for their lives during the frightening series of race riots that seemed to erupt each summer. Again, not only was the police response violent, but the police were often the provocateurs of riots.

Especially in major cities, the rates of serious crime exploded. Because reformers had transformed the police into a crime fighting institution whose major performance measure was crime rates, the image of the police as efficient and effective crime-fighters was tarnished. Something seemed to have gone terribly wrong not only with the police institution but with the American dream, as more and more social inequities and contradictions began to come to the public's attention. The visible presence of the police on the front lines of the battles taking place on all fronts for social change made them the symbol of society's frustration with the escalating domestic upheaval and a lack of governmental responsiveness that seemed unstoppable.

In the early 1960s, mainstream America still expressed overwhelming optimism that scientific and technological progress ensured an unbroken march toward utopia. There were still problems to be conquered. Racial integration and equality had not been achieved, but Dr. Martin Luther King Jr.'s non-violent approach offered hope of peaceful progress toward that goal. The war in Vietnam continued to escalate, but military leaders assured the country of victory and that they could see light at end of the tunnel. Technology and science advanced almost as fast as the government's inability to listen to peoples concerns about the direction the country had taken. Science and the war metaphor became firmly entrenched in the American view of social problems. Many people still thought that human and social problems were solvable by waging technological and scientific warfare.

Community policing arose, in part, as a response to concerns about rising crime and the volatility of police-community relations. Rates of serious crime, particularly violent crime, had risen to levels virtually unthinkable decades before, and people worried that there appeared to be no relief in sight. Newark had suffered a devastating riot, and the Flint Police Department experienced a series of disturbing incidents with racial overtones. Almost every large American city experienced similar problems. There was an overall crisis of confidence that American society could pull itself back from the brink of anarchy portended by the rising tide of violence. There was tremendous pressure on the police to do more, to do something different, and, most of all, to do something that would help rather than fuel problems.

Important as well is the lesson that the impetus for community policing came from unavoidable pressures from outside the system more than from insiders who were eager to explore new ideas. In fact, the unwillingness of police departments to respond to changing needs and times is what allowed them to be caught off guard. Police departments were also beginning to struggle with the need to address minority concerns and they were bracing for the anticipated rise in crime as those Baby Boomers started to hit their most crime-prone years. But they were shocked to find themselves figuratively under fire from so many groups at the same time. The police were stunned at the degree of hostility they faced from college students and minorities, but they were perhaps most shocked at criticism leveled at them by those whom they saw as their primary base of support—the middle-class, white majority.

Community Policing Strategies: Preventing False Alarms in Phoenix

Patricia M. Rea
Alarm Coordinator
Phoenix Police Department Alarm Unit

Rea discussed the Phoenix Police Department's False Alarm Tracking System (FATS), which was implemented in 1990 at a cost of $17,500. In 1995-96, FATS cut the department's expected false alarm responses in half, a savings of $4.4 million.

Each year, Rea said, police departments in cities across the country waste thousands of hours—and millions of dollars—responding to repeated false alarms. In Phoenix, the city code traditionally allows businesses and residences to have a certain number of false alarms without assessment of a fine. Once an alarm system triggers an excessive number, however, both subscribers and their alarm companies are fined. Enforcement of this code is handled by the Phoenix Police Department's alarm unit.

Before the introduction of FATS in 1990, the unit's enforcement of alarms was a manual, labor-intensive process that wasted an extraordinary amount of personnel hours and led to complacency on the part of officers who were weary of responding to more and more false activations at the same locations. After an alarm activated, 9-1-1 operators asked standard questions about the type of alarm, business or residence, and alarm company involved. This information was entered into the department's computer-aided dispatch (CAD) system and sent to radio for dispatch. Responding officers then retrieved the information on their patrol car's mobile data terminal (MDT).

After their investigation, officers completed a false alarm report that essentially duplicated the information they had obtained from the CAD screen. These reports were then forwarded to the alarm unit where incidents were compared to address histories to determine if enforcement was needed. Enforcement procedures required manually typing warning letters and invoices and checking addresses at each stage of the process.

The burden of alarm enforcement on the department's resources and personnel became unmanageable when false alarm activations paralleled the city's explosive growth in the late 1980s and rose dramatically. In 1989, more than 80,000 false alarms were reported in the city, and increase of 60,000 over 1985.

In response, the department radically rethought its alarm enforcement process. At the heart of the new strategy was FATS, a tracking system developed in 1990 that automated the entire alarm call process and educated alarm subscribers through public awareness.

Built to follow all department and city code procedures and guidelines on alarm enforcement, FATS generates and displays all information needed by officers from the moment an alarm is activated through follow-up enforcement. It is tied to the department's CAD system and to patrol officers' mobile data terminals, linking officers and dispatchers to data bases with information on addresses, alarm ownership, and residence and business ownership. Every automated activity in the system is triggered by a simple permit number assigned to subscribers when they apply for an alarm license. Using a permit system streamlines the involvement of 9-1-1 operators once a call is received by eliminating the need to type repetitive information into CAD as well as the errors dispatchers and alarm company operators make through miscommunication.

FATS also automated officers' false alarm reports, allowing this information to be entered on MDT's and downloaded directly to the system every 24 hours. This step alone has eliminated 6 person-hours previously needed each day for data entry. After CAD and MDT false alarm information is received, FATS calculates the oldest alarm activation for that permit within a 365-day cycle and counts the number of false alarms. The system then generates any correspondence required by city code, including warning letters and assessment notices. In addition, FATS tracks the monetary value of assessments and operates an accounting feature that displays payments received and balance due information.

Through FATS, the department has studied when, where, and why false alarms are activated in Phoenix and used that information to dramatically reduce their occurrence.

Source: *Technology for Community Policing* (1997). Pp. 67-70.

Fears that strained race relations could mean new riots meant much of the attention focused on ways the police could reach out to minorities. Many departments faced increasing pressure to adopt civilian review boards as a way to address abuses of authority. While minorities often correctly viewed a department's willingness to accept such proposals as a bellwether of its sincerity in addressing their concerns, many police chiefs resisted them, arguing that they allowed people who did not understand policing unwarranted intrusion in determining police policy and procedures. Remnants of this type of thinking still haunt police departments today. Many police departments initially tried to ignore the mounting pressures to change, and dismissed citizens' concerns. The surprising passage of the Jarvis Amendment in California, which cut property taxes in half overnight, sent a brutal message to all government institutions that the people paying bills could revolt in ways that had both political and institutional consequences for the police.

The police also began to see the burgeoning growth in the private security industry as a growing threat, an ominous indication that people who could afford to pay more to feel safer were turning to the private, not the public, sector. Public policing had steadily lost ground to private policing, though few outside police circles realize that there were far more people employed in private security than there were public police officers.

Even many within policing did not recognize the full ramifications of this trend. One consequence is that those who want more protection and can afford to pay more to feel safer often choose to buy service from private sources. Those who cannot afford to pay more therefore must make do with the level of service that the public police can provide. The added irony, of course, is that those who can afford to buy more private security are often those who are already less likely to be victimized.

Private policing tended to mirror the class distinctions found in American society. On one end of the social spectrum is a family in an exclusive apartment building (or suburban enclave) where a hired security guard monitors the entrance with a video camera, challenging anyone who tries to enter to prove they have a valid reason for being there. On the other end is the inner-city welfare mother who has no phone to dial 911 if she hears someone breaking in. The harsh reality is that we have a two-tiered system of police protection, one in which the poorest and most crime-riddled areas depend on public policing, while the middle and upper classes must spend more and more of what they make on a mix of public and private services.

Advantages tend to multiply the further up the economic pyramid a person climbs. Affluent areas benefit from a higher tax base, which means more tax dollars for public protection. Those who earn more also have more to spend for extra security, whether that means buying a burglar alarm or sharing the fee for a doorman or security guard. Even if someone penetrates those superior defenses, money can insulate people of means from many of the consequences of crime. Such people usually have insurance—medical, homeowner's or renter's, disability—in addition to being better able to bear any out-of-pocket losses in the first place.

As the split between classes in American society became greater and as the public began to lose confidence in the police, the institution was thrown into a state of crisis. The crisis in legitimacy and a growing trend by the public to seek alternative means by which to ensure their safety forced the police institution to once again revisit its mission and rethink its social role. The police had to modify its mission to become socially useful to the vast majority of people as well as political leaders. Facing a crisis, how was policing to regain public confidence? How was the emerging philosophy of community policing to become a reality?

Turning the Spirit of Community Policing into Practice

Trojanowicz viewed community policing as the vanguard that would stabilize our cities and bring the police institution out of crisis. The philosophy of community policing was to be turned into action by creating Neighborhood Community Policing Centers that could grow into Community Resource Centers, as new social service agencies sent representatives to reach people where they live. Depending on local needs, not federally directed programs that had been seen as failures, it made sense to move professionals like parole officers into centers, so that they could work together, share information, and share staffing the local office. The next step would be to employ drug counselors, who could work with the CPOs and the area parole officer to coordinate workable proactive outreach efforts.

By allowing those three new outreach professionals to work together as a community team would allow them to be far more effective together than they hope to be individually. Operating out of such a center, the drug counselor could work with the parole officer to field a roster of former drug offenders who will work the CPO on making presentations to kids at risk, warning them of the potential consequences they face, and reminding them of the power they have in making positive choices. Unlike the *Scared Straight* or DARE approaches of dubious value, where the goal is to frighten kids away from bad behavior, such an effort could encourage both ex-cons and reformed drug addicts and kids at risk to work together on helping each other stay drug-free.

The center would also allow CPOs and parole officers to share information. Being in the same facility would give them a chance to work together on helping people on parole readjust and get their lives back together so that they do not fall back on bad habits. This would involve working with area businesses to find jobs, or enlisting the help of adult education teachers to help them sharpen their job skills. The center might provide a home for a volunteer-supported literacy effort.

Trojanowicz envisioned an explosion of possibilities if these professionals were joined by a public health nurse. The nurse could work with everyone in the center on identifying and helping pregnant women get off drugs, because of the urgent need to prevent the damage that drugs can do. Public health nurses could also work with the CPO to develop community-based initiatives to help single parents struggling to raise infants alone. The public health nurse could play a vital role in helping prevent the spread of AIDS among the IV drug users that the drug counselor sees.

The opportunities would multiply exponentially each time a new outreach specialist joins the team—social workers, adult education teachers, parks, and recreation specialists. Perhaps some spend a day each week, while others might move into the facility full-time. With the CPO leading the way to ensure their safety, these professionals may be able to enlist others in the cause. Perhaps a physician would visit once a month, to provide immunizations and physicals to youngsters. Maybe a corporation would free a personnel specialist one afternoon a week to help counsel people in how to find and hold jobs. Businesses who recruit employees from the area might be persuaded that their long-term future depends on allowing their successful employees time off to spend working with minority youth in the area, to provide them positive role models.

The Community Resource Center could become the hub of neighborhood activity, the outreach center where local churches and civic organizations hold meetings, coordinate projects, and disseminate information. It would become the place that people turn to for help first, because even if the help is not available there directly, there will always be someone there who can tell people where to go or whom to call. Perhaps the concern is finding safe shelter for the homeless or abused women and children. Maybe the challenge is to address minority health concerns, ranging from sickle-cell anemia to high blood pressure. The focus and scope of each effort would be bounded only by the collective imagination of the people involved and the particular needs of the community. And all would benefit from the involvement of the CPO's provision of continuity.

Ironically, of course, this hope for the future harkened back to the past, not of policing, but of social service. Not that long ago, social workers visited clients in their homes; the public health nurse made calls on the elderly, the sick, and young mothers; and truant officers tracked down kids who skipped school. Since then, however, we have pulled back from providing decentralized and personalized service, where professionals worked directly in the community. Pressures to become more efficient and more "modern" have favored a centralized system, where the clients came to the professionals. But just as putting police officers into patrol cars inadvertently spawned isolation from the community, centralizing other public services has alienated these professionals from the people they serve.

The first thing that happened when the public system pulled back from direct involvement in the community was that the burden of receiving service fell onto those with the fewest resources. When the social workers of the past visited homes, their transportation expenses were covered as part of the job. Now instead, we demand that welfare clients must pay to take the bus, often with their children in tow, and they often have to wait for hours to be seen. This change sends a message that the system no longer cares about the client's wants and needs.

Pulling social agents out of the community also removed the visible symbols of social control. Though it may be somewhat unfashionable to say so, a visiting social worker was in some sense both a role model and a snoop. The social worker typically brought with him or her a middle-class set of values about what constituted proper behavior, backed with the power to approve or disapprove certain benefits. When the system worked properly, those spot checks could uncover obvious cases of physical, mental, and sexual child abuse and neglect. The downside was the thought of an imperious bureaucrat, arriving unannounced, threatening fearful clients that they would lose their benefits simply because the social worker found the person's lifestyle or customs distasteful. Recall that many initiatives labeled community policing suffered similar undesirable effects when the police and community elites attempted to impose their vision of community revitalization on people.

Another concern was that personalized service led to uneven distribution of aid. A kind-hearted social worker might bend the rules to find a way to give enough money to a struggling mother whose kids needed shoes to go to school. Another might slash benefits to the children of a mother deemed promiscuous. The line between offering help and interfering with individual freedom and dignity has never been easy to draw, which made it easier to retreat from a personalized approach that allowed professionals the opportunity both to use—and abuse—individual discretion.. Community policing is also fraught with the potential for abuse when officers are afforded greater autonomy and power to function in the community. Will some citizens become the preferred customers of community policing service? Will others becomes the geographically targeted consumers of law enforcement services?

Adding to our uneasiness about personalized service was the tinge of racism. In the past, many social workers were white, while many clients were minorities. The white majority saw this system as a way to use economic coercion as a means of imposing its will and its customs on minorities, in the guise of providing charity and assistance. Yet reform has created a centralized system where people's benefits are determined purely "by the numbers," a system so impersonal that common sense plays no role. The issues of racism and the loss of personalized service is also a concern with current trends in community and problem-solving policing. As we will discuss later, the criminal justice system's move toward actuarial justice and the police institution's emphasis on problem solving may make service less personal, and practices such as location-oriented policing and sweeping "hot spots" could have an adverse impact on minorities, particularly the poor who live in the nation's urban centers.

Challenges to the Spirit of Community Policing

Many supporters naively believe that community policing ensures a bright future for both communities and the police. Many also believe the movement is too firmly entrenched to be denied. Yet, this ignores the fierce competition in the marketplace of ideas as well as the power of more than half a decade of indoctrinating police in their crime fighting role. The history of modern policing is littered with the remains of promising ideas that faltered and died. Police Community Relations and Team Policing are only two of the more obvious examples. Both undeniably addressed important problems and were launched with great fanfare and enthusiasm. Both failed to change the basic values and operations of the police institution and have all but disappeared.

There are lessons to be learned from these extinct attempts to transform the police institution. Most of these programs failed because they merely repackaged policing without modifying the core function and values of the police institution. For more than half a century, police have been socialized into their crime fighting role, political leaders have pandered to citizens' fear of crime, and the media has distorted our view of the realities of both crime and the proper response to it (Kappeler, Blumberg & Potter, 1996). With such powerful forces shaping our vision of society and the means to improve it, it may be overly optimistic to hope that any philosophy, no matter how revolutionary, can transform social institutions in a single decade. History would seem to instruct otherwise. There have been relatively few social revolutions in America that have transformed the very fabric of our society. History more accurately instructs that change is a slow process that might be better characterized as a chain rather than a revolution—each social transformation constitutes another link in the chain becoming both dependent on the previous link and making future links dependent upon it.

From this perspective, the spirit of community policing is more likely to become absorbed by the traditional orientation of the police institution rather than to become a replacement orientation. While the introduction of community policing will change the nature of the police institution, it may not fundamentally alter the institution's most basic values and core operations. The community policing movement faces many challenges and difficulties and it is fraught with obstacles both inherent in the police institution and society.

Contemporary Issues and Questions About Community Policing

While community policing in its purest form represents one of the most profound changes facing the police institution, there are serious issues and questions to be raised about the ability of the police institution to transcend its own past and bring about a revolution rather than merely forging another link in the chain of the relationships between police and society. Some of these difficult questions include:

- Community policing involves a detachment of the police institution from the rule of law and its professional crime fighting orientation to develop a true service ethos (Kappeler & Kraska, 1998; 1998a). This means police officers derive their sense of what constitutes acceptable police practice from their perception of community need, desire, and will rather than from legal dictates or professional desires. In this situation, will police be able to accurately read and discern between their own professional agenda, what is legally permissible, and what all (not just the majority) members of the community want? Will police be able to set aside their desire to achieve the mantel of professionalism by increasing their specialization and technological efficiency to become social servants?

- Community policing entails a shifting of responsibility for crime control from the police institution to citizens and other service agencies (Kappeler & Kraska, 1998; 1998a). Could this shift result in an inability of citizens to make the police accountable for crime control? Will other social service agencies' primary function be adversely affected by an exposure to or transplanting of police objectives into their agencies? Would every social service agency then have a law enforcement agenda? Will citizens still avail themselves of social services knowing that these agencies not carry out a crime control function?

- Community policing involves a dramatic shifting of police orientation and public preoccupation with crime control to a broader range of human activities (Kappeler & Kraska, 1998; 1998a). If the police are free to determine what constitutes disorder and problem behavior, will the police institution become more controlling and invasive? Could this mean a dramatic challenge to existing civil rights and liberties? Will the behaviors of the least powerful members of the community become defined as the disorder that "causes" crime?

- Modern policing has embraced the high-rationality of science along with its tendency toward bureaucratic efficiency. If this movement continues, will the value of "what works" supplant the value of "what *should* be done"? There are many law enforcement tactics that can be used to reduce crime and make law enforcement more efficient, but what is the price tag for such endeavors?

- The police adoption of the imagery of service provision and problem solving constitutes a hierarchical positioning of police as directors of the community (Kappeler & Kraska, 1998; 1998a). Will police be allowed to both direct community will and interpret the quality of their own performance? Will the police claim credit for declines in crime rates even though they have instructed citizens and political leaders that this is not the proper measure of police performance, nor is it their sole responsibility?

- Community policing entails the language of community-based accountability (Kappeler & Kraska, 1998; 1998a). Will the police institution surrender its power to define what constitutes a valid citizen complaint about the police and what actions are appropriate to address police abuses of community trust? Are the police really willing to allow citizens to determine what constitutes proper police behavior and to make decisions on how to sanction violations of proper police conduct?

These questions are not easily answered or resolved. In many ways they represent the basic paradox of policing in a democratic society. While on the one hand the police represent one of society's greatest assets for the protection of civil rights, liberties, and freedoms, yet they remain one of the greatest threats to those same rights, liberties, and freedoms (Kappeler, Sluder & Alpert, 1994). The language of community policing contains these conflicts.

As the title of this chapter indicates, community policing in America stands at a crossroads—somewhere between a community model and a hyper-rational crime fighting model (Kappeler & Kraska, 1998). While remarkable strides have been made in our knowledge about crime, policing, and criminality over the last decade, there are certainly some disturbing practices, dialogues, and trends taking place in society and policing today. Consider a few trends that undermine the spirit of community policing.

- **Disorder and pathology are dangerous metaphors** – The public discussion on community policing has replaced the language of "waging war" on crime with the language of conducting "scientific experiments" into the control of urban decay through the deployment of police forces to disorderly "hot-spots." Unfortunately, these tactics are packaged as "enforcing the community's quality of life and civility" as expressed in academic theses touted as "fixing broken windows" (Wilson & Kelling, 1982), "acquiring a taste for order" (Kelling, 1987), and "developing a climate of order" (Bayley, 1994). What we must remember is that the imposition of order creates disorder. Disorder and urban pathology, rather than poor public policy and shifts in the economic base of American society, are incorrectly seen as the root causes of crime. As such, policing has taken a tactical rather than true social problem-solving turn (Kraska & Kappeler, 1997). This language, while appealing to the public and political leaders in its simplicity, cannot be empirically supported and is often used to restrict civil liberties and promote aggressive rather than service practices by the police (see, Kraska & Kappeler, 1997; Kappeler & Kraska, 1998, 1998a). The language of disorder and decay has freed the police from some burdensome constitutional constraints that previously limited their proactive authority. More and more cities are enacting statutes that restrict peoples behaviors. Now the police enterprise is instructed to scientifically identify and fix "broken windows," "uncivil people," and "decaying urban" places not through the provision of service but through the use of aggressive law enforcement tactics.

- **Police have failed to adequately define and address "quality of life"** – Within policing and academic circles, the language of policy science is focusing on urban space. Refinements in law enforcement have been advanced with media crime talk, police disorder speech, and an emerging criminology of place. Targets of police control have become scientifically identified "hot spots" (Koper, 1995; Sherman & Weisburd, 1995; Sherman & Rogan, 1995), and intrusions into public and residential space are rationalized using "street sweeps," "crack house raids" and "weeding and seeding." This language has taken on an Orwellian flavor in programs promoted by the Harvard School of Government (HSG) and the New York City Police Department (NYPD). In a novel, albeit distorted, adaptation to the call by police reformers to enhance community's' quality of life, NYPD and HSG have sponsored a national training conference (titled COMPSTAT) for police administrators. The program includes a learning module labeled "quality of life enforcement" as opposed to 'law enforcement' or 'service provision'" (Kappeler & Kraska, 1998, in press).

- **We are becoming a society of safety seekers and risk managers** – Because of the unrealistic fear of crime, society has developed an obsession with safety and an aversion to risk. People now more than in the past want to make every aspect of life risk free and predictable. This theme resonates in our desire for uniformity in many aspects of social life from the fast foods we eat to our daily interactions with others. In a our highly modern "society of strangers," prediction becomes both increasingly more desirable and more difficult. These desires have arisen alongside a culturally induced dependence and indifference among many citizens. The police have become the premiere problem-solvers for some of society's most complex difficulties. Politicians and the bulk of the public fall back on juvenile curfews, increasing regulations, order enforcement, and target-hardening as a means to bring order and predictability to a largely unpredictable circumstance—modern living. This trend is destroying the possibility of creating communities where people interact in meaningful ways to solve their own problems without governmental control (Kappeler & Kraska, 1998; 1998a).

- **We are destroying community as we reorder policing and society** – Society is moving in the direction of defensible social ordering. Gated bedroom communities and carefully administered residential areas, isolated by the simulation of nature, punctuate the modern blend of people, places, and purposes. Individual-based suspicion (Skolnick, 1966), the cornerstone of police action, is being replaced by surveillance and the control of populations and places threatening or defying the new rationality of place and purpose (Kappeler & Kraska, 1998; 1998a). A newly found correlation between public intoxication and robberies can serve as the meager proof of the disorder and broken windows thesis without much thought being given to both relationships to public policy. Residential and formerly private spaces have become well defined and more receptive to intrusion by social control agents through the language of disorder, drug epidemics, and family violence. Police activities are moving further into previously undefined, unregulated space, and the daily lives of citizens (Kappeler & Kraska, 1998; 1998a).

- **Policing may not be more democratic** – Community police reformers repeatedly call for the reading of the community's needs and concerns. Meetings with well-positioned members of the community, discussions with media and political representatives, and especially citizen surveys, have become popular forums for citizen involvement. The U.S. Department of Justice has heavily promoted this trend as a type of "democracy in action" (Bureau of Justice Assistance, 1994:4). Yet, business owners, corporate executives, community leaders, and the affluent have always been able to make their wishes known through formal and informal contacts. A police executive cannot make time for every private citizen who might call for an appointment, but most will try to make time to meet with the president of a major corporation or the elected leader of a powerful community group.

    The traditional system also discourages average citizens from asking for a formal appointment, especially unless they have a pressing concern. In contrast, the power brokers in the community often interact informally or socialize with police officials, at meetings, at luncheons, or as friends. This not only gives them the chance to air specific concerns, but also to share opinions and general impressions. Because the top command in the department often shares much in common with other successful people in the community, in terms of education, values, and current lifestyle, they often reinforce each other's perceptions—and biases.

- **We may not be reading community needs and desires** – The citizen survey approach is packaged as a type of market analysis. It is by far the most popular method by which the police ostensibly allow the citizenry to participate in setting police priorities and it is used to demonstrate to the community an ethic of public accountability. In addition these surveys are used as a major indicator of whether or not a police department is "doing community policing," making them an integral part of community policing reform efforts.

   Supported by some police academics and by the resources of the federal government, police agencies are using citizen surveys which have contained within them a traditional law enforcement agenda rather than a service agenda (Kappeler & Kraska, 1998; 1998a). Detailed consideration of the instruments used by the police (see for example, Tempe Police Department, 1993; Bradshaw, 1989; Henderson, 1995; NCCP, 1994), demonstrates how the law enforcement agenda encoded into most community survey measures. These surveys articulate for citizens the notion that the police are the providers of community solutions to police-identified problems. We can find within these instruments basic tenets of problem solving, but they also instruct citizens that fear of crime is to be found among distinct populations and activities, that this is the best measure of police productivity; and that solutions to social problems should be enforcement based. Citizens are to interpret the causes of police-represented problems as stemming from local disorder, the circulation of drugs, violent gangs, unsupervised youths, and community outsiders. Many of the current measures of citizen concerns function as pedagogical tools, framing for the citizen the central tenets of the law enforcement agenda rather than the service agenda.

- **Not all police partnerships are created equal** – Traditionally, in discussions of policing, one could make a pretty clear distinction between formal and informal social control. One was able to quite effectively argue that police represent one of the most formal institutions of social control and that this institution only had a distant or indirect effect on organizing, managing, and influencing more informal systems and agencies of social control. Today, one of the most dramatic changes in the police institution since is the emergence of the police as the organizers and managers of an array of social controls. This phenomena represents a fundamental change in the alignment of social control. Policing, historically a reactive institution, is emerging as a proactive institution that directs and organizes many social control efforts.

   Two examples are informative as to the organized nature of social control. Promoted under community policing partnerships, these descriptions evidence the nature of how police-citizen partnerships are constructed, ordered, and serve police interests in both constructing and solving social problems.

San Diego Problem Analysis Advisory Committee (PAAC)

PAAC, provides a monthly forum in the San Diego Police Department where participants—problem-solving officers and members of other governmental agencies—collaboratively problem-solve complex crime, fear, and disorder problems. Problems are brought to the attention of PAAC by individual officers. Participating agencies include the Departments of Probation, Parole, Parks, Fire, Social Services, and Codes. Other agencies, organizations, and businesses are brought in on an as-needed basis depending on the particular POP project under discussion. . . .

San Diego's Committee is housed in the police department rather than in a neutral or community site. While potentially practical, this may evidence a symbolic framing of the problem-solution origin. It at least serves to reinforce law enforcement as the solution to social problems. Second, participants in the process are organizationally derived rather than individual citizens, government agencies as participants in community problem identification are emphasized, and in some sense community is only represented as it is culled from organized interests on an "as needed basis." Inherent in the description is a method of controlling how problems are brought to the attention of the committee. Problem-solving officers bring to the committee their selection of concerns. One can only assume that law enforcement officers acting as the collectors of problems to be placed on the committee's agenda will advance concerns based on their background assumptions and world view. This assumption seems bolstered by the fact that the description clearly identifies complex crime, fear, and disorder as problems that are taken for granted. The communication of community desires is filtered through law enforcement mediums. In this configuration, not only is the ideology of law enforcement implanted in the process, but the ability to select, define, and address problems is controlled by law enforcement, not the community, as the spirit of community policing suggests.

Norfolk Support Services Committee

The Support Services Committee is a citywide body that provides services and resolves neighborhood problems. Agencies, organizations, and citizens are represented on the Support Services Committee. Municipal agencies participating include the Department of Human Services, the Norfolk Police Department, the Juvenile Services Bureau, Department of Public Works, Norfolk Public Schools, Parks, Public Health, City Planning and Codes and the Norfolk Housing Authority. In addition, non-government agencies and organizations participate as well, including the Federation of Civic Leagues, Neighborhood Crime Prevention Coalition, and the Norfolk Resident Organization. Bureau heads (not agency heads) attend, allowing business to get done quickly without going through layers of bureaucracy. The Committee meets twice a month and hears progress reports on neighborhood crime and police problems, social service and health needs, and environmental issues like street lighting, trash pick-up and code enforcement for different neighborhoods. Agency employees can refer problems to the committee, so can neighborhood residents through a variety of mechanisms. Norfolk's Support Services Committee is part of a larger effort designed to realign Norfolk to a community-oriented government model of service delivery.

The Norfolk models evidence a similar pattern although individual citizens are mentioned. The model, however, clearly places emphasis on a government model of service delivery and describes concerns in the language of police products—street lighting, trash pick-up, and code enforcement. Even "police problems" are emphasized in the model. Like the San Diego model, governmental agencies and their employees are the communicative link between community and problem identification.

Figure 12.1
Problem Solving: Guide to Collaboration

General Background
1. Develop personal networks with members of other agencies who can give you information and help you with problems you may be working on.
2. Become familiar with the workings of your local government, private businesses, citizen organizations, and other groups and institutions that you may need to call upon for help in the future.
3. Develop skills as a negotiator.

Getting Other Agencies To Help
1. Identify agencies that have a role (or could have a role) in addressing the problem early in the problem-solving process.
2. Determine whether these other agencies perceive that there is a problem.
   a. Which agency members perceive the problem and which do not?
   b. Why is it (or isn't it) a problem for them? How are police perceptions of the problem similar to and different from the perceptions of members of other agencies?
3. Determine if there is a legal or political mandate for collaboration.
   a. To which agencies does this legal mandate apply?
   b. What are the requirements needed to demonstrate collaboration?
   c. Who is checking to determine if collaboration is taking place?

4. Look for difficulties that these other agencies face that can be redressed through collaboration on this problem.
   a. Are there internal difficulties that provide an incentive to collaborate?
   b. Are there external crises affecting agencies that collaboration may help redress?
5. Determine how much these other agencies use police services.
6. Assess the resource capabilities of these agencies to help.
   a. Do they have the money?
   b. Do they have the staff expertise?
   c. Do they have the enthusiasm?
7. Assess the legal authority of these other agencies.
   a. Do they have special enforcement powers?
   b. Do they control critical resources?
8. Determine the administrative capacity of these agencies to collaborate.
   a. Do they have the legal authority to intervene in the problem?
   b. What are the internal procedures and policies of the stakeholders that help or hinder collaboration?

Working With Other Agencies
1. Include representatives from all affected agencies possible in the problem-solving process.
2. Look for responses to the problem that maximize the gains to all agencies and distribute costs equitably.
3. Reinforce awareness of the interdependence of all agencies.
4. Be prepared to mediate among agencies that have a history of conflict.
5. Develop problem information-sharing mechanisms and promote discussion over the meaning and interpretation of this information.
6. Share problem-solving decisions among stakeholders and do not surprise others with already made decisions.
7. Develop a clear explanation as to why collaboration is needed.
8. Assess the resource capabilities of these agencies to help.
   a. Do they have the money?
   b. Do they have the staff expertise?
   c. Do they have the enthusiasm?
9. Assess the legal authority of these other agencies.
   a. Do they have special enforcement powers?
   b. Do they control critical resources?
10. Determine the administrative capacity of these agencies to collaborate.
    a. Do they have the legal authority to intervene in the problem?
    b. What are the internal procedures and policies of the stakeholders that help or hinder collaboration?

When Collaboration Does Not Work
1. Always be prepared for collaboration to fail.
2. Have alternative plans.
3. Assess the costs and benefits of unilateral action.
4. Be very patient.

Source: (BJA, 1994a:99-100); Adapted from J.E. Eck (1990 draft). *Implementing a Problem-Oriented Approach: A Management Guide.* Washington, DC: Police Executive Research Forum, pp. 69-70.

References

Bayley, D. (1994). *Police for the Future*, New York, NY: Oxford University Press.

Bittner, E. (1970). *The Functions of the Police in Modern Society*, Washington, DC: National Institute of Mental Health.

Black, D. (1970). "Production of Crime Rates." *American Sociological Review*, 35:733-748.

Bourdieu, P. (1982[1994]). *Language and Symbolic Power*, Cambridge, MA: Harvard University Press.

Bradshaw, R.V. (1989). *Reno Police Department's Community Oriented Policing—Plus.* Reno, NV: City of Reno.

Bratton, W.J. (1995). "The New York City Police Department's Civil Enforcement of Quality-of-Life Crimes." *Journal of Law and Policy*, 3(2):447-464.

Brodeur, J. (1981). "Legitimizing Police Deviance." In C.D. Shearing (ed.) *Organizational Police Deviance.* Toronto, Canada: Butterworths and Company.

Bureau of Justice Assistance (1994). *Neighborhood-Oriented Policing in Rural Communities: A Program Planning Guide.* Washington, DC: U.S. Department of Justice.

Crank, J.P. (1994). "Watchman and Community: Myth and Institutionalization in Policing." *Law and Society*, 28(2):325-351.

Eck, J.E. (1990 [draft]). *Implementing a Problem-Oriented Approach: A Management Guide.* Washington, DC: Police Executive Research Forum.

Ericson, R.V. (1981). "Rules for Police Deviance." In C.D. Shearing (ed.) *Organizational Police Deviance.* Toronto, Canada: Butterworths and Company.

Gaffigan, S. (1994). "The Community Policing Consortium Announces Availability of Practical Primer on Community Policing." *New Release*, (October, 3):1-2.

Goldstein, H. (1990). *Problem-Oriented Policing.* New York, NY: McGraw-Hill.

Goldstein, H. (1979). "Improving the Police: A Problem-Oriented Approach." *Crime & Delinquency*, 25:236-258.

Green, L. (1996). *Policing Places with Drug Problems.* London, England: Sage Publications.

Harring, S.L. (1983). *Policing a Class Society: The Experience of American Cities, 1865-1915.* New Brunswick, NJ: Rutgers University Press.

Henderson, C. (1995). *Community Resource Areas: A Residential Survey.* Hillsborough County, FL: Sheriff's Office.

Kappeler, V.E. (1996). "Making Police History in Light of Modernity: A Sign of the Times?" *Police Forum*, 6(3):1-6.

Kappeler, V.E., M. Blumberg & G.W. Potter (1996). *The Mythology of Crime and Criminal Justice*, Second Edition. Prospect Heights, IL: Waveland Press.

Kappeler, V.E. & P.B. Kraska (1998). "A Textual Critique of Community Policing: Police Adaption to High Modernity." *Policing: An International Journal of Police Strategies and Management.* In press.

Kappeler, V.E. & P.B. Kraska (1998a). "Policing Modernity: Scientific and Community Based Violence on Symbolic Playing Fields." In S. Henry & D. Milovanovic (eds.) *Constitutive Criminology at Work*. Albany, NY: SUNY Press.

Kelling, G.L. (1988). *Police and Communities: The Quiet Revolution*. Washington, DC: U.S. Department of Justice.

Kelling, G.L. (1987 [1995]). "Acquiring a Taste for Order: The Community and the Police." In V.E. Kappeler (ed.) *The Police & Society: Touch Stone Readings*. Prospect Heights, IL: Waveland Press.

Kelling, G.L. & M.H. Moore (1988 [1995]). "The Evolving Strategy of Policing." In V.E. Kappeler (ed.) *The Police & Society: Touch Stone Readings*, pp. 3-28. Prospect Heights, IL: Waveland Press.

Kelling, G.L. & J.K. Stewart (1989). *Neighborhood and Police: The Maintenance of Civil Authority*. Washington, DC: U.S. Department of Justice.

Kelling, G.L., R. Wasserman & H. Williams (1988). *Police Accountability and Community Policing*. Washington, DC: U.S. Department of Justice.

Klockars, C.B. (1988). "The Rhetoric of Community Policing." In J.R. Green & S.D. Mastrofski (eds.) *Community Policing Rhetoric or Reality*, pp. 239-254. New York, NY: Praeger.

Klockars, C.B. (1986 [1995]). "Street Justice: Some Micro-Moral Reservations-Comment on Sykes." In V.E. Kappeler (ed.) *The Police & Society: Touch Stone Readings*, pp. 155-158. Prospect Heights, IL: Waveland Press.

Koper, C.S. (1995). "Just Enough Police Presence: Reducing Crime and Disorderly Behavior by Optimizing Patrol Time in Crime Hot Spots." *Justice Quarterly*, 2(4):649-672.

Kraska, P.B. & L. Cubellis (1997). "Militarizing Mayberry and Beyond: Making Sense of Paramilitary Policing." *Justice Quarterly*, 14(4), in press.

Kraska, P.B. & V.E. Kappeler (1997). "Militarizing American Police: The Rise and Normalization of Paramilitary Units." *Social Problems*, 44(1):1-28.

Kuhn, T.S. (1962). *The Structure of Scientific Revolutions*. Chicago, IL: The University of Chicago Press.

Lefebvre, H. (1991 Eng. Trans.). *The Production of Space*. Oxford, England: Blackwell.

Manning, P.K. (1996). "Policing and Reflection." *Police Forum*, 7(3):1-6.

Manning, P.K. (1994). "The Police: Symbolic Capital, Class and Control." In G.S. Bridges & M.A. Myers (eds.) *Inequity, Crime and Social Control*. Boulder, CO: Westview Press.

Manning, P.K. (1993 [1995]). "Violence and Symbolic Violence." In V.E. Kappeler (ed.) *The Police & Society: Touch Stone Readings*, pp. 357-364. Prospect Heights, IL: Waveland Press.

Manning, P.K. (1992 [1995]). "Economic Rhetoric and Policing Reform." In V.E. Kappeler (ed.) *The Police & Society: Touch Stone Readings*, pp. 375-392. Prospect Heights, IL: Waveland Press.

Manning, P.K. (1988). "Community Policing as a Drama of Control." In J.R. Green & S.D. Mastrofski (eds.) *Community Policing Rhetoric or Reality*, pp. 27-46. New York, NY: Praeger.

Manning, P.K. (1971 [1995]). "The Police: Mandate, Strategies and Appearances." In V.E. Kappeler (ed.) *The Police & Society: Touch Stone Readings*, pp. 97-126. Prospect Heights, IL: Waveland Press.

Marx, G.T. (1992). "Under-the-Covers Investigations: Some Reflections on the State Use of Sex and Deception in Law Enforcement." *Criminal Justice Ethics*, Winter/Spring:13-24.

Mastrofski, S. (1988). "Community Policing Reform." In J. Green & S. Mastrofski (eds.) *Community Policing*. New York, NY: Praeger.

Moore, M.H. & G.L. Kelling (1983). "To Serve and Protect: Learning from Police History." *The Public Interest*, 70:49-65.

Moore, M.H. & R.C. Trojanowicz (1988). *Corporate Strategies for Policing*. Washington, DC: U.S. Department of Justice.

Murphy, C. (1988). "The Development, Impact, and Implications of Community Policing in Canada." In J.R. Green & S.D. Mastrofski (eds.) *Community Policing Rhetoric or Reality*, pp. 177-190. New York, NY: Praeger.

National Center for Community Policing (1994). *Police Department Community Survey*. East Lansing, MI: Michigan State University.

National Institute of Justice (1996a). "Policing Drug Hot Spots." *Research Preview*. Washington, DC: National Institute of Justice.

National Institute of Justice (1996b). "Communities: Mobilizing Against Crime—Making Partnerships Work." *National Institute of Justice Journal*, (August):1-56.

Sherman, L.W., P.R. Gartin & M.E. Buerger (1989). "Hot Spots of Predatory Crime: Routine Activities and the Criminology of Police." *Criminology*, 27:27-55.

Sherman, L.W. & D.P. Rogan (1995a). "Effects of Gun Seizures on Gun Violence: 'Hot Spots' Patrol in Kansas City." *Justice Quarterly*, 12(4):673-710.

Sherman, L.W. & D.P. Rogan (1995b). "Deterrent Effects of Police Raids on Crack Houses: A Randomized, Controlled Experiment." *Justice Quarterly*, 12(4):755-781.

Sherman, L.W. & D. Weisburd (1995). "General Deterrent Effects of Police Patrol in Crime 'Hot Spots': A Randomized Control Trial." *Justice Quarterly*, 12(4):625-648.

Skogan, W. (1975). "Pubic Policy and Public Evaluations of Criminal Justice System Performance." In J.A. Gardiner & M.A. Mulkey (eds.) *Crime and Criminal Justice*, pp. 53-61. Lexington, MA: D.C. Heath.

Skolnick, J.H. (1966). *Justice Without Trial: Law Enforcement in a Democratic Society*. New York, NY: John Wiley and Sons.

Sparrow, M.K. (1988). *Implementing Community Policing*. Perspectives on Policing, Vol. 9. Washington, DC: National Institute of Justice and Harvard University, pp. 8-9.

Stedman, J. (1992). "Taking a Closer Look at Gangs." *Problem Solving Quarterly*, 5(1):11-17.

Strecher, V.G. (1991 [1995]). "Revising the Histories and Futures of Policing." In V.E. Kappeler (ed.) *The Police & Society: Touch Stone Readings*, pp. 69-82. Prospect Heights, IL: Waveland Press.

Sykes, G. (1986 [1995]). "Street Justice: A Moral Defense of Order Maintenance Policing." In V.E. Kappeler (ed.) *The Police & Society: Touch Stone Readings*, pp. 139-154. Prospect Heights, IL: Waveland Press.

Walker, S. (1992). *The Police in America*, Second Edition. New York, NY: McGraw-Hill.

Walker, S. (1983 [1995]). "Broken Windows and Fractured History: The Use and Misuse of History in Recent Police Patrol Analysis." In V.E. Kappeler (ed.) *The Police & Society: Touch Stone Readings*, pp. 53-68. Prospect Heights, IL: Waveland Press.

Wallace, H., C. Roberson & C. Steckler (1995). *Fundamentals of Police Administration.* Englewood Cliffs, NJ: Prentice Hall.

Wilson, J.Q. & G.L. Kelling (1982). "Broken Windows: Police and Neighborhood Safety." *Atlantic Monthly*, 249 (March):29-38.

COMMUNITY CLOSE-UP
Buffalo's Neighborhood Initiatives

R. Gil Kerlikowske, Police Commissioner

Buffalo, New York is a city of strong neighborhoods. In a 1994 housing survey conducted by the U.S. Census Bureau in 15 cities, Buffalo beat Dallas and tied with Tampa in residents' degree of satisfaction with their neighborhoods. The study found that 36 percent of Buffalo residents rated their neighborhood a perfect "10," while only 27 percent did so in Dallas.[1] Buffalo is a city with what is now being called human or social capital, a term invented by Nobel laureate economist Gary Becker to describe "activities that influence future monetary and psychic income by increasing the resources in people."[2] Like Chicago, a strong sense of neighborhood and ethnic identity still flourishes in Buffalo and what it may currently lack in economic capital, it makes up for in a web of informal networks, a social fabric of families who have lived in the area for generations, and a healthy history of community activism. Despite the infamous weather, people who leave the area do so reluctantly because they leave behind this strong sense of community, distinctive identity, and cohesive social system.

But like other rust belt cities that lost their industrial economy in the late 1970s and were hit with the crack epidemics of the 1990s, Buffalo and its neighborhoods have suffered decay and decline. Street-level drug dealers took over certain neighborhoods, commercial strips lost vitality and appeal, and abandoned houses littering the area served as the locations of criminal activity. To address these crime and disorder problems, the Buffalo Police Department developed a Neighborhood Initiative plan to stabilize key neighborhood and commercial areas throughout the city of Buffalo by strengthening the connection between the police and block clubs, businesses, and community organizations. The Initiative program had three primary objectives: strict enforcement, high visibility, and increased communication and coordi-

---

[1] Zremski, Jerry. "Census Survey: Residents feel most at home in Buffalo area." *Buffalo News*, June 30, 1996. The survey was conducted for 3,659 households in the Erie and Niagara counties and shows that "residents see both the city and the suburbs as good places to live." City residents rated their homes an 8.1 while suburban residents rated them 8.5. The study has a 1.3% margin of error.

[2] Becker, Gary. *Human Capital: A Theoretical and Empirical Analysis.* New York: Columbia (1964), 1.

nation with the community and other city agencies. As an officer in one of the Initiative areas said, "Policing is an information business," and the community is one of the best sources of good information. Information flow between the police and the community is necessary in order to achieve the mutual goal of stable neighborhoods.

Initiatives: The Initiatives have proven very successful in bringing together the police, community groups, and other public agencies to address problems in targeted areas of the city. In the Broadway-Fillmore Initiative, officers have targeted worst offenders, worked with the community to identify problems surrounding corner stores and networked with other agencies to address those problems. They have also begun a juvenile follow-up program to keep track of at-risk youth that police officers contact. In the Jefferson Avenue Initiative, police worked with community members to reverse years of decay through strict enforcement of city ordinances combined with clean-up efforts to restore order to the area. A police officer and a business woman established a group called "50 Women with a Vision" that began cleaning up the area every Saturday and has grown into a neighborhood revitalization effort. In University Heights, the police are working closely with a community center to identify and address quality of life concerns in the neighborhood. Recently, police, the district councilman, and community organizers took a walk to talk to business owners on one of the main commercial streets in the area only to discover to their amazement that crime was no longer much of a concern. On Buffalo's Lower West Side, police are working together with the community and University of Buffalo researchers to create short- and long-term solutions to the problem of prostitution, and in the Downtown business district the combined efforts of the police and the business community have reduced crime and the fear of crime.

Broadway-Fillmore Initiative: Key Elements for Success

Located on the east side of Buffalo is a historic district known as Broadway-Fillmore, an old Polish neighborhood that in the past few decades has become an economically distressed, transitional, urban neighborhood noted for drug activity, crime, and poverty. The area leads the city in priority one calls and repeat calls have been high, especially to blocks with numerous abandoned houses where drugs and gangs proliferate because nobody seems to care. The once flourishing business district has been slowly dying, and small "Mom & Pop" groceries have been driven out by high crime and by other stores that profit from illicit activity. At a neighborhood summit conducted by the mayor of Buffalo, residents identified some of these businesses as places that generated or harbored much of the area crime. The area has a significant number of senior citizens and many of these elderly people have been de facto prisoners in their homes due to fear of crime.

Responsibility for the Initiative was given to the district captain, who solicited suggestions from officers for methods and resources necessary to achieve the objectives. The Initiative's success depended on this effort to include police personnel in the design and implementation. Another key to the success of the program was a collaboration with a local college. In the Hilbert Internship Program coordinated by Dr. Martin Floss, five student interns each semester have assisted the police to survey citizens, tutor juveniles at risk, computerize the Detective Unit, and produce a comprehensive and detailed summary report of the Initiative's activities. The captain also identified and contacted anchor organizations in the area, such as the Broadway Market (a historic Polish market established in 1888) and the Polish Community Center, to help formulate the plan.

Strict enforcement and targeting: The centerpiece of the Initiative was a detail car that targeted the worst offenders in the area and developed an information network with community members and street youth; as a result, many career criminals have been driven out of the area or arrested. The detail car conducts on-the-spot investigations of major crimes, freeing up patrol cars to answer calls and gather information while witnesses and evidence are fresh. In a recent high-profile homicide, information the detail car developed through the network led to the arrest of the suspect. In another case, the DA's office was unable to find a witness to testify at a homicide trial. The young man had no permanent address, but the officers knew him and quickly located him on the streets.

Initiative officers found that strict enforcement of violations of city ordinances and employing other civil remedies often proved more effective than pursuing criminal charges. For instance, officers discovered a city ordinance that allowed them to remove or modify pay phones used for drug trafficking. They also worked with other federal, state, and local agencies to enforce health and licensing codes in corner stores that were the site of illicit activity and a high volume of repeat calls.

High visibility: To target the problem of repeated purse snatchings and other low-level crimes around the Broadway Market, a daytime foot patrol was dedicated to a two-block area. The presence of the officer, who speaks Polish and lives in the neighborhood, has encouraged senior citizens who previously felt locked in their homes to come more often to the Market, which serves as a social gathering point for the elderly. In the evenings, the detail car patrols the area at closing time and the officers are aware of the regularly scheduled events and meetings. Citizens now know these officers, and often flag them down to discuss problems on their street.

Increased communication and cooperation with the community: A coalition of citizens, non-profit agencies, city officials, and police established a Neighborhood Initiative Center (NIC) at the Polish Community Center. The NIC was used to receive and distribute Initiative information (including criminal activity information forms) and to meet and consult with citizens.

Initiative meetings for the entire community were held at the Polish Community Center every other month. The Broadway Market manager arranged for flyers for the meeting to be placed in shoppers' bags. Attended by police officers, the community, and representatives from the numerous agencies that became involved in the effort, these meetings allowed for information exchange between community members and the police, kept the community apprised of the progress of the Initiative, and educated citizens about services available to them. Initiative officers also met with more than 100 businesses to discuss the Initiative and to update the police business files for the area, and Initiative information was disseminated at the monthly meetings of the Broadway Area Business Association.

Coordination with other agencies: Initiative officers worked closely with the District Attorney's Community Prosecution Unit to target misdemeanor offenses. This effort resulted in the first successful prosecution for the sale of drug paraphernalia in New York State. Officers also teamed up with Housing Inspectors to identify and demolish abandoned houses used for criminal activity, and they worked with Streets and Sanitation to cite for trash and debris. A model problem-solving effort was developed by two officers who created a Deli Task Force to focus on illegal activity surrounding corner stores. The problem was identified by the community, the locations were the site of a high number of calls for service, the worst offending stores were targeted, the effort was coordinated between federal, state, and local agencies, and both civil and criminal remedies were invoked.

End results: In 1996, arrests increased 46.5 percent and 77 guns were seized. According to the district captain, the number of violent felonies has dropped 15 percent, and by targeting a few of the career burglars, burglaries are also down considerably. Purse snatches dropped by 200 percent, and there was a 22 percent reduction in calls for service to the area. Information exchange is growing between the police and the community, complaints against the police have plummeted, and the police are increasingly considered a trusted and reliable source of help. Perhaps most significant is the renewed energy and hope in the target neighborhood: people have growing interest in their block clubs, merchants are witnessing an increase in their business, senior citizens are less fearful of coming out of their homes, and spin-off projects have taken on a life of their own. One such project is a collaboration between the police department, Hilbert college, and a local high school to prevent juvenile problems before they start through tutoring, team building, and recreational activities. The Broadway-Fillmore Initiative is a good example of the police leading a cooperative effort with the community, businesses, and other agencies to stabilize an urban neighborhood.

Submitted by: Dr. Pamela Beal, Captain James Cudney, and Dr. Martin Floss.

COMMUNITY CLOSE-UP
Philadelphia Police Department
Philadelphia, Pennsylvania

Willie L. Williams, Commissioner

Community policing as a managerial and tactical police program has taken many forms across the United States. In Philadelphia, community policing means police accountability to the community for the quality of life in neighborhoods. This has involved the implementation of three interrelated programs to accomplish the mission of the department: to improve community quality of life; neighborhood advisory councils, decentralized experimentation; and the adoption of a problem-focus for management and tactical operations.

In each of Philadelphia's 23 police patrol districts, neighborhood advisory councils have been formed with the explicit purposes of (1) providing community access to police policymaking and (2) establishing an accountability linkage between the police and the consumers of police services, the public. These advisory councils meet regularly with district captains to identify and assess community problems, and jointly to determine strategies (police and community) to resolve those problems.

Linked to neighborhood advisory councils is broadening of operational discretion at the patrol district level, and the mandate that captains have the managerial latitude to experiment in programs aimed at reducing crime, fear of crime, and community disorder. In several instances, that has resulted in opening *mini-stations* to anchor deteriorating neighborhoods and to strengthen civic development. In others, this has resulted in the full-scale decentralization of a police division as an alternative to traditional, and, oftentimes, centralized, police functioning in the city. The central theme of this "spirit of experimentation" within the Philadelphia Police Department recognizes that problems and programs will, of necessity, vary according to community needs and available resources.

Finally, the Philadelphia Police Department has embraced a problem-oriented approach to policing, wherein managers, supervisors, and patrol officers are challenged to solve community crime and disorder problems, rather than reactively responding to problems once they are identified by the community. Here, the department is in the process of elaborating on communications and analytic systems to better capture demand, conduct repeat call analysis, and isolate persistent problems confronting the community.

The theme of community policing in Philadelphia is establishing a partnership with the community to reduce crime, disorder, and fear, and to improve community quality of life. Many individual efforts and programs contribute to this theme. Preliminary assessments of the effectiveness of these programs have been encouraging. The challenge of community policing in a large, urban police department is not to reduce the concept to a listing of programs that are implemented citywide. We have resisted this approach in favor of a strategy that provides incentive and initiative for local commanders to tailor programs to local needs. Each patrol district has a team of specialists that help to fulfill the many missions of community policing. In addition to the patrol force, Victim Assistance Officers, Police and Community Relations Officers, and Community Crime Prevention Officers are assigned to each patrol district. This core of community-oriented officers is not expected to become just another specialization within the department. Instead, the ultimate goal is to transfuse the patrol force with the community policing idea and practice, so that community-oriented and problem-focused policing become the *normal* operational practice of the department.

Community leaders have access to police decision-making that they did not have in the past. Command officers, most particularly those who are in the patrol and detective bureaus, have begun to make the transition from policing as reaction to policing as problem identification, analysis, and resolution. The police themselves have developed a better appreciation for community policing, although acceptance of this strategy in the face of drastically reduced manpower remains a problem. Business and residential communities, however, are squarely behind this initiative.

Submitted by: William T. Bergman, Inspector.

COMMUNITY CLOSE-UP
Mapping and Analyzing Crime as a Public Health Crisis, Colorado Division of Criminal Justice

Kim English, Research Director

In 1991, English said, the Centers for Disease Control and Prevention declared violence a public health crisis in the United States. The result of that action and the widespread embrace of the concept of community policing in U.S. law enforcement was a change in focus for some researchers studying crime and violence.

English noted that the field of public health employs a different perspective than that of traditional crime analysis. To study crime and violence through the prism of public health, she said, requires first determining the risk factors for individuals to become perpetrators or victims of crime. The public health perspective brings a new strategy to crime prevention that fits well with the philosophy of community policing: violence can be averted through simple, low-cost solutions to specific local problems that lead to repeated incidents of violence.

English cited two important studies—by the National Institute of Medicine and the Office of Juvenile Justice and Delinquency Prevention in the Department of Justice—that stressed the accumulation of risk factors in the lives of those affected most by violence. These studies reach conclusions that echo the most powerful objective of community policing: that by taking a community-wide approach, key members of the community will take ownership of strategies to reduce violence and juvenile delinquency.

According to the studies, English said, the past 30 years of criminological research into violence has identified 13 risk factors at four levels:

- Community;
- Family;
- School; and
- Individual/peer.

English analyzes data on particular types of crime as an indicator of risk factors in a community, not merely as an indicator of the crime itself. As crime data links risk factors for people in a certain geographical area, crime prevention strategies that address those factors can be selected and employed. Research has found, for example, that communities with greater availability of firearms experience higher rates of violent crime. An obvious and important strategy for those communities would therefore be reducing access to firearms for those most at risk of violence.

An important family risk indicator, she said, is domestic violence. Violence in a family increases the likelihood that young people will engage in violent behavior themselves. A researcher using the public health model would study police arrest data to find evidence that domestic abuse is a neighborhood risk indicator.

Once these risk indicators have been identified for a community and data supporting their existence collected, mapping software can be used with that data to pinpoint law enforcement problems and needs for services at the address level. English highlighted innovative approaches to mapping risk factors that are overlaying population density and crime incidents as well as maps of Weed and Seed areas, AFDC recipients, and domestic violence.

In the end, English said, risk factor data and mapping correlations are only valuable if law enforcement, community members, and service providers use them to develop crime and violence prevention strategies. Data can be a powerful vehicle to get people talking about and owning problems in their communities.

Source: NIJ (1996). *Technology for Community Policing*. Washington, DC: National Institute of Justice.

COMMUNITY CLOSE-UP
Reno Police Department
Reno, Nevada

Jerry Hoover, Chief of Police

Introduction

In the mid-1980s, the Reno, Nevada, Police Department (RPD) faced the challenges confronting many law enforcement agencies. A lagging economy had forced administrators to make significant reductions in staffing and resources, while calls for service continued to rise dramatically. In this 24-hour gaming community of 60 square miles and a tourist-inflated population exceeding 250,000, the situation was untenable. Further, community relations were poor at best, as evidenced by the defeat of two tax initiatives that would have provided sorely needed police personnel and equipment. Clearly, the policing strategies of the 1970s were unsuited for present needs and change was necessary.

As the department struggled to cope with these challenges, community support eroded. A survey in 1987 revealed that citizens viewed the police departments as being uncaring and heavy-handed. Two municipal bond issues that would have replaced officers lost to attrition failed because of a lack of voter support. Department administrators saw the need for broad-based change. In May 1987, the RPD adopted a department-wide strategy it labeled Community-Oriented Policing Plus (COP+). Administrators realized that the department must engage the community and city agencies in a shared approach to problem solving if it hoped to repair its relationship with the community and properly address the problems of increased crime and disorder.

Keys to Successful Implementation

Implementation began with a 40-hour block of training for every employee from chief of police to custodian. This was followed by a training on problem-oriented policing for officers and supervisors by the Police Executive Research Forum. Following training, planning teams were developed representing employees from every rank and area of the organization to begin the difficult task of reengineering the entire department toward its new COP+ philosophy.

Moving the RPD from its reactive, incident-driven mode to COP+ was no simple endeavor. The RPD's implementation efforts focused on four key components that were believed to profoundly affect the way the agency did business: leadership and management, human resources, field operations, and external relations.

Leadership and Management

COP+ required a change in philosophy of leadership and management throughout the entire organization. This change began with a committee of employees (consisting of a cross-section of ranks and divisions) to develop *vision/values/mission statements*. Next, all *policies and procedures* were reviewed to ensure they comported with the department's COP+ objectives. The department's staff encouraged *leadership* at all levels of the organization, and a shift in *management style* from controller to facilitator was promoted. The department invested in *information systems* for crime analysis, crime mapping, and mobile computer terminals in police vehicles to assist officers in identifying patterns of crime and to support the problem-solving efforts. Recently appointed Chief Jerry Hoover has tasked the department to revisit its long-term *strategic plans* and *evaluation processes* and to make any changes necessary to meet current and future challenges. The organizational design was flattened and two ranks (assistant chief and captain) were eliminated; financial accountability was pushed down to subordinate commanders. The sharing of personnel and financial resources across the organization and with other city departments promoted effective problem solving as well.

Human Resources

The RPD learned that COP+ required new skills, knowledge, and abilities for everyone in the organization. Therefore, a review of human resources was necessary.

This began with major changes in the department's *recruiting, testing, and hiring* processes, which were modified to attract candidates with problem-solving and decision-making skills. A community policing and problem-solving course was included in the recruit academy. Field training officers (FTOs) were provided additional training in COP+, and new recruits' daily evaluation criteria were changed to better reflect its tenets. *Performance evaluations* were changed so that less attention was given to boilerplate measures such as numbers of arrests and citations and more attention was given to identifying and solving problems.

Testing for all *promotions* was changed to reflect knowledge of readings and research on community policing and problem solving as well as basic management and tactical skills. *Honors and awards* were also changed to provide recognition to those employees engaged in COP+ efforts. A more progressive system of *discipline* was developed to ensure that problem behaviors were dealt with as quickly as possible. Finally, monthly *labor-management* meetings were held between the chief's staff and representatives from employee labor organizations to work out concerns (this activity alone has resulted in a significant reduction in employee grievances over the years). Also, labor representatives were included in the planning and implementation process from its inception.

Field Operations

One of the biggest changes made was the complete reorganization of *geo-graphic districts* and renewed interest in the importance of field operations. Numerous specialty positions were disbanded or civilianized, and those officers were reassigned to patrol. Officers and a supervisor work in teams in the same district for six months, with the same days off. The supervisor has significant authority to manage the district as needed and based on the problems identified.

The department has developed three neighborhood stations staffed by civilian police services technicians (PSTs). These *decentralized neighborhood stations* provide the residents with more convenient services and a place to conduct community meetings. PSTs are also assigned to unmarked police vehicles and assist patrol officers with a variety of field duties, including crime scene investigations, minor traffic investigations, and traffic control. Currently, PSTs handle more than 68 percent of the departments reports, allowing patrol officers more time to engage in community policing and problem-solving activities.

In addition, a *community-based approach* to gangs, the homeless, violent and repeat offenders, and other major social issues involve the RPD and other local and federal law enforcement agencies, schools, businesses, and social service organizations, replacing the parochial attitudes and duplication of efforts of the past.

External Relations

Improving community relations and forging collaborative partnerships were principal objectives at the beginning of implementation. Several approaches helped the police department accomplish these objectives. First, *neighborhood advisory groups* (NAGs) consisting of residents from each division of patrol were formed to meet with operations personnel on a quarterly basis, or as needed, to discuss neighborhood problems. This forum greatly contributed to improved education and communication between the police and the community. Each meeting is preceded by a newsletter containing general information about the department and specific information concerning the area. The NAGs have proved valuable in the resolution of many neighborhood problem-solving efforts. Aside from newsletters and NAG meetings, the department also utilizes public service announcements and community surveys to educate and communicate with the public. The *media* have also provided an excellent opportunity for the RPD to educate the community. Press releases are routinely sent to the media concerning collaborative problem-solving efforts, and various agency programs and news conferences are held to discuss major crime reduction efforts.

The department has also improved its partnership with other city government organizations. Monthly *Problem Analysis Advisory Board* (PAAC) meetings are chaired by the patrol commander and involve sworn officers and representatives from various city organizations who brainstorm problem-solving efforts. Throughout the years, this process has greatly improved the agency's knowledge of potential problem-solving resources and the speed with which neighborhood issues are handled by multiple government agencies.

Neighborhood Problem Solving

As indicated above, all RPD officers received training in the problem-solving concept and the SARA model (for scanning, analysis, response, and assessment). Officers soon applied their new skills to a variety of crime and neighborhood disorder concerns (gangs, homelessness, prostitution, abandoned vehicles, and bar problems). Examples of officers' problem-solving efforts include:

Taking back the park. A small neighborhood park in a low-income area had become unfit for public use, being transformed into a hangout for drug dealers and gang members. Following meetings of the area NAG, the police, and local ministries, patrols and arrests were increased, changes were made to the environment of the park (including signage and lighting); these changes served to reduce the problems, and the community organized a "We took back the park" parade to celebrate their success.

Reduction of drug traffic. A convenience store was a popular hangout for drug dealers, who used pay telephones to receive calls from drug users. Officers worked with the business, local schools, residents, and telephone company, and arranged for the phones to be programmed to receive no incoming calls—thus removing the problem from the area and reducing the threat of general drug trafficking exposure to local school children.

Attending to gang issues. A low-income area with a high density percentage of non-English speaking population was plagued with drug and gang members. Business leaders formed a coalition to increase bilingual officer presence and work with schools and parents to reduce the incidence of gang violence.

Employing social services. A row of rent-by-the-week motels outside the downtown area were typically rented by working, two-parent families. While the parents worked, young children were left alone, creating truancy and other juvenile problems. Officers engaged the support of social services, schools, and other city agencies to provide needed services and care for the children, thus reducing the incidence of juvenile problems in that area.

Conclusion

The RPD has been committed to COP+ for more than a decade. The results of biannual surveys indicate that this type of policing is widely supported by police officers and the public alike. However, implementation is no easy task. Police chief executives who commit to implementation face two critical problems—overcoming organizational resistance to innovation and gauging and managing the pace of change once it is undertaken. The RPD has learned that implementation is evolutionary; it occurred as a result of refining past practices, implementing new strategies, and, at times, accepting "small wins" to major changes. Simply stated, it takes planning, patience, and time.

Does community policing work? In 1987, a public survey determined the police department's performance had a dismal 39 percent approval rating. Today—10 years after the inception of COP+—the department's performance approval rating stands at 84 percent. The full effects and potential of COP+ are not yet known; therefore ongoing surveys, the nurturing of community-based partnerships, and collaborative problem solving will continue, and will guide the RPD into the next millennium.

Submitted by: Deputy Chief Ronald W. Glensor, Ph.D.

COMMUNITY CLOSE-UP
Arvada, Colorado, Police Department

Ronald C. Sloan, Police Chief

How can technology help police be more effective in community policing?

"The challenge for police is to embrace technology," Sloan said, "but they must do it intelligently. Police must become more knowledgeable about what technology can really do. Often, they are faced with prolonged implementation, then questionable utility once the technology is in place. It is critical that users be involved during the initial stages of developing and implementing technology."

Sloan suggested combining two principles: define the objective and ensure that form follows function. Police must ensure that the form technology takes follows the function they are charged with carrying out. They must assess their most basic function as police agencies and redefine their role in pursuit of that function. How police prioritize and use technology will be shaped by what they prioritize in their departments.

The term "law enforcement" itself connotes a narrow and distorted view of police functions, according to Sloan. Caution must be taken to ensure that technological advances that police develop and implement support not only the law enforcement components of police activities, but also all the other roles that a community policing practitioner has to carry out: mediator, facilitator, community mobilizer, organizer, crime prevention monitor, and mitigator. Function should not be altered to meet the form of technological advances. It is critical not to sacrifice effectiveness of policing for greater efficiency.

Examples Sloan cited of how technology has been employed at cross-purposes with community policing include:

- The combination of computer-aided dispatch technology and computerized data in the patrol car has tethered officers to the automobile rather than facilitated the face-to-face interaction in the community that is so integral to community policing. Not only do officers feel tied to machines in their patrol units, but dispatchers can't reach officers who are out of their cars;

- Automated records management systems have improved the efficiency of data entry and storage but have complicated the retrieval of vital information;

- Deployment and scheduling software do a good job of computing optimum manpower needs but with traditional, incident-driven measures; and

- Systems that analyze police workload and help devise strategies to deal with it also are based solely on traditional measures. These data are incredibly valuable, but basing decisions solely on them causes police to continue to adhere to the traditional mindset.

Technological innovations can be tremendous tools for law enforcement: concealed weapons detection and sharing information between police agencies about crime trends and criminals have tremendous potential. Police must explore technology that enhances their ability to diagnose community problems in a systematic manner. They must be able to better analyze the cause of crime and the quality of life in communities across the country.

In addition, communications technology can open policing to the community to facilitate information sharing and prevent crime, mobilize the community around salient crime and quality of life issues, help the community better understand policing, and help police better understand community issues and restraints.

COPS programs can help officers become more effective in policing their communities. Technology can help police marshal resources and synthesize service providers to solve community problems. "Police are in the community 24 hours a day, 7 days a week, 365 days a year. Who better to coordinate community services?" Sloan said.

Source: NIJ (1996). *Technology for Community Policing*. Washington, DC: National Institute of Justice.

COMMUNITY CLOSE-UP
Edmonton Police Service
Canada

P.J. Duggan, Staff Sergeant

The Shift to Community Policing

To successfully implement this model, law enforcement agencies must rethink and restructure all information systems to support the work of officers in the community. Problem solving in policing requires that officers have the ability to identify neighborhood problems and recognize recurring incidents as symptoms of a bigger problem.

Echoing the words of Edmonton Police Chief John Lindsay, Duggan said that operational effectiveness depends on practical applications of technology that parallel major shifts in community policing. "Information technology," Lindsay believes, "must therefore be selected, structured, and used . . . to support local neighborhood problem solving."

The experience of the Edmonton Police Service (EPS) has suggested that neighborhood problem solving will work only when based on these principles:

- Urban areas consist of individual neighborhoods with individual problems;

- Some neighborhoods legitimately require more police attention than others;

- Specific locations in a neighborhood often become repeat problems;

- The community's constant demand for service makes the police incident-driven and reactive; and

- Information is the lifeblood of policing.

Although some have noted that increased reliance on technology separates police and the community they serve, the success of Edmonton's experiment has shown that the opposite is true: properly managed information technology can bring the police and the community closer together.

Old Information Systems No Longer Meet Community Needs

While an excellent tool to support rapid response to calls, the Computer Aided Dispatch (CAD) systems traditionally used by police seldom are flexible enough to supply the kind of information managers and community officers need in a community policing model. CAD systems function as, in the words of Chief Lindsay, "electronic filing cabinets" that do not focus on the information most vital to neighborhood officers—repeat problems.

According to Duggan, community policing requires a much broader information path that moves law enforcement beyond its preoccupation with calls for service, dispatch, response, and incident reports and toward an understanding of community problems and the resources to solve them.

Community policing requires a new information delivery system on the street and on computers that support crime analysis.

Prior to 1988, EPS was a conservative, process-oriented model of traditional policing that employed three strategies that had little effect on crime or police workload: random patrol, rapid response, and investigation after the fact. As Edmonton's population and crime rose sharply in the 1980s, this approach unraveled as budget cuts took a toll on the department's resources and manpower. As a street manager in the downtown area, Duggan found it impossible to catch up to the calls his group received each day for service.

In response, the department attempted a radical change. Using research that challenged the command and control approach, Edmonton police built a neighborhood foot patrol program that concentrated on solving problems in the city's hot spots of crime. Duggan highlighted two aspects of the program's successful implementation:

- EPS had the program evaluated by independent researchers to show the community and officers throughout the department that problem solving policing works; and

- The process revealed the importance that an information system plays in organizational change. The old CAD system was manipulated to identify hot spots based on workload and repeat calls for service.

Edmonton's rewired CAD system classified data by volume of occurrence at specific locations, repeat address, dispatched calls, and dispatched units. By looking at this basic information in a new way, EPS found that for nearly 75 percent of all police responses calls for service originated from repeat addresses and much of the police activity occurred at relatively few locations. Solving problems in these hot spots of crime became the focus of community officers' assignments and what they considered as their beats.

The success of Edmonton's foray into community policing led to a rethinking of every aspect of the organization's operations. Every decision and commitment of resources was examined in light of meeting community needs. This standard, the department's core value, became a powerful tool to move more officers onto the street and several million dollars into the budget supporting them.

EPS became an information-based organization that focused on the patrol officer as the cornerstone of the police delivery system.

To help patrol officers carry out this responsibility, the department made a commitment to community policing in four key areas:

- Assigning each community officer to a particular area;

- Requiring that officers take ownership of those areas and their problems;

- Giving officers freedom to make decisions; and

- Encouraging policing in collaboration with local residents, not as a service to them.

Duggan pointed out that a community officer's assignment could extend beyond a geographical problem area to groups of residents with shared problems or concerns.

The New Service Delivery

Although Edmonton's new community-oriented philosophy won the support of the community and officers on the beat, the department was still operating largely in a reactive mode, overwhelmed by calls for service. A new approach to service delivery was needed. The heart of that approach recognized that rapid response to most nonemergency calls made little difference. Instead, the community agreed to bring nonemergency needs to police at 1 of 16 community stations. Patrol officers would then have more time to respond to real emergencies and to solve problems before they became emergencies.

In addition to the requirement that residents report calls to community stations, Duggan highlighted other elements of the strategy that have been effective:

- A computerized call path chart that determines if a request for service will be handled by a community station or dispatched. By tracking backlog in the dispatch system, the chart helps determine the best resources for solving problems;

- Expanded ownership of community policing within the department. Every officer, manager, and volunteer working in a neighborhood must respond to the needs of that neighborhood;

- Self-assignment of calls. Patrol officers, who are familiar with the problems of trouble spots in the community, are given a role in deciding which calls they will take and when they will meet the complainant;

- Accountability through on-street managers; and

- The use of volunteers, who, as a vital link to the neighborhoods EPS serves, are now an indispensable part of community policing in Edmonton.

The new strategy worked. According to Duggan, Edmonton citizens now report more than 62 percent of occurrences to community station officers and the volunteers they supervise.

A New Strategy Requires New Technology

Devoting the time of patrol officers to community problem solving, however, also heightened the department's need for greater technological support. OSCAR, the Operational Support, Communications, and Records system, was designed to support community-based service delivery. OSCAR's complaint handling and dispatch system, CHAD, has significantly enhanced community officers' safety and ability to solve problems by providing them access to a wealth of information about a location's criminal history. OSCAR's other component, a records and data management system called PROBE, uses mapping technology to perform data and intelligence analysis by area. Officers use PROBE to identify problem locations within their neighborhood assignments. Through the system, data are available from a wide variety of police reports, including case investigations, traffic violations, arrest bookings, street information reports, and intelligence analysis.

In policing, time and information are an officer's most precious resources. OSCAR has given the Edmonton Police Service and the community it serves much more of both and an opportunity to make life healthier and safer.

What Community Policing Has Accomplished in Edmonton

- Criminal code violations: ▼ 45%
- Clearance rates for crimes against persons: ▲ 13%
- Clearance rates for crimes against property: ▲ 23%
- Insurance claims for residential break-ins: ▼ 42%
- Insurance claims for vandalism: ▼ 53%
- Complaints against EPS officers: ▼ 47%
- Citizen satisfaction with community stations: 93%
- Significantly reduced workloads in communications.
- Increase in police-citizen contact.
- Decrease in insurance fraud.
- More than 850 citizen volunteers working at community stations.

Source: NIJ (1996). *Technology for Community Policing*. Washington, DC: National Institute of Justice.

Index